LATIMER:
Apostle to the English

LATIMER:
Apostle to the English

CLARA H. STUART

Zondervan Books
Zondervan Publishing House
Grand Rapids, Michigan

Latimer: Apostle to the English

Copyright © 1986 by Clara H. Stuart

This is a Zondervan Book
Published by the Zondervan Publishing House
1415 Lake Drive, S.E., Grand Rapids, Michigan 49506

Library of Congress Cataloging in Publication Data

Stuart, Clara H.
  Latimer, apostle to the English.

  Bibliography: p.
  Includes index.
  1. Latimer, Hugh, 1485?–1555. 2. Church of England—Bishops—Biography. 3. Anglican Communion—Bishops—Biography. I. Title.
BX5199.L2S78   1986   283'.092'4   [B]   86-13269
ISBN 0-310-41370-2

Edited by John D. Sloan
Designed by Carole Parrish

Printed in the United States of America

86 87 88 89 90 91 / 10 9 8 7 6 5 4 3 2 1

To my lifelong friend
LILLY SIBLEY EVANS
Whose interest and enthusiasm undergirded this work
from start to finish

CONTENTS

PREFACE

A biography need not be uninteresting or limited to quoted material. It is written about a life, and any life, whether lived in the twentieth century or in the first, is marked by tides of interest, adventure, and fascination. My aim in presenting this biography of Hugh Latimer has been to make him live and breathe and become as real as a reader's closest friend in daily life.

A biography must also be true to the facts. In retelling the story of this great but relatively unknown man in our times, I have not contradicted any of the historical materials available to me during this five-year writing project. But when a biographer must research more than four hundred years, the records may leave gaps. I have not permitted my imagination to run wild, however. Where it has been necessary to bridge the gaps, I have written what most likely took place and at the very least was a possibility. Using the knowledge of Latimer's character and personality as found in his letters and sermons and in the recorded comments of his contemporaries, I have written from "inside" his life.

One does not write a book like this without help from a great many people. I would like to express my appreciation to each one. A few I must mention by name.

Dr. Philip Edgcumbe Hughes encouraged me to begin this work, gave assistance along the way, and took time from a crowded schedule to read the manuscript and to make helpful suggestions and corrections.

My friend Robbie Lee Gore, a court reporter, undertook with incredible patience the proofreading of not one but three successive rewrites.

Lilly Evans aided me in countless ways, especially on a research trip to England.

The Right Reverend Robin Woods, Bishop of Worcester, permitted me to visit Hartlebury Castle where Mr. Leonard Greenwood, former librarian of the Hurd Library at the castle, provided me with useful historical information.

Miss Henderson at the Worcester Record Office arranged for me to examine the registers of the Bishops of Worcester from the time of Latimer's bishopric.

My husband George has quietly endured, never begrudging the time and the expense that this project involved.

I have found John Sloan, my editor at Zondervan, easy to work with, kind, helpful, and always patient in the difficult job of readying the book for publication.

CHARACTERS

THOMAS ARTHUR: One of the early Reformers at Cambridge, accompanied Bilney on a preaching tour.

ANNE ASKEW: A lady of good standing, much attached to Reformed doctrine.

JAMES BAINHAM: Got in trouble for his preaching of Reformed doctrine.

ROBERT BARNES: Prior of Augustine Friary at Cambridge, outstanding member of a group of Reformers.

SIR EDWARD BAYNTON: Lord of the manor at Bromeham, near West Kington, influential at Court.

THOMAS BECON: A younger Reformer, Cambridge man, one of Cranmer's chaplains and an outstanding preacher.

AUGUSTINE BERNHER: A young Swiss, attached to the Reformation, who made himself Latimer's faithful servant.

RICHARD BERTIE: Gentleman-Usher to Lady Katherine, the Dowager-Duchess of Suffolk, at Grimsthorpe.

THOMAS BILNEY: Fellow of Trinity Hall, in whose heart was born the Reformation at Cambridge.

ANNE BOLEYN: Second wife of Henry VIII, friend of Reformers.

EDMUND BONNER: Bishop of London, following Stokesley.

JOHN BRADFORD: Young Reformer, close friend of Latimer in his later years, chaplain in Bishop Ridley's household.

DR. RUDOLPH BRADFORD: One of Bishop Latimer's chaplains.

BUCKENHAM: Antagonist of Latimer in "The Card" incident.

DR. BUCKMASTER: Vice Chancellor at Cambridge in Latimer's time.

SIR WILLIAM BUTTS: Physician to Henry VIII, friendly to the Reformers, Latimer's special friend.

JOHN CARELESS: Of Coventry, friend of the Glovers at Baxterley Hall, admirer of Latimer, strong in Reformed views.

MILES COVERDALE: A friar of the Augustinian order, Reformer at Cambridge, translator and editor of the English Bible which bears his name.

THOMAS CRANMER: Succeeded Warham as Archbishop of Canterbury under Henry VIII, actively involved in Reformation.

EDWARD CROME: Early Reformer at Cambridge, courageous preacher, but usually recanted when brought to trial for his views.

THOMAS CROMWELL: Secretary to Wolsey until his death, attached himself to Henry VIII, became powerful, held many offices, notably that of Lord Privy Seal; friend of the Reformers.

JOHN DUDLEY: Duke of Warwick, became Duke of Northumberland in reign of Edward VI.

PRINCE EDWARD: Son of Henry VIII and his third wife, Jane Seymour; succeeded Henry to the throne, when a child not yet nine, as Edward VI.

PRINCESS ELIZABETH: Daughter of Henry VIII and Anne Boleyn.

JOHN FISHER: Bishop of Rochester, opponent of Reformation.

JOHN FOREST: A friar who was tried for heresy and treason.

EDWARD FOX: King's almoner, joined the Reformers, became Bishop of Hereford.

STEPHEN GARDINER: A secretary of Henry VIII, became Bishop of Winchester, remained a confirmed papist, vigorously fought the Reformers and Reformation.

THOMAS GARRETT: Young Reformer, one of Bishop Latimer's chaplains.

JOHN GLOVER: Wealthy landowner lived at Baxterley Hall, devoted friend of Reformed doctrine and Reformers.

ROBERT GLOVER: Brother to John Glover, husband of Latimer's niece, lived at Mancetter, ardent friend of Reformation.

GREENWOOD: Of St. John's, Cambridge, one who opposed Latimer in the controversy over "The Card."

PHILIP HAWFORD: Abbot of Benedictine Abbey at Evesham.

HENRY VIII: King of England.

RICHARD HILEY: Vicar-general of the Diocese of Salisbury, Latimer's superior in his parish at West Kington.

DR. JOHN HILSEY: Prior of the Dominican Friars at Bristol, later Bishop of Rochester, succeeding Fisher; a Reformer.

HENRY HOLBEACH: Prior of Worcester, became Latimer's suffragan bishop at Bristol.

JOHN HOOPER: Younger Reformer, King's preacher to Edward VI, became Bishop of Gloucester.

LADY KATHERINE: Dowager-Duchess of Suffolk, at Grimsthorpe Castle, great friend and benefactor of the Reformers.

HUGH LATIMER: Fellow of Clare Hall, Cambridge, a priest who held tenaciously to the "old order" until his conversion, after which he fought with vigor for the Reformation, whether as King's preacher, parish priest, or Bishop of Worcester, becoming the greatest preacher of the era.

JOHN LAMBERT: Member of early group of Reformers at Cambridge, whose views advanced too far and too fast.

PRINCESS MARY: Daughter of Henry VIII and Catherine of Aragon; succeeded Edward VI to the throne. Opposed reformers. Became known as "Bloody Mary."

SIR THOMAS MORE: Succeeded Wolsey as Lord Chancellor, staunch opponent of the Reformation.

RALPH MORICE: Secretary to Archbishop Cranmer, friend of Latimer.

MATTHEW PARKER: One of the early Reformers at Cambridge.

KATHERINE PARR: Henry VIII's sixth wife, friend of Reformation.

DR. EDWARD POWELL: Prebendary of Salisbury, opposed Latimer in the controversy at Bristol.

NICHOLAS RIDLEY: Great Reformed preacher, Prebendary of Westminster, King's chaplain, Bishop of Rochester, then Bishop of London, succeeding Bonner.

JOHN ROGERS: One of early Reformers at Cambridge, responsible for the English Bible known as the *Matthew* Bible.

RICHARD SAMPSON: Dean of the Chapel Royal under Henry VIII.

EDWARD SEYMOUR: Earl of Hertford, brother of Jane Seymour, (Henry VIII's third wife), uncle to Edward VI, made Duke of Somerset at Edward's succession, and Protector of the Realm.

JANE SEYMOUR: Third wife of Henry VIII. Died shortly after giving birth to Edward VI.

THOMAS SEYMOUR: Brother of Jane and Edward Seymour, uncle of Edward VI, became Lord High Admiral.

NICHOLAS SHAXTON: One of early Reformers at Cambridge, became Bishop of Salisbury.

WILLIAM SHERWOOD: A priest who gave Latimer trouble at West Kington.

GEORGE STAFFORD: Fellow of Pembroke, Cambridge, one of early Reformers, outstanding teacher and preacher.

MRS. STATHAM: A friend of the Reformers in London, nursed Latimer back to health in time of illness.

JOHN STOKESLEY: Succeeded Tunstal as Bishop of London, gave Latimer and other Reformers much trouble.

ROWLAND TAYLOR: Preacher of the Reformed group, Vicar of Hadleigh.

CUTHBERT TUNSTAL: Bishop of London, then of Durham; opposed the Reformers.

WILLIAM WARHAM: Archbishop of Canterbury.

NICHOLAS WEST: Bishop of Ely, opposed the Reformers.

DR. HUGH WESTON: Dean of Westminster, Prolocutor at the Disputations at Oxford.

DR. NICHOLAS WILSON: One of King's chaplains, opposed Latimer at Bristol.

THOMAS WOLSEY: Cardinal and Papal Legate, Archbishop of York, Lord Chancellor under Henry VIII.

WRIOTHESLEY: Succeeded Sir Thomas More as Lord Chancellor.

INTRODUCTION

Following upon the heels of the Renaissance, and overlapping it to some extent, came the sixteenth-century Reformation of the church. Although it appeared in a number of places in Europe at about the same time, each movement happened independently and followed a somewhat different pattern. The English Reformation was no exception. Its slow growth can be attributed partly to the nature of the English people: They enjoy things as they are and as they have been; change is difficult for them.

Two popular misconceptions about the origin of the English Reformation have persisted through the years and should be set straight in the beginning: First, it was not an importation of Luther's Reformation. Second, it was not a result of Henry VIII's break with the Pope over the question of the King's divorce.

Henry VIII came to the throne in 1509, a young man of eighteen years. His father, Henry VII, had earlier requested of Pope Julius II and been granted a dispensation by which the young Henry could marry Catherine of Aragon, his brother's widow. In the year that he became King, this marriage took place.

In 1515 Francis I succeeded Louis XII as King of France. Four years later the death of the Holy Roman Emperor Maximilian necessitated the choice of his replacement. A grandson of Maximilian, who was also a grandson of Ferdinand and Isabella of Spain, succeeded in edging out Henry and Francis, both of whom were eager candidates. Charles V became the new emperor. The fact that he was a nephew of Catherine of Aragon had some bearing on later events. These three young kings were intermittently at war with one another during the next quarter century. Sides were changed frequently as the political situation shifted.

Henry took his religion seriously and considered himself a loyal son of the church. When Luther's writings began to make their way across the channel into England, he placed a firm ban on them. In 1521 he wrote and published a paper against the teaching of Luther, which won for him the title "Defender of the Faith" from Pope Leo X.

But Henry had a problem that posed a serious threat to the stability of his throne. Catherine gave birth to one short-lived or stillborn infant after the other. The only living child was Mary. Henry desperately needed a male heir to insure the succession and to ward off the possibility of civil war should he die with Mary his only heir.

By 1527 he was voicing the inner qualms he had already felt about the validity of his marriage. Perhaps the Pope had had no right to grant a dispensation for him to marry Catherine. Was the death of all these children a punishment from God for entering into a marriage that Scripture seemed to prohibit in the Book of Leviticus?

About this time Henry made the acquaintance of Anne Boleyn and fell deeply in love with her. If he could manage to obtain a divorce from Catherine, he could marry Anne, and she would no doubt produce the needed male heir to the throne.

Thus began Henry's long struggle with the Pope, now Clement VII, over the question of the divorce. Clement had his problems too. Under normal circumstances he would probably have granted Henry a divorce or annulment, but times were not normal. The Pope was under the thumb or, more precisely, the iron fist of Charles V, and Charles was not about to have his aunt's marriage set aside.

By the time this drama had played itself out and Henry had made his break with the Pope, the Reformation in England was well under way, although Henry was not aware of it. For this was a quiet Reformation, at least in its beginning stages.

So quiet was it that it is difficult to pinpoint the exact year of its birth. It may have been as early as 1519. Certainly it was not more than a year or two later. The English Reformation was born in the heart of one gentle scholar at Cambridge University. Thomas Bilney, who was a graduate in Law, an ordained priest of the church, and a Fellow of Trinity Hall, first read the New Testament of Erasmus in Latin for the beauty of the language. But his troubled soul, which had found no peace in any of the remedies recommended by the church, soon came upon a passage that changed his life. He became a new man. From the moment of his discovery he knew no law but Scripture and owned no master but Christ.

He shared his discovery with his friends. Soon he had gathered about him a little group of like-minded men, eager to study the Scriptures and learn more of what true Christianity was meant to be. If the movement was born in Bilney's heart, the cradle that nurtured it in its infancy was the White Horse Inn at Cambridge where the group met secretly for study and discussion. But word leaked out. Any such zeal for the Scriptures was associated in the popular mind with Luther, so the inn was referred to as "Little Germany."

14

Bilney had a keen eye for men of character, intelligence, and leadership ability. He concentrated on winning these, one-by-one, until he had assembled the best minds at Cambridge about him at the White Horse Inn. From this group came a great majority of the men who were to be the Reformers of the church during the next quarter century.

By far Bilney's best single work was the discussion and personal plea he placed before Hugh Latimer late one evening. For the Reformation was promoted largely by preaching, and Latimer became the greatest preacher of the era, one of the greatest of all time. Preaching the Truth included the denunciation of abuses in the church and the promotion of efforts to correct them. None was more zealous than Latimer in this. The Reformation was marked by an unceasing effort to obtain for the English people a Bible in their own language, freely available to all. This became one of Latimer's greatest dreams and an end for which he labored tirelessly.

But at this time Hugh Latimer is still a priest of the old order, clinging firmly to the doctrines and practices he has always known. Among opponents of heresy, especially the type coming across from Germany, none was more fiercely outspoken than Hugh Latimer. Certainly he was a most unlikely candidate for membership in the group of Reformers; Bilney, however, thought otherwise and dared to follow him home one evening. And there our story begins. . . .

Part One

CLASHES AT CAMBRIDGE

"I'm just 'little Bilney.'"
[1524–1531]

1

[1524]

Hugh Latimer closed the door of his small study at Clare Hall and leaned against it. Flashing eyes and the set of his angular features evidenced his excitement. As he paced the floor, he reviewed the evening's activity. Later he would feel drained and exhausted. But not now.

The discourse given in St. Mary's Cathedral had accomplished two purposes. It had met a final requirement for his next degree in theology. At the same time he had refuted the teachings of the German heretic Philipp Melanchthon about reliability of the early church Fathers and such men as Thomas Aquinas, Peter Lombard, and Duns Scotus. Latimer had upheld his reputation as defender of the traditional teachings of the church.

The excitement subsided. Seated now at his table, he gazed with unseeing eyes at the books before him. Something in a hidden corner of his mind gnawed at the satisfaction he had previously felt. Weariness engulfed him. The guttering candle at his elbow reminded him of the lateness of the hour.

One person had listened with particularly keen interest to the evening's oration against Melanchthon. Thomas Bilney, the man in whose heart the Reformation now in progress at Cambridge was born, had detected a trace of "zeal without knowledge"; it was a possible chink in the armor of the speaker. Always on the alert for an outstanding man who might be won to the faith in Christ that had changed his own life, Bilney had been eyeing Latimer for some time. He now followed him to his rooms.

Latimer opened to the knocking on his door and found a small figure standing before him. In the darkness he could not identify his caller.

"Master Latimer, the hour is late, but I have great need to talk with you, if you will allow me."

Inviting him in, Latimer turned to light a candle in place of the one that had sputtered out. He almost dropped the candle as he recognized Thomas Bilney, leader of the group responsible for spreading such teachings as he had this day refuted.

Before he recovered sufficiently for speech, Bilney fell to his knees, seized Latimer's hand, and cried, "Oh, sir, for God's sake, hear my confession!"

Bewildered, Latimer gave consent and sat down, prepared to listen. Bilney remained on his knees.

What poured from Bilney's lips in the next hour was anything but what Latimer could have expected. A confession? Indeed, he laid bare his heart to this unlikely confessor.

"Oh sir, for many years I sought the Lord God. With all my heart I wanted to know him and his Christ, to walk in his ways, to do his will. For this cause I forsook the study of Law to become a priest, so I might find how to please him. But in spite of all I learned and all I could do, my soul continued torn and distressed, with no assurance that I had by any means reached God. My sins piled higher and higher, forever obscuring his face. Only judgment remained, for how could I ever do enough to pay for my sins, so they might be removed and God's face revealed? I went from one confessor to another, seeking help for my pitiful condition."

As the words tumbled out, they caught at Latimer's heart and evoked a familiar echo from within. He fixed his eyes intently upon the pleading form. His own longing for peace was intense. He had sought it in vain just where Bilney had sought.

"All they could ever prescribe was that I should fast, do penance, pray to the Virgin and the saints, mortify the body, pay for masses, purchase pardons. I followed faithfully all their remedies but found no relief. I fasted until I was nearer death than life, but to no avail. My soul remained as sick and hopeless as ever."

Again the sensation of listening to his own voice assailed Latimer, not the voice with which he had given that day's address, but the voice of his secret sufferings and fears.

"Then one day," continued Bilney, "I chanced upon a book, one you denounce as dangerous to the soul, the New Testament of Erasmus in Greek and Latin. As I read, I came upon St. Paul's words, 'It is a true saying, and worthy of all men to be embraced, that Christ Jesus came into the world to save sinners.'

"Oh, Master Latimer, you cannot imagine the joy and peace those words brought to my soul. My eyes seemed to open for the first time upon the true light. Think of it! Christ Jesus came into the world *to save sinners!* That means Thomas Bilney. His death on the cross effected peace with God. It was all done for me long ago. I can do nothing to add to it.

"You, Master Latimer, send me for peace and wholeness only to the remedies already found useless. You say that for me to read the Scriptures is not pleasing to God. Yet in them I find peace and power, renewal for each day's duties, and life with a new dimension. Must I return to the old, barren ways?"

Reaching into his sleeve, he withdrew a worn volume. "See for yourself," he cried. The book fell open to a heavily underlined passage. As if in a dream, *this is a faithful saying & worthy of all acceptation that Christ Jesus came into the world to save sinners of whom I am chief.*

Latimer reached for it. His eyes fell upon the words of 1 Timothy 1:15, *"Fidelis sermo, et dignus omnino qui accipiatur, quod Christus Iesus venit in mundum, ut peccatores salvos faceret, quorum primus sum ego."*

The words pierced his heart like an arrow. They crashed against his stubborn defense of the church's teaching about man's salvation. Countless hours he had spent to produce convincing arguments against the Reformers in defense of the church while he had remained unconvinced in his own heart. Wonder not at that *now*, Hugh Latimer! His armor was shattered. He could only lay down his bow and arrows at the feet of the Conqueror. He had been fighting on the wrong side.

He tried in vain to speak. Tears poured down his cheeks. His inner vision cleared, as if he truly saw for the first time. He had thought Reformers proud and obstinate heretics, bent on destroying what the church stood for and changing the old ways and practices. How wrong he had been! Here was this earnest soul before him, an honest seeker after God who cared enough to come and light a candle in his soul's darkness.

Tears gleamed in Bilney's eyes as well. He took Latimer's hand and with a smile that seemed mingled with rays of light, whispered, "Thank God!"

As Bilney turned to go, Latimer managed to say in a broken voice, "Would you . . . would you find me a copy of the Book?"

2

[1524]

In some ways the change that took place in the heart of Hugh Latimer on that late spring evening in 1524 at Cambridge University was as cataclysmic as the conversion of the apostle Paul. For almost a week he scarcely left his rooms. He spent hours absorbed in the Testament Bilney obtained for him. The light from the Cross streamed into his soul with dazzling brilliance. The power of God's love overwhelmed him and brought tears again and again.

Over and over he read the words Bilney had pointed out, *"Christ Jesus came into the world to save sinners."* He felt them written in letters of flame upon his heart. In John's gospel he discovered, *"I am the Way, the Truth, and the Life. No man cometh unto the Father but by me."* In Romans he read, *"But God commendeth his love toward us, in that, while we were yet sinners, Christ died for us,"* and *"Being now justified by his blood, we shall be saved from wrath through him."*

Not all his time was spent devouring Scripture. He had to look back and then forward to visualize the difference this change would make in his life. A definite reorientation was necessary, but some things would remain the same. Sorting it all out was not easy. Seeking order in his thoughts, he relived certain portions of his life.

A boy of ten, he stood in a meadow in Leicestershire. He clutched a longbow from which an arrow had just flown. As the arrow fell short of its goal, his eyes clouded. He would never be an archer. His shoulders slumped in an attitude of defeat.

But his father was firm. "You use only the strength of your arms, Hugh. Lay your body in the bow. When you draw with the strength of your whole body, you will give wings to your arrow."

The lad pushed his fair hair back and looked into his father's face to find the confidence he needed. He fitted another arrow. All the strength of his body! The arrow flew straight to the target. A smile lit his face. His eyes shone.

In all the years since, he had tried to apply in every situation the lesson he learned that day. Your body in the bow!

Old Hugh never wavered in his intention. He meant this boy for the church. So young Hugh took the path to Cambridge. Not four years later, still an undergraduate, he became a Fellow of Clare Hall and achieved a growing reputation as a scholar.

The fellowship paid a meager stipend upon which he was able to live. He proceeded with all speed from the B.A. to M.A. degree. In nine years of his coming to Cambridge, he had reached the goal his father had set. He had knelt in the cathedral at Lincoln and taken his ordination vows as a priest of the church.

Nine more years had passed. An outstanding preacher, he was chosen one of the twelve University men licensed to preach anywhere in the realm.

Yet success had not brought peace. He thought of a day a few weeks earlier. A wild, wintry wind had swept down from the fens that spread across the eastern landscape of England. The scene seemed appropriate to his condition. For the wind wrung a silent protest from field and forest where crocuses had bloomed for weeks. Daffodils sprinkled their gold beside the River Cam and across the meadows. To all appearances spring had arrived, but winter insisted on one last fling.

After tramping for miles, he had sat upon a fallen tree in a clump of maples. Here he reached a decision about how to deal with the problem that had sent him flying off across the fields. He found himself increasingly engaged in a struggle against heresy in the University. It had begun with what some called the "new learning." Now a flood of heretical literature creeping across from Germany posed a larger threat against orthodoxy. He met with students in their sophistry gatherings and pleaded with them not to pervert their minds with such matter.

On that afternoon he had decided upon an open attack on the teaching of George Stafford, Reader of Divinity. Instead of following the usual program of the *Sentences* of Peter Lombard, Stafford was reading from the New Testament in Greek and Latin and daring to interpret what he read for his students.

As he now recalled that day, he dropped his head in his hands. It had begun a course of action of which he was now ashamed and for which he would have to try to make amends.

"And Stafford was right," he muttered to himself, "in his statement about justification by faith. Even while I was shouting against him, disrupting his lecture, I was trying to silence my own inner longing to believe it true." Latimer relived those and other memories as the chaos in his thoughts continued.

One day Bilney reappeared. "Come, my friend," he said with the bright smile Latimer would come to love. "You can't continue to hide your light under a bushel. Let it be seen."

Thus began the daily walks. So often did the two climb the slope of Castle Hill that the wags began to refer to it as "Heretics' Hill." All Cambridge was soon aware that something had happened to the strong defender of the church and the "old learning."

3

[1524]

Latimer found that he must somehow stretch the hours of each day. Of greatest importance was the study of the New Testament, from which he could scarcely tear himself away. Next in importance was the time spent with Bilney. So much to discuss, so much to learn. Yet his conscientious disposition would not allow any less scrupulous attention than before to his other duties.

An honor that he prized was his election two years before as Keeper of the Silver Cross. The great crucifix, a University treasure, was carried in official processions and displayed on important occasions. Latimer took great pride in rubbing and polishing it to a lustrous shine.

The crosskeeper was also chaplain of the University's New Chapel, a post that required the saying of mass on anniversary dates of benefactors who had bequeathed properties to the University. The position paid a sizeable stipend. Latimer was able to employ an undergraduate to clean the lecture halls and make repairs on the properties under his care.

He preached in his turn at Great St. Mary's, the University Church. He did the teaching that his fellowship required. Pursuit of his next degree meant continuation of his studies.

"How do you find time for everything?" he asked Bilney. "You never seem rushed. Yet you get your work done."

"I have a small secret," replied Bilney. "I require little sleep. Four hours does me admirably. That gives me an advantage. But surely God does not intend you to be under undue pressure. What activities could you dispense with?"

"I have considered and I see the mastery of the school men as less important. Why should I study Aquinas when I have the Scriptures?"

"You could leave them off for a time. Later you might consider those studies worth returning to."

"A different sort of problem causes me concern. What must I do about Stafford?"

"Ah, yes," said Bilney. "Perhaps we should discuss that."

"I entered his classroom and rudely disrupted his lecture. In indignation over his reading the Scriptures and daring to proclaim the doctrine of justification by faith, I urged his students to cease listening to him."

"The incident had all Cambridge in an uproar. Even your Master of Clare felt you acted with unwarranted vehemence."

"Dr. Natares understood my position but he realizes the need for caution in these times. He did express confidence in my 'stability,' as he put it. I wonder what he thinks now . . . now . . ."

As he faltered, Bilney smiled. ". . . Now that you are seen so often in my company? I imagine his confidence is shaken."

"About Stafford," continued Latimer, "I knew, even as I planned my attack, that under different circumstances I could like the man. His warm nature attracts people. He is a true scholar. As I awaited the proper moment to pounce upon his words, I could not but admire the beautiful cadence of his Latin. When he read in Greek, though I understood little of that language, the musical flow of his voice was captivating."

"His smile has a winning quality," said Bilney. "He has drawn a number of young students to an interest in the Scriptures and to a knowledge of the Truth found there."

"What must I do to make amends?"

"Don't force things. You will find an opportunity."

They moved down Castle Hill toward Cambridge. Absently twirling a new leaf in his fingers, Latimer said, "Thomas, how could I have thought of God as cold and austere, needing to be propitiated by my feeble acts of penance, my mumbling prayers and watchings? He had already made forgiveness available through faith by the blood of Christ. I thought he stood ready to strike me down for my sins, but in love he waited to receive me into his open arms, if only I would come."

"You were not alone, Hugh. I stood in the same error. How many others? Aids to worship have turned into obstacles to keep us from reaching God at all. Ceremonies intended to help us show our devotion to Christ have become means of winning his love and forgiveness, even of earning salvation. His lovely face is obscured by the wrong use of ceremonial aids."

At the bridge Bilney laid his hand upon his friend's arm and spoke softly. "It's time now for you to join us at the White Horse Inn. Will you come this evening and meet the others?"

Latimer did not reply at once. He dropped his oak leaf into the stream and watched it swirl past. "I feel a reluctance, a fear that they might not accept me. Will Stafford be there?"

"He'll be there."

They continued a few paces before Latimer spoke again. "I'll come. You'll be with me. I am really eager to come. It's just that I rather dread the first encounter."

Bilney smiled. "You needn't. There's nothing to fear."

Encouraged him & brought him into Bill's Study

[1524]

Latimer scarcely noticed the chill that had come with darkness. Excitement filled him, but a slight fear remained. He followed Bilney along the river's edge behind Trinity and Clare Halls, past King's College and into Cholis Lane. Turning right into Milne Street, they found the square belonging to Catherine Hall on the left. Bilney lifted the latch of a small postern gate, and they slipped inside. Across the court they climbed a stair. Bilney rapped a signal on the door. It opened for them to enter and immediately closed behind them.

A fire on the hearth provided illumination and welcome warmth this April evening. Beside the fireplace stood two heavy oak settles at right angles to the wall. Windows were carefully shuttered. The point of interest for Latimer was a long table bearing two or three flickering candles. Upon rough benches on either side sat the men he was eager, yet hesitant to meet.

Bilney led him to the end of the table. Some faces he had expected to see; others were a surprise. On one side sat Thomas Arthur, John Thixtill, Matthew Parker, and John Lambert. Beyond them were Richard Smith, William Paget, and two he did not know. On the other side he recognized

Edward Crome, Nicholas Shaxton, John Rogers, George Stafford, and Miles Coverdale.

Fellows and doctors, masters and undergraduates, all assembled for one purpose. Each held a copy of the same *Novum Testamentum* he found so compelling.

"Friends," said Bilney, "I have told you how the light broke for Latimer a short time ago. He has found what each of us finds in the Scriptures. He comes to join us. You will welcome him."

All eyes were upon him as a murmur of welcome rippled around the table. Their expressions put him at ease. Bilney guided him to where, as if by prearrangement, places opened for them. As they seated themselves, Bilney involved himself in conversation with his neighbor on the right. On Latimer's left sat Stafford.

He turned to find Stafford looking intently at his book. In a low voice Latimer said, "I must ask your forgiveness. Truly, I am sorry. I was blind, but the Lord has seen fit to open my eyes. What I did must seem unpardonable, but . . . but . . ." He trailed off into silence, not knowing what more to say, since Stafford gave no sign of hearing.

Stafford turned to face him. His eyes gleamed softly in the candlelight. "Of course I forgive you, Latimer. I was ready to do so as soon as the first shock wore off. I was angry but I asked the Lord to forgive *me*. So I must forgive *you*. You acted in ignorance. I prayed that God would enlighten you, and he did. Give me your hand, for we are brothers now."

As he felt Stafford's firm grip, tears of relief came to Latimer's eyes. "I should tell you," he said, "that God used what I overheard in your lectures to stab me to an awareness of the Truth. Not at once, but after Bilney made his 'confession.' Your lucid explanation of the Scripture kept coming back to me."

"For that I am grateful. God works in strange ways."

As leader for the evening, he then made ready to begin. "We'll resume our reading where we left off last night in the fourth chapter of the Epistle to the Romans."

The next hour would remain bright in Latimer's memory to the end of his days. They read in Latin, then in Greek. The discussion that followed thrilled his heart.

The closing time of prayer was a revelation to Latimer. He knew the Latin prayers of the prayer book. But these men poured out their hearts to God in English, speaking as to one present in the room. Latimer was convinced that he was indeed present. The glow from hearts drawn together before the Savior produced an almost visible brightness.

Parker extinguished the fire, which already burned low. Rogers blew out the candles, lifted the bar from the door and opened it. "As usual," he said, "leave by ones and twos."

In the darkness someone spoke into Latimer's ear. "We'll listen to your next sermon with interest. God will doubtless turn your tremendous gift for preaching in a different way."

Latimer was a bit startled. He knew he must face up to his preaching, but he wasn't sure how to go about it. A heart change is one thing; to fit that change into every facet of daily life is another. His turn to preach at Great St. Mary's was little more than a week off. He recalled Bilney's words, *"You can't keep hiding your light under a bushel."*

5

[1524]

Spring had arrived in its full glory. Every little garden had its hyacinths and tulips. Early roses, the delicate pink ones with the soft fragrance, bloomed along the bridge. Bilney picked his way lightly up the hill ahead of Latimer.

Latimer's back was giving him pain. Glancing at the slight form of his friend, he called out, "You have an advantage in being small. You don't have as much to carry up the hill as I."

Bilney slowed his pace a bit. "How's the sermon coming?" he asked. "It is significant that you preach first at the University Church. You will be taking an official stand. Your Latin is as good as your English, so that presents no problem."

"As for the tongue," replied Latimer, "it's easier to preach in Latin than in English. You doubtless find the same true."

"What do you plan for your sermon?"

"My text is from St. John's gospel where Jesus says, *'I am the light of the world; he who followeth me shall not walk in darkness, but shall have the light of life.'* Jesus has burst in upon me as the very Light. Beginning to know him fully and freely is nothing short of the brilliant sunrise of a new day."

"Most appropriate. I knew you would find the right one."

"An official stand? I'm not sure. Certainly I plan to preach no heresy. Contrary to what I thought, reform does not mean overthrowing the church or changing its doctrines, but making the Truth plain and clearing away the obstacles."

"When you stop attacking the Reformers and warning against heresy, your listeners will know that something has happened. Seeing you in my company day after day has already raised questions. They'll be out in full force to hear you."

"We must make them understand," protested Latimer. "They must recognize the Truth."

"The difficulties are greater than you imagine. But God undoubtedly raised you up for a special purpose."

"So many think, as I did, that Reformers mean to destroy the old faith. When they learn better, they'll be in accord."

"What's going to happen about your sudden devotion to the Scriptures? Your Master of Clare will not approve."

"Dr. Natares will be unhappy. He will deplore my new position, unless I can convince him of the Truth. His conviction was strong that my stability would prove unshakable against the Reformers and their heresy."

"He just turns out to be a false prophet," said Bilney.

"Maybe he was not so badly mistaken. He said he felt certain I would never fall away from *the true faith.* I have no intention of falling away from the *true* faith. I merely have a clearer understanding of it. I *do* mean to stand firm."

"It's not what he meant."

"I'll work hard on the sermon. Pray that I may say the right things." Latimer reached out to touch his friend's shoulder. "I don't know how to thank you, Thomas, not only for your confession that changed my life, but also for your daily support and friendship. I have never known anyone like you."

"Look at it this way: I'm just 'little Bilney.' Timid and fearful, I'll never accomplish mighty deeds. But if I can give you a push, God can do no end of great things through you."

6

[1524]

Excitement ran high at Great St. Mary's on the morning of Latimer's sermon. His preaching always drew a crowd. Today promised to set a record.

The excitement stirred Latimer as well. *I feel as eager,* he thought, *and as uncertain, as a new priest about to preach his first sermon.* An inner voice seemed to reply, "You *are* a new priest about to preach your first sermon. *New* you certainly are in your understanding of the gospel. You stand today to preach your *first* sermon as a soul set free by the living Lord."

He was conscious of a difference in his preaching. He sensed a power not his own and felt little need to rely upon his natural persuasiveness or facility with words. He stuck to his text and drew illustrations from Scripture, with a few from his own experience. While he made no direct reference to the change in his own life, the evidence was there.

Those who came expecting heresy were disappointed. Perhaps his

Hoopula

message left unanswered questions, but no flaw could be found in his doctrinal stand. Yet henceforth his words and actions would be held under close scrutiny. The company he kept and the subtle change in the content of his sermon made him suspect.

At the next meeting at the White Horse Latimer found that he was in the limelight. The men had been pleased with his sermon. Most understood the caution he felt it necessary to exercise at first.

"You made a fine beginning," said Crome. "We'll expect greater things in the future."

"Don't get carried away and say more than wisdom permits," said Coverdale. "You could harm the cause as well as yourself."

"He's right," agreed Bilney. "Guard against language that could be twisted to any semblance of heresy."

"It wasn't as hard as I expected," said Latimer. "A power not my own makes it easy to speak the words of the message Scripture has revealed to me. I preach next at St. Edward the Martyr in fulfillment of a commitment made some weeks ago." *then at Hoopula*

Latimer observed a peculiarity in Bilney's behavior. "You enter the hall for dinner empty-handed but you often leave carrying a parcel. You take your dinner away with you?"

"My appetite is small," said Bilney. "I require only one meal a day. I give the other to someone in need of it."

"And who is this 'someone'?"

"I visit poor wretches in the hospitals who have no one to care for them. They lie on their miserable cots day after day with only their barest needs met. I do what I can to ease their suffering. Some are always hungry."

Latimer murmured, "'I was hungry, and you gave me to eat . . . I was sick, and you visited me.' It's relatively easy to drop money in the 'poor' box. But you, Thomas—you give yourself, as Jesus did."

"They need to hear of his love. They listen more readily if someone demonstrates it in practical ways."

"Might I accompany you?"

"I've been waiting for you to ask."

Leaving the White Horse surroundings behind, they made their way to a hospital. Latimer involuntarily drew back in horror as he followed Bilney into a filthy room filled with the most wretched pieces of humanity he had ever seen. The stench was overpowering. The loathsome sores dressed in dirty rags or left uncovered repelled him. An almost uncontrollable wave of nausea swept over him.

"How can you stand it, Thomas?"

"You learn to look beneath the outward circumstances, Hugh. On each cot lies a redeemable soul, needing to hear of Jesus."

Faces lit up as Bilney approached. He laid his hand upon a fevered brow, or drew thin covers about a shivering sufferer, or lifted one that he might drink. To each he spoke some word of Jesus. As he prayed, tears flowed from many an eye.

Before leaving, Bilney divided his food between two who seemed most needy. The ravenous manner in which they consumed it was frightening. Latimer could but ponder upon the insufficiency in relation to such a terrible need.

He followed Bilney out in silence. "I go now," said Bilney, "to the prison across the way."

Here Latimer found matters worse, if possible, than in the hospital. A powerful mixture of odors assailed him, odors of unwashed bodies, filthy clothing, and human waste. Even breathing was difficult. People might exist here, but no real living was possible under such conditions.

What struck Latimer most forcibly was the hopeless expression in the eyes. Many had remained long without a trial. Rejected by friends and loved ones, what hope could they have?

"How can I ever feel love for such as these?" he asked.

Bilney turned to face him with a sad smile. "You don't *feel* it, Hugh; you *show* it. What could God find in me, a miserable sinner, that would make him *feel* love? But he *showed* it in sending his Son."

Latimer continued to observe Bilney's procedure. He seemed to know something about each man. He paused to speak quietly to individuals about hope in Christ. Then standing where the largest number could see, he preached a simple sermon. He closed with a prayer, committing them to God's tender mercies.

"If I'm not careful," said Bilney, as they moved down the hill toward the river, "I spend more time here than I can afford."

They reached the bridge and crossed it before either spoke. Then Bilney turned with an inquiring look. "You remain silent, Hugh? I thought you would be exploding with impressions."

"I am at a loss for words, Thomas. I am deeply affected. I scarcely know how to deal with my conflicting emotions."

"It was not easy for me at first. Only the compelling love of Jesus made me go. But now I look forward to going."

"What I have seen today underscores what God has been teaching me," said Latimer. "As I read the Gospels, I follow Jesus along the shores of Galilee and into the streets of Jerusalem. He preached and he taught, even as he has called us to do. But, too, he is always thronged by the poor, the hungry, the lame, the blind, the lepers, the ignorant, the crafty, the grasping, the needy. He took time to demonstrate the love of God to individuals, as well as masses."

"Yes, I know," said Bilney. "Strange how we never saw that so clearly before. He reveals it in the reading of his Word."

"Peter and Paul set forth the same example. How different from the usual picture of the life of devotion. How inadequate such things as burning candles, praying before saints' shrines, and going on pilgrimages seem. Whom do these exercises benefit? Today I saw in action such a life of love as Jesus surely means us to live. I perceived the true meaning of charity."

A deep sadness filled him. "What distresses me beyond words," he continued, "is my reaction to what I saw. I shrink with all my being from the thought of touching those diseased wretches as you did. When I would speak of the love of Jesus, I find a barrier I cannot cross. In short, I am a hypocrite."

Bilney's eyes grew soft with compassion. "Give yourself time, Hugh," he said gently. "The Christian life is a growth. You are not alone. The Holy Spirit stands ready to make the changes within you. It is his work, not yours. Let him do it."

Latimer's mind remained uneasy. He was unable to sleep. The faces he had seen kept coming before him. The unspeakable odors filled his nostrils and threatened to choke him. He struggled against his feeling of disgust. The compassion he should feel refused to come. He spent a miserable night.

7

[1524–1525]

Morning brought a result Latimer could have predicted. One of his fierce headaches assailed him. Any unusual stress was likely to produce one. He was unable to think, almost immobilized while the agonizing pain continued.

When he had first arrived at Cambridge, they occurred with such frequency that he almost despaired of being able to remain at his studies.

He could now see the connection between the headaches and the stress of those early days. He had been used to simple but plentiful food on his father's farm. His ailing body suffered from the monotony of boiled beef and oatmeal, never in sufficient quantity. When he crept shivering to bed in a damp, cell-like room shared with three other students, he longed for the warmth of the hearth at Thurcaston. The hours dragged, lectures were often dull, and he had to memorize prodigious amounts of materials.

"But I persevered," he murmured, as these memories stirred. "I remembered my father's voice, 'Your body in the bow.'"

Late in the day the pain diminished. But any jarring movement could renew the stabs of agony. Bilney commented on his paleness. He was more subdued until the effects wore off.

The daily walks continued. The two spent hours discussing the New Testament. Latimer committed to the Lord his reluctance to visit the hospital and prison. Then he drew his forces together and became Bilney's regular companion in this labor. The feeling of revulsion lessened. The day came when he looked forward to the visits as much as Bilney did.

It was the summer of 1525. Bilney and Stafford sat one day in Latimer's study discussing the growing interest of many students in the Scriptures. Increasingly they came to the Reformers with questions. A few had joined the group.

"We should concentrate our efforts," said Stafford, "upon winning Dr. Robert Barnes to the cause."

"Coverdale has spoken of him," said Latimer. "Both are of the monastery of the Augustine Friars. Barnes is prior there."

"Isn't he the one," asked Bilney, "who studied at Louvain and distinguished himself as such a brilliant scholar?"

"The same," said Stafford. "Admirers of the classics flocked to his lectures here on Cicero, Terence, and Plautus."

"What makes you think we should concentrate on him?" asked Latimer, somewhat puzzled.

Stafford flashed him a smile. "Just recently he has begun to expound St. Paul's epistles."

"Ah!" cried Bilney and Latimer, almost with one voice.

"But," continued Stafford, "he fails to understand well the Apostle's meaning. Some say he lectures on St. Paul out of a love for controversial subjects, rather than a love of Scripture."

Bilney suggested that they attend one of his lectures. At this Latimer and Stafford exchanged glances and laughed.

Bilney hastened to add, "Of course, we must go with a more kindly attitude than—"

"Than that with which I attended Stafford's lecture," concluded Latimer.

Barnes delighted them with his wit and charm. A friendly relationship developed, and they were soon able to bring him to a better understanding of St. Paul.

Tall and broad-shouldered, Barnes had a booming voice, which could not fail to command attention. He was popular with members of his House and far beyond. He attracted Latimer at once.

He displayed an intractable nature, however. Happy as he was to fellowship with them and to attend an occasional meeting at the White Horse, he was not inclined to identify with them.

"Give him time," said Bilney. "He'll come around."

The Pope had now seen fit to provide for the financing of Cardinal

Wolsey's proposed college at Oxford. His emissaries arrived with instructions to search out the finest minds at Cambridge. They were to offer liberal rewards to those who would transfer to Oxford and become the nucleus of the new college.

When the agents had concluded their investigation, they began to issue secret invitations. It was soon common knowledge that two of the chosen had declined the honor. One was Thomas Cranmer, a Fellow of Jesus College, known to be a great lover of Scripture. The other was Matthew Parker, a well-loved member of the White Horse assembly.

Meetings at the White Horse Inn continued. The men had begun to include in their study writings of the Continental Reformers. Not everything they read was acceptable, but it was helpful to know what other Reformers were thinking.

One evening several men appeared unduly excited. "We know," said Coverdale, "to whom the cardinal's other invitations went."

Holding a paper near the candle, he read, "Richard Cox, John Clarke, John Fryer, Godfrey Harman, Henry Sumner, William Betts, John Frith, Goodman, and Radley."

Before he finished reading, the group had dissolved into helpless laughter. Such an uproar followed that it took a worried Parker several minutes to restore order.

"This could bring someone to investigate," he remonstrated. "Then they catch us red-handed with our reading matter, after all our precautions of the past months."

Several of the men on the list were even present in the room, but all maintained a firm commitment to the spread of Reformed ideas. The company found the situation hilarious.

"What would the cardinal say," asked Cox, "if he knew his 'able men' were all tainted with heresy?"

Looking thoughtful, Stafford replied, "He's willing to overlook a bit of harmless heresy if only he gets the best men for his purpose. He likes to frustrate the bishops who are eager to hunt heretics. And he does not want the waters muddied just when he is planning to get his college under way."

"When do you go?" asked Latimer, turning to Frith.

"Probably not for several months. The building that will house us is still under construction. We are to remain ready."

The joke had to be kept private, of course. Not only was it a source of joy but of serious thanksgiving to them all. A nucleus of Reformers at Oxford!

A certain cessation of activity against the Reformers marked that summer. Bilney, Stafford, and Latimer preached as never before. West, Bishop of Ely and no lover of heresy, licensed Bilney to preach anywhere in the diocese.

All their preaching was on the same general theme: the free forgiveness of sins by the atonement of Christ, a message many had never heard before. On the negative side, they attacked the abuses that tended to conceal Christ and salvation.

Men might be suspicious of such teaching, but it would have been difficult to base a charge of heresy. As the year moved into autumn and peace prevailed, Latimer grew apprehensive. Could it be that this lull preceded some storm?

8

[1525]

The first Sunday in December dawned frosty, but clear. Worshipers were gathering at Great St. Mary's as Latimer approached. The hour for the sermon found the preacher in high spirits. He had a good sermon prepared and a large congregation to hear it: a satisfactory combination.

He read the Scripture and then repeated the words of his text several times. A manuscript lay before him, but careful planning made it unnecessary for him to refer to it. He sometimes made changes as he preached.

As he completed his introduction and moved into the first point, a group of latecomers entered, causing a disturbance. He paused for the restoration of order. The Bishop of Ely and his attendants advanced in all ostentation to occupy the foremost seats, which were hastily vacated for their use.

As the surprised murmurs died away, Latimer said, with a smile in the direction of the Bishop West, "A new audience, and especially one of such rank, deserves a new theme."

He turned in his Bible to the ninth chapter of Hebrews and read a portion of the eleventh verse, *"Christus autem superveniens pontifex futurorum bonorum. . . ."* Then he threw his head back and lifted his eyes up past the stately arches of the clerestoried nave to the vaulted oak ceiling. Turning his head slightly to one side, he appeared to be listening. After a moment he returned his gaze to his audience.

"Listen to what God has to say, 'Christ being a high priest of good things to come . . .' Our Lord himself is a priest, a High Priest. Some of us are priests. It is a goodly and should be a godly calling. Some are even high priests— bishops we call them. Christ, our great High Priest, sets for us an example."

He sketched the life of Christ as the supreme model for all bishops and priests. He elaborated upon the sacredness of the office and the awesomeness of being named to the same office, although to a lesser degree, as our Lord. He enumerated the duties and responsibilities such an office entailed.

"Alas! How widely some depart from the model. How far short they come of being true pastors of Christ's people. Could it be that some resemble more nearly the line of priests headed by Annas and Caiphas?"

The bishop, with a half-smile, kept his eyes fixed on Latimer. At the end of the hour he lost no time in summoning him to the room beside the west door, the usual meeting place of the Consistory Court of the Diocese. Latimer paused a moment at the door. Then with head held high, he stepped into the bishop's presence. As the two men eyed each other, Latimer could sense the other's antagonism.

"I thank you, Master Latimer," West began, "for your most excellent sermon. Never have I heard my office so admirably expounded. Indeed, if you will do one more thing, I will kneel and kiss your feet for the good admonition I have received."

The exaggerated politeness of the words did not match the expression in his eyes. Latimer replied with caution. "What is your lordship's pleasure that I should do for you?"

"A simple matter," said the bishop. "I wish only that you preach me one sermon against Martin Luther and his doctrine."

"My lord, I am not acquainted with the doctrines of Luther, nor are we permitted here to read his works. How could I refute his doctrine when I am ignorant of what he has written?"

West made no reply to this. He seemed to be waiting. His eyes never left Latimer's.

"Sure I am," continued Latimer, "that I preached before you this day no man's doctrine, but only that of God from the Scriptures. If Luther does the same, no confutation of his doctrine is needed. If I am led to see that he teaches against Scripture, I will be quite ready to confound his doctrine."

Unable to make objection to this shrewd reply, West broke off the conversation with the remark that Latimer would one day repent of his course. Abruptly he dismissed him.

Latimer felt somewhat shaken. He went in search of Bilney but failed to find him. Nor could he find Stafford. Only in midafternoon did he come upon the two of them together.

Their expressions informed him that they already knew of the morning's events. He hastened to acquaint them with his version and with the outcome of his summons before the bishop.

"What will he do now?" he asked. "He won't let it drop."

"We can only wait," said Stafford. "I am not sure just what he *can* do but I agree that he will not drop the matter."

"Waiting is the hardest part," murmured Bilney. "We must remember to pray while we wait."

9

[1525]

A week dragged by. Then on Sunday afternoon a monk from Barnwell Abbey, highly excited, burst into Latimer's room. "The Bishop of Ely preached at the abbey today," he said. "He denounced you and said, 'That voice will no longer be heard in this diocese.'"

A formal document arrived the next day. It curtly prohibited Latimer from officiating in any part of the diocese or in any of the University pulpits until further notice.

Latimer paced the floor like a caged animal. *"Until further notice"— what does that mean? I have to preach.*

He seized his cap and clapped it on his head. Buttoning it beneath his chin with one hand, he reached for his cloak with the other. Out he strode in search of Bilney.

Bilney listened in silence to his angry tirade. When Latimer had run out of words, he gave his friend a puzzled look. "How can you remain so calm? Don't you see what this means?"

"I see quite clearly," replied Bilney. "It is bad, but not as bad as it might be. We need to see Barnes."

"Barnes! What does Barnes have to do with it? He's not even quite one of us. He is certainly no friend of the Bishop of Ely." Latimer was a bit indignant over Bilney's attitude.

Bilney did not elucidate. With an enigmatic smile, he bundled into his cloak and opened the door. "Come," he said. Something in his manner compelled a doubtful Latimer to follow.

As they passed St. Edward's Church, a figure hurtled around the corner and almost collided with them. It was Barnes.

"Just the people I was looking for!" he said. "Now we need Stafford. Some discussion and some plans are in order."

Stafford was in his rooms beside a roaring fire. They were barely seated when Barnes burst out, "I've decided at last to join you openly."

"What brought you to this decision?" asked Stafford. "You've been *with* us but not *of* us for some time."

"At Louvain I came in contact with Lutherans. My understanding remained a bit hazy until you set me straight on St. Paul. I'm a stubborn fellow. I refused to step out on your side because I am basically a 'loner.' But the time has come."

To Latimer he said, "I heard about the bishop. I offer you the freedom of my pulpit at the monastery chapel. It's a 'peculiar' and not subject to the jurisdiction of the bishop. West forgets that his power is limited."

Latimer cast a quick glance at Bilney, who was smiling.

"Words fail me, Barnes. You provide relief for a troubled man. I hasten to accept with gratitude. How can I thank you?"

"The only thanks I need is for you to preach," said Barnes. "I have never felt too kindly toward West. I take perverse delight in this opportunity to frustrate him."

"The news that you ally yourself with us is welcome," said Bilney. "Your ability, your status among the intellectuals, your popularity with the students—all this will make you an asset."

Reaching into Stafford's small hoard in the corner, Barnes selected a lump of coal and cast it on the fire. "I could turn out to be a liability. You know I fly off at tangents."

"St. James reminds us," said Stafford, "that the tongue is a member hard to control. But you have help. As you step forward to take a firmer stand for Christ, he will give you control."

"If I let him," mused Barnes. "My next scheduled preaching is Sunday at St. Edward's. I selected my text from the epistle for the day, 'Rejoice in the Lord alway; and again I say, Rejoice. Let your moderation be known to all men.'"

Latimer recalled his own first appearance as a Reformer. He looked at the young man with the flashing eyes and eager enthusiasm. "We need to heed well the latter part of the text."

Barnes' expression grew more serious, and his eyes softened. "Thank you, Latimer. Now as I identify myself publicly with the Reformers, I will try to be careful."

Latimer preached on Christmas Eve in the little chapel at the Augustine Friary. The fact that he preached in defiance of the Bishop of Ely might have drawn comment. Any attention that might have been turned his way, however, was completely overshadowed by the explosion Barnes caused.

10

[1525–1526]

A hastily called meeting at the White Horse drew full attendance. Several members had been at St. Edward's. Matthew Parker was given the floor.

"Seeing faces of so many opponents of the Reformation evidently caused Barnes to cast caution to the wind. He was already excited over Latimer's matter. He began with caustic remarks, but soon he moved into an attack on the clergy, particularly bishops. He likened bishops to Judas, who loved the purse but not Christ. Like Balaam, they ride upon asses, who are the ignorant people whom they rob and abuse."

"Did he actually say all that, Matthew?" demanded Bilney. "Surely you exaggerate. Barnes would have better sense."

"All that and more," Parker assured him. "He claimed the horns of the bishops' miters resemble the horns of the false prophets, and the pastoral staff is used to knock the sheep on the head.

"He attacked Cardinal Wolsey. He denounced him for his many offices, his great dioceses, the pomp in which he carries himself about, his magnificent clothing, his pillars, his cushions, his two crosses, his golden shoes, his red gloves. All these he held up to the scorn and ridicule of his hearers. I can tell you, after a short silence at the conclusion, all hell broke loose."

"He made it possible for Latimer to preach," said Thomas Arthur, "but the harm he has done may be too great a price to pay, even for that good."

"You are right that he has done us no good," said Bilney. "But we must not desert him. He let his hot head get him into trouble, and he is in serious need of our support."

"He insists that he was misunderstood," said Parker. "He asked for a chance to preach next Sunday so that he may explain himself. The vice chancellor vetoed that."

"He is not officially under arrest," said Stafford, "but they have him hidden away for questioning. That can't go on."

"First thing in the morning, Stafford," said Bilney, "you and I must go to the vice chancellor. Barnes should either be released or put under arrest and given a fair trial. Secret questioning must not go unchallenged."

Barnes was released but his troubles were not over. The University divided into opposing factions, as it often did with a live controversy. Many lined up on the side of Barnes. No one remained neutral. The opposition drew up twenty-five articles from Barnes' sermon and insisted that he recant.

He was ready to admit to being indiscreet. But recantation was preposterous. The opposition seemed determined to bring him to recantation without a public trial. His friends were equally determined that his trial must be public. Latimer and Bilney led in his defense and protection. They regretted the sermon but meant to stand by their brother at whatever the cost.

Finally, on the advice of his friends, Barnes threw himself on the mercy of the vice chancellor and agreed to read from St. Edward's a recantation of the offensive matter.

11

[1526]

Barnes remained calm up to the moment the paper was put in his hand. His friends in the assembly could almost breathe a sigh of relief. Barnes would read and here the matter would end.

As Barnes scanned the paper, his face darkened. He returned the sheet to the vice chancellor, saying in a firm voice, "Sir, I refuse to read anything so grossly unfair as that." He turned and strode from the building. No one offered to detain him.

Latimer and Bilney hastened to the monastery, where they found Barnes pacing the floor of his study in a fine rage.

"What on earth came over you?" asked Bilney in a voice somewhat less loving than his usual tone.

Latimer threw an arm about Barnes' shoulders, saying, "We're not blaming you, for we know there is a logical explanation."

Making an effort at self-control, Barnes said hoarsely, "You never saw anything as unjust. The terms of the proposed recantation were impossible. They wanted me to admit saying things I never said and then to repent for having said them. As unwise as my words were, they had twisted them to make it appear I had said horrid and indecent things. They wished to put into my mouth heresy and even blasphemy. They knew I could not read such a paper. They haven't had their fun yet."

A storm broke from other directions. An Englishman, working on the Continent, had produced a translation of the New Testament in English that he would attempt to circulate throughout England. Furthermore, it was claimed that not only Cambridge but all England was filled with Luther's books. This, in the public mind, was wrapped up and made part and parcel of Barnes' dilemma.

"The translator of that New Testament could only be William Tyndale," said Bilney.

On February 5 at midmorning Parker rushed up to Latimer. "Barnes has been arrested. They have hurried him off toward London. Coverdale intends to follow. He is to appear before the cardinal."

At that moment Stafford burst in. "Quickly! We must move the books. Farman says the hiding place is known."

Only a handful of men knew where the forbidden books were stored. But the secret had leaked out. Latimer, Bilney, Stafford, and three others moved toward the hiding place, not too quickly lest they arouse suspicion. Then each man went his way, carrying what appeared to be books for his studies.

The sergeant-at-arms who had arrested Barnes came striding down the street with his underlings. He jerked open the postern gate leading to the court outside the White Horse and marched directly to a coal bin under the stairway. He threw up the lid, only to stare blankly at emptiness. His face flushed, and he hastily departed.

12

[1526]

By common consent the White Horse meetings were suspended until the noise concerning Barnes and the missing books died down. It was impossible to suppress a certain anxiety over Barnes.

On February 13, eight days after the arrest, Coverdale and two companions returned. Word spread and a cautious movement began toward the White Horse. A fire burned on the hearth, and the benches were drawn toward it. Fear of what they were about to hear hung heavy. When the shifting and moving had ceased, Bilney prayed.

Coverdale then rose, the flames behind him casting an elongated, dancing shadow across the room. He moved his hands in excited gestures as he began to speak.

"You know how Barnes was arrested in the Chapter House of the monastery. I followed with Goodwin and Field. We lost time finding horses but overtook them before dark. We rode with them but were permitted no conversation."

"Coverdale," cried Matthew Parker, "will you please move on and tell us what happened to Barnes?"

"All in good time, my dear Parker," replied Coverdale, inclining his shaggy head in Parker's direction. "Some of our brethren desire a full report, and who knows when and whether we may obtain another opportunity to speak thus?"

"A full report," said Stafford, "but move along a bit faster. Who knows whether we have even one uninterrupted hour?"

Coverdale nodded. "In London they conferred with Stephen Gardiner, the cardinal's secretary. He permitted Barnes to spend the night with Thomas Parnell, a former student of his. Gardiner was one of Barnes' tutors at Cambridge and has great respect for him. He and Edward Fox did all they could for Barnes."

Coverdale pressed on with the tale. Barnes had waited all day at Westminster Palace. Late in the afternoon he was summoned before Wolsey in the gallery he uses at the palace. Only Fox and Gardiner were present. It was not the cardinal's custom to become excited over a bit of heresy. But Barnes had wounded his well-known vanity. He was unwilling to pass over the attack on his personal dignity and habits.

"What! Master Doctor," he had cried, "had you not sufficient scope in the Scriptures to teach the people, but that my golden shoes, my pillars, my golden cushions, my crosses did so offend you, that you must make us *'ridiculum caput'* amongst the people? That day we were jollily laughed to scorn. Verily, it was a sermon fitter to be preached on a stage than in a pulpit."

Fox and Gardiner probably saved him. They knelt before the cardinal and pleaded for him, promising that he would conform.

The cardinal said, "Stand up! For your sakes, and the University's, we will be good to him." He then asked Barnes whether he would acknowledge the legatine powers that were his.

"I thank Your Grace for your good will," Barnes replied. "I will stick to the Holy Scriptures, according to the simple talent God has lent me."

"Well," the cardinal answered, "you shall have your learning tried to the uttermost and you shall have the law."

Back at Parnell's, Coverdale and those with him spent the night helping Barnes write out his defense. After that they were not allowed to see him again until Sunday.

On Thursday and Friday Barnes faced four bishops who were his judges. He was repeatedly commanded to confess heresy, which he refused to do. On Saturday they ordered him to read and sign a paper handed to him or stand in jeopardy of his life.

"I will not read," declared Barnes.

At this the bishops changed their tactics. They insisted that it was a small matter merely to read a few words. They stressed the mercy of the cardinal, if only Barnes would submit.

Sympathy accomplished what threats had not. Barnes seized the roll, read it, subscribed to it, and marked a cross upon it. He agreed to submit to any penance inflicted and was returned to the Fleet Prison.

At first light on Sunday Barnes and other prisoners were given fagots to carry and then marched through the streets of London from the Fleet to St. Paul's Cathedral.

A high scaffold stood at the top of the stairs. Here the cardinal sat with his mitered abbots, priors, and bishops in all the pomp against which Barnes had spoken. The cardinal was arrayed in rich purple; the others in gowns of damask and satin.

After the sermon Barnes and the others were made to kneel and ask forgiveness of God, of the church, and of the cardinal, in his gold shoes, red gloves and all. Then they were required to state that they had been more charitably treated than they deserved.

Barnes marched three times about the fire and threw his fagot into the flames. He then knelt before Rochester, received absolution, and was declared received again into the church.

Here Coverdale ended. "We had only a word with him before he was returned to prison to await the cardinal's pleasure."

"I fear we won't see Barnes again soon," said Bilney. "He will not likely be allowed to return to Cambridge even when he is released from the Fleet. Wolsey may not be through with us here. He will have the names of those who spoke out for Barnes."

13

[1526]

Latimer was troubled. He felt Barnes was wrong to agree to what they required him to read. He had acted against his conscience in thus recanting. The lying statements wrung from him must have distressed him greatly. But was the wretched sermon worth dying for? Barnes was no heretic. His words had wounded human vanity. They were extravagant, foolish, but not heretical. Yet the statements he had been forced to make had no relation to the content of his sermon.

What if I had been in his place? Latimer asked himself. *Would I have acted differently? What is worth dying for? Death at the stake is not to be embraced lightly.*

Bilney was not wrong in his surmise that the cardinal meant to deal with Barnes' friends. A few weeks later both Bilney and Latimer received a summons to appear before the cardinal.

Spring was in the air as they rode toward London. A bit of green peeped through the brown earth of the fields. Beeches and elms unfurled their leaves. Early hyacinths and crocuses painted bright spots along the way.

"How can we be utterly downcast," asked Latimer, "in view of the beauty of God's earth?" Yet they felt apprehensive.

Bilney was called first. In a surprisingly brief time he reappeared, relief written on his face. The cardinal had questioned him about his teaching, but in no detail. After brief consideration he required him to swear that he would not preach Luther's doctrine. He had his man reimburse Bilney for his expenses in coming to London, a gesture that left him amazed.

A few moments later the cardinal's small bell sounded, summoning Latimer into his presence. The cardinal was arrayed in his usual splendor. Two of his chaplains, Dr. Capon and Dr. Marshal, attended him.

He began by asking Latimer his name. Then he commented on his appearance, noting that he was no youth.

"I may inform Your Grace that I have passed my fortieth birthday," said Latimer.

"Yet I am told," said Wolsey, "that you are infected with the fantastic heresy of Luther. A man of your years should know better. The report is that you do much harm with your teaching."

"Your Grace is misinformed," replied Latimer with dignity. "I ought to have more knowledge than such as has been reported to you. I have been for many years a student of the ancient Fathers of the church and also of the school doctors."

The cardinal seemed surprised. He turned to his chaplains and bade them question Latimer on Duns. Each of them propounded questions of Latimer, who answered with no hesitation. At one point Dr. Capon stumbled in trying to state his question. Latimer helped him frame it and then promptly answered. Clearly he knew his schoolmen better than the chaplains.

"What do you mean, my masters," demanded Wolsey, "in bringing such a man before me? I thought he must be some light-headed fellow who had never studied such doctrines as these. Tell me, Latimer, what has the Bishop of Ely against you?"

"I would inform Your Grace that some time ago I preached a sermon in his presence on the duties of a bishop. My text was Hebrews 9:11. Since that time the bishop has forbidden me to preach anywhere in his diocese or in any University pulpit."

Upon being asked what he preached on the text, Latimer summarized his teaching.

"You preached nothing more than that?" asked the cardinal.

Assured that such was the case, he asked a few more questions and consulted with his chaplains. With an ironic smile he said to Latimer, "If the Bishop of Ely cannot abide such doctrine, you shall have my license and preach it unto his beard, let him say what he will."

A few moments later Latimer was ushered out, clutching the cardinal's license to preach anywhere in the realm. He almost knocked Bilney down as he seized his arm and burst into an excited recital of what had taken place.

Barnes may have injured the cause of the Reformation, but today the great Cardinal Wolsey had unwittingly been of the greatest assistance to it. They could not explain his benevolent mood, but with grateful hearts, they took the road to Cambridge.

14

[1526]

On the following Sunday Latimer appeared at St. Edward's. Before the astonished congregation he climbed the five steps to the pulpit. He reached into his sleeve, producing a paper. This he smoothed out with great care, aware of the growing suspense. In a clear voice he read the words from the cardinal's license. He then took up his Bible, read the lesson for the day, and proceeded with the service in his ordinary manner.

After the shock of his return to the pulpit wore off, a period of calm descended upon the University. Latimer received more and more calls to preach.

As his love for Jesus Christ grew, so did his love for the Scriptures. Or perhaps it was the other way round. The two went hand-in-hand. During this period he developed a devotional habit from which he was not to vary for the rest of his life. He arose long before daybreak. These early hours he spent in deep study of the Scriptures and in prayer.

In spite of the outward calm of this period, Latimer experienced a lack of inner peace. Questions arose in his own mind for which he found no satisfactory answers. When he attempted to share his difficulties with Bilney and others, they could not help him. They faced the same problems.

What troubled him most were the abuses in the church. All along he had been gently censuring them, while he insisted on the necessity of faith in Christ for forgiveness of sins. Yet the abuses were not easily abolished. He remembered how he had naively assured Bilney a week after his conversion that all they needed to do to set matters straight was to proclaim the Truth.

Neither clergy nor people accepted his designation of "voluntary works" as such. Most considered praying to the saints a necessity. Giving money at the shrines assured them of merit that would help pay for their sins. The people, at least, were sincere in believing so.

Latimer had doubts about the clergy. Did true belief in such practices inspire their zeal? He feared many had their eyes only on the money that poured in at the shrines. Little was made of Christ's atoning death on the cross.

The priests put pressure on the people to pay large sums for masses for their dead. Latimer was not yet clear in his own mind whether the practice itself was wrong. What disturbed him was to see a man spend money in this fashion while his family suffered from hunger. Was the concern of the priests for the souls in purgatory or for the money?

In traveling about the countryside, Latimer found little preaching being done. At the University churches men were assigned to preach. But in small parish churches the time was too often spent in saying mass, reciting Pater Nosters and Ave Marias and Latin prayers, and in leading processions. Even bishops seldom preached but spent time in secular affairs and in making a show of their wealth. Exceptions such as Bishop Fisher, who preached and told others to do the same, were rare.

Multitudes would never hear the gospel if the present state of affairs continued. Latimer and others who were preaching the finished work of Christ would reach only a fraction of those who sat in darkness. The Scriptures *must* be made available to people in their own language. Even for priests it was a necessity.

Inevitably this crept into Latimer's sermons. It was well that he had the protection of the cardinal's license. His friends urged moderation, and he made a genuine effort at restraint. But the depth of his concern and his basic sense of honesty required him to voice his thoughts. Men's lives were at stake.

One summer evening as Latimer and Bilney took their walk, they paused to look back at Cambridge, shimmering in the heat. The colleges stretched along the riverbank, willows and sycamores making a backdrop of green. King's College Chapel presented a magnificent spectacle with its slender double turrets. Great St. Mary's and the other churches nestled along the familiar streets. At a distance the scene manifested a beauty that diminished at close range. The filth of the streets and of the King's Ditch offended sense of sight and smell.

"It's the same with the church," said Latimer. "From afar it appears beautiful, peaceful, stately. At close range its imperfections show up. The greed, accretions, and refuse make it necessary to be on guard at every step."

"Yet," said Bilney, "the University could be cleansed of its filth."

"And the church *must* be cleansed of its overgrowth. I wonder I never saw this until after my conversion."

"My dear Hugh, you were so intent on your busy life that you had little time to look about you. With your true nature, you assumed others to be as faithful to duty as yourself. A part of the price one pays for having eyes opened is that he beholds not only the face of Christ but also man's clay feet."

They wandered down the hill's slope toward the river, away from the path. Under a tall elm they sat for a brief rest.

"I have something to show you, Hugh," said Bilney. "I saved it until we were well away from curious eye or listening ear."

From his gown he drew a small volume. Latimer gasped as he saw that it was a New Testament in English. He turned page after page. At last he tore his eyes from the book to gaze at Bilney.

"Thomas! A dream come true! God's Word, available for any man to read and study for himself. This is the most wonderful thing that has happened since your confession."

"It is as gratifying to me as to you. It was long a dream for Tyndale before it became a reality."

Latimer's eyes moved unseeing down across the river. "How shall we go about getting permission for this to be circulated?"

"Not so fast, Hugh! It is a banned book, the same as any other 'heretical' publication from the Continent. You could no more get approval for its distribution than for Luther's *Bondage of the Will.*

"Yet copies will circulate. No efforts will suppress it. Sooner or later things will change and it will be approved. In the meantime it may make some martyrs."

He stood up, took the book, and placed it back in his gown. Latimer extended his hand for some help in rising. They paused at the crest of the hill for another glance at the town, bathed now in the rays of the setting sun. They continued in silence toward the bridge and their rendezvous at the White Horse.

15

[1526–1527]

Latimer's physical ills usually intensified with cold weather. The winter of 1526 was no exception. Long before the new year arrived he yearned for spring.

Tyndale's New Testament was enjoying extensive popularity. Tunstal, Bishop of London, was almost beside himself at finding quantities of proscribed books, of which Tyndale's work made up the major portion, circulating in London despite all Tunstal's preventative work.

The existence of a number of Lollards was not unknown to the bishops. More than a century after his death, these followers of John Wycliffe persisted. They had no known leadership and were in large part, though not entirely, from among the working classes. They were generally ignored. They met in twos and threes to read portions of Wycliffe's translation of the Bible. Occasionally a few came to trial for refusing to attend mass or confession. A recantation usually ended the matter.

But Tunstal now discovered that Lollards had become the chief patrons of dealers in Tyndale's book. With no known connection to the Reformers at Cambridge or Lutherans on the Continent, they represented a hidden force, large and dangerous.

Coverdale, just back from London, imparted this information to the White Horse group. He spoke of his deep personal interest in the English New Testament. He mentioned avenues he had followed in agitating for its acceptance. So far he had failed.

In his dramatic way he shifted his position and smiled a tantalizing smile. At last he said, "I have seen Barnes. He has been released but he is not free. He is closely confined at the Augustinian Friary in London."

"But he *is* allowed to see visitors?" asked Bilney.

"His friends may visit him. A number have already availed themselves of that privilege. Any of us who have occasion to go to London should not fail to see him. He is eager to talk."

"He is certainly better off than in the Fleet," said Parker. "But confinement must go hard with a man like Barnes."

"Actually," said Coverdale, "he is enjoying himself. He has become the largest dispenser of the New Testament in London."

"What!" cried Latimer. "I can't believe he would be so foolish. Has he learned nothing from all he has suffered?"

"Barnes will never change," said Parker. "His rash spirit cannot be tamed."

"But right under Tunstal's nose!" cried Latimer. "Where does he get the books?"

"He has connections on the Continent. The books are concealed in bales of cloth or crates of merchandise at Antwerp. The eastern ports are notorious strongholds of Lollardy. So the books come into Barnes' hands. He does a thriving business."

"I warrant," said Arthur, "he gets fully as much enjoyment from outwitting the bishop as from distributing the books."

"I didn't ever bother to warn him that he treads on dangerous ground," said Coverdale.

"It would have done no good," said Latimer. "He knows the danger. Parker is right. It is his nature to live dangerously."

"Let us hope," said Bilney, "that he is at least scrupulously careful. I shudder to think what will happen if his activity becomes known to Wolsey or Tunstal."

Coverdale's smile exuded confidence. "Have no fear. He *is* careful. He has no intention of being found out."

16

[1527]

Bilney had grown restless during the winter and more so with the coming of spring. One afternoon he confided his state of mind to Latimer. They sat in their favorite spot on Heretics' Hill, overlooking the Cam.

"I feel the need to move out from here with the teaching," he said. "Years pass, and we remain concentrated in one spot."

"You forget those who have gone out from our group. Quite a few hold benefices in and around London and in a number of scattered parishes."

"I do not forget. Students we reach will continue to go out with the teaching. Our strongest emphasis must still be here. But you and Stafford and others can carry on that work."

"How and where do you mean to go? You will not go alone?"

"Thomas Arthur has agreed to accompany me on a preaching tour. We both have friends who can offer us opportunities to preach. Other places will open up as we proceed."

Latimer felt uneasy. He thought of Tunstal's zeal. He had recently made Sir Thomas More his heresy hunter.

"Thomas," he said, concern evident in his voice, "you will be careful, won't you?"

His friend's luminous smile caused a slight abatement of his fears. "Hugh, when the light of the gospel comes so clearly to us, should we let fear keep us from passing on the message?"

Latimer knew the question needed no answer.

"I do not plan to preach heresy," continued Bilney.

Latimer seized his hand and cried, "Thomas, I know that! You are no heretic."

"I only want to remove the obstacles that obscure the Truth. This means speaking against superstitious worship of images, adoration of the Virgin, and fruitless pilgrimages to the shrines of the saints. This I will do only to make way for the message of life found in the sole mediation of Christ."

"In what direction will you go?" asked Latimer.

"I mean to spend some time in the country places around Norwich, where I grew up. Eventually we hope to go to London."

"How long will you be gone?"

"We expect to spend the rest of the year on the mission." Seeing Latimer's sadness, he said, "Don't be downcast, old friend! The New Year should see us together again. What tales I will have to share with you of the power of the preached Word and of the risen Christ!"

The last meeting at the White Horse before they left was a lengthy one. "Little Bilney" was beloved of all. Diminutive in stature, he was a spiritual giant. In spite of Bilney's reassurances they knew the dangers involved. Even here in comparative safety the ear was alert for a strange step on the stair, and the heartbeat quickened at any unusual sound. In more than one mind must have lurked the unvoiced question, "Shall we of this group ever assemble thus again?"

As farewells were said, unashamed tears appeared in many eyes. Bilney, the dear man who never put himself forward or took any note of his special position among them, was quite overcome by their love and concern. Tears streamed down his cheeks as he embraced each one in parting.

Nor was Thomas Arthur forgotten. He would be a protection and a guiding force to steer Bilney back if he grew too zealous for dangerous subjects.

They planned to leave at daybreak. Latimer was at Bilney's door in the darkness before dawn. Glancing at a bundle on the floor, he asked in astonishment, "Is that all you are taking?"

"What need have I for things? The necessities are there. My Latin Bible goes with me. I reluctantly leave the English New Testament behind. It would be dangerous to carry it."

When Arthur arrived, Latimer walked with them down the High Ward. The rising sun painted the eastern sky and cast a reflection across to the west. A light mistiness in the atmosphere took up the glow and bathed everything in a rosy hue. A radiance from within glowed on Bilney's face as well.

As they reached the corner by St. Edward's, Bilney stopped. Laying his hand on Latimer's shoulder, he said, "Dear friend, go back now. Going farther will make the parting no easier."

Latimer clung to his arm as if he would not let him go. Bilney regarded him tenderly. "We go, sent forth like Paul and Barnabas, by the Holy Spirit and with the blessing of the brethren. You remain with as great or greater mission by order of the same Spirit. Let us each stand obedient to his calling."

Latimer stood watching as they walked away, heads held high, steps buoyant. After a bit they turned and looked back. He raised his hand; they did the same. They disappeared down Pennyfarthing Lane. They would pick up horses in Dowdivers Lane. The journey lay eastward to Newmarket and Bury St. Edmonds.

With a sense of foreboding Latimer turned back. As Bilney said, they went at the Spirit's bidding. He should not fear for them. Yet his mind continued troubled. His friendship with Little Bilney was precious. He had depended upon him, perhaps more than he realized. When would they meet again?

17

[1527]

He raised his eyes from his sermon notes to glance out the window. Coverdale came into view, hurrying across the court. Latimer's first thought was, "He has news of Bilney."

He burst through the door crying, "Barnes has escaped!" In his excitement he kept giving unrelated bits of information. Finally Latimer begged him to begin at the beginning.

He took a deep breath and dropped to a stool. "A Lollard was arrested at Steeple Bumpstead for possessing an English New Testament. At his trial he told where he obtained it."

Latimer groaned. "Of course he got it from Barnes."

"He related how he and a friend had visited 'that leading colporteur Robert Barnes' with the intention of acquiring a copy. To convince Barnes that they were not spies they showed him some pages of their Lollard Bible. 'I can offer you a new, printed copy in much better English,' he told them. They paid him three shillings, two pence for a copy. He urged them to keep the matter close."

"Which they failed to do," muttered Latimer.

"Messengers rode to the friary to arrest Barnes. But the news of their coming traveled faster. Barnes pretended suicide. The dejected officers could only report finding a corpse. Barnes made his escape and headed for the Continent."

"A narrow escape!" cried Latimer. "I rejoice that he is safely away." Then wistfully, "Did you hear no news of Bilney?"

"None. But don't worry."

Word finally came that the missionaries had met with difficulties and even physical mistreatment at Ipswich. When forced to leave that area, they headed for London.

Parker journeyed to London in late June. He discovered that Bilney and Arthur were prisoners in the Tower.

"I talked to a man," he said, "who heard Bilney preach at Willesden. He spoke boldly against image worship. But the focus of his message was Christ, whom he held up as 'our wisdom, righteousness, sanctification, and redemption.'"

"Yes, it would be," murmured Latimer. "It is the passion of his life."

"In Whitsun week he spoke at St. Magnus against image worship, intercession of saints, and authority of Popes."

"Surely he knew," said Coverdale, "that this last matter must inevitably put him in trouble."

"After the sermon both he and Arthur were seized. In the Tower they await trial."

"And who knows when that may be!" cried Latimer.

"I have posted a friend," said Parker, "to get word to me immediately when the time for the trial is set."

Latimer in his lonely walks watched the plowing of the fields about Cambridge and the planting of the winter wheat and rye in the rich brown soil.

Then winter came. Latimer's digestive problems intensified. Headaches came and went. But the worst was severe back trouble, which made it almost impossible for him to move about. He yearned for news from Bilney.

Parker came the last week of November to say, "The trial takes place this week. We are off to London."

18

[1527]

Parker returned on December 10. Latimer apologized for remaining in bed during the visit.

"Replenish the fire and draw up a chair. I see by your face that the news is not good. He isn't ... Bilney isn't ... ?"

"No, he's not dead. He's in prison, and it *is* bad. I've had to piece the story together.

"The preliminary hearing was on November 27, with the Lord Cardinal in charge. You can imagine the pomp with which they assembled at Westminster Abbey. I was able to get in for a few minutes. The gray arches and walls of the Chapter House provided a fine backdrop for the red and gold apparel of the dignitaries. Scarlet gloves and gold cushions for Wolsey as usual."

"But what of Bilney, what of Bilney?" demanded Latimer.

"Such a contrast! His shrunken body, his somber garments. Even his speech seemed unimpressive in such surroundings."

"Did the cardinal remember that Bilney had been before him earlier?" asked Latimer.

"Undoubtedly. He asked him whether he had preached opinions of Luther or of others condemned by the church. Bilney replied that he had not knowingly preached anything contrary to the teaching of the church. The cardinal then asked whether he remembered taking an oath that he would not proclaim Luther's opinions but would impugn them. Bilney hesitated."

"I can see his dilemma," said Latimer. "He preached his own opinions, arrived at independently. Yet on the whole, he agrees with Luther. So he did preach what Luther believes."

"The answer he gave was that he had taken such an oath, but not 'judicially.' He did not consider the oath binding, since it was sworn in a private interrogation and not in a law court."

"Certainly an unwise answer."

"Then the cardinal made him swear again," said Parker, "this time that he would answer plainly, without any craft, qualification, or partial truth."

"What about Arthur?"

"They questioned him about something he said to Sir Thomas More. Then they were given time to prepare written statements."

"The old cat-and-mouse game," said Latimer. "Tossing them about with no injury, letting them know that more is to follow."

Parker continued with a faraway look in his eyes, as if he were reliving the events he described. He and the others had been allowed to visit the prisoners. Bilney spent time writing letters to Tunstal, the Bishop of London, pleading his case.

Wolsey had turned the case over to the bishops, instructing them to proceed against all men and all writings favorable to the spread of Lutheran heresies. He ordered them to force the guilty to a solemn abjuration, else they were to be given over to the arm of the state for suitable punishment.

Yet Bilney felt he could count on a measure of mildness from Tunstal. He poured his heart into these letters, much as he had in his "confession" to Latimer. If he could just convince the Bishop of London of the truth of the statements he made from Scripture!

On December 2 the court convened and called Arthur again. They forced him to repudiate certain articles he had previously confessed and to submit to the bishops. He must perform public penance and spend time in prison.

Next day thirty-four counts of heresy were brought against Bilney. He stood his ground bravely. Most of his answers were acceptable. His judges found unsatisfactory his answers on the use of images, the perpetual virginity of Mary, the need for the Lord's Prayer and Creed in English, and the advisability of making available an English Bible.

The Bishop of London was in a dilemma. He refused Bilney a private hearing but probably read his letters. Tunstal was not a harsh man but, fearing the cardinal's ire, he could not acquit Bilney. To save him from burning, he must force him to recant. But this Bilney refused to do.

Tunstal took the step he found necessary. "I do by the consent and counsel of my brethren here present pronounce thee, Thomas Bilney, to be convicted of heresy. For the rest of the sentence, we take deliberation till tomorrow."

Seven days passed and seven almost sleepless nights. Bilney was near the point of complete exhaustion.

Next morning Tunstal asked if he would revoke his errors and return to the church. Bilney protested that he had never separated from the church. He was sent out to his friends and urged to reconsider and abjure.

His friends were in great perplexity. Bilney had stood so nobly. Sentence had not been pronounced, but they knew what it would be. Could they send Little Bilney to a horrible death at the stake for stating beliefs that each of them also held?

Recalled again and again, Bilney still refused to recant. Tunstal granted him two nights in which to reach a decision.

It was at this point that his friends found it too hard to support his stand further. They begged him to give in. He wept and said he could not deny his Lord. They told him he would not be denying his Lord, but merely changing his stand on nonessential matters.

Bilney was near the breaking point. Quiet and unassuming, he was never meant to stand before bishops and oppose them. He simply knew his Savior and wanted to make him known.

The next morning Tunstal asked him again if he would revoke the errors for which he stood condemned and return to the church. He submitted. Tunstal handed him the form of abjuration. He read it to himself, then aloud, and signed his name. Tunstal spoke the words of absolution. For penance he was to bear a fagot and then lie in prison until it pleased the cardinal to release him.

Next day Bilney walked from his prison to St. Paul's, carrying on his shoulder the usual fagot. He stood before the cross while the preacher expounded upon the wickedness of heresy and the triumph of reclaiming a penitent heretic.

His friends were not allowed to speak to him again. He was returned to prison and transferred the next day to the Tower.

At the end of this recital Parker paused for a long moment. Then in a broken voice he cried, "Oh, Latimer! The misery in his eyes! Were we wrong to advise him as we did? He was a soul in torment. I wonder . . . I wonder if he wouldn't have been better off *dead.*" He sobbed uncontrollably.

19

[1527]

When Parker had gone, Latimer gave way to his own feelings. His inner agony was such that he could hardly bear it. Heart and mind, he was almost as one with Bilney. He suffered through the trial himself as he relived the scenes Parker had described.

What would he have done in Bilney's place? He might well be in the same situation before long. Relentless tracking down of heretics would continue. Yet he could no more muzzle his conscience and curtail his witness than Bilney had done.

What, after all, was worth giving one's life for? The old question: Was it the matter of images—or pilgrimages? Why should one's loyalty to the church and to Christ hang on such issues?

Bilney had no desire to depart from the church; he had never doubted its authority. He believed in its power to bless and condemn. To be cast out of the church meant to die in unbelief and to suffer in hell forever. Yet could he deny what he had learned from the Holy Scriptures? Could the church and the Bible be opposed to each other? All he wanted was to share the love of Christ, the certainty of salvation, the comfort of the Scriptures with the lost. Could the church call that heresy?

He could understand Bilney's struggle about recantation. He had clung to the Truth revealed in God's Word. The matters to which he had taken exception might not be in the Word, but they contradicted it in the normal working out. How, for instance, could one pay for forgiveness for sins? Christ had paid.

How dreadfully lonely Bilney must have felt. And he stood on an even lonelier precipice. For if he were condemned as a heretic and cast out of the church, would it be not only for time but for eternity? Would he be separated from his Lord, in hell forever? The church claimed that power. Dear Little Bilney!

He had stood firm, with no wavering, until the last. Consulting his friends had been his undoing. How could they have advised him otherwise? The choice was so terrible. To burn in the body would be indescribable agony. But infinitely worse, the possibility of burning in hell forever. How could he declare repentance for beliefs he still held? Which was worse?

The cardinal must count his recantation a great victory. Why was it a victory to make an earnest believer *lie* to save his life and remain in the church? Was hypocrisy the way, after all, in spite of what Jesus so plainly taught?

Latimer never knew how long he spent in this private hell. His thoughts contradicted one another and ended up making no sense. Groans, sobs, tears—all were a part of his soul's agony.

At last he knelt and surrendered his insupportable burden to the Lord. He thought of Little Bilney alone in a cold and cheerless cell, perhaps likewise at prayer. He begged that his friend might know the peace and comfort of the Holy Spirit.

A measure of relief came just at dawn. But he still had no answer to the old question: What is worth giving one's life for?

20

[1528]

No great changes at Cambridge marked the early months of 1528. Latimer still preached. Opposition was negligible. A growing number of young students flocked to him. His urgency in the insistence on an English Bible increased.

But a storm was breaking at Oxford. At Bilney's trial Farman of Honey Lane had testified on Bilney's behalf. On cross-examination he revealed that his curate, Thomas Garrett, had sold a number of Tyndale's New Testaments at Oxford. Garrett was arrested. He recanted and bore his fagot.

This focused the attention of the authorities on Oxford. It came to light that the cardinal's new college housed the purchasers of the New Testaments. They were all the men who had left Cambridge with the blessing of the Reformers three years earlier. Clarke, Frith, and others were thrown in prison. By late autumn Clarke and two others had died. A number, including Frith, escaped to the Continent.

The whole story came out. Almost since their arrival these men had pushed the cause of the Reformation. They had secretly spread the principles now openly proclaimed at Cambridge.

In meetings similar to those at the White Horse Inn, they gathered to read the New Testament. They were regularly supplied with writings of Continental Reformers, presumably by Garrett.

Because of Clarke's insistence on caution, they had escaped detection and had brought into their group a number of the most outstanding scholars at Oxford.

This fiasco led the White Horse group to extend their precautions. They always posted a sentry to signal approaching danger. Now the constant presence of danger drew the group closer. With Bilney gone, Stafford assumed leadership.

One evening near the end of January as Latimer sat in his customary spot with his Bible open, a knock sounded at the door. A vague familiarity about the sound jolted him. He almost fell in his haste to open the door. There stood a diminutive form, unbelievably shrunken and emaciated. It was Bilney.

21

[1529]

Bilney had returned, yet he seemed almost a stranger. He had come to Latimer, but Latimer was unable to reach him. A solid wall shut him off. Bilney was completely crushed under his burden of guilt. He believed he had committed the unpardonable sin. His agony was pitiful to behold.

Latimer tried to bring to him the promises of the Word, but the passages he had been so eager to share with others were now as a sword in his heart. Truth that had once brought peace now pointed at his guilt and twisted the knife in his grievous wound.

His friends rallied round with deep concern. They feared to leave him alone, lest he take his life. It was Latimer who spent the most time with him. It was Latimer's voice at last that broke through. Slowly through weary weeks, it was Latimer who led him back.

First came the renewal of walks upon Heretics' Hill. The familiarity of the old routine worked in his favor. Latimer refused to let slow progress discourage him. His quiet persuasion finally gained Bilney's consent to return to the sick and the prisoners. Engaged in these activities of comforting, teaching, and reclaiming the lost, he bloomed once more.

He expressed to Latimer his determination to do all in his power to wipe away the memory of the weakness that made him fall. He declared a deep-rooted resolve to show, with the help of his Lord, that he was not ashamed of the great Truth he preached.

One day Bilney began to show enthusiastic concern for one particular prisoner, a case in which Latimer too had become interested. The prisoner was accused of murdering her child, a crime she denied. Both Latimer and Bilney tried in vain to get her to confess her guilt.

One evening as they left the prison Latimer said to Bilney, "I believe she is telling the truth. She stands condemned and has nothing to gain by lying."

"So do I," said Bilney. "Her words have the ring of truth. Yet she will perhaps die for a crime she never committed. What a world is this where such injustice is possible! But what can two 'heretical' preachers do?"

22

[1529]

All England was swept up in discussion of an emotionally charged question. King Henry VIII proposed to divorce his Queen, Catherine of

Aragon. Talk of the King's "Great Cause" took precedence in all gatherings. The population of Cambridge came out mostly against the divorce.

Latimer and Bilney agreed that the King had scriptural grounds for ending the marriage, inasmuch as he should never have entered into it in the first place. They saw evidence in the Book of Leviticus that such a marriage was forbidden. Catherine had been the wife of Henry's older brother Arthur, who had died. Latimer doubted a Pope's authority to grant a dispensation contrary to Scripture.

The Princess Mary was the only living child of the union. Such a state of affairs they could only interpret as being God's judgment upon a union entered into contrary to his Word.

When Cardinal Campeggio arrived from Rome to confer with Cardinal Wolsey, the Papal legates were expected to rule on the divorce. In July the legatine court met with both the King and Queen in attendance. Instead of declaring for the divorce as the King expected, Campeggio adjourned the case. Speculation arose as to whether this would precipitate Wolsey's fall from power.

An epidemic of the "sweating sickness" swept across Cambridgeshire, sending a general exodus of students and fellows before it. Latimer, Bilney, and Stafford chose to remain.

"The sick and dying are in need of comfort," said Latimer. "The bereaved will require support. Why should we run away?"

Stafford had been working for some time with a priest who was involved in black magic and witchcraft. Stafford had reasoned with him repeatedly and tried to turn him to the Truth. When he heard that the man had fallen victim to the plague, he hurried to his side. The priest confessed his sin, put his faith in Christ, and died. Soon after, Stafford lay dead as well.

Latimer's grief was overwhelming. Stafford had been his friend for more than five years. Yet he could rejoice in the memory of his friend's faithfulness. "Greater love hath no man than this, that a man lay down his life for his friend." The Reformation had lost a strong supporter and Cambridge an outstanding leader.

The coming of autumn saw the end of the plague. Latimer and Bilney spent their free time as usual among the sick and imprisoned. They walked on the Hill; they preached. Life was full. Yet a restlessness fell upon them both. The heavy quietness around them could only presage a brewing storm.

23

[1529]

On October 19 Wolsey, the most powerful man in the realm, surrendered the Great Seal to the Dukes of Norfolk and Suffolk upon written instructions from the King. Sir Thomas More succeeded him as chancellor. Wolsey confessed to *praemunire*, the offense of obeying other authority than that of the Crown, meaning the Pope. He yielded up his possessions without a murmur. Though the Archbishopric of York remained to him, his power was broken. He moved toward his diocese and province to begin duties never before attended to.

Latimer's enemies expected his wings to be clipped with Wolsey's fall. From the pulpit, he said, "You think my license decays with my Lord Cardinal's temporal fall. I take it not so. For I trust he is now reconciled to God from his pomp and vanities. I therefore set more store by his license than when he was in happier circumstances."

He felt sad at the man's fall. Although disagreeing with him on many points, especially his practice and example, he had felt respect for a strong man, who made plans and carried them out.

The Advent season arrived. Latimer would preach at St. Edward's on December 19. He wanted desperately to win the young undergraduates to a true faith in Jesus Christ. His heart ached as he thought of the superstitious practices to which they were exposed. He knew he must use pointed language to achieve his double purpose of preaching Christ and warning of error.

As he sat, pen in hand, paper before him, he discarded one idea after another. Then a smile spread across his face. A truly ingenious thought had come to him.

At Christmastide the students were allowed to play at cards. He would preach about "The Card." But his cards would be different. He would deal with Christ's cards. The gospel reading for the day was the passage in which the Jews came to ask John the Baptist, "Who are you?" This question he would turn upon his hearers. Each must answer, "I am a man under condemnation because of my sin." But if they came to Christ, repenting and seeking forgiveness, each answer would be "I am a Christian man."

Then the game would begin. All could win if they played properly. For Christ's cards were dealt to show what he required of us. Taking his departure from the card dealt, he would teach them what it meant to live as a true Christian. In the afternoon sermon he would continue the game by dealing another card. He seized his pen, dipped it in the ink, and wrote rapidly.

A light snow had fallen. He walked to the church with a buoyant step. No one was about as he opened the heavy door. Sunlight streamed across the altar through the east window. How he loved this beautiful little church that was also the chapel for Clare and Trinity Halls. He entered the vestry to the left of the altar to make his preparations.

As he approached the little hexagonal pulpit, he noted with satisfaction that the building was crowded. The faces before him represented not only his friends, but many who opposed him.

He read the Scripture from the Latin Bible, translating directly into English. With enthusiasm he moved into his sermon. He was sensitive to the reaction of any audience. Today he discerned eager interest and a receptive spirit, though an undercurrent of opposition was not lacking. He had no fear that his congregation would fail to return in the afternoon.

24

[1529–1530]

Latimer was scarcely prepared for the violent reaction. His opponents attacked him with vigor; his friends defended him with equal force. The warfare remained verbal, but it threatened to become physical.

Buckenham, Prior of the Black Friars, undertook to reply to the sermons on "The Card" with his own version of a Christmas game of dice. He called his sermon *"Cinque-quatre."* *Cinque* was a group of five Scripture passages; *quatre* were the four doctors of the ancient church: Ambrose, Augustine, Jerome, and Gregory. He objected to Latimer's implied teaching that every man should be able to read the Scriptures in his own tongue, saying that the four doctors did not agree with this position. His support was weak; his argument was ridiculous.

"The common man will not understand the figurative language of Scripture," he said. "For example, 'If thine eye offend thee, pluck it out and cast it from thee' might lead men to take this command literally. We could become a nation of blind beggars."

Latimer responded that he had faith in his fellow Englishmen and they would not be so foolish. He pointed out that figurative language is commonly employed in everyday life.

"For example," he said, looking directly at Buckenham, "when a painter pictures a fox in a friar's cowl, no one supposes for a moment that he pictures an actual fox preaching. What he means to point out is the hypocrisy, craft, and subtle dissimulation that often lie hidden in a friar's cowl."

Effective use of words was a gift of which Latimer was aware. He frequently employed keen wit to make a point, and his sarcasm could cut his opponents down. Perhaps he went too far upon this occasion: He made Buckenham a laughingstock.

Those at St. John's College opposed Latimer, not only on account of the sermons but because he favored the King's divorce. Sharp words continued. The whole University became involved, and the animosity grew so strong that riots were feared.

Dr. Buckmaster, Vice Chancellor of the University, received a letter that threw him into a panic. The eyes of the Crown were upon Buckmaster, and the King was not pleased.

The King's intention, wrote Dr. Edward Fox, the King's almoner, was that order be restored. Some private malice was doubtless involved on the part of the men at St. John's, and the fact that Latimer favored the King's Great Cause might have some bearing. Yet Latimer's actions and words seemed to have exceeded what an evangelist should have employed, and his zeal may have given personal offense.

On January 29 the vice chancellor informed the parties involved that open dissensions must cease, at the King's order. He threatened excommunication if such spectacular preaching was again heard. He informed Greenwood and others of St. John's that Latimer had answered satisfactorily the questions brought against him. He warned Latimer to show more discretion in his preaching.

Buckmaster succeeded in smothering the open personal attacks, but controversy over the divorce continued. The Reformers stood in favor of it; a vocal majority, including the men from St. John's, argued boldly against it.

"I wonder," said Latimer one evening at the White Horse, "why they feel so strongly about the divorce. They are sure to incur the King's wrath by speaking out as they do."

"I think it's fear that moves them," said Bilney.

"I should think fear would cause them to remain silent," said Parker. "The King doesn't react kindly to opposition."

"You don't understand," said Bilney. "These men are loyal to the King, but their loyalty to the Pope and the church's ceremonies is stronger. They fear whatever threatens the *status quo.* They want no reformation of such basic matters."

"But we're not talking about reformation," insisted Parker. "We're talking about the King's divorce."

"And the divorce depends upon overturning a Pope's decision," said Bilney. "That would indicate that a Pope is not inerrant. *That* is what frightens these outspoken opponents. Once it is admitted that the Pope can err, the door will open to other such admissions. Their system may begin to crumble."

"You have to admit they are right in that," said Latimer. "It will certainly lay open the matter of the need for reform."

In February the appearance of the King's ministers, headed by Gardiner and Fox, promised to bring things to a head.

25

[1530]

The delegation's arrival threw Buckmaster into a quandary. He had not expected them at this time. Upon the suggestion of Thomas Cranmer, the King had decided to put the question of the divorce to the universities. But Buckmaster knew it would be difficult to obtain at Cambridge the response the King desired.

Instead of putting the question to the University as a whole, a committee was appointed. Latimer and Crome were among those chosen. The question to be decided: Can a Pope dispense contrary to Scripture? Does Scripture teach that a man may not marry his brother's widow?

When the vote was taken, the decision went against the King. Gardiner undertook to reason with the committee. In the heated discussion Latimer was not silent. Another vote gave the same results. The opponents were determined.

Gardiner was more determined. He gained the withdrawal of the more timid and appointed others. Gardiner knew that the University as a whole opposed the King's Great Cause, but he had done his duty.

"I had interesting contact with Sir William Butts, the King's physician," said Latimer. "One wonders why he is with the delegation. He listened intently to the discussion. I understand he leans in the direction of the Reformation."

Butts must have brought Latimer sharply to the King's attention. He received an invitation to preach before the King at Windsor on the second Sunday in Lent.

"His Highness doesn't miss much," remarked Bilney. "I'd say he knows pretty well about your sermons on 'The Card.' He wants to find out whether you live up to your reputation."

"I don't know what he expects," said Latimer, "but I know what I must try to do. I shall make as clear an exposition of Scripture as I know how. I shall emphasize a ruler's particular responsibilities in living a Christian life before his subjects."

"You will not fail to make a deep impression. May His Majesty receive the Word into his heart as God means it."

"Pray," said Latimer, "that I find opportunity to speak to His Majesty about the woman prisoner who we believe is innocent."

Latimer found it awesome to be within the cold, gray walls surrounding Windsor Castle. Nothing seemed expected of him on the day before he was to preach. He spent some time wandering through St. George's Chapel with its turrets and towers. This, he knew, was one of the wealthiest establishments in the land, surpassed only by Westminster Abbey and Canterbury Cathedral.

The splendor somewhat depressed Latimer when he recalled the poverty just outside the gates. This was a great center for pilgrimages. The shrines were even now hung with votive offerings made by pilgrims in hope of obtaining merit. Latimer looked upon all this with a heavy heart.

As yet he had had no glimpse of the King. He wondered how he would feel when the moment came. Perhaps a great deal hung upon the reception given his message.

26

[1530]

The hour for the service arrived. Gardiner and Fox had recognized his presence with no great show of warmth. He had seen Dr. Butts. Now the head chaplain conducted him to his place. All must be in readiness before the King entered.

A large assemblage of worshipers waited in silence. Then the royal party entered. Latimer saw at once that His Majesty was half a head taller than any of the company. He was attired in a blue velvet doublet, lighter blue hose, and a white silk shirt with much embroidery in gold and jewels. He took his place, along with the lords and ladies of the court.

Latimer stood to read the Scripture. He let his eyes move from one face to another, coming to rest upon the King's, whose eyes met his with a steady, not unfriendly gaze.

He began a brief introduction, then he paused, stood silent for a moment, and turned his head as if listening. In a clearly audible voice he said, "Latimer! Latimer! Latimer! Be careful what you say! Henry the King is here!" Stepping back a bit, he again paused. In a louder voice he said, "Latimer! Latimer! Latimer! Be careful what you say! *The King of Kings is here!*"

Such a dramatic gesture was not for show. It expressed his feelings as to whom he should try to please. His words came freely, and his whole heart was in the message. He preached directly to the King.

At the end he felt limp, but he had not long to consider his feelings. Fox came to usher him into a gallery for a meeting with His Majesty. He was quite at ease with the King, who complimented him on his sermon and asked a question or two.

Latimer was on the alert. When the moment came, he knelt before the King and poured out the story of the woman prisoner. Then he humbly petitioned for her pardon. To his delight, the King agreed. The document would be in his hand on the morrow.

By now Latimer was in high spirits and made pleasant conversation not only with the King but with others of the court, particularly Mistress Anne Boleyn. She was not beautiful, but Latimer was attracted by her youth and vivacity. She was attentive to him and said kind things about the sermon.

Later, in thinking the matter over, he had some qualms. True, it was reported that no immorality was involved between the King and the lady. Still, until the divorce was granted, Queen Catherine was the King's wife.

In due course he received from the hands of an agent a pound as thanks for his preaching. This was the normal gift for preaching before the King. To his surprise he was later handed an envelope containing five pounds.

Upon reflection he decided that the additional gift represented an expression of thanks for his activity on behalf of the King's Great Cause at Cambridge. Gardiner would not have mentioned Latimer's strong stand in the committee. Dr. Butts must have given the King the details. He felt drawn to Butts and believed the feeling was mutual. Butts was a powerful man, a good friend to have "at court."

27

[1530]

Back at Cambridge he hastened to find Bilney to share with him the news of the pardon for the prisoner. Wanting to make sure of her innocence, they withheld the news for some time. When they were convinced beyond doubt, they produced the pardon. The overjoyed woman was soon released.

In early May the King sent a letter instructing the vice chancellor at Cambridge to choose twelve capable men and send them to London for a special task. A like number would come from Oxford, and the King himself would choose others to complete the group. He would commission them to examine the books about religious subjects now in wide circulation. Their task would be to reprove any error or seditious material and to approve what they found good.

Latimer, Crome, Shaxton, and Thixtill were among those chosen. The

Reformers were thus a minority, but a vocal minority. Latimer wondered whether Buckmaster had any malicious intent in the selection. He surely knew they would tend to favor the books being considered while the majority would not.

The work began May 10. Each was to state his opinion with frankness. Latimer did not agree with all Luther wrote, but he saw no need to suppress the material. He found it generally in accord with Scripture. To some of Tyndale's opinions he took exception, but his excellent New Testament should be circulated freely. The Reformers proved too few. Sir Thomas More, Gardiner, and Tunstal argued so persuasively they carried the day.

After two weeks the commission closed its labors in the King's presence at Westminster in St. Edward's chamber. Warham, Archbishop of Canterbury, read the report. It listed the books examined and pointed out the errors and heresies discovered. The document was signed by the archbishop and three notaries. Appended was a list of those present. Latimer was relieved that he was not required to sign.

"At least we made ourselves heard," said Latimer to the others as the assembly broke up. "But as often happens, the most overcame the better."

"Why did they have to present the report as unanimous?" inquired Shaxton. "What should we have done about that?"

"Nothing," said Latimer. "But be assured, everyone knows about such a fictional variety of unanimity."

"They succeeded in giving Tyndale's New Testament a bad report," said Crome. "His Pentateuch in English fared even worse. Both are absolutely forbidden."

"And there's the royal proclamation being issued against the books," said Latimer. "At least none of us was chosen to read it publicly. Imagine! The people are to purge their hearts of 'any contagious doctrines and pestiferous traditions' absorbed from reading the New Testament in English."

"His Majesty did promise that he would cause the New Testament to be faithfully translated into English," said Thixtill, "so it may be freely given to the people. But he left himself a loophole. He will do this when he sees by their behavior that they are fitted to receive it."

"So he approves in theory," said Shaxton, "of the use of an English Bible. He merely opposes Tyndale's translation."

With the summer before him and nothing of importance to call him back to Cambridge, Latimer saw no reason not to accept the invitation of Sir William Butts to spend some time as his guest.

Old Cambridge friends of the Reformed group now occupying London posts welcomed Latimer to their pulpits. Everywhere his preaching attracted crowds. The See of London was temporarily vacant, since Bishop-elect

Stokesley was engaged in business for the King on the Continent. No one offered any hindrance to his preaching.

28

[1530]

September found him back at Cambridge, reunited with Bilney. As they resumed their usual pursuits, Bilney showed a tendency to lapse rather too often into spells of melancholy. Latimer's tales of London experiences sometimes succeeded in cheering him.

They spoke of the King's promise of an English translation of the Scriptures. "If he waits until he thinks the people are ready," said Bilney, "he may put it off indefinitely."

"Someone needs to prod him," said Latimer. "I feel guilty that I lacked boldness to express the Truth to His Majesty in so many words. You will recall St. Augustine's statement about one who hides the Truth because of his fear of some power."

"He said that such a man is likely to provoke the wrath of God. St. John Chrysostom goes even further. Not only is one who for Truth teaches a lie betraying the Truth, but also one who fails to freely speak the Truth he knows."

"That stings my conscience," said Latimer. "I have no desire to provoke the wrath of God nor to betray the Truth."

"Don't blame yourself. You had no opportunity to speak. After all, who are you to instruct the King? Between a high ruler and a common man is almost as much difference as between God and man. He stands, in a sense, in the place of God to us. It is difficult to argue with him, the distance being so great."

"Yet he is a man, even though in a special position. He is born in sin, as we are. He needs the cleansing blood of the Savior, as we do. He needs instruction for what is right and wrong, as we do. On that ground we stand the same before God."

"So we do," replied Bilney. "He is a higher member of the same body of Christ. He must not disdain a lower member."

They found themselves far across the fields, past their usual stopping point. A sheltered spot in a copse of beech trees offered a place to rest. The autumn wind already brought a damp chill from the fens, but Latimer was almost oblivious to it.

"With the knowledge of Latin, don't you suppose His Grace reads the

Gospels? He *must* see the contrast between Jesus' life of poverty and the lives of his supposed followers today, who take vows of poverty and then pile up riches. The King must have observed the avarice of high clergymen in the last year's Parliament sessions. How they howled when the Commons wanted to cut off the fees extorted for probates of will and exaction of burial fees, even from the most poverty-stricken."

"A few good Christian men are in the group," said Bilney, "but too few. Perhaps the need is not so much for the King to take away the goods due the church as to take away the evil persons from the goods. Then, better men could replace them."

Latimer stood up to relieve a cramped leg. "Could the Savior who sent his preachers with the Word to comfort sin-sick souls allow that same saving Word to cause insurrections and heresies? Gardiner and Tunstal and More presented to the King their opinions of the books examined. I should like to present mine. They threatened dire consequences to those who read the Book. They are likely to send a thousand men to hell before they send one to God. How *I* would like to get hold of the King's ear."

"Lacking other means," said Bilney, heading toward the path, "you must write a letter to His Majesty. He needs to make his decision on the basis of the Word itself, not by his opinion or that of others. He must not only consider the souls of his subjects, but his own soul as well. One day he too must stand before the judgment seat of God. He must prove himself faithful to the trust God has placed in him as ruler of this great realm."

"Write a letter?" cried Latimer. "What would I say?"

Bilney smiled. "What would you say? Just what we have been saying here. Through your words set on paper, the Holy Spirit can lead the King to the Truth."

Latimer sat late at his desk, struggling to recall the points of their conversation. His thoughts tumbled about as he sought to set them in order. At last he dipped his pen and began to write: "The holy doctor St. Augustine says that he who for fear of any power hides the Truth . . ."

29

[1530–1531]

He labored long at writing, then at revising the letter. When he at last inscribed the date on the copy he meant for the King's hand, it was December 1, 1530. Now that the task was complete, he was eager to get it before His Majesty's eyes.

Only Bilney read it before he left. No other eyes must see it before it reached the King. Latimer had not seen his friend so jubilant since the early days of their friendship. If only the King would respond with half as much enthusiasm.

In London he went at once to Sir William Butts. The doctor registered genuine pleasure at learning of his mission. He would escort Latimer to the palace the next day.

"Cromwell is the man you want to see," Butts said. "He'll get the letter to the King. And he'll put in any good word he can for *this* cause."

Latimer had met Thomas Cromwell at Windsor. His position was difficult to define. He had been a secretary to Cardinal Wolsey. At Wolsey's fall he had accompanied him north. A year later came Wolsey's arrest on the charge of high treason. He had sent Cromwell to London to plead with the King on his behalf. Wolsey never reached London; old and ill, he had died at Leicester Abbey. It was as well. In London he would have faced almost certain execution. Cromwell could not have helped.

An efficient and intelligent man, Cromwell had set about making himself indispensable to the King. Little services called forth greater. He got elected to the House of Commons, where he would serve the King's purposes. He had men strategically placed to bring him any information he needed in the King's business. Yes, he would be the man to get the letter to the King.

His Majesty summoned Latimer and thanked him but gave no hint of intended action on the letter's content. Within a few days Latimer received word that he was to become one of the King's chaplains. This honor took him by surprise.

The weeks of December and early January he spent at court. He fit in well and made himself agreeable. Lady Anne took pains to cultivate his friendship. She was aware of his helpfulness in promoting the divorce. Cromwell paid Latimer marked attention. He was pleased to find Cromwell favorable toward the Reformation.

For a while the excitement of court life dazzled Latimer, then the glamor wore off. He was out of his element. The undercurrent of intrigue disturbed him. This was no better than the bickerings at Cambridge. Such a life was not for him. The court atmosphere offered no time for serious thinking.

He took his problem first to Butts, who was sympathetic with Latimer's dilemma but reluctant to think of his leaving court. He then went to Cromwell. What he wanted was an appointment to a benefice in a country area where he could preach and do his pastoral work, yet have time to study and think. Failing to shake his determination, Cromwell promised to try to locate a post that fit Latimer's description.

Part Two

A CHURCH IN THE COUNTRY

"You requested a country parish."
[1531–1535]

1

[1531]

"Latimer, you requested a country parish," said Cromwell with a wry smile. "You are getting exactly that. The benefice of West Kington is so remote that you need expect no visitors except those who come by deliberate intent."

"That sounds entirely satisfactory," said Latimer. "What is the location?"

"It's in Wiltshire on the edge of the Diocese of Salisbury. Bristol, fourteen miles west, is in the See of Worcester."

"When may I take possession?"

"The service of institution can take place at any time we arrange with Richard Hiley, the vicar-general. Your bishop, Cardinal Campeggio, has never seen fit to visit his diocese."

"I should like to proceed immediately."

"In spite of all you have said, surely you don't intend to *live* there? Get yourself installed, leave a curate in charge, and come back to London. You can't bury yourself there."

Latimer smiled. "I see I did not make myself clear. A man should reside on his living. London holds no charms for me."

Cromwell shook his head in utter lack of comprehension. But he agreed to arrange things with Hiley. "You're a rare man, Latimer. King's chaplain, court preacher, prospects for advancement—and you choose to leave it all for a place nobody ever heard of."

The first sight of his new field of labor brought a throb of joy to Latimer's heart. He followed the narrow road over the last miles through the hills with a fresh spurt of energy. At a turn in the road stood the rectory, an ordinary cruck cottage with a weatherworn thatched roof. All was neat and in order.

Among those assembled to welcome him was an elderly woman of authoritative mien. She greeted him with proper courtesy and said, "Father, I care for the rectory. With your permission, sir, I shall care for you as well. I am a widow with few home duties. I come each morning and stay until all is done."

She seemed to expect no discussion. Latimer acquiesced.

He said to Hiley, who had accompanied him, "Could I see the church?"

Hiley shrugged. "Since the service of institution is tomorrow, you could wait until then. Are you not weary?"

"Not too weary to offer my thanks before the altar."

Hiley led him through a farmyard and up a hill. Within a low wall of fieldstone stood the ancient Church of St. Mary the Virgin. Constructed of stone from the neighboring hills, it took the shape of a Greek cross. A weathered slate roof rose in peaks of varying height. The square bell tower bore a curious feature, not uncommon in old churches. On its sides were small, cross-shaped slits. In the old days when an enemy might creep in to do battle, an archer with drawn bow had stood behind each of these slits while the people huddled in the church for protection.

Inside the building late afternoon sunlight poured through the diamond-shaped panes in the triple-arched windows. In the city the splendor of stained glass had seemed appropriate; here the little translucent panes were more suitable. The pulpit of dark carved wood gleamed with a soft sheen. He sensed a stateliness even in its simplicity.

Turning his back on Hiley, he approached the chancel, advanced to the altar, and knelt. He must have remained for some minutes. At last Hiley's repeated clearing of his throat reminded him that it was time to leave.

2

[1531]

He threw himself at once into the work of his "little cure," as he called it. Preaching claimed first place. He felt immediate kinship with these simple country folk. His message remained the same, though he adapted his language to his hearers.

On foot or on horseback, he became a familiar figure. He soon knew each parishioner by name. Inner tension vanished, and he relaxed in a way he had forgotten possible.

A couple asking to be married presented themselves. He not only spoke with the couple about the meaning of Christian marriage, he preached on the subject. Christian living must begin in the home.

He began to teach the children in the catechumenal class to read and write. When the English Bible became available, they should be prepared to read it. To combat illiteracy among the adults, he started a class for young men to teach them to read.

He drew his sermons from the Scriptures, based on the needs of the people. The baptism of a baby gave occasion for preaching on the meaning of this sacrament and the responsibility of the parents and of the whole family of God toward the child.

A few weeks after his arrival he recalled a bit wistfully his vision of long, unbroken hours for study. *How does one with a large parish ever keep up with his work?* he asked.

Yet the strains and frustrations that had plagued him for the last seven years were absent. His parishioners accepted him. He loved them and they returned his love in full measure.

A scant quarter mile behind the rectory lay the old Roman Fossway. Latimer let his imagination travel along its route past Gloucester, through Warwickshire, by his father's old farm in Leicestershire, and on to Lincoln. He had tramped many miles along it as a boy. His heart grew heavy now at the sight of pilgrims hastening along toward the great shrines to the north.

The remoteness of the region might delay the news from London, but not all communication was cut off. Whispers about the new rector at West Kington, a favorite of the King, and his somewhat heretical views spread far beyond the borders of the parish.

Cromwell wrote that Stokesley had returned from abroad and occupied his See. His first act was to register a complaint about the preaching of Bilney, Latimer, and Crome. Crome, serving a London church, had made a pitiful recantation the year before. No evidence of a relapse was found now. Stokesley could bring no action against Bilney and Latimer as they were not in his diocese. But the news disturbed Latimer and brought back all too vividly the former antagonisms from which he had hoped to escape.

The parish priest at Marshfield, four miles away, issued an invitation for him to preach there. He selected his text from the tenth chapter of St. John's gospel, "All that ever came before me were thieves and robbers."

Marshfield was a larger community than West Kington. Houses and shops lay along a straight street, at the end of which stood the church. Overcast skies threatened rain, but the church was crowded. A number had come from neighboring parishes.

"All that ever came before me were thieves and robbers." Even as he was beginning his sermon, thoughts of Stokesley moved into a much too prominent place in his mind. He launched forth into a more violent tirade than he intended against rulers of the church. His excitement was carrying him beyond what he had planned to say, but he seemed unable to stop.

Sensitive as usual to his hearers' reaction, he was aware of antagonism. The priest who had invited him treated him coldly and allowed him to depart with no offer of refreshment.

That evening he sat before his fire and sought to piece together the reaction to his sermon. He could recall having made no statement that might be interpreted as heretical. Yet he knew that he had spoken more strongly than he intended. His heart sank. Would the old conflicts follow him even here? He blamed himself. Why could he not have banished Stokesley from his mind and preached the Word of God purely?

3

[1531]

The sermon had caused no small ferment. Latimer now believed that the priest at Marshfield had invited him to test his preaching, not to be friendly. Probably he had invited outsiders who would be incensed by any hint of heresy.

"And I played right into his hands," moaned Latimer. "What I said, though no heresy, would be objectionable to some."

As often happened, people heard what they wanted to hear. Exaggerated reports soon circulated freely. No one was more shocked than Latimer at what was being said.

Neighboring priests who had not even heard the sermon were making him the subject of conversation as they congregated in their local alehouses. Derisive remarks came back to him.

He received a letter from William Sherwood, a priest from the parish of Dyrham. Sherwood, apparently undisputed leader in the neighborhood, felt it his duty to set Latimer straight. His letter, written in Latin, seemed courteous enough, but an offensive rudeness lay behind his words.

"I should like to give you," he wrote, "a little Christian admonition about that unchristian sermon, or rather mad satire of yours, lately preached at Marshfield. You said that *all* bishops, popes, rectors, and curates were thieves and robbers and worthy only to be hanged. I suppose you mean all except yourself and others of your class. Do you really believe there are more thieves than shepherds in the church?" He urged Latimer to heed the advice of St. Paul and Christ and not to judge others.

"You also said," he continued, "that everyone who with Peter confesses Christ to be the Son of the living God is a Peter, as if the passage belonged no more to Peter, the Supreme Vicar of Christ on earth, than to any Christian. The very error of the Lutherans, who maintain that all Christians are priests! You said that a baptized man who followed the lusts of the flesh was no more Christian than a Jew or a Turk, a horrible doctrine worthy only of such heretics as Zwingli and Ecolampadius."

Latimer was indignant over the letter, both its content and its bitter tone. "He seeks to bring disrepute upon me," he cried, "by classing me with the great Continental heretics. I agree with some of Luther's ideas, but I have no intention of breaking with the church. I have no quarrel with the doctrines of the church, only insofar as voluntary works are substituted for works that Christ truly requires. My quarrel in the sermon was with leaders who fail to live by the church's teachings."

Sherwood found that he had more than met his match. Latimer had not taken part in the many debates and disputations at Cambridge without gaining considerable skill.

As for *all* being thieves and robbers, he had said *all those who climb up some other way* are such. "I judge not the men," he wrote, "but their mode of entry, even as Christ did. You advise against judging others. Does it seem to you that *all do* enter some other way, and for that reason, *you* call them thieves and robbers? If so, that is *your judgment, not my statement.*"

As to Peter's primacy, Latimer had not mentioned the subject. "I did remind my hearers," he said, "that the church is built on rock, not sand. I warned not to trust in a dead faith, lest they be overcome by the gates of hell. They should show their faith by their works, thus being sure of everlasting life."

He then turned Sherwood's statement back upon him. "You seem more ready to defend the primacy of Peter, even when there is no occasion, than to renew the blessed confession of Peter in suitable works of holiness."

He admitted saying that a baptized person who lives by the lusts of the flesh is no more a Christian than a Jew or a Turk.

"A fornicator, you say, is a servant of Christ because he is baptized. But he is also a servant of sin. Therefore the same man *can* serve two masters, which Christ says he cannot. If dead faith makes a Catholic, the devils belong to the church, since according to St. James, 'they believe and tremble.'"

Sherwood wrote again in a more cautious vein. He denied having reviled Latimer but had only warned his people about him when he heard that he spoke disrespectfully of the Ave Maria. "I have no anger," he insisted. "I try, rather, to love even my enemies, as Christ said. So naturally I love a brother such as you. I am glad to know your true statements about which I had been misinformed." Sherwood seemed eager to quit the arena without losing face. He had underestimated his adversary.

Latimer recognized some underlying causes for the antagonism expressed by Sherwood. Tyndale had a few years before lived nearby when he was tutor to the sons of Sir John Walsh. He had made enemies here and in Bristol with his talk of the Bible in English. The local inhabitants would know of his New Testament, which the King had made it treason to read. Now appeared a new priest, with a reputation for heresy, talking about the need for a Bible in English. No wonder their suspicions caused them to snatch at every word he uttered.

Latimer wanted to get away from controversy and strife, but could he? Preaching the Truth produced it in this remote spot the same as at Cambridge and London. What could he do?

If he persisted in preaching the Truth—as he must—he would inevitably offend someone. His teaching would clash with what was being practiced and taught. Debate and controversy would follow. A country parish could offer no insurance against reactions produced by the offense of the gospel. Must he then resign himself to a life of endless strife? He thought of the apostle Paul with a more sympathetic heart than ever before.

4

[1531]

In the summer Latimer received a pressing invitation from Butts and Cromwell. They could not approve of his burying himself any longer in the country. The urge to accept was strong, for he found himself in a strange position at West Kington. He had no one to talk to, no one like the Cambridge friends who were of the same mind. So as quickly as he could arrange to be away for a few weeks, he took the road to London.

In January when Latimer had left London, Parliament had convened. Cromwell welcomed the chance to discuss with him some momentous actions.

Cromwell, armed with the King's own signet ring, had gone before the Convocation of the clergy. He had informed its members that they were guilty under the law of *praemunire,* even as Cardinal Wolsey had been. They had sworn allegiance to a power outside the realm, an action inconsistent with their duty as loyal subjects of the King. Furthermore, they had recognized the late cardinal as Papal legate. The penalty that had been imposed was to deliver all of their goods to the King. They were now subject to imprisonment at His Majesty's discretion.

Naturally this came as a shock. No one had enforced the law for years until Wolsey's case. But it *was* a law. Having no alternative, they submitted, pled guilty, and implored the King's forgiveness. They obtained pardon by a promise to pay 144,000 pounds into the royal treasury.

Latimer sat speechless as Cromwell finished the unbelievable story. But more startling news was to come.

The paper proclaiming their pardon referred to the King as "protector and Supreme Head of the Church and clergy in England." The clergy protested in vain; His Majesty remained firm. On February 11 the archbishop gloomily declared that all gave consent to recognize the King as "sole protector, only sovereign Lord, and, *as far as by the law of Christ is lawful,* Supreme Head of the English Church."

"This could make things easier for you Reformers," said Cromwell. "You will be dealing with the King rather than the Pope. The timing and approach, however, will be important; otherwise it could become *more* rather than *less* difficult."

"Was it after that," asked Latimer, "that Bishop Stokesley tried to start proceedings against Bilney, Crome, and me?"

"That's right. But it came to nothing, as you know."

"I heard that Bilney left Cambridge in the spring on a preaching tour," said Latimer. "Have you heard anything?"

"I was reluctant to speak of it. Your friend acted foolishly. He not only preached but distributed copies of Tyndale's New Testament. A short time ago he was at Greenwich. When he returned to Norwich, Bishop Nix was waiting for him. He is now Nix's prisoner. I am afraid you know what that means."

Latimer was shattered. In a stricken tone he asked, "Could you not make a plea to the King for him?"

But he knew the answer even before Cromwell shook his head.

Information had previously come to Latimer in a letter from Parker. He had no inclination to share this with Cromwell.

Bilney had called the remaining members of the old group to his room one evening in early spring. "I must go up to Jerusalem," he had said. They knew what he had meant. He still carried a burden of guilt for his recantation. The hour had been ten at night. After a moving prayer with his friends Bilney had walked out the door, down the path, and through the gate.

He had gone first to friends' homes and preached, giving out copies of the New Testament. Later he had preached in the fields and wherever he could find listeners. His themes were the same as before, but his distribution of the New Testaments was sufficient offense. There was no escape for a lapsed heretic.

After some minutes of silence Cromwell said, "A writ will have to be procured from the Lord Chancellor More to proceed to his punishment. More and Stokesley have now joined forces in pushing the persecution of heretics to the extreme."

Latimer could not restrain a shudder. Bilney had indeed brought it upon himself. To die was his deliberate intention.

The dreaded news soon came. On August 19 Bilney perished in flames in the Lollard's Pit at Norwich. He had died bravely in the assurance that he was in the keeping of the Lord he loved so well. His testimony remained strong to the end, never faltering. Latimer kept to himself for some days. His loss was inestimable; his grief was the deepest he had ever known.

Then came an invitation for Latimer to preach at Kent, which was outside the Diocese of London. He preached to a large crowd and found many old friends in the congregation.

Soon after, a group of merchants approached him about preaching at St. Mary Abchurch. He was quick to refuse, for he had no permission from the Bishop of London to preach there. The men returned a second and yet a third time, insisting that many desired to hear the preaching of the Word of God.

At his third refusal one of them said, "This church is attached to an abbey. Is it not perhaps a 'peculiar' and exempt from the jurisdiction of the Bishop of London?"

Latimer let them persuade him but he laid down certain conditions. The parson and the curate must understand that he had no license from Stokesley. He had only his license as a preacher of Cambridge, which did give him the right to preach anywhere in the realm. All seemed in order and a date was set.

A nagging suspicion gnawed at the back of his mind. Was this a trap set by Stokesley? But he had already committed himself. He determined to preach what he felt was right.

He chose his text from the epistle reading for the day, "Ye are not under the law." Just that and nothing more would be bound to startle any listener, which was his intention.

"Christians not under the law?" he began. "Surely this is a dangerous saying unless it be rightly understood. It sounds as if Christians are at liberty to break the law. What if the adversaries of St. Paul had so understood his words and had accused him before the Bishop of London for his preaching?"

As he proceeded, the old reckless spirit took control. So what if it were a trap! He would make it worth their efforts.

"If my lord of London had listened to St. Paul explaining his meaning, then he would have escaped. But suppose my lord had listened only to the words of the accusers and given sentence accordingly? Then good St. Paul would have borne a fagot, even to Paul's Cross. What a sight it would have been!"

He urged judges to take care in proceeding against teachers of religion. They should not rely on ignorant and dishonest persons, who misunderstood or misrepresented what was spoken. To the end he continued to make full use of his sarcastic wit.

If it was a trap, the bishop was slow to act. Latimer was sure the content of the sermon had been reported. Stokesley could not fail to see that the words had been aimed at him. He and More were now in the midst of some questionable proceedings against certain heretics.

Latimer's indignation mounted when he heard that Stokesley had gone to the King with the matter. He represented Latimer's remarks as a defense of heretics presently under trial. He suggested that he spoke against the way Bilney's case had been handled. But the King refused to concern himself with the bishop's complaints.

Latimer and Cromwell seemed to be taking each other's measure. Latimer was not sure their relationship would ever be close, but he was coming to admire certain things about this man on the rise. He could speak his mind to him and be understood.

"I had no thought of Bilney's trial and death," he said to Cromwell. "The route he took distressed me. I had no direct contact with him for some months before his death. He would know my feeling about his distribution of the New Testament. He knew he was breaking the law; he was prepared to suffer for it."

"I have some thoughts and some plans," Cromwell confided to Latimer, "about the eventual production of an English Bible. But the time is not yet ripe. Patience is required."

In early autumn Latimer headed home. It had been good to be in London among friends; it was even better to be leaving. The farmer heart in him beat faster as his horse carried him along toward the harvesting he would find under way. The pastor heart thought of the possible harvest of souls that awaited him.

5

[1531]

The children held back at first, overcome by shyness. But their eagerness for the catechizing and the lessons soon prevailed. These were his people, the kind he grew up among and he loved the land and its fruits. He was at home among the animals: His father had kept a hundred sheep and had cultivated enough land to keep a dozen men employed; his mother cared for the milking of thirty cows. No aspect of rural life was foreign.

His parishioners set him apart as their priest and revered him in his relationship to God, yet they appreciated the fact that he understood their lives. They could get close to him and count on him for help.

In his time at court Latimer had made the acquaintance of Sir Edward Baynton, lord of the manor at nearby Bromeham. When he heard that Latimer was to come to West Kington, he assured him that he would see him whenever he was home from London. Latimer had heard that he had a mild interest in the Reformation.

Soon after his return from London he received a letter from Sir Edward telling him of complaints the Bishop of London was making against him. He specially advised Latimer what he should do if he were summoned before the bishop. He would arrive at Bromeham within a few days. Should this problem come up, Latimer was to let him know, and he would further advise him.

As winter came, Latimer suffered from his old ailments and some new ones. A pain in his side plagued him constantly. His back was bad once more. He suspected that some of his troubles were due to uneasiness about the matter Sir Edward had mentioned.

He thought often of Bilney. He grieved for the loss of this friend no one could replace. If he, with all his goodness, could come to such an end, how could Hugh Latimer hope to escape? Was his own hour of darkness even now approaching?

The Bishop of London requested the chancellor of the diocese to send Latimer to him for examination. Had Hiley been bishop, he might have resented such interference with one under his jurisdiction. But he was only the chancellor; he felt obliged to do as Stokesley asked.

Latimer meant to avoid complying if possible. He notified Sir Edward Baynton, who offered to accompany him to talk with Hiley. He expressed concern over Latimer's condition and was sympathetic toward his desire not to go to London.

"You are my ordinary," said Latimer as he faced Hiley. "If I am in error, you are capable of correcting me."

Upon consideration, Hiley seemed inclined to view the matter in that light.

"It is deep winter," continued Latimer, "and travel is precarious. I suffer from several ailments, as you see. It would go hard with me to have the trouble and expense of such a trip. I have plans to keep Christmas with my flock. If you *order* me to go, however, I will obey."

Sir Edward thought Latimer should discuss his doctrine with Hiley. He suggested that he explain fully his teaching on purgatory and saint worship. Hiley might then be able to satisfy Stokesley as to Latimer's orthodoxy.

Latimer made his explanations, and Hiley seemed convinced. "I will write to the bishop," he said, "and tell him I have examined you here. Perhaps you need not go to London."

Latimer had no confidence that Hiley would be able to hold out against Stokesley. Hiley was a good man but he realized his subordinate position.

As Latimer left, he said, "This is no light matter. My very life may be involved. I know no other course to follow except to pray to my Lord God that as he has made me bold to preach his Truth, so he will strengthen me to suffer for it, if need be."

In the days before Christmas he grew ever more despondent. One evening, unable to find peace, he left his fireside and through the bitter cold took the path to the church. The chill was only slightly less within the stone walls of the building.

He thought of Bilney and wept. He thought of Richard Bayfield, won by reading Tyndale's books. When discovered importing more books, Bayfield was confronted by Stokesley who tried by cruel measures to force him to reveal the names of accomplices. He refused. In anger Stokesley struck him a savage blow with his crozier, knocking him senseless. He died at the stake in late November.

He thought of John Tewkesbury, a leather merchant who was seized in late autumn and received barbarous treatment at the hands of the lord chancellor. He was tied to the famous "Jesus Tree" in More's garden and whipped. Cords were tied about his head and tightened until blood came from his eyes. When he still refused to recant, More had him tortured upon the rack in the Tower. This proved more than the prisoner could bear. He abjured and was dismissed. But when he saw the constancy of Bayfield, remorse drove him to preach as he had before. More and Stokesley condemned him. He was burnt at Smithfield.

Latimer lay prostrate before the altar. Fear clutched his heart. Would he be next? If Stokesley got him in his clutches, he would never let him go.

Suddenly he rose to his knees. There was a way out! He could leave England and take refuge on the Continent. Barnes was there and would help him. He could still study and preach. As he stood up, he found his legs quite numb. He walked up and down until circulation was restored.

Returning to the altar, he knelt once more. He would commit his decision and his journey—for he must go quickly—to God. As he raised his eyes to the crucifix, moonlight poured through the diamond-shaped panes across the figure of Christ.

Like a piercing sword came the words of St. Peter, "For even hereunto were ye called, because Christ also suffered for us, leaving us an example, that ye should follow his steps."

He bowed his head and wept. How had he thought he could flee? "I must follow his steps," he whispered.

6

[1531]

He sat next day to compose a letter to Sir Edward Baynton. "I fail to understand," he wrote, "why Stokesley does not preach in his own diocese, rather than trouble those who do preach.

"If his lordship would come and preach in my little bishopric, I would thank him heartily. I would not dispute or demand by what authority he came, as long as his preaching was faithful and edifying to my parishioners."

Latimer insisted that he had done no wrong by preaching in London. His license issued by the University was as good as any Stokesley could give him. Furthermore, the King had recently granted liberty to those admitted in this way to preach anywhere in the realm. Could he ask better than royal authority?

As to his preaching, if Stokesley would take it as Latimer spoke it, he would find nothing to condemn. It was true Latimer had reproved the abuses and superstitions connected with voluntary things, such as pilgrimages and image worship, but he did not condemn the things themselves. Those who accused him of this were they who had found the offerings in the boxes diminished following his preaching.

In all honesty he must admit that if Stokesley inquired into his opinions, what he found might displease him, for in many things Latimer had changed due to a deeper study of the Scriptures.

"I have thought in times past," he wrote, "that the Pope was lord of all the world as Christ is. If he should have deprived the King of his crown—or you of your lordship of Bromeham—who could have spoken? For he could do no wrong. *Now* I might be hired to think otherwise."

He had once thought there was help for physical ailments in the worship of images of saints; now it grieved him to see such as his lord of London encouraging belief in these things. Latimer wrote how he regretted the long time it had taken him to come to the Truth, which he had done by constant prayer, study of the Scriptures, and communing with men better informed than he.

Lastly, he mentioned the matter of the King's divorce. Many had thought such a marriage as the King had made was according to the will of God and would have been in great danger to have stated otherwise. Now even Stokesley was bold to say that the marriage was contrary to God's Word.

He closed the letter with an earnest plea to Sir Edward to pray for him. Without the help that only God could give, he would not be able to stand when the blow fell. He confessed that he had almost yielded to the temptation to put the ocean between him and the Bishop of London. Only God had kept him from this error.

Having dispatched a messenger with the letter, he entered wholeheartedly into the Christmas festivities. It was a time for rejoicing and praising God as well as being thankful and loving God and one another, not only in the worship and related ceremonies but in the feasting and merrymaking that followed.

7

[1532]

Baynton replied to Latimer's letter in terms that were anything but what he expected. Latimer was startled to learn that Baynton had shared his letter with friends. The coolness of his tone was disappointing.

"I am only a layman," Baynton wrote. "My views must be with the majority, since I am incapable of making decisions in such matters. My friends censure you and accuse you of arrogance."

Baynton was an influential landowner of high standing. Were the conservative priests among these friends? Perhaps Sherwood?

"You should not say that you preach the Truth," wrote Sir Edward, "for only God knows the Truth for sure." This statement Latimer found particularly galling.

"If a man's preaching excites contention rather than charity," Sir Edward continued, "it cannot be of God. It makes rather for division."

Latimer snorted in disgust at this statement. He felt certain Baynton had not arrived at it alone.

In conclusion Baynton recommended caution and submission. He added, "Should God see fit to add large numbers of converts to your opinion, I could be induced to come over to that opinion. But for now I must be prudent and remain with the majority."

Again Latimer snorted. "Such a show of honesty and prudence! It is really only laziness and unwillingness to know the Truth, if it puts one out of step with the majority."

Busy as he was with the cares of his parish at the end of this first year, he took time to write again. He must defend himself against the charges Baynton had made at the insistence of his friends. A flood of loneliness swept over him. He needed the help of *his* friends. Again, he thought of Barnes.

He gripped his pen with grim determination. He addressed Sir Edward, but in his mind, he saw the group behind him, waiting to pick apart what he might say.

"You dislike my saying *I am sure* that I preach the Truth," he began. "You say that only God knows certain Truth. I agree that only God knows *all* certain Truth. Yet either I am *certain* or *uncertain* that it is the Truth I preach. If it *is* the Truth, why may I not say so, encouraging my hearers to receive it and follow it? If I am uncertain, why should I preach at all?"

Assuming that some of Baynton's friends were priests, he continued, "Ask your friends, if they preach, whether *they* are sure that what they give *you* in their sermons is Truth. Perhaps I can learn from them. If they say they are *sure,* is it possible that they too are *arrogant?* If they are *not* sure, how will *you* be sure that Christ is your Savior?"

Latimer insisted that in his own preaching he had taught nothing out of accord with Scripture, the Fathers, and long-established interpretation. If such preaching caused dissension, he was sorry. Yet it was unsafe to conclude, as Baynton's friends did, that such preaching was necessarily of the Devil.

He cited the example of St. Paul's preaching to the Galatians and the dissension it caused. Was St. Paul not a true apostle? St. Jerome's writings stirred up dissension. For that reason was his teaching not of God? Closer at home, consider the case of the doctrine that marriage with a deceased brother's wife is illegal. This had caused great controversy. Were those who gave expression to this doctrine, even the King and Bishop Stokesley, to be condemned as of the Devil?

"You pray for agreement between Truth and uttering of Truth," he wrote. "How can it be, as long as we will not hear Truth but muzzle preachers of Truth who reprove our evil?"

Before he had finished, a knock came at his door. With unsteady hand he broke the seal of the paper handed him. Hiley had given in to Stokesley's insistence. Latimer must appear before the Bishop of London to answer for the "crimes and grave excesses committed by him within the Diocese of London." He must present himself at St. Paul's on Monday, January 29, between the hours of nine and eleven in the forenoon.

With heavy heart he began his preparations for the dreaded journey. Ill or not, deep winter notwithstanding, he must go.

8

[1532]

The road seemed endless. On the fourth day he reached the home of Sir William Butts; he was cold, weary, and ill. Butts welcomed him warmly and set about ministering to his ills. It was a relief to have the sympathetic ear of Sir William. Cromwell was tied up in Parliament.

"Don't be hard-headed, Latimer," Butts said. "Keep your statements moderate. You face a dangerous man. Remember Bayfield and Tewkesbury. And Bainham still lies in prison. They whipped him and racked him. Be warned and walk in wisdom."

"But I am only called on the charge of preaching in the diocese without permission of the bishop," said Latimer.

"You are a fool if you think Stokesley will stop there. It was the pretext upon which to get you here. He'll find more upon which to act—unless you make sure there *is* nothing more."

He had no illusions of the matter being dealt with swiftly. Stokesley began in a mild way. On the first day they gained nothing. On Wednesday the questioning took a more vigorous turn. Still he answered calmly and well. He took time in replying and left nothing for them to accuse. They bade him return on Saturday. This thrice-a-week pattern continued for some time.

One day as he entered, a difference in the arrangement struck him. Generally a fire burned on the hearth. Today, a piece of tapestry of the same type as covered the walls hung over the fireplace, and Latimer was required to stand near it.

One of the bishops put a question. Latimer recognized a possible trap, so he hesitated. As he began to speak, the bishop interrupted, "Speak up! I am hard of hearing."

At other times he had heard well enough. A suspicion grew in Latimer's mind. The covered fireplace! He tuned his ear in that direction. Someone behind the arras was writing down his answers. They hoped to trick him into saying something upon which they could condemn him.

He breathed a prayer for guidance. The question was, "Master Latimer, do you not think on your conscience that you have been suspected of heresy?"

"Speak up!" demanded Stokesley. "Surely you can answer either yes or no."

That was exactly what he could not do. To answer either way would incriminate him. He allowed a twinkle to come into his eyes.

"My lord, the question you have asked is like asking a man, 'Have you stopped beating your wife?' If he answers yes, he seems to admit that he *has been* beating her. If he says no, he indicates that he is still beating her. You have put to me a shrewd question. Inasmuch as I am innocent of heresy, I cannot answer either way. I beg you to excuse me."

With an angry glare Stokesley squelched the laughter that ran through the group. But the question was dropped.

Matters now before Parliament caused Stokesley to act with caution. In the House of Commons complaints were still being registered against abuses concerning mortuaries. The custom of presenting infants to church living was drawing fire. Also, there was the large number of holidays, termed holy days, but not kept as such.

The divorce question dragged on. A permanent rupture between the Pope and the King threatened. Henry was orthodox in all matters except his attitude toward a Pope who refused to make the decision he wanted. Everyone knew where Latimer's sympathies lay and of the King's esteem of him.

Thus, the situation with Latimer reached a stalemate. Stokesley was unwilling to defy public opinion by acting too strongly, nor did he dare risk the King's displeasure. In an unexpected action he referred the case to Convocation.

9

[1532]

On March 11 Latimer stood before Convocation at Westminster. Warham, Archbishop of Canterbury, presented him with a list of articles. Latimer's heart sank. The articles were those to which Crome had assented in his abjuration before Stokesley:

1. There is a purgatory to purge the souls of the dead.
2. Souls in purgatory are helped by masses, prayers, and alms-deeds.
3. The holy apostles and martyrs are in heaven.
4. The same saints pray for us in heaven.
5. The saints should be honored.
6. Pilgrimages and oblations to the relics and sepulchers of saints are meritorious.
7. One who has vowed chastity may not marry, nor break his vow, without the dispensation of the high bishop.
8. St. Peter's keys of binding and loosing remain to his successors the bishops, even though they live wickedly, and were never given to laymen.
9. It is profitable to invoke saints, so that they, as mediators, may pray unto God.
10. Men by almsdeeds, prayer, and other good works may obtain merit at God's hands.
11. Persons forbidden by the bishop to preach should not preach till they have purged themselves before him.
12. Lent and fasting days should be kept.
13. God gives grace in all the seven sacraments to the lawful receiver.
14. The consecration, sanctification, and benedictions received in the Christian church are laudable and profitable.
15. The crucifix and other images of saints should be kept in churches as memorials, and to the honor and worship of Jesus Christ and his saints.

16. It is profitable for them to be decked and trimmed and have candles set before them.

Not one of the articles would he deny categorically, yet he had preached for years against the *abuses* of these things. How could he blot out his years of preaching and give his approval to the old "voluntary things" that were of far less importance than the plain duties commanded in Scripture?

He answered that he would not sign. Warham put the question a second and a third time. He continued to refuse. Warham then pronounced him contumacious and excommunicated him. He must now remain in custody of the archbishop at Lambeth Palace.

For days they did not call him. Mental distress plunged him into the depths; uncertainty tore at him. The greatest torment was his excommunication. Cut off from the church! Was he doomed to hell should he die without being reinstated? Surely he would die unless he obtained some relief for his ailments. Would he suffer the penalty Bilney had suffered? He was willing to die for his Lord, but these articles concerned matters not even mentioned in Scripture. He tried to pray but found no relief; God seemed to have gone away.

He wrote a letter to the archbishop. He explained the precarious condition of his health, intensified by the excitement of the present ordeal. His flock needed the care of their pastor. Already he was away from them for two months.

He complained of unfair treatment. He had been cited to appear before the Bishop of London on a specific charge. Now he stood before Convocation with many questions added to the original accusation. Why must he subscribe to opinions others wished to put upon him when he had not been called by them?

"If you wish to question me about my preaching," he wrote, "I will be happy to clarify any statement. I have not preached contrary to the Truth, nor to the decrees of the Fathers nor, so far as I know, to the Catholic faith." He admitted a desire to reform the judgment of the common people, to teach them to distinguish between duties God required and such as were voluntary, undertaken by men of their own strength and pleasure.

"Images," he continued, "are lawful, as are pilgrimages and prayer to saints. It is lawful to care for souls in purgatory. But these things are to be kept in moderation. Thus, God's *necessary* commandments will not be deprived of a right place."

He concluded with, "Therefore, Most Reverend Father, I dare not subscribe the propositions submitted to me. I am unwilling to perpetuate popular superstition, lest I bring damnation on myself. It is not pride that keeps me from subscribing. It is blameworthy not to obey the rulers of the church. But there are occasions when one must obey God rather than man."

10

[1532]

Butts and Cromwell came to talk with him. Cromwell had spoken with the bishops, urging them to diminish their demands. Butts had used his influence where it might count. But they insisted that Latimer must moderate his opinions. If each side would give a little, the dilemma might be resolved.

Such concern did much to revive Latimer's spirits. Their influence would do more than any words he had written to Warham.

Apparently their intercession had its effect. He came March 21 into a different atmosphere. He stood before a panel of bishops acting for Convocation. Stokesley sat as deputy for the archbishop, who was ill. No doubt he found satisfaction in forcing Latimer to face him again. This court was more powerful than that of a diocese.

They handed him the same articles. An awkward moment followed in which no one spoke. Stokesley cleared his throat and asked Latimer to withdraw. He was advised to spend the time in consideration of the articles.

He knew the content of the articles well enough. He spent the time wondering what they must yet discuss.

At his return Stokesley told him that if he would subscribe to articles eleven and fourteen, he would be released from excommunication. "We also require you," rasped Stokesley, "to apologize for preaching against these articles and to make full submission to the court. Then you must beg the forgiveness of your judges."

Latimer needed little time for consideration. The terms were lenient indeed, considering Stokesley's previous actions against Bayfield and Tewkesbury.

He looked Stokesley in the face, did reverence to him as president of the court, and expressed acceptance of the terms. He was about to continue with a recognition of his error and a request for forgiveness when a paper was thrust into his hand. A new voice ordered him to kneel and ask forgiveness of the Bishop of London. Then he must read the confession handed him.

In complying he read, "My lords, I confess that I have misordered myself very far. I have presumptuously and boldly preached, reproving some things by which the weak have been misled. Wherefore I ask forgiveness. I will be glad to make amends. I have spoken with an unwarranted vehemence. I have erred in some things and have lacked discretion in many."

He then made a humble plea that he be absolved from the sentence of excommunication. They set a date three weeks ahead for the signing of the articles and for his absolution. By such an exasperating delay they apparently sought to add to his humiliation and their own partial victory.

He ground his teeth at what they had forced him into. Yet he realized he was getting off lightly. His conscience troubled him about the confession he had read. He could sign the specified articles without compromising himself greatly: submitting to a bishop who told him not to preach; confessing belief in the church's consecrations.

The days of waiting saw his mood swing like a pendulum between hopefulness and despair; irritability replaced patience. Why this delay? He had given in to their demands and read their wretched confession. Did they really mean to absolve him and release him? What more could they want?

Each day his restlessness increased. Then came word that Greenwood was rejoicing wildly at his fall. He was spreading the tale that Latimer had made a full recantation and abandoned his doctrines. Greenwood of St. John's had been among those who opposed him in the controversy over "The Card."

Latimer could not let this pass. He decided to set Greenwood straight by means of a letter. His old recklessness gained the upper hand. He would not admit that his need to act was an attempt to silence the voice of his own conscience, which was making almost the same accusations against him.

"Master Greenwood," he wrote, "if what I hear is true, I must accuse you of a grievous lack of Christian charity. As to my preaching, I was not conscious of having preached any error, so I have made no public acknowledgment of such. Perhaps I have been more outspoken than advisable. My lack of discretion may have led the people to a misunderstanding of my teaching. In the future I will have more respect to their capacity but in my preaching, I will not change the Truth."

On April 10 he appeared for what he hoped was the last time. Stokesley ordered the paper presented to him. A sudden wildness seized him. He began at the top and signed every one of the articles. He was intent only on getting free. What did it matter? He heard the intonation of the formal words absolving him from excommunication and restoring him to the sacraments.

With tremendous relief he rose from his knees. The next words must surely be those of dismissal. He would be free.

Stokesley cleared his throat, according to an irritating habit, and with a malicious smile, shattered Latimer's world. "You must remain in custody, Master Latimer. We have some new information that requires you to appear on April 15."

11

[1532]

The letter to Greenwood. The bishops must know of it. How foolish he had been to write it. He berated himself, using all the foul names in his vocabulary. His stupid, foolish pride! He couldn't bear to have Greenwood laugh at him. Freedom had been within his grasp and he had thrown it away.

On the 15th he listened to the charge without surprise. "You have written a letter to one Master Greenwood, which has come to our hands. You will appear on the 19th for questioning."

When he thought about it in a rational manner—which was difficult—he knew they had not altogether planned it this way. Both Houses of Parliament were in the midst of debates on subjects in which Convocation had much at stake. The bishops would be concerned with these matters. His case could be put off. This knowledge made the waiting no easier.

Butts reported that Bainham had been freed in mid-February, after a recantation, extracted under torture, and the payment of a fine. But his conscience gave him no rest. He confessed to his friends with tears that he had denied his Savior. He preached in his parish church, holding aloft a copy of Tyndale's New Testament. Arrest followed. Preparations for his trial were even now under way. This news added to Latimer's depression.

That he should be put off again was incredible. Yet on the 19th, he was told, "You will appear again on the 22nd." He became frantic. In desperation he appealed his case to the King.

This was a daring step. Yet, in the previous year had not Convocation declared His Majesty the Supreme Head of the Church in England? As such, he might look kindly upon Latimer's plea and react favorably.

The King had Latimer brought before him. Latimer studied his face for some sign of his state of mind. Then he knelt and made the plea that His Majesty intervene on his behalf.

It was plain that the King was in no expansive mood. Yet by his questions, he showed a full knowledge of the affair, which indicated his interest. Apparently, His Majesty too had in mind his position as Supreme Head of the Church. Would he choose this occasion to make clear to the bishops that it was no formality?

His voice was stern. "You will make a full apology to the bishops. And you will promise to preach with more care in the future." He dropped his voice and added, "See that you keep the promise." He then dismissed him. Latimer heard him instruct the Bishop of Winchester to inform Convocation of his desire.

On April 22 when the matter of Latimer's appeal came up, the Bishop of Winchester stated the King's desire, that the case be returned to Convocation.

Now the situation was almost the same as before, but the difference was a significant one. The King was now interested: He obviously wanted Latimer forgiven and received into favor.

His apology and confession went much further than before. On his knees, he read from the script handed him: "Whereas I before confessed that I had erred, meaning only error of discretion, I have since better seen and searched more deeply my own acts. I now acknowledge that I have erred in doctrine as well as discretion. I was called before the lords upon just grounds and have been by them charitably treated. Whereas I before misreported of the lords, I acknowledge in this that I have done ill. I desire them humbly to forgive me. Whereas I am not of ability to make them recompense, I will pray for them."

Once he had made this wretched statement and since it was the King's express desire, the action proceeded smoothly. They sternly warned that, should he relapse, the old charges would be revived. After Stokesley extracted a promise of obedience to the law and to the mandates of the church, the bishop absolved him.

The three long months were over. He was free. Yet he felt no exultation, no joy. His mind ran back over the endless questioning. Had he been right in his actions? Still the old question: What is worth giving one's life for? Had he persisted in his refusal to submit, Stokesley would have condemned him as a heretic. He would have met Bilney's fate. Were the articles worth giving one's life for?

12

[1532]

He remained in London the rest of the week. Friends were kind. Cromwell assured him that he had been fortunate to obtain his release so easily. He urged him to remember his promise to be careful of his future preaching.

On the morning of April 29 Edward Isaac came to call, along with Ralph and William Morice. Bainham lay in Newgate Prison, awaiting execution the next day.

"We plan to visit him after dark," said Isaac. "He will need comfort and encouragement for his final ordeal."

"But will you be allowed to see him?" asked Latimer.

"By inquiry, through a certain channel, we gained permission," said Ralph

Morice. "We mean to hear from his own lips the truth as to the matter for which he is condemned. Rumors and contradictory statements make it impossible to establish."

"We have come," said Isaac, "to urge you to accompany us, Latimer. You should know the truth as to his condemnation before you leave London. Besides, you will know better than we just how to speak to him so as to strengthen him in his last hours."

Reluctantly Latimer agreed to go with them. He had no wish to have it known that he was showing sympathy for a condemned heretic. He was free, but he was still in London.

At the prison gate the younger Morice showed his pass to the keeper, who allowed them to enter. A guard led them down a steep stair and along a filthy corridor to a small dungeon.

Bainham sat in a corner upon a couch of straw. He clutched a candle in his right hand, while holding a book in his left. As they entered, he laid aside his book and extinguished his candle. They had a lantern. He would need his candle later.

The situation was awkward. Greetings exchanged, the visitors stood silent. Then Isaac nudged Latimer to indicate that he should open the conversation.

Latimer was on the defensive, a fact he concealed by a condescending manner. "Master Bainham, we hear that you are condemned for heresy to be burnt. We have some doubt as to the cause of your condemnation. A man should not consent to his own death unless it be for a right cause. Do not let vainglory overcome you. If you give up your life in a cause not worthy of death, you shall neither please God nor do good to yourself or your neighbor. Would you acquaint us with the articles for which you are condemned?"

The man replied in a quiet tone that he had spoken of Thomas à Becket, the great saint, as a traitor.

"Surely that is no cause worthy for a man's death."

"I also spoke against purgatory," said Bainham, "declaring that there is no such thing, but that it picks men's purses. I spoke against the doctrine of the mass as a sacrifice for sins."

"Truly," said Latimer, "your conscience as to these matters may make it seem your duty to die in their defense. You may feel that to recant goes against your conscience and the Scriptures. Yet beware of vainglory. The Devil will be ready to infect you with it when you come into the multitude of people."

Latimer grew more and more uncomfortable. How much did Bainham know of his trial and of what had led to his release? The others gave him no help. In desperation he plunged on. He advised Bainham to take his death quietly.

Bainham thanked him, then looking intently at Latimer, he said, "I likewise exhort *you* to *stand to the defense of the Truth.* For you who be left behind have need of strength also, the world being so dangerous as it is."

A flush of shame crept up Latimer's neck and into his face.

When Bainham mentioned his wife, he broke down and wept. She had been sent to the Fleet Prison when he was arrested. Repeated questioning had failed to obtain the names of associates or the hiding place of the books. What would happen to her?

Latimer launched forth into what he realized was a self-righteous attack on Bainham's lack of faith.

"You are ready to die," he said, "yet unable to trust your wife to the goodness of God. Truly, she shall be better provided for than any provision you could make if you were here."

The words had a hollow ring. Latimer fell silent. Bainham again thanked him and asked for their prayers. Embarrassment hindered speech as they reached the street. Their ways parted and Latimer was relieved to move off into the darkness alone.

Next day he turned his back on London streets and headed into the country. His mind went over and over his trial, the advice his friends had given, and the course he had taken. As he rode along, he was only dimly aware of the beauty of English Maytime. He heard the thrush's song but with no glad response.

13

[1532–1533]

He buried himself in his parish duties, thankful for definite tasks that must be performed. He occupied his mind with the needs of his people and the means by which he could meet them. He was not tempted to preach outside his parish. Life fell into a pattern, and he was glad to have it so.

Yet in the night hours when sleep eluded him, unwelcome thoughts crowded into his mind. The death of Bilney continued to weigh on him; Bainham's words returned.

At last he could bear it no longer. He would force himself to pass judgment upon his own conduct. To do this, he must examine more fully his own doctrines in the light of Scripture.

Could it be that Bainham was right—that purgatory is only a cruel pickpurse, that no scriptural sanction upholds this doctrine? He had preached against the abuses that accompanied the belief. Could the doctrine itself be the real abuse?

If Bainham was right, what about his own action in rashly signing the sixteen articles? These were painful questions. He must find answers. God would give them to him if he persevered in his search. God's Truth was what mattered.

A letter from Cromwell arrived. Convocation had been forced to cancel with finality its legislative powers. The action read, "No constitution shall be promulgated by the clergy unless the King first approve the same." A day later Sir Thomas More resigned his post as lord chancellor.

So the King had actually become the Supreme Head of the Church in England. It was no empty title. Latimer recognized the connection between Convocation's clipped wings and More's resignation. Sir Thomas would not remain in power beside a church that was rendered powerless and had lost its glory.

The King still maneuvered about the divorce. News of Latimer's trial had reached Rome. The Pope complained that a priest who had been imprisoned by the Archbishop of Canterbury had been set free upon appealing to the King.

In August Warham, the Archbishop of Canterbury, died. Latimer felt it must have been a relief to the unhappy old man. He had suffered at the hands of Wolsey, who overshadowed and overpowered him. He did not approve of the actions of the King to which he was required to voice assent.

As to his successor, Latimer learned that the King's choice had fallen upon Thomas Cranmer, an unexpected but not unwelcome move. With the submission of the clergy accomplished, the choice was firmly in the King's hand. He would expect Cranmer to complete the divorce proceedings. Now Latimer would hope for his help in furthering the Reformation.

For the moment the King did nothing further to ruffle the Pope's feathers. He wanted no breach of order in the important matter of securing the bulls for Cranmer's consecration.

His Majesty's insistence finally overcame Cranmer's reluctance to accept the appointment. His humility was well known to his friends. In piety, integrity, and prudence he could not be matched. He seemed eminently qualified.

The new year promised new hope for the Reformation. Even Latimer's inner problems were beginning to clear up.

Hardly had a messenger from the King departed for Rome with a request for the bulls for Cranmer's consecration than an agent from the Pope arrived. A Papal bull demanded that Lady Anne Boleyn be dismissed from the court immediately.

In defiance of the order the King immediately married the lady. Of course, this step must be kept secret until the bulls for the consecration of the archbishop were safely in hand. The idea of the King marrying before a divorce from Queen Catherine had been legally determined shocked Latimer profoundly.

14

[1533]

Growing optimism led Latimer to give in to the temptation to preach outside his parish. He agreed to preach at Bristol. On the morning of March 9 he preached at St. Nicholas. "I observe the reverence you do Our Lady. Yet you must not believe that she is a savioress. Only Christ is savior of sinners. Does so saying make him Our Lady's Savior? Does this make her a sinner?"

Angry murmurs swept through the congregation.

"Wait!" he cried, raising a hand. "I do not say she was a sinner. I say that either she *was* or she *was not.* If she *was* a sinner, then Christ redeemed her as he does all sinners. If she *was not,* it was because Christ preserved her from sin. In either case he was her savior. I remind you that, worthy of honor as she is, Our Lady is not our savior. Only Christ saves."

In the afternoon he was to preach at Black Friars. How would he be received in this Dominican establishment? He sensed a coolness in the Prior, Dr. John Hilsey. A good portion of his congregation was the same as that of the morning.

The images gave him a point of departure. "Do you worship saints or do you worship images?" he asked. "Be careful in answering. What one frequently understands by 'saint' is the image such as this." He pointed to a richly robed and bejeweled image of St. Dominic.

"What you see is an image made by man's hands. St. Dominic, the saint, is in heaven. Why do we put images before us? To represent to our eyes and to bring to our remembrance one whom we cannot see. To worship the dead image is to be guilty of idol worship. Give your honor to the living saint."

He sensed unrest. "If praying to an image makes me an idolator, how may I use the image? No image has power to relieve my headache or cure my toothache. Yet it serves as a kind of 'laymen's book.' As I 'read' it, I call to mind all the good the saint did in his life on earth. I think of the good being done by the friars of his order, even in this place in which we worship." He paused to smile and bow toward the friars seated in their choir stalls.

"But tell me, does a dead image need raiment and jewels? All men are created in the image of God. Is it not better to use one's wealth to feed and clothe the living images who lie in desperate circumstances in your city streets?"

He ignored a few protesting voices. "Since the image is in a sense a book, does it not stand to reason that we can read the book as well whether or not its pages are gilded and embossed? So the lighting of candles is useless. Does one need a light in broad daylight? With candles so dear, the money is better spent in charitable deeds to one's neighbors."

They allowed him to finish, but their anger was evident. Yet he had his champions, nor were they all of the lower classes. A number of prominent men, including the mayor and a group of priests, applauded his message.

Next day at St. Thomas things began to get out of hand. At his preaching against pilgrimages, the crowd became unruly. By the time he had completed his message, a veritable explosion was taking place in the streets.

A voice cried out, "He called Our Lady a sinner." Other voices joined in, "He accuses us of idolatry"; "He says the saints can perform no miracles"; "He makes pilgrimages a sin."

The whole city divided into two armed camps. The zeal of his defenders horrified the opposing priests, so in haste they sent off a letter to Convocation.

On March 26 the complaint against Latimer came before that body. He had broken his promise of the previous year by preaching against the teaching of the church in Bristol.

Convocation was aware of its diminished powers. At Gardiner's advice they sent a copy of Latimer's submission to Bristol with instructions to use it against him as seemed wisest. To Latimer went a prohibition against preaching again in the Diocese of Worcester without license from the bishop.

15

[1533]

His opponents launched into new attacks with all confidence, since Latimer could not reply. The Bristol zealots brought in outside help to reinforce the efforts of the local talent.

On April 6, Palm Sunday, the most theatrical of the imported preachers appeared. Hubberdin was somewhat of a clown. He used vulgar language and exaggerated gestures. Latimer's opponents counted on this to attract the common people to their cause.

He almost outdid himself. He preached for Papal supremacy. Christ's death, he claimed, was not sufficient without the blood of martyrs. The Scriptures in English would breed heresy.

His statements grew wilder. "The church knows everything Christ preached and did, even things not recorded in the Scriptures. Scripture need not have been written at all. Latimer is a heretic, almost an atheist."

Latimer's sympathizers entered the fray, rebutting all accusations. The city became one mad scene of theological debate, and the authorities feared riots. Even the news of Cranmer's consecration as Archbishop of Canterbury went unnoticed. All eyes were fixed on the local scene.

Late in April Dr. Edward Powell, a Prebendary of Salisbury, preached in opposition to Latimer. He allowed zeal to overcome good sense by censuring the King's divorce, calling it adultery. He asserted that all kings are subject to priests and prelates.

Dr. Nicholas Wilson added his fiery oratory. He continued to uphold Papal supremacy. He played upon Latimer's supposed assertion that the Virgin Mary was a sinner.

Latimer became frantic as his accusers twisted his words with complete dishonesty. The absurdity of their extravagant statements made him wonder that anyone continued to listen.

He sought to bring his opponents before the Mayor or Council of Bristol. If they established openly their accusations against him, he might make reply. They refused to answer.

The next day brought proof that at least one man was wearied of the falsity of Latimer's opponents. Dr. John Hilsey, Prior of the Black Friars, requested a private conversation, that he might hear the details of Latimer's beliefs. He was completely satisfied with what he heard and proffered his friendship.

Cromwell instigated an investigation. His importance had grown. He was a member of the council, master of the King's jewels, clerk of the hanaper, and chancellor of the exchequer.

His commission reached Bristol in July and sought to get to the bottom of things. They interviewed key people, took copious notes, and forwarded them to London without delay.

The reports made it clear that Latimer's opponents had censured the King's divorce, denied the royal supremacy, and upheld Papal infallibility and supremacy. Hubberdin, Wilson, and Powell were imprisoned, along with others. The rest found it wise to slip quietly away from the vicinity.

The silencing of his opponents vindicated Latimer, but he remained bound by the prohibition against preaching in the Diocese of Worcester. How could he set the record straight?

The new archbishop was already at work. He had annulled the marriage of Henry to Catherine; he had recognized the marriage to Anne Boleyn. At a magnificent ceremony in Westminster Abbey he crowned the new Queen. His latest action was to issue to Hugh Latimer a license to preach anywhere in the Province of Canterbury, which of course included Bristol.

Latimer lost no time in taking advantage of the freedom provided by his new license.

16

[1533]

The archbishop was making a visitation and would include Bristol in his itinerary. The churches made hasty preparations. Some had misgivings as to what his attitude would be, in light of the recent disturbances.

Latimer hoped for time with the archbishop. Would it be too much to expect to find a friendly ear into which he could pour his explanation of the Bristol affair? He felt a desperate need to establish clearly that he was no heretic.

Cranmer dealt rather quickly with what the situation at Bristol demanded. Then he had time for Latimer.

The archbishop wore his robes of office with quiet dignity. A clean-shaven man, he appeared younger than his years. One felt the weightiness of his presence, yet at the same time, sensed a humility of spirit. His gentle smile, reflected in his gray eyes, put Latimer entirely at ease.

"I am sure these six months have been trying," he said to Latimer at their first meeting.

"Rather an understatement, Excellency. To be muzzled as I was . . . you have no idea. At the same time I had to hear my words twisted into something unrecognizable, to have put into my mouth statements I had never made. Then they came back in defense of their own stand with the most preposterous misinterpretations of the Truth."

"I would like to know what you actually said. I am eager to hear what your beliefs really are at this point."

"Where would you like me to begin?"

"Why not take the doctrines touched on? Start with the statement about the Virgin. Did you say she was a sinner?"

Cranmer had doubtless read the report of the commission. His interviews in Bristol would have further informed him. Latimer rejoiced at this chance to set the record straight.

As he finished his brief sketch, Cranmer smiled. "I see nothing to criticize there. But an adversary could twist the words and make your meaning different. You must exercise care."

"They said I spoke disrespectfully of the Ave Maria. I merely pointed out that only superstition can lead one to think a Pater Noster cannot be properly said without an Ave Maria at its heels. Nor does the Word of God anywhere teach that men should say twenty Ave Marias for one Pater Noster. Surely *one*, reverently said, is better than hurrying through a dozen in such a garble that no word is understood."

"I want to know for my own satisfaction," said Cranmer, "what your beliefs are on the controversial points. I will also be in position to set the King's mind at rest, if he inquires."

Latimer leaned forward in his chair. What joy to find a keen mind ready to give his views an honest hearing. He raised his eyes to meet the steady gaze of the gray ones across from him. With strong feeling he launched into an explanation of his teaching on images and saints, on gilding, decking, and candles.

"I suppose your beliefs on pilgrimages follow from that?"

"Naturally. All idolatry, superstition, false faith and hope in the image must be pared away. A man must care for his own household before he takes off on pilgrimage. He must provide charitably for his needy neighbor. He must make restitution to anyone he has wronged. Only then, if he is able, may he go on pilgrimage. Yet there is no requirement that he ever go."

Cranmer nodded thoughtfully.

"As for saints in heaven," continued Latimer, "they are not mediators by way of redemption. Only Christ is that mediator. The blood of Christ is enough for a thousand worlds. But by way of intercession, saints in heaven may be mediators and pray for us. I have an idea they do this whether we ask them or not."

"The same thought had occurred to me," said the archbishop.

"I don't deny that we may pray to saints. But I consider it preferable to pray to the One who made them saints and who can make us saints. The best honoring of saints is to know their holy living and to follow them as they followed Christ."

"Well said," exclaimed Cranmer. "Now I must hear you on the subject of purgatory, though the hour grows late."

Latimer stood up and pressed his hand to the small of his back to ease the pain that rarely left. "I do not deny the existence of purgatory," he said. "Those who are there are in charity, which they cannot lose. They cannot dishonor God, nor can they displease him or be displeased by him. They cannot be cut off from God and cannot die. Their salvation is certain."

"You know," said Cranmer, "you are right. We seldom see it that way because we concentrate on the thought of suffering."

"I admit that I would prefer being in purgatory to being in the Bishop of London's coal house. In that prison I might die bodily for lack of food and drink; in purgatory, I could not. In prison I might die spiritually for fear of pain or lack of counsel; in purgatory, I could not. In prison I could be made to bear a fagot; in purgatory, I could not."

"Ah, friend Latimer, your wit is never far away, is it?" said Cranmer, laughing. "But be careful where you speak thus."

Resuming his chair, Latimer continued, "It is my opinion that provision for purgatory has brought thousands to hell. Debts are left unpaid. Restitution of ill-gotten goods is not made. Christian people are neglected and allowed to perish. Last wills are broken. God's ordinances are set aside. Thus, we have gone to hell with masses, dirges, and ringing of many a bell.

"Unless we do what God commands, mass-priests may sing till they are blear-eyed, say till they have worn their tongues to stumps, but neither singing nor saying shall bring us out of hell, where we shall go for being contemptuous of God's forbiddings. Purgatory's iniquity has replenished hell and left heaven almost empty. If purgatory were purged of all that it has gotten by setting aside restitution and robbing Christ, it would be a poor purgatory. So poor that it could not feed so fat and enrich so many idle and slothful lubbers."

"Those are bold words, Latimer," said Cranmer. "If you spoke like that in Bristol, I can understand the reaction of the conservative priests. But you speak truth. Yet even truth can be softened a little. People must have time to get used to new ideas when they have been force-fed the old ones for so long."

"But many are ready to hear the Truth," said Latimer. "They have long been pillaged by a corrupt clergy. Every occasion of life offers an opportunity to force the adding of something to the enormous treasures that the clergy pile up for their own luxurious living."

"No wonder the clergy become indignant at your preaching against practices that provide a profitable source of income."

"This, indeed," said Latimer, his eyes flashing, "is the wasp that stings them and makes them swell."

Before Cranmer returned to London, Latimer broached another subject. He longed for an opportunity to preach again before the King. Would the archbishop seek to arrange for such an occasion?

As they parted, Latimer clasped Cranmer's hand in both his own and spoke with deep emotion. "I feel like a new man. You have done me more good than all Butts' medicines. I praise God and thank both him and you."

17

[1533]

Stacks of golden hay stood in the fields. Latimer's parishioners planted their winter wheat and barley in plots that had lain fallow the previous year, following the three-field cycle in use of the land. They talked freely as he sat with them in the evenings. As he discerned needs, he planned his sermons to meet them.

In hours of study and meditation he took a deeper look into his own heart and mind. He was astonished when he considered the nine and a half years since Bilney had turned him to the Truth.

In the early days he had said—how many times?—"*Only* clear away the abuses. . . ." That and preaching the Word with clarity would result in Reformation.

He had found it not so simple. As often as he stated his position, accusations of heresy followed. Why? Because the abuses of the practices provided much of the church's income. Every petty abuse filled someone's pockets. An almost demonic hatred sprang up against the Reformers and against the Truth.

He had told Cranmer that many were ready to be released from bondage. But in truth, many were so deeply entrenched in the old errors, it was difficult to break them loose. They clung to old ideas with a fierce tenacity. In spite of all his explanation about images he feared that most still worshiped the image and not the saint. What else could all the rich clothing and jewels piled upon every image mean? Must he now deny the validity of the use of images because they were so misused?

He knew that he was growing, so he supposed he must expect "growing pains." The ordeal at Bristol had taxed him to the uttermost. Yet being forced to defend his position had driven him to a fuller knowledge of the Truth. A great soul-searching had been required: He had to find out where he stood and why. The struggle had strengthened him. Thank God for that.

He stood in the pulpit on Sunday morning searching the faces of his people. Late September sunshine streamed through the east windows, touching with a golden glow the baptismal font by the door and falling upon faces with a softer radiance.

He spoke on the relative unimportance of paying to have masses said for souls in purgatory. First things must come first, if they would please God.

"If I had a thousand pounds to give, where could I best use it for God's glory? To try to help souls in purgatory? No, I would use part of it in repairing that dangerous stretch of road beyond Nettleton. You know it well. I know a poor man whose daughter has no dowry. I would slip money into that father's hand, that he might provide for his daughter's marriage. I would think of a man I know in Bristol who is unemployed and unable to supply his family with necessities. I would think of the sick and suffering who lie uncared for. These would come higher on my list of concerns than souls in purgatory."

That week a letter from the archbishop brought word of the birth of Princess Elizabeth. The royal parents had hoped for a prince, but the King seemed happy over his little daughter.

"I urge you to come to London for a visit," he wrote. "Both Cromwell and I feel the need to have you here. I expect you as my guest at Lambeth Palace. Do not delay."

He disliked leaving his people again, but an invitation from the archbishop was not to be treated lightly. Things were astir in the land. Was he to play a larger part?

18

[1533]

He climbed the steps from the Lambeth landing dock and looked up at the red brick walls and arch of the main gate. He recalled the time spent here as Archbishop Warham's unwilling "guest." How different to arrive as Archbishop Cranmer's friend.

Cranmer was away. Ralph Morice, serving as Cranmer's secretary, welcomed him. They found much to talk of.

"At Westminster," said Latimer, "I was handed a letter from George Brown, Prior of the Augustine Friars. He invites me to preach there two days from now. Is my license from the archbishop sufficient to overthrow Stokesley's inhibition?"

"You may be sure of it," said Morice.

"What I desire above all else is to preach before the King. How I wish I might preach before him every Sunday for a year."

"Such ambition is a bit excessive, I fear. But I rather expect a part of your wish will be fulfilled ere long."

On October 3 Latimer preached in the Church of the Augustine Friars. A part of his pleasure stemmed from the knowledge that he was defying Stokesley.

Stokesley was furious. But all his thunderings were noise without power. He no longer enjoyed the status that Warham's archbishopric had afforded him. His friend Sir Thomas More was now unable to help. Times had changed.

Cranmer and Cromwell were in favor. The wrath of the Bishop of London went unheeded.

Cranmer had summoned Latimer to London to assist in the trial of a famous case, now approaching its final stages. Some years earlier a simple servant girl by the name of Elizabeth Barton had become subject to convulsive seizures during which she uttered strange sounds. Edward Bockyng, a monk who lived nearby, evidently saw certain possibilities in her condition. He undertook her care and claimed for her a miraculous cure.

The priest obviously practiced deception in what followed; however, he at least gained the girl's cooperation. The "Maid of Kent's" claim to visions of heaven, purgatory, and hell led to her recognition as a channel through which God made his will known. The area of Kent in which she lived soon swarmed with pilgrims.

She managed to gain the ears of both Wolsey and Warham for a time. Under her influence, they slowed almost to a standstill their efforts in effecting the King's divorce. The Papal party found her an effective mouthpiece. She declared that the King would not live a month if he married Anne. When the passage of time proved her wrong, she affirmed that the King's situation was like that of King Saul, whom God disowned but allowed to hold the throne for a short period.

Bishop Fisher and Sir Thomas More came briefly under her influence. She communicated with the Pope. When a report came of a conspiracy against the throne and life of the Sovereign due to her "visions," it received ready credence.

In July Cranmer had begun proceedings against the Maid. Both he and Cromwell had questioned her. Now Cranmer was gathering witnesses. Her accomplices were put under arrest. Cranmer planned to hold a final examination at Lambeth.

Latimer joined with enthusiasm in the efforts to unravel the affair. She had included Latimer, Cranmer, and Cromwell in her denunciations.

When the hearings dragged on for days, Latimer's enthusiasm waned. He suspected that torture extracted the confessions of the accomplices. They revealed a plot to remove Henry and replace him with his daughter Mary. Such evidence was sufficient to seal their doom. Parliament would act.

Latimer considered the time in London well-spent. He could preach in the metropolis without fear of the Bishop of London. His friendship with Cranmer was stronger. He and Cromwell had a growing respect for each other. It pleased him to be accorded a welcome in Cranmer's household. Not that he craved prestige, but after all the unhappy experiences he had endured, he found comfort in being accepted in these circles. Only one shadow marred his satisfaction: Nothing had been said about his preaching before the King.

19

[1534]

A third Christmas at West Kington passed. Latimer continued to agonize over the lack of an English Bible. Preaching was essential and must come first, but daily feeding upon God's Word was necessary for each household if the flames kindled by preaching were to burn brightly.

Tyndale's New Testament continued to circulate. But he could not permit his people to break the law even in so important a matter. The King *must* come through on his promise.

Then Cranmer's letter dissipated all dark thoughts. He was to preach before the King on the Wednesdays of Lent. He made a rapid calculation. Ash Wednesday would fall on February 18, barely five weeks away.

He read Cranmer's letter again. Then he laughed aloud. "Cranmer is afraid to give me free rein. He wants to tell me what to say. He even warns against preaching overlong. Dear, cautious Cranmer. He can't understand what it is to be Latimer."

To leave his flock again made him uncomfortable, yet his absences all seemed necessary. No one could doubt the importance of the present commission.

Cranmer welcomed him with warmth; Cromwell with his usual reserve. "You seem afraid to turn me loose on my own," said Latimer to Cranmer. "Such instructions and warnings you gave!"

"Indiscretion could spoil everything. More than your reputation is involved. We must think of the whole future of the church. But I meant no slur on your judgment."

"You have some confidence in me," said Latimer, "or you would not have arranged this opportunity for me."

"You may be coldly received by the Dean of the Chapel Royal. Sampson could not conceal his displeasure when I told him of your appointment. He had invited someone else for Wednesdays and had to withdraw the invitation. Besides, he was on Stokesley's court at your trial two years ago and still doubts your soundness."

"Don't worry about Sampson. His lack of friendliness will not upset me."

"Could we enlarge upon the points I outlined in my letter?" asked Cranmer. "I asked Cromwell to give us his advice."

"Remember," said Cromwell, "I'm no preacher."

"But," said Cranmer, "you are privy to undercurrents of opinion. You can advise as to where to place emphasis and where to tread lightly."

Cromwell murmured a gruff assent.

"As to the Scripture you use," said Cranmer, "I suppose by now you have made your choice. My concern is that you stay with the Scripture. Bring out the true sense of the meaning."

"In other words my text must not become a pretext," said Latimer. "I think I can live with that."

"Need you mention the disturbance at Bristol at all?" asked Cromwell. "Can you not accomplish more by keeping your preaching straightforward? Your teaching should stand on its own, apart from any accusation made against you in Bristol."

"My thoughts are the same," said Cranmer.

Latimer looked from one to the other. At last he said, "For one who lived through that nightmare, it won't be easy."

"You should avoid at all costs," said Cranmer, "any mention of a specific adversary by name."

"Sound advice," agreed Cromwell. "No need to deal in personalities. Offending people at this time will be unwise. Avoidable offense, that is."

"You wrote," said Latimer, with a certain grimness, "that if the Word of God gave occasion to rebuke some offense, I might do so in general terms. You advise more caution than I customarily employ. My habit is to voice what I consider right, without special regard to whom it offends. However, considering the importance of the occasion, I shall try to restrain myself."

Cranmer said, with a sympathetic look, "We do not mean to bind you. Just strive to temper your manner of speaking a bit."

"His Majesty has no love for long preaching," said Cromwell. "Limit yourself to an hour, perhaps a bit more, in the pulpit."

"Cranmer mentioned that. He hinted that the King and Queen might walk out if I preach too long. That would be awkward."

"Here again," said Cranmer, "we don't want to make the limits too strict. Be guided by the feel of the situation. But an hour and a half should be your outside limit."

"I shall try to stay in line," said Latimer. "It would be unusual for anyone to walk out. Whatever else may be true of my preaching, it holds the attention of the listeners."

"In the complaints against you," said Cromwell dryly, "no one has ever accused you of being boring." With that he excused himself, saying that another matter pressed for his attention.

Latimer handed Cranmer a sheaf of papers. "My sermon outlines. I seldom prepare a complete manuscript. But I shall write each of these sermons out, show you the manuscript, and then try to hold myself to the words as written."

Cranmer approved the outlines. "I am sure things will go well. I do have confidence in you. You represent not only yourself but the Reformation movement in the church."

Latimer straightened his shoulders. "I represent Jesus Christ. I am his ambassador. *That* I shall try to remember."

Latimer was not comfortable about being hovered over and restricted. He needed freedom—freedom to expound the Word of God as he understood it. In spite of his high expectations, perhaps this would not be his happiest assignment.

20

[1534]

Ash Wednesday found Latimer with some perplexity of mind. He ascended the steps of the pulpit in the Royal Chapel. As he encountered the firm gaze of the King, he thought, "I'm on trial!" His eyes shifted to the face of the Queen. Her dark eyes lit up, and a brief smile passed over her face.

He read the Scripture and began with the opening words from the manuscript. Then he paused and took a deep breath. His heart soared as if restrictive bands had burst. A surge of urgency to preach in his own terms swept over him, so he laid the manuscript aside and began to pour out his message with all the vigor of his soul. He was aware only of the special two before him and the need to proclaim the Word that lay on his heart.

Then the service was over, and he stood with Cranmer and Cromwell in a corner of the vestry. Cranmer's excitement and Cromwell's tight smile reassured him.

"You never lost the attention of the King and Queen for an instant," cried Cranmer. "All went well. I am pleased."

"You put aside your manuscript," said Cromwell. "Even so, you kept to your subject. I noted no indiscretions. Do as well on six future occasions."

He duly wrote out the next sermon, and again it lay unnoticed. The King made no attempt to conceal his pleasure in the sermons. The Queen was generous in her praise. She discussed the content of his messages and asked questions of a theological nature. The depth of her thinking came as a surprise. He had supposed that she was like most of the other ladies at court—attractive and polite, but of little depth.

Because of the favor shown him, he grew bolder. He forgot himself and moved dangerously close to forbidden areas in the succeeding weeks. Cranmer grew nervous and protested. Cromwell thought he should be allowed to pursue his own course. At length Cranmer realized that he could not control Latimer. The pleasure of the King and Queen was what counted.

21

[1534]

After Easter Latimer was eager to be on his way home. Cranmer had other ideas. "It will better serve the church as a whole, Latimer, if you remain here for a time."

"I have already been away from my flock for three months."

"During January," Cranmer said, "while you were deep in sermon preparation, Parliament took some momentous actions of which you should know before you leave. And I have a plan concerning your future that I must discuss with you."

Latimer threw up his hands in resignation. He could not oppose Cranmer. Besides, Cranmer had piqued his curiosity.

The archbishop's time was not his own. Days passed before he could spare time for Latimer. The mildness of the April evening drew them into the garden.

"I hardly know where to begin," said Cranmer. "I suppose the root of the matter is that His Majesty found himself pushed into adopting a stronger policy than he first intended. Pushed by circumstances, you understand."

"Certainly he is not a man to be pushed by people."

"From the time of my consecration as archbishop, a loose understanding existed with regard to outside interference. No control by a foreign power would be tolerated."

"Once Papal supremacy was denied," said Latimer, "laws had to define the meaning of the statement. Was that it?"

"The King discovered activity among Catherine's supporters, including the Pope, which was definitely treasonable."

"Could the Pope have been testing the King to see what he actually meant by 'supremacy'?"

"Possibly. His Majesty was reluctant to cut all ties with Rome, but recent actions have amounted to that. No appeal may be made to Rome. No longer will *the Bishop of Rome, otherwise called the Pope,* have a word in the naming or consecration of bishops. No more payments of pensions, Peter pence, and the like to Rome. The power and jurisdiction the Pope formerly claimed now belong to the King, including the power of visitation of the religious houses. He may inspect and reform them as he pleases."

"How then will bishops be elected and consecrated?" Latimer was having difficulty assimilating all this.

"Dean and chapter in a diocese will elect the bishop, but only upon royal recommendation."

"So no trace of Papal supremacy is to remain in church or state," commented Latimer. "How did the clergy react? I can hardly see Stokesley taking it calmly."

"They were pretty grim about it, but what could they do except give assent?"

"A verbal assent that does not go very deep?"

"Easy escape was not permitted. Each member of Convocation was required to answer a question. Each answer was recorded."

"And the question?"

" 'Does the Bishop of Rome have, *by Scripture*, any more jurisdiction within the realm than any other foreign bishop?' "

"And every member gave the expected negative reply?"

"Almost. A few refused to answer."

Darkness had fallen. The paschal moon had waned, but the brilliance of a myriad stars lighted the cloudless sky.

Cranmer sighed. "A shame to go in on a night like this. But another full day lies ahead."

22

[1534]

Latimer had some questions to put to Cromwell. The man's schedule allowed little leisure, but at length he found an hour.

Latimer let his eyes roam around Cromwell's well-appointed study. "How does the Reformation stand in the light of recent actions?" he asked.

"Where it stood before," replied Cromwell. "Parliament aimed to remove a yoke of tyranny. They decried the thought of abandoning any doctrine or practice of the church. They intend to keep the church 'Popish' without acknowledging the Pope."

"They mean to hold onto all the dogmas brought in by the Papal See, while disavowing its authority?" asked Latimer.

"Do I detect a note of doubt as to their ability to do so? You are right. They will discover it is an impossible position. Meanwhile, I am learning to be a patient man. Patience is essential if one expects to reach one's goals."

"Is there no practical gain, then, for the Reformers?"

"Strangely enough, there is. Not that Parliament meant it so. But we must be grateful for the crumbs that fall to us."

"And these crumbs?" inquired Latimer.

"No longer is it heresy to speak against the Pope and his pretended authority. No procedure against a person accused of heresy can be made without at least two lawful witnesses. Trial must be in open court. No more secret conclaves such as Stokesley employed in the beginning of your trial."

"What about the punishment of heretics?" asked Latimer.

"One found guilty of heresy may not be burned without a royal writ. This law precludes hasty, unauthorized burnings. Some prisoners, kept on suspicion of heresy, have been released."

"His Majesty has learned, then, that tightening up on many things makes necessary the loosening up on a few other things."

"It would seem so," said Cromwell, with his tight smile.

"How was the passing of the Act of Succession received? Adherents to the Papacy, with their zeal to uphold the claims of the Lady Mary, must have found that hard to swallow."

"Little *open* objection was voiced," said Cromwell. "Mental reservation is another question. His Majesty remains adamant. The succession is to be limited to his heirs by Queen Anne."

Cromwell nodded and rose abruptly from his chair. The interview was at an end.

23

[1534]

Two days later Latimer again walked in the gardens at Lambeth. Violets filled the carefully tended beds along the path. From over near the wall came the fragrance of lilies mixed with a softer scent of cloves from gillyflowers.

He was not alone. With him were Ralph Morice and several doctors and chaplains of the archbishop's staff. A lighter mood prevailed than one might expect in so august a company.

"Can you believe," asked Latimer, "that I have so recently preached seven sermons with no manifestations of bitter opposition? No arguments, no misquoting, no charge of heresy."

"Maybe you have found the right company, Latimer."

The conversation continued, with laughter and joking. *We are acting,* thought Latimer, *like Cambridge undergraduates on holiday.* For the moment he felt content with his situation among like-minded men and the fellowship it nourished.

Suddenly a burst of laughter was cut short and silence fell. From an upper chamber a figure appeared on the balcony. They recognized Sir Thomas More. He stood rather uncertainly for a moment. Then he descended the stairs and disappeared into a small room at the bottom.

"They must have brought him from the Tower for questioning," said Morice.

"Why is More in the Tower?" asked Latimer in surprise.

"Both More and Bishop Fisher declined to take the Oath of Succession," said Morice. "The form was set by Parliament and the language was specific. Neither spoke against it; they simply refused to subscribe. Such an example by men of high position could not be overlooked."

Morice said that the archbishop had tried to work things out. He begged that they be allowed to take the oath in a modified form. This was denied. Others joined Cranmer in an attempt to persuade the men to subscribe. Nothing availed. The King saw no alternative to imprisonment in the Tower.

Later Sir Thomas was recalled to the room above. At supper Cranmer related the conclusion of the matter. During the afternoon, he had used every logical persuasion to get More to swear. All was in vain. More was returned to the Tower.

"I have great respect for Sir Thomas More," said Cranmer with sadness in his tone. "Why does he have to be so stubborn?"

A chill had come into the air. Cranmer invited Latimer and a few others into his small sitting room where a fire burned on the hearth. The conversation continued.

"The execution of the Maid of Kent is set for a week from today," said Cranmer. "She and her accomplices have been convicted of high treason. The penalty is death by hanging. A bad business. I confess I am glad to see it finished."

The high spirits of the afternoon had vanished. A chill wind swept into the room through some outside door left open. The flames on the hearth flickered wildly, settling back to a steady burning as the door closed. Silence fell over the group. The hour grew late. Still they sat.

24

[1534]

Latimer had heard Cranmer say, "Cromwell has done more than all others together in what has been accomplished toward the Reformation of religion and the clergy." Since Cranmer was not one to exaggerate, this increased Latimer's interest in Cromwell. With each succeeding contact Cromwell loosened up a bit more. Their relationship began to develop into friendship.

The recent legislation had produced great dissatisfaction among the clergy. A few had chosen to face death rather than perjure their consciences. Many had no doubt submitted with inner reservations. Treasonable utterances were whispered in the confessional. Members of the various religious orders expressed their disapproval with what boldness they could muster.

"His Majesty is aware of this smoldering discontent," said Cromwell. "He was forced to take further action than he had anticipated, but he must stand by it. Opposition must cease."

Cromwell more than anyone had guided the King's actions. Thus, he was responsible for the results. He had a distinct aim, and he bent all efforts to pursue it to a specific end.

"Until now," he confessed to Latimer, "I have found no one who could cooperate with me. *You* could be the like-minded friend for whom I have searched. I have listened to you, in the pulpit and out of it. I have given attention to your discussions with the King. You have ability. I am convinced that your zeal and eloquence can sway the mind of the nation as can no other."

As Latimer started to reply, Cromwell said, "I speak also for the King. May he count on your support in the policy upon which he has entered? It will be difficult and dangerous."

"I appreciate what you have said," replied Latimer. "What God has given me I am eager to use in his service. I do have a certain facility in speaking and a persuasiveness of manner that seem effective. If as I employ these gifts in God's service I can at the same time serve the King, I shall be happy. But we can travel the same road only if it is God's way for me. I will promote no man's views unless they are also my own, arrived at through prayer and the guidance of Scripture."

"I would not respect you otherwise. You are too honest to be a tool in any hand, save God's. You would never support a man merely for political reasons. We already travel the same road, each spurred by his own convictions. Let us recognize that fact and give conscious aid to each other, as we are able."

"Then it is agreed. You are in a position to render me more aid than I can render in return. But I shall do what I can."

Near the end of May, Cranmer was ready for the conference with Latimer. He insisted that Cromwell be present.

Latimer arrived early and waited in Cranmer's study. A scent of roses drifted through the open casement windows. Near the windows stood a desk of polished oak and a heavily carved chair, with two similar chairs facing. Bookshelves lined three walls. Cranmer's library contained more volumes than either university library and even exceeded that of Sir Thomas More.

Cromwell arrived, then the archbishop, who immediately got down to business. "The preaching during Easter week produced dangerous results," he said. "Some of the clergy seized the occasion to speak against the King's marriage. We are, therefore, suppressing all preaching. No variant opinions may be discussed. Parliament has acted and law is in force."

"No preaching at all?" asked Latimer in alarm.

Cranmer smiled. "Each person must have his license renewed. Some will be renewed immediately without question."

Cromwell turned to Latimer. "Every clergyman, including bishops, will be required to preach every Sunday upon set material. The King is now Supreme Head of the Church. The name and any reference to the authority of the Bishop of Rome must be removed from the prayer books and quite forgotten."

"Those measures," said Cranmer, "should help remove from the people's minds such firmly entrenched errors. Only priests committed to the present order will have their licenses renewed. We cannot permit a hostile clergy."

"Justices of the peace and county magistrates," said Cromwell, "are to note any failure to comply and to report it. All loyal subjects must observe whether compliance is made."

Latimer nodded in understanding. "Certainly, a perilous course lies ahead for His Majesty. I can foresee tremendous difficulties in putting this into force."

"That," said Cranmer, "is where you come in. I intend to send you back as my agent, armed with unofficial episcopal authority. You will see that the injunctions are observed. At any failure you are empowered to return the license of the individual. It will thus be your duty to supply spiritual teachers for all the West of England."

"The Dioceses of Worcester and Salisbury are without bishops," said Cromwell. "Parliament declared the posts vacant, since Ghinucci and Campeggio reside at Rome. They are given four months' grace, within which they may come to England, reclaim their dioceses, and take oaths to obey the law of the land. There is no likelihood that either will respond. So you will be in no danger of stepping on any toes."

Latimer was elated. This fitted in exactly with what he had longed to bring about in the area around his own parish.

"It is more than I could have dared ask. Just think, I will be able to preach anywhere in that vast region. No opposition can stop me. I may instruct preachers and set them an example of true, scriptural preaching. What an opportunity you are giving me." Suddenly he found tears in his eyes.

As he set out toward his parish, his horse could not move fast enough to please him. How eager he was to be reunited with his people and to stand once more in his own pulpit.

His hands would be full. What plans he had to make and begin to carry out! He would find scant time for relaxing on the bench under the oak by the front walk of his parsonage.

25

[1534–1535]

The weeks flew. Latimer wished that his work reached definitive conclusions as often as did that of his parishioners. For them the hay was in, harvesting was over, and the fruit stored away. Now they readied their fields for winter wheat.

What of his own work? He was saddle-weary from endless journeys. He had preached more times than he could recall. He had questioned hundreds of priests. The inadequacy of the preaching was appalling. Many priests knew little Latin beyond the Ave Maria and Pater Noster. How could they read the lectionary or follow the prayers? They had little idea what the gospel was. Yet he approved their licensing and did his best for them. Reports went regularly to London.

As he celebrated his fourth Christmas at West Kington, his people expressed fears that it would be his last among them.

In early 1535 the King appointed Cromwell vice regent, vicar-general, and special commissary. This gave him, as representative of the Supreme Head of the English Church, almost unlimited ecclesiastical jurisdiction. Latimer was not surprised to hear that Cromwell meant to reorganize ecclesiastical taxes and to initiate a visitation of the monasteries.

Neither Parliament nor Convocation met. It became high treason to deny the royal supremacy or to decline the Oath of Succession. His Majesty insisted that it be heresy to deny the corporeal presence in the mass or to question any of the traditional teachings of the church. He was still determined to keep the church as it had been, except for having a Pope.

In early May five ecclesiastics were executed for treason. Later in the month fourteen Dutch Anabaptists were convicted of heresy and burned at Smithfield. As a warning to others, the King felt it necessary to mete out stern punishment. No one could remain neutral. He had laid out the path, and his subjects were expected to tread it without question.

In June Latimer received a summons to London. He had no craving for high position and no intention of maneuvering for it. His proper occupation was preaching the Word, aiming at the reformation of the church. A relentless force pushed him on to fight fiercely for an English translation of the Bible.

As he rode into London, he heard that three monks of Charterhouse had that day been hanged as traitors. This too was a warning to any inclined to withstand the King's orders.

Bishop Fisher's trial was in progress. He quietly refused, even after months in the Tower, to take the Oath of Succession. Henry played no favorites. He could not afford to do otherwise than assent to the verdict of high treason. Fisher went to the block on June 22. Two weeks later Sir Thomas More followed him.

Latimer pondered deeply upon this latter death. Cardinal Wolsey had admitted that he served his King better than his God, yet his downfall came from the King. Sir Thomas More had thought to serve the King *and* his God. His own conscience had made this impossible: To serve his God according to his own beliefs, he departed from the King. His downfall was inevitable.

Latimer recalled his words to Cromwell: He must first serve God; if he could at the same time aid Cromwell and the King, he would. A dark foreboding stirred within him. *Could* one really serve at one and the same time God and the King?

His thoughts returned to More. He could not help remembering that this man had heartlessly consigned Bilney to the flames with a jest. Later he had done his utmost to establish the slanders upon Bilney's reputation that had absolutely no basis in fact. Latimer found it hard to think charitably of such a man or to regret overmuch his death.

When Cromwell called him for a conference, Latimer felt concern over the harsh expression on Cromwell's face. This man walked a difficult path. It had not been easy to direct the course of the recent trials. There seemed no alternative to the verdict rendered. Fisher and More were men of high reputation and great learning. Cromwell must know that the reverberations of their deaths would echo all over Europe. He was alone, but for the King. And for the King's actions, he was responsible.

Latimer looked upon him with compassion. He thought of the year since he left London as Cranmer's deputy. Had he been forced to stand alone in what he had faced, the task would have been impossible. The archbishop had stood behind him. Latimer must now offer Cromwell his support, as far as he was able.

Cromwell made no reference to recent events. He talked of the visitation of the monasteries.

"The army of regular clergy in the monasteries still resists the King's position. They are loyal to the Pope and will use every subversive tactic they can. They opposed the divorce and the marriage to Queen Anne. In spite of the recent executions, the resistance will continue. This the King cannot tolerate."

"What do you expect to establish by the visitation?"

"We both know that all is not well in the monasteries. Once looked upon as the highest point of holiness, learning, and Christian charity in the land, they have departed from that condition. What we plan to do is to uncover the facts as to the debauchery, the absolute divergence from the Christian ethic."

"With a view to reform?" asked Latimer.

Cromwell hesitated only a moment. "If that be possible."

Latimer slept little that night. So much darkness—the darkness of ignorance, immorality, greed, lust, laziness, pride, craving for power and position. Where was the knowledge of the gospel of Christ? One man, alone, preaching—what could he do? But one man, *not* alone, preaching—would there be any limit to how far he could go? What did Cranmer and Cromwell have in mind?

Part Three

THE BISHOP OF WORCESTER

"Worcester is an extensive see."
[1535–1539]

1

[1535]

Latimer walked into Cranmer's study on a sunny July morning to hear the news he had waited a month to receive. Cranmer's eyes sparkled as he greeted him. "Rumors have been flying," he said, "concerning the identity of the next Bishop of Worcester. Would you find that appointment agreeable?"

Latimer took his time about replying. Shaxton, his comrade of the White Horse, was already Bishop of Salisbury. But when he pictured himself as Bishop of Worcester, he shrank back.

"Worcester is an extensive see."

"Extensive geographically, yes," replied Cranmer. "Not the most important of dioceses, but possibly the most neglected."

"Let me explain my reluctance," said Latimer. "I am fifty years old. I possess no executive ability. Preaching has been my major concern. In my small parish the work is never finished. What happens with a whole diocese for a parish?"

"You learned something as my deputy. As bishop, the responsibility will be increased, but so will the authority."

"I am not certain I am cut out to exercise such authority."

Cranmer ignored this. "Except for Shaxton, no Reforming bishop sits on the bench. As parish priest, you deal with individuals and leave a mark on a parish; as bishop, you will deal with entire parishes and control the men who serve them."

"As archbishop, you must keep the whole church in view. I see your point about the need for Reforming bishops."

"You can influence the other bishops. As a member of Parliament, you will have a chance to guide official actions."

"The only influence I could have on the Bishop of London would be to increase his animosity toward me."

"In England," said Cranmer, "the bishops have for centuries been agents of the Crown. If the Reformation is to accomplish what we intend, men like you will be essential in the government. No remote voice in a small country parish can carry weight. God and the church need you. England needs you."

His voice grew low and almost broke. "And God knows *I* need you, Latimer. Can you refuse?"

A lump rose in Latimer's throat. His eyes sought those of his friend. "You show me my ingratitude and reveal my smallness of vision. The call is of God. Of course, I cannot refuse."

The wheels of hierarchy turned slowly. Latimer served as one of the King's chaplains during the summer and found opportunities to preach. Cromwell questioned him in detail about the opinions he had found among the people in his work of the past year.

"I suggest you keep an official register of the names of landowners and gentry who take the Oath of Succession," said Latimer. "If a man's name is not on record, his loyalty is suspect."

"An excellent idea," said Cromwell.

"It will cause a man to think twice before declining to swear," said Latimer. "I found some who refused but hoped no one would know. Others hid out to avoid confrontation."

Latimer was pleased to find Barnes again in London and in the good graces of the King. Barnes had changed little in his years on the Continent. He did express an intention to temper his words and actions sufficiently to keep out of trouble.

Then one morning came word that the royal assent had been given to Latimer's election as bishop. This was only the first step. Now his name went to the Prior and Chapter at Worcester. Latimer went for his installation on August 20 and immediately returned to London to do what he could to hasten the next step.

His consecration should have come next, but there was a delay. A necessary document requiring the King's signature was lacking. Latimer knew full well the reason.

A bishop's first year's income had originally been paid in advance to the Pope; now it went to the King. His Majesty was withholding his signature until he received the money. And Latimer was having trouble raising it.

Then came an invitation to dine with the Queen. He and Shaxton had more than once been guests at the royal table that summer. He asked the Queen whether he should request the King to allow him to pay the first fruits later after they were gathered.

With a swift glance at Shaxton the Queen said, "I believe you would be ill-advised to take that course."

"I explored that avenue," explained Shaxton. "My request met with cold disapproval from His Majesty."

Latimer could not hide his dismay. The Queen gave him one of her winning smiles, saying, "Let us see what we can work out. You may expect some word in a few days." Within a week he received the Queen's gracious offer to advance him the needed sum. He need only inform Cromwell.

Once this difficulty was removed, things moved swiftly. On Monday,

September 26, 1535, Hugh Latimer stood in Winchester Cathedral for the solemn ceremony of consecration. The Archbishop of Canterbury presided. Gardiner of Winchester and Shaxton of Salisbury were co-consecrators.

A sense of unworthiness swept over Latimer. With the placing of the miter on his head and the staff in his hand came the weight of responsibility. He straightened his shoulders at the realization of the honor Christ did him. His inability must give way to God's ability. It was a high moment.

2

[1535]

All the bishops gathered at this same time at Winchester, summoned by the King. He wished to insure that they understood the importance of what he was commissioning them to do. In their preaching they were to emphasize the royal supremacy. Priests and people must have a clear explanation as to why the Pope was now excluded from any jurisdiction within the King's realm. Repetition would be necessary.

Latimer was delighted. The King's directive would provide him with an admirable opening wedge as he took up his duties. As bishop, he could claim the privilege of any pulpit. But an order direct from the King's hand must open wide the doors.

Cromwell had arranged that he should receive half the year's rent from the bishopric, the other half going to the King. Finances would continue to be a problem. From so large a diocese, the income should be considerable. Every day, however, seemed to reveal some new and unexpected expense. As bishop, would he still be forced to scrimp and cut corners?

There was the matter of the properties belonging to the bishopric. Upkeep would necessitate substantial outlays. Then there were the residences. He was already familiar with the London house, Stroud Place, a relatively unpretentious residence on the river. For centuries the chief dwelling of the bishops of Worcester had been Hartlebury Castle, ten miles north of Worcester on the banks of the Severn. There were also various manors in scattered parts of the diocese. Housekeeping expenses would probably be enormous.

Tithes would provide the greater part of his income. He began to wonder whether he might find himself with little more than he had known as parish priest.

On October 4 at Westminster, the King signed the final deed recording that his "beloved and faithful chaplain" had been duly elected, confirmed, and consecrated. He ordered the Royal Escheator in Worcestershire to transfer the temporalities of the diocese to the new bishop.

"Surely now," said Latimer, "I can hasten to my diocese."

Cranmer shook his head. "Not yet, Latimer. Cromwell and I have still some matters to go over with you. And there are preaching engagements that you must fill before you depart."

At last Cranmer and Cromwell had finished with him. He had met all the preaching engagements, including one at Westminster Abbey. He was free to leave.

The journey he began in early November was different from any of his previous trips. A student at Cambridge or a poor country priest may ride alone. Not so a bishop. A large company traveled the westward road with him.

Always a gregarious soul, he found the three days' journey passing rapidly. Stops for the night provided better accommodations for a bishop than for an unknown parson. Such small hidden benefits did exist.

3

[1535–1536]

Hartlebury Castle. He was coming home. Emotion welled up within him as his horse moved up the leaf-strewn avenue between rows of plane trees, standing like sentinels. They pulled their horses to a halt just before they reached the bridge. A moat surrounded the sandstone cliff on which the castle stood.

"The stables are there to the left, my lord," said his attendant, "apart from the other buildings."

All buildings were of pink sandstone cut from the cliff itself. The afternoon sun cast a rosy glow over the whole.

"The chapel is at the southernmost end," continued the man. "Next comes the part in which you'll be living, my lord. In the center stands the Great Hall. Beyond it, just at the end there, are the fortifications, in very bad repair now."

Latimer crossed the bridge and rode slowly up to the main entrance. He greeted the household staff, assembled to welcome him, in a manner befitting his new dignity. No bishop had resided here for fifty years, though passing dignitaries had stopped upon occasion. The number on the staff appeared excessive, but then it was a large establishment.

The immensity of the Great Hall was breath-taking. The emptiness made its vastness more noticeable. His immediate thought was of a community Christmas celebration.

A few days later he set about mapping out plans for Christmas, which he then turned over to his staff. He was determined that this should be the merriest Christmas the resources of Hartlebury could afford. He meant to make up for all the years the castle had stood dark and silent.

The Hall would lend itself to lavish hangings of greens, holly, and mistletoe. Bishops customarily adorned their walls with tapestries, a custom he would not follow. Better to feed a multitude than impress a few, so an abundance of food would be prepared. The Hall would ring with the sounds of merrymaking. Their bishop would receive his people with open heart. The "tidings of great joy" once told by angels should be on all lips as they remembered the Gift of gifts, the Babe of Bethlehem.

4

[1536]

Before the end of January Latimer rode again to London for the reassembling of Parliament and Convocation where he would take his seat as a Peer of the Realm. He looked forward to the new experience with excitement. The thought of sitting in the House of Lords had never occurred to him. His only connection with Convocation was the period when his fate had rested in the hands of the Bishop of London. Now he would sit beside Stokesley as an equal and speak his mind with no interference from his lord of London.

Parliament had not met the year before. Their last action at the close of 1534 had been to transfer to the Crown the authority for visiting and reforming religious houses. Cromwell, as the King's viceregent, had appointed Ecclesiastical Visitors to begin an inspection of the monasteries and abbeys.

As Latimer sat through the opening sessions savoring his position, he wondered whether he would have opportunity to speak on the issue. He had not been opposed to the religious houses as such. Barnes had permitted him to preach in the Church of the Augustine Friars. Coverdale belonged to the same order.

The Ecclesiastical Visitors reported first on the few houses found relatively above reproach. As they proceeded, Latimer listened more attentively. He had known of cases of immorality in monasteries. But he could scarcely believe what he now heard: stories of vice and abominable living in one monastery after another; debauchery and misuse of funds and of lands and properties. Before the Visitors had completed their reports, voices were crying, "Down with them! Down with them!"

The statement proposed was passed immediately without discussion. It called for the suppression of the smaller monasteries. The property was to be turned over to the King.

Latimer spent much time with Cranmer and Cromwell. The feeling of superiority this gave him troubled his mind when he recognized it for what it was. The possession of power and authority was heady stuff. Pride would get the better of him yet. Still, he couldn't help remembering how he had been forced to kneel abjectly before Stokesley and the others and beg forgiveness for his errors. He could not suppress the feelings, unworthy as he knew them to be.

Soon after the action on the monasteries, he invited Cranmer, Cromwell, and Shaxton to Stroud Place to supper. It pleased him to be able to return the hospitality so often extended him and to give a good appearance to his London friends.

Conversation turned to the matters in which they were involved. Latimer had been having troubled thoughts. Shaxton did not appear altogether comfortable.

"Do you suppose things are as bad as the Ecclesiastical Visitors' report made them out?" asked Latimer.

"Surely," said Shaxton, "there are *some* good men in the monasteries. The report makes each house a den of iniquity."

"There are probably good men," said Cromwell, "but such a minority as makes no impression on the whole. The Visitors reported what they gathered from monks and friars, from servants and people who live about them."

"My concern," said Latimer, "is for the members of the houses that are to be suppressed. No plans were made for them."

"Something will be worked out," said Cranmer. "The ones who wish to remain in orders may attach themselves to other houses; those who wish to leave will be allowed to go where they please."

"Won't this turn loose a number with nowhere to go?" asked Shaxton. "I'm thinking also of the household help, the people who work the lands and care for the animals belonging to the monasteries, the artisans, and others. Already I am appalled at the number of beggars on the streets of London."

"It is natural that there should be questions," said Cromwell, "but I have plans. Rest assured that they will be put into effect. This has not been done hurriedly. We had an idea what to expect from the Ecclesiastical Visitation. But we could not act until the facts were in hand.

"As for the people you mentioned, most will stay where they are. The King's agents will need workers to operate the farms. Should the King dispose of the properties, new owners will need the same sort of help. As for the domestics, they will be pensioned. His Majesty does not intend his subjects to suffer."

Latimer perceived a coldness in Cromwell's tone. He took this as an indication that the conversation should turn to other subjects. The hour grew late and his guests departed.

He resumed his chair near the fire. In spite of the lateness of the hour he could not sleep until he had thought this out. Something bothered him. All the bits and pieces did not fit together into a full picture.

Was the dissolution of the monasteries necessary? He had given his vote to the action. In retrospect he questioned it. The shocking conditions could not continue. But what of schools? The poor and needy required a refuge. Travelers depended upon the hospitality of monasteries. The original intention was to show the love and mercy of Christ to those in need of it. The properties had been established for that purpose.

Now they were to be turned over to the King. His Majesty's need for money was no secret. Further taxation would not be supported. So the monasteries would be stripped to replenish the monarch's treasury. Would the lands and houses pass into the hands of men whose support the King found important? How did God view robbing monasteries for the enrichment of such men?

Cromwell had spoken as if his plans had been made even before the Ecclesiastical Visitation. Was a calculated plan to destroy the monasteries formulated solely for the enrichment of the Crown? Was the report of the Visitors merely an instrument to prod Parliament into action? When the treasury again became empty, would the larger houses follow the smaller?

He would seek an early opportunity to talk again with Cromwell. In a private conversation he might get at the truth.

5

[1536]

It was the second week in March before Latimer found Cromwell free to see him. They sat in Cromwell's study in the house he had recently acquired. From a lowly background, Cromwell had obtained an excellent education by his own efforts. In each position he had held, he had learned all he could and filed the information away in his amazing mind. The paintings on the walls and the objects of art about the room evidenced an appreciation of fine things.

"I never like to waste time," he said to Latimer. "Even in travel, one can do something constructive with the mind. In my journeying back and forth to Rome, it was no great task to memorize Erasmus' Latin New Testament. This increased my knowledge of Scripture, and it also gave me a familiarity with the finest Latin. This I find helpful in my present position."

He did not brag. He merely stated facts. Such a mind excited Latimer's admiration, yet a barrier remained between them. Latimer wondered whether anyone ever found a close approach to this man possible. In his loneliness and aloneness he closed himself off still more from others. He had talked of friendship but continued to hold Latimer at arm's length.

Cromwell permitted Latimer to ask questions and express doubts. Near the end he said, "I am sure you can understand my perplexity. My humble mind cannot comprehend all the workings of government and church. Still, I must think my own thoughts and try to see the direction in which I am headed. It would be foolhardy to charge off without knowing where the path leads."

Cromwell smiled what was the closest thing to a warm smile that Latimer had ever seen. "Latimer, I understand your perplexity. I wish I could answer all your questions. I cannot. The weight of my responsibility is far greater than yours. I have to muster all my strength to carry it. The battles are fierce and require all my mental faculties, if I am to come out the victor."

Difficult as it was to feel compassion for him, Latimer found that emotion welling up in his heart.

"We spoke before of our need of each other's help," Cromwell said. "More than ever I need your support. It is likely that you will need mine. May we not renew the agreement of that earlier hour and trust each other? We said it was a question of serving God's interests and serving the King's interests. This matter of the monasteries points up the case. Two facts stand out: The monasteries are corrupt and must go; the Crown is in need of money if the realm is to prosper. The first fact tends to serve God's purposes. If it can at the same time serve the Crown, is that not also serving God?

"Perhaps the question you really mean to ask is, 'Is the dissolution of the monasteries merely an excuse to get the property for the Crown?' The answer is no. As for rescuing some of the monasteries for Christian purposes, I shall keep it in mind. When you find a specific instance where such a need can be well met, you may notify me."

Latimer was relieved to have their relationship back on a more comfortable footing.

"It may appear at times," said Cromwell, "that I put the affairs of the realm first. This is not necessarily so. Sometimes there are hidden purposes that serve God well but cannot immediately be brought into the open. I am as much in favor of a Reformation as you or Cranmer, but I cannot speak as openly, if I am to continue to be able to speak at all. These are precarious times, as no one knows better than you."

6

[1536]

On the following Sunday Latimer was to preach at Paul's Cross. He prepared a sermon on Christian charity, particularly as it related to the poor. He would echo Shaxton's thoughts about the beggars in the streets. Those who have should share with those who have not. He took his notes into the pulpit, though his eyesight was becoming too poor to read them easily.

In the crowd he noted a few noblemen and a number of the higher clergy. He heard himself saying, "Bishops, abbots, priors, parsons, canons, resident priests—all are thieves, along with dukes and lords who parade about in Parliament and at court. See how they live while the poor die at their doors for hunger. I heard that the King will urge an act of Parliament requiring certain men to each sow two acres of hemp. Even so, I doubt there would be enough to hang all the thieves in England. Bishops and abbots make a show of their pomp with many servants when fewer would suffice. At table they require many dishes to satisfy their gluttonous appetites. It would be better if they would feed the needy."

Later he was appalled at the terms in which he had spoken. *Yet I said nothing untrue,* he thought, seeking to justify himself.

The archbishop summoned him a few days later and went straight to the point. "I hear you made quite an attack on your fellow clergymen at Paul's Cross. You also took to task the courtiers with whom we must try to get along. Was it wise?"

Latimer took the defensive. "I spoke only truth. I said nothing I would not say to their faces, if I had opportunity."

"Perhaps what you said was true. You spoke of a lack of charity. Did it not occur to you that you were less than charitable to point out so rudely any man's sins in so public a fashion? Are the people you attacked not worthy by their position of a measure of respect from the common people? Did not our Lord say that if a man sin you should go to him and show him his sin between you and him alone?"

Latimer sat silent. The shield he had thrown up in self-defense slowly vanished. He felt ashamed. Cranmer was right.

"I let myself get carried away," he said in a low tone. "It is a common fault of mine. You warned me against this when I was to preach before the King. What can I say?"

"I know your zeal for just treatment of the poor and for the rights of the common man," replied Cranmer. "My chief concern now is about your reputation as a bishop. You need not follow the actions of the other bishops, but you should not alienate them. Why not show something of your loving nature rather than the acrimonious side that often comes to the fore?"

"You are right," said a contrite Latimer. "Yet I have difficulty loving some of the brethren. I wonder at times whether they *are* brethren. Pray for me, that I may control my tongue and show humility toward those with whom I differ. I struggle against pride. It has often been my downfall."

"You said you would express yourself to their faces as freely as you did in public on Sunday, given an opportunity. I can provide that opportunity. Parliament is about to be dissolved. When a new one is called in June, I should like you to preach the opening sermon at Convocation."

In a voice that was not quite steady, Latimer replied, "Thank you. You give me an opportunity, even more a responsibility. I shall try not to fail either God or you."

7

[1536]

The Parliament that had sat for nearly seven years was dissolved on April 14. In its accomplishments Latimer saw little that appeared to forward the Reformation. Cromwell pointed out that considerable groundwork had been laid.

Papal supremacy had vanished. A move had been made toward relief of the spiritual bondage of the people. The smaller monasteries had been suppressed. The most distinguished defenders of the Papal system had gone to the block. The clergy had suffered curtailment of its former wealth and prerogatives. In establishing the supremacy of the Crown, Parliament had laid a firm foundation upon which the Reformers could hope, in time, to build a solid structure.

In its final days Parliament had dealt with some matters to which Latimer gave unqualified support. The universities were included in the official Ecclesiastical Visitation of the previous year. Upon recommendations made in the Visitors' report, the program was to undergo basic changes. Old textbooks were banned, including Peter Lombard's *Sentences*. A study of Old and New Testaments would be mandatory. Lectureships were established in Latin, Greek, and Hebrew with exegesis to conform to the new learning. Cromwell was appointed Chancellor of Cambridge.

One measure pleased Latimer greatly. Each university must appoint and pay a King Henry VIII Lecturer in a subject chosen by the King. The King gave a word of assurance that he would not "by any means hinder the setting forth of the living Word of God, whereby his people must be fed, nourished, and instructed."

Latimer was jubilant. "For this," he declared to Cromwell, "I have hoped and worked and prayed for twelve years."

"Don't expect too much," growled Cromwell. "The conservatives will bow reluctantly to His Majesty's will. They will attempt to salvage as much as possible of the old learning."

Latimer gave up any thought of returning to Worcester. He remained at Stroud Place and applied himself to the task of preparing his sermon. Before Convocation it must be in Latin. For several years he had preached almost entirely in English.

"No haphazard notes this time," he said. "Cranmer will expect to approve a complete manuscript. And I must preach what is on the paper. No deviation. I won't find that easy."

A servant burst into the room in a state of excitement. The words that tumbled from his lips proved quite incoherent.

"Calm yourself, man," cried Latimer. "Talk sense."

At last one sentence came from the man's lips. The fellow must be mad. Latimer's chair toppled as he stood up.

"Go at once to the boat dock," he said to the man. "Have a wherry waiting. I must hasten to Lambeth without delay."

8

[1536]

He climbed the steps from the water and reached the gate quite out of breath. An astonished gatekeeper responded in the negative to his question as to whether the archbishop was in. With an exclamation of disappointment Latimer hurried through the gate and across the lawn.

"I'll find Morice," he said through set teeth. "He'll know something about this lunacy." But Morice was not to be found.

He turned toward the gardens. He must find a means of occupying his time until someone could dispel the horror engulfing him. He strode up one path and down another.

The sun was sinking behind the abbey across the Thames before Cranmer returned. When the two men faced each other, neither spoke for a moment.

"Thomas!" cried Latimer at last. "What is this insane word that comes to my ears? The Queen, a prisoner in the Tower?"

"I can tell you little, Hugh," said the archbishop hoarsely. "Cromwell will not see me. The King has not called me. I am uncertain as to the truth of what I gathered at court, but that the Queen is in the Tower is an indisputable fact."

"But why, why? What is the charge?"

"I refuse to repeat gossip. When I know anything, I will tell you. Discuss this with no one. Do not permit yourself to listen to rumors. Stay in your study. I will send for you."

The hours seemed endless. Latimer sought to keep his mind on his sermon but he accomplished little. When Cranmer's message finally arrived, it contained but one word: "Come."

The two men faced each other across the familiar desk. Cranmer's face was haggard.

"I have talked with Cromwell," he said. "His commission has questioned me. How to say it? The charge is adultery."

"Adultery! That's not possible."

"So I believe. I merely state the charge."

"But . . . with whom?"

"Several have been questioned: Mark Smeaton, her musician; Harry Norris, the King's secretary; Brereton and Weston. Worst of all, the charge of incest with her brother, Lord Rochford. All are in the Tower."

"Impossible! Surely they can have no evidence."

"Cromwell has means of obtaining information," said Cranmer. "Means that you or I might hesitate to employ. He has a job and he does it. He seems certain of his ground. I am in such a state that I do not know what to think."

"But the King—what is he saying? How can he permit such a charge? Can he possibly believe it?"

"He acts as if nothing has happened. His barge is on the river at night with music and the sound of revelry. I have written him a letter. He *must* see me."

"A good and gentle lady I always found the Queen," said Latimer. "She graciously befriended me. I doubt not that her word helped me obtain the bishopric. A devout lady, she possesses a copy of Tyndale's New Testament, printed on vellum with illuminated capitals and woodcuts, a remarkable book."

"I know the book well," said Cranmer. "We may hope that she is relying upon the Lord whose Truth she finds there."

"Your letter to the King—what did you write?"

"I told him plainly that I am in such perplexity that my mind is clean amazed. I never had better opinion of a woman than of her. I told him that, next to himself, I am more attached to her than to any creature living. I expressed my hope that she would yet be found innocent. I reminded him that his own life is not without blame before God."

"No one could have written more wisely," said Latimer. "Who but you would have the courage to make that final statement?"

Latimer refused to return to Stroud Place. He begged leave of Cranmer to remain at Lambeth until the affair was decided.

The King at last sent for Cranmer. When he returned, he was no less distraught than before. "You understand," he said to Latimer, "that some things must remain unshared, even with you. What I reveal is for your ears alone. Your lips will be sealed."

Latimer nodded his assent.

"I urged His Majesty to be merciful, to spare her life. At the trial she was found guilty, but sentence has not been passed. He could send her into exile, perhaps to Antwerp."

A prolonged silence followed. Latimer broke it at last. "What does Cromwell say?" he asked.

"He is sending me to the Queen tomorrow on a special mission. I am not certain that our conversation will be private. All her words are being recorded. She has committed the little princess to the care of Matthew Parker, her chaplain."

"Morice tells me that the five men accused with her went to the block today," said Latimer.

Cranmer nodded. "They died quietly and bravely. Only Smeaton confessed to wrongdoing with the Queen. I suspect the use of torture in extracting such a confession."

After his meeting with the Queen, Cranmer only said, "In the light of what I have learned, I can only declare the marriage between the King and the Lady Anne null and void. I have indisputable evidence that it was never legal for them to wed."

Tears filled his eyes. Latimer found his own cheeks wet. They looked at each other in mute agony.

"Cromwell says she is guilty," said Cranmer. "The King believes her guilty. In the face of that and of my ignorance of the facts, does it matter that I still believe her innocent?"

"Then ... she will die?"

"No hope of clemency remains. She will die tomorrow. She requested a swordsman from Calais. He arrives this evening."

The Lady Anne Boleyn went to the block on the morning of May 19. Latimer and Cranmer never spoke of her again. Latimer kept locked in his heart the memories of one he still considered a great lady. He clung to his belief in her innocence.

On May 30 the King married Lady Jane Seymour.

9

[1536]

Today Latimer would stand before both houses of Convocation to preach. He donned his episcopal robes with unusual care. The white linen rochet was requisite for all public appearances. Over this went the scarlet chimere with its long full sleeves of white lawn. Across his shoulders he draped the velvet tippet which hung down the front. His man set the white linen miter upon his head. No chains or jewels, only on a ribbon about his neck hung the eyeglasses, which made reading easier.

He counted thirteen bishops, besides the two archbishops. Gardiner was absent, being in Paris on His Majesty's business. Only four of the bishops had been on the bench in 1532, when Latimer underwent his trial. Certainly Stokesley and Tunstal had not changed their opinion of him. He noted a number of mitered abbots and priors. Most from the Lower House were archdeacons, with a sprinkling of deans and proctors and at least one master of a college. The total was something more than a hundred, including a few lesser clergy who were serving their superiors.

When the moment arrived, he did not lack confidence. His Scripture was from the 16th chapter of St. Luke's gospel. He removed his spectacles and, with a now familiar gesture, lifted his eyes upward and stood as if listening. After a moment his eyes came back to his listeners, and he began to speak.

"We heard how, at the close of the parable, our Lord was not afraid to pronounce the children of this world more prudent than the children of light in their generation. Neither do I fear, trusting that he will guide me to use this sentence as a good foundation for such things of which I shall speak to you."

He exhorted his brethren to examine their walk. Were they living as children of this world? Were they following a wisdom that came from the Devil? Such worldly wisdom had nothing to do with children of light, who were of God's kingdom. He emphasized life rather than beliefs, practices more than teachings.

The church was full of abuses that the children of this world had introduced for their own gain. In vivid language he painted pictures of the suffering of poor, ignorant people at the hands of priest and prelate. He delineated the abuses connected with image worship, relics, pilgrimages, purgatory teaching, and masses for the dead.

He deplored the use of Latin, which the people could not understand, in services. Preaching should be the chief thing but was rarely done. Rich living for the clergy seemed unfitting when God's poorer children suffered for the want of necessities.

In the afternoon he preached with even greater passion. He begged them to consider whether in the work of seven years they had accomplished anything in keeping with a status as children of light. He could not resist a thinly veiled reference to his own treatment at the hands of Convocation in that time.

Then he turned to their present duty. "Let us do something so as to be known to be children of light. Men call us prelates. Let us *be* prelates in honor and dignity, in holiness, benevolence, diligence, and sincerity. Lift up your eyes, brethren. Spy out what needs reform in the Church of England."

He drove home the reason for the reluctance to correct abuses: "We be so hot in all things that have any gain in them, though they be not commanded us. It is as though we had rather the abuse tarry still than, taken away, we lose our profit."

He warned of judgment unless matters were reformed. "But God will come upon such a day as we nothing look for him, at such an hour as we know not. He will come and cut us to pieces. He will reward us as he does the hypocrites."

He concluded with a heartfelt plea. "If ye will not die eternally, live not worldly. Leave the love of your profit. Study for the glory and profit of Christ. Seek in your consultations such things as pertain to Christ. Bring forth at last something that may please him. Feed ye tenderly, with all diligence the flock of Christ. Preach truly the Word of God. Love the light, walk in the light, and so be children of light."

10

[1536]

"I knew I could trust you," said Cranmer. "I warned against excessive zeal. I knew you would not err through an excess of timidity. You have a clearer view than any man in England of the situation of the church and its need for a real reformation. Your gift with words made it possible for you to present the picture to those most involved and best able to help remedy the situation. Even the vehemence of your attack on the brethren was tempered by the gentleness of your pleading and the tone of your exhortation. No one could have done it better."

"I doubt," said Latimer, "that too many share your sentiments. Stokesley varied between a studied indifference and an icy stare. As we dispersed, someone said, 'Latimer's flying too high. Being a bishop has gone to his head.'"

"Some resentment must result from so strong a message from a new bishop. But one older head found echoes of Dean Colet's sermon before Convocation twenty-five years ago. He spoke of the same matters, and his sermon was long remembered. So will yours be. May those in whose power it lies to act be moved to do so!"

Some question may have existed as to how the sermon was received by members of Convocation, but not so with the man on the street. The message was translated into English, printed, and widely distributed. It received enthusiastic acclaim. Latimer became the popular hero of the day.

Those of the Papal party raised as loud a cry as they dared in support of the old practices, in direct opposition to all Latimer preached.

His was not the only voice they must counteract. Parliament might express unshaken attachment to the old creeds and worship, but the growth of public opinion was not under Parliament's control. Cries for reform were already being raised about the country. The influence of Latimer's preaching in the west and around London had been considerable.

Other Reformers appeared in London, pushing for a more comprehensive Reformation. Well-acquainted with the teaching of the Continental Reformers, they clamored not just for the abolition of abuses but for the removal from the forms of worship the doctrinal error that had spawned the abuses. Theological debate waxed furious.

The King was not one to permit variety of opinion. Cromwell appeared on the second day of Convocation. As vicar-general, he represented the King in ecclesiastical matters. The assembly rose to do him the reverence due his office. He returned the salutation and seated himself in the highest place, above the archbishop. By this calculated move he would remind them that the royal supremacy was a reality.

He assured the assembly that the King pondered day and night upon means of restoring quietness to the church. Religious controversy distressed him deeply. Convocation was to give priority to the consideration of this problem. They were to debate controversial matters and end them by the action of Convocation and Parliament.

"He desires you to put aside, for Christ's sake, malice and obstinacy. Debate in a friendly manner. Reach your conclusions by the Word of God and without offensive speaking. His Majesty warns you not to twist Scripture by any Papistical laws or any authority of doctors and councils. You may not introduce any articles or doctrines approved only by continuance of time, old custom, and as unwritten verities. His Majesty will give you high thanks if you will effectuate a godly and perfect unity. You must determine all things by the Scriptures. God commands it, and His Majesty exhorts and desires it of you."

"Noble sentiments," murmured Latimer. "He calls us to follow the only path by which a godly and perfect unity can ever be established." He took a look about the table and considered any possibility of achieving such a goal remote.

The bishops did not proceed far before their differences surfaced. The first subject discussed was the sacraments. What of their efficacy and nature? How many shall they be?

Stokesley insisted that they retain the same sacraments and with the same nature as presently held. Ignoring the King's instruction that they appeal only to Scripture, he upheld his position by referring to unwritten verities and quotations from the doctors. He received immediate support from several others.

Cranmer, Fox, and Latimer spoke in opposition. Debate grew fierce, and speeches diverged from the point under discussion.

Stokesley, in direct opposition to the King's instructions, insisted, "It is a delusion to believe that no other Word of God exists but that which a man can read in his mother tongue. The doctors of the church made mention of unwritten verities, received from the apostles, of equal authority with Scripture. These may be called 'the Word of God unwritten.' "

What was intended to lead to "a godly unity" ended in angry warfare. Convocation had failed. The meeting was adjourned.

11

[1536]

The King refused to be discouraged by the failures of his prelates. He felt a responsibility as Supreme Head of the Church. He would personally pen the articles to be set forth, read, and taught as a means of avoiding further contention.

Cranmer and Latimer wondered what the outcome would be. Which way was the Sovereign leaning at the moment? Cromwell said with a wry smile, "He will *begin* the work himself. He expects to consult the archbishop. On some points he will seek the opinion of the Bishop of Worcester."

In the end neither man contributed significantly. The King questioned Latimer on the matter of purgatory. He instructed him to write his beliefs on the subject and reasons for so believing. As the paper passed back and forth, the King wrote remarks on the edge of the paper and asked Latimer to comment further.

At last His Majesty submitted all the articles to Cranmer for his opinion. He proved unwilling to permit any significant changes, although he did allow Cranmer to improve the wording.

Cromwell brought the Ten Articles before Convocation, assuring his listeners that the King knew the controversies well. He read to that body the first authoritative statement of doctrine of the Church of England since it had thrown off the yoke of the Papacy.

Discussion should have followed. Inasmuch as their opinions had already been stated and rejected, silence hung over the chamber. His Majesty had taken the matter out of their hands.

The articles embodied opinions of neither of the opposing groups. No compromise had been achieved. As Cranmer and Latimer had foreseen, the Articles represented the beliefs of the King at the time. He found himself compelled to depart from some of the orthodoxy of his earlier years, but he was reluctant to accept anything new as to ideas or practice.

The first article stated that all should hold as true the things included in the canon of Scripture and the creeds. The next three dealt with the sacraments, of which only baptism, penance, and that of the altar were retained. The doctrine of justification was handled with a weak statement. Three more dealt with images, honoring of saints, and praying to saints. The matter here was almost the same as what Latimer had been preaching. Then came one about rites and ceremonies, which retained most of the old practices opposed by Latimer. The final article dealt with purgatory. It was upheld in modified form but with warnings against abuses of the teaching.

The outcome satisfied neither Latimer nor Cranmer. But they found reason to be hopeful. When the time came for signing, Latimer took particular pains to make his signature legible.

12

[1536]

Cromwell sought out Cranmer and Latimer a few days later. "The Papal party has renewed its determination to draw the King back toward Rome. In fact, Rome has made direct overtures. Cardinal Campeggio approached His Majesty with an epistle to which he appeared to listen. My concern began to grow."

He paused here, shifted his position in his chair and smiled before continuing. "About the same time as Campeggio's letter, a book came to His Majesty's hand. Why it arrived just then I do not know, for it is not new. It is Cardinal Pole's *Unity of the Church,* written as the King was struggling about the divorce."

"Pole strongly opposed the divorce," said Latimer.

"You and I know," said Cromwell, "that Pole's remarks applied to the divorce controversy. The King assumes that the work has only recently appeared and that its inflammatory remarks and seditious advice relate to a more recent situation."

"Then His Majesty thinks Pole is showing himself an advocate of the late Queen Anne?" asked Cranmer.

"Precisely," said Cromwell. "It makes impossible any hope of reconciliation with Rome. The fond expectations of Stokesley and his friends have been, at least for the present, cast down."

"God's ways are mysterious," said Latimer. "Only his hand could have withheld the book until now."

13

[1536]

When Parliament and Convocation ceased their labors in late July, Latimer hurried toward his diocese, driven by an optimistic impatience. He carried with him the King's Injunctions, which Cromwell had just completed. These, with the Ten Articles, would provide ammunition for the battle. A battle it was sure to be, this attempt to set right the affairs of the diocese.

At Hartlebury he found Thomas Garrett, whom he had named one of his chaplains. Dr. Rudolph Bradford, who had traveled with him from London, was another.

"I can feel optimistic about some matters," said Latimer as they sat about the table in his study. "All is not bright, but solid gains are visible."

Bradford looked up from the papers. "The Injunctions seem to provide for slow but definite advancement. The English mind cannot accept a complete overthrow of lifelong customs all at once. We must be content with small steps and seek to cultivate patience. We are permitted to discourage pilgrimage and to encourage using the money to help the poor. Priests will not be easily persuaded to follow such injunctions."

"We shall instruct the people to report to us any failure on the part of the priests to follow them," said Latimer.

"This one seems simple enough," said Bradford, reading further. "The priest is to teach the Lord's Prayer, the Creed, and the Ten Commandments in English. Fathers are to follow up by teaching them at home to their children and servants."

"There are priests," said Latimer, "who cannot repeat the Ten Commandments either in Latin *or* English. As for the Creed and Prayer, each priest should use them at the beginning and end of his sermon until every one of his people knows them. Such repetition will insure that the priest learns them too."

"Some," said Garrett, "will balk at the requirement that priests must reside on their livings."

"You notice," said Latimer, "that they have an alternative. They may, instead, contribute a set portion of their income to the poor and to the support of students at the universities."

"Ha!" exlaimed Bradford. "I see that the clergy are to improve their conduct. That's a matter worth pressing for. Their time is to be spent in reading the Scriptures and in setting a good example for their people."

"I fear we shall find few," said Garrett, "who can read the Scriptures in Latin, or even in English, with understanding."

"A disgraceful number do not even possess a copy of the Scriptures," said Latimer. "They will have to purchase copies."

"By the way," said Garrett, "have you heard about Coverdale's Bible?"

"Cromwell disclosed to me," replied Latimer, "that Coverdale has completed a translation of the Bible into English. He used much of Tyndale's New Testament, as well as the completed portions of his Old Testament. Coverdale himself is no mean scholar."

"Did Cromwell hope to obtain permission for its free use?" asked Bradford.

"He had hoped to include that item in the Injunctions. But inasmuch as Queen Anne had favored the use of such a Bible, it seemed wiser not to mention it to His Majesty at present."

"It will be printed anyway," said Garrett. "We might distribute it ourselves. I've had considerable experience along that line. My old contacts could still supply me."

"None of that!" said his bishop. "We exercise that patience of which Bradford spoke. If we are to place the matter in the hand of God, we do not snatch it out. I know of your former ventures in that field. See to it that you do not enter into such undertakings again."

"When the trade in forbidden books got too hot at Oxford," said Bradford, "you moved along to London. You worked with Barnes, I believe."

"We supplied not only London," said Garrett, darting a glance at Latimer, "but the whole of the Thames Valley."

"Barnes is back in London," said Bradford, "as an obedient subject of the King. He serves on commissions at times and he preaches. He is quite in the good graces of His Majesty."

"The fires of his rash zeal may be banked for the moment," said Garrett, "but they still burn. They will flare up when the occasion arises. I know Barnes well."

138

Going on to the next Injunction, Bradford exclaimed, "You struggled hard enough in Convocation for cutting the number of holy days. I'm glad Cromwell got that one past the King."

Latimer smiled. "They had become mere holidays with nothing holy about them. The upper classes will have not so much time in which to drink and gamble. The poor will have extra days for honest labor to support their families better."

They would travel together to a general area, then separate for distribution of the material to various parishes.

"Explain the Ten Articles to each man as if he had never seen them before," said Latimer. "By now each priest should have his copy. Inform them that all the anti-Papal laws are to be obeyed as previously stated. The pretended powers of the Bishop of Rome must not only be blotted out of the books but from the minds of priest and people. Repetition will be essential."

"We must remove one idea and replace it with another," said Bradford. "Establish the King's authority. Confirm his jurisdiction over ecclesiastical matters. We must hammer it home. Otherwise the old teaching will return."

"Next," said Latimer, "the priests must be urged to expound the Ten Articles by sermons. The problem will be getting them to carry out the simple instruction. You must go over each article in detail and give it the turn it should have."

"There is a nice thing about the articles," said Garrett. "They are just vague enough that we may fill in with as much Reformation meat as we dare. The meaning is so unclear in places that we can readily give it the most radical Reformation twist."

"That is a two-edged sword," said Latimer. "The opposition can turn them in the same way to their ends. The vagueness can be misused, as well as used. Therefore, pound the right meaning well into the heads of the priests."

14

[1536]

As day broke, Latimer put aside his books and slipped out behind the castle. He leaned over the stone wall and looked down the reed-covered bank to the waters of the moat. Wisps of fog floated above the surface, moving slowly as if loath to be dispersed by the rising sun. He lifted his eyes to the low green hill on the other side and to the oak, which crowned it. The sky beyond reflected the rosy glow from the east and mingled it with silver. It was as if he stood at the hidden heart of Hartlebury. With this spot to return to, he could face any difficulty. He murmured an expression of gratitude.

Later the bishop's party rode off on what was intended to be a quick trip through the diocese. Latimer had reluctantly put aside until later the thought of an official Ecclesiastical Visitation.

Latimer always sent word of his intended arrival time. He expected priest and people to be on hand to hear the bishop preach and to receive his admonitions.

One sunny morning he rode up to a church that appeared deserted. When at length the verger could be found, Latimer said, "Ring the bell, man! Call the people to church."

"But the bell has no clapper," responded the verger.

"And why have you not restored the clapper, so the bell may resume its normal function?" inquired Latimer.

The building was in bad repair. A thick layer of dust covered the pulpit. He wiped his finger across it and displayed it to the verger, who had avoided replying to his question.

Nodding toward the pulpit, the man said, "That too is a bell with no clapper. Our priest never preaches. We might restore the clapper to the bell in the tower, but *this* bell would remain silent."

Latimer's exasperation was greater in the knowledge that the situation was not unique. How could you tell a man to reside on his living when he could not be found? How could you tell him to read the Scriptures when not a copy existed in the parish?

Latimer found his high hopes fading. So many priests turned out to be either lazy or ignorant; they showed little desire to take in what he tried to tell them. Occasionally he met belligerence, but more often, apathy.

The response of the people was often little better. They appeared to listen, but without interest or understanding. After he left, all would likely revert to its former state. They preferred the light of a candle before a shrine to the Light of the World in their hearts!

"We *must* have better priests," he exploded to his chaplains. "Men who know the Lord and who are trained to teach and preach. We may have to train them ourselves. Beyond that, we *must* have an English Bible to put into the hands of the people."

Garrett and Bradford sympathized but could offer little encouragement. The weather held for several weeks, but Latimer's back did not. The long days and weary miles proved too much. Reluctantly he turned back, leaving the others to continue.

15

[1536]

Disturbances in the North had taken on serious proportions. The rebels claimed religious reasons as their basis, calling their effort the "Pilgrimage of Grace." But there were deep political overtones. The House of Tudor was trembling on its foundations and could fall. If these advocates of the old order succeeded, the Reformers could find all they had attained wiped out in one blow. Cromwell intended to exploit every means of shoring up the shaky situation. The Bishop of Worcester was to proceed at once to London to preach against the rebellion.

The thought of such results as Cromwell suggested filled Latimer with despair. Was the work of twelve years to be destroyed? Was England again to see bloody civil war such as that of his father's time? Was the Bishop of Rome to regain his powers over the English Church? Then Latimer's fighting spirit prevailed. If Cromwell thought he could be useful in heading off disaster, he would hasten to London.

Cromwell had assured Latimer that his eloquence and popularity made him a fit instrument to stir the devotion of loyal subjects to the royal cause. But he urged the use of discretion and warned him to say nothing that might offend any who might be useful to the King in this emergency.

"Restrictions!" cried Latimer. "Why must I always be cramped? I need freedom to preach the Truth in such a way that the people may see and follow it." Yet he dared not disregard Cromwell's instructions.

He consulted the lectionary and found that the epistle reading for the day he was to preach came from Ephesians 6. That was it! His text would be: "Put on the whole armor of God."

On a gloomy November morning Latimer stood in the pulpit beneath the cross at St. Paul's. His popularity with the common folk drew them out in full force. Cromwell was with the King at Windsor, but a number of council members and courtiers joined the throng. The rebellion was the outstanding issue of the day.

Latimer had the feeling that he was about to give a "command performance." Still, a large crowd never failed to stimulate him. He felt confident that he was preaching well and to the point, but he lacked his usual power. Once or twice he threw off discretion and lashed out with his customary fire. Each time he caught himself up short and returned to safer ground.

Later he smiled ruefully as he discussed the response with Ralph Morice. "Something was greatly wrong. I pleased all my hearers, both high and low. A good sermon should anger someone."

"Whatever you say," said Morice, "it accomplished what Cromwell intended. Its effectiveness will be reported to the King."

Latimer did not tarry. The needs of his diocese tugged at him. Unrest prevailed in Gloucester and Bristol.

16

[1536–1537]

Bristol had been quiet since Latimer's accession to the bishopric. The troublemakers of 1533 had given assent to the Ten Articles and Injunctions. The presence of a number of Reformers kept the lid on activities of priests who had Romish leanings.

But news of the northern rebellion brought them into the open. They neglected to preach against the Pope's authority. Some omitted prayer for the King, expecting him to be overthrown.

Those attached to the Reformation refused to take this. Violence proceeded beyond the exchange of words; black eyes were reported. The old accusations against Latimer surfaced again.

The Bristol priests got their controversy into full swing just as the rebellion in the North was quelled. The hand of God apparently intervened on behalf of the King's forces. A torrential rainfall caused such flooding of the Don River as to prevent the troops from crossing to join the battle with Norfolk and his men. With the bad weather and long delay the rebel troops melted away until only a handful remained. The leaders agreed to accompany Norfolk to London to meet with the King.

But the rioting in Bristol continued. After the Christmas celebrations at Hartlebury Latimer hurried to Bristol. He received a warm welcome from the majority of the population. He preached in most of the city churches. The noise diminished.

Yet reports soon followed him to Hartlebury, indicating that nothing had improved. Latimer wrote a full report to Cromwell, who would take the necessary steps. Before the letter was fairly on its way, a King's messenger arrived. The Ten Articles required fuller explanation to make them intelligible to the clergy. Latimer was appointed to the commission charged with the task.

He did not doubt the necessity for the work. He had seen the weakness of the articles. An ingenious priest could interpret them in a way far different from the intention. As an instrument designed to promote unity, they had failed; they tended rather to increase division. Some commentary should be added for the benefit of the priests. The King's Injunctions had helped but little. But why must he be chosen? There were others who had a talent for such work and found it congenial.

In the middle of April he turned reluctant steps toward London. Stokesley stood as chief advocate of the Romish side. Hilsey, Fox, and Cranmer were the pillars of the Reformed view. Latimer took little part in the debate. The fine points of theological discussion escaped him. His particular interest lay in a practical Christianity, though he recognized the importance of right doctrine. The fact was, his thoughts were elsewhere.

I wish I were back in West Kington, he cried one day. *For all I am accomplishing, I might as well be. There I got something done. Now I spend my time either in London or traveling back and forth.*

The weeks ground wearily on. With summer came the plague to London and the vicinity. The King and Cromwell fled to healthier surroundings, slowing the progress of the work, for Cromwell had a knack for keeping things moving. Stifling heat, the smell of death, and fear of the plague shortened tempers.

People were dying in the streets of London and Westminster. At Cranmer's gates and in the house next to him, death took its toll. Latimer's household was invaded, as two in the gatekeeper's family died. His undercook fell ill.

They determined to hasten the conclusion of the work, each side giving a bit. By the end of July it was ready to send off to Cromwell, who would inspect it and pass it along to the King. The commission breathed a corporate sigh of relief.

17

[1537]

The King's instruction had been that they prepare a plain exposition upon the subjects touched in the Ten Articles. He wanted them to set forth the Truth, purging away all heresies and errors. The men had honestly tried to fill this difficult order.

Looking at the finished work, Latimer thought he detected a more Romish flavor than in the Ten Articles. "Why did we go back to seven sacraments, when the Ten Articles named only three?" he asked.

"If we go beyond baptism and the Lord's Supper, the only two set forth in Scripture," said Cranmer, "we may as well have five more as one more."

"Even some of the practices not mentioned before have crept back in," complained Latimer.

"True," said Cranmer. "But look more closely. It is urged in strongest terms that the people be guarded against ignorant and superstitious abuses. At a glance even the most ardent adherents of the old religion may rejoice at what they consider a victory, declaring that the new book restores all things to their old use. But they are wrong."

"I don't see it," said Latimer.

"Look again. If you will read impartially, you will see that the whole list, from purgatory to merits, is *not* restored to the late accustomed abuses. The Word of God now has the upper hand and has put all these things to their proper use and in their proper place. The Word of God makes the difference."

The members of the commission could not leave until word from the King dismissed them. They looked daily to hear what his estimate of their work would be. He seemed in no hurry.

One day Cranmer placed a book in Latimer's hands. "Behold!" he said. "A complete English Bible. The Matthew Bible."

Latimer exclaimed with pleasure as he examined the book, quickly turning the pages to read bits here and there. "Where did it come from? Why the *Matthew* Bible?"

"I am told that Matthew is a pseudonym for your friend John Rogers. In my opinion it is the best translation yet. It borrows from Tyndale and Coverdale but differs in some points from either."

"Must you have it back immediately? I should like a chance to go deeply into it."

"Keep it a day or so," said Cranmer. "I am eager to send it to Cromwell. If he likes it, he may consider this an appropriate time to request the King to approve its circulation."

Latimer stayed up the greater part of the night, reading enough to get the flavor of it. The next day he hurried to Cranmer and thrust the book into his hands. "Get it off to Cromwell. I hardly dare hope, but this could be the time."

In the meantime the book the bishops had produced came back without the King's stamp of approval. Apparently he had not read it with any care. Why he withheld approval remained a mystery. He said nothing against it; he merely returned it.

The commission decided to endorse the book by signing their own names and publishing it. They gave it the name *The Pious and Godly Institution of a Christian Man.* Cromwell made arrangements to have it printed in sufficient quantity for wide circulation. In spite of disappointment, the bishops felt they had produced a worthy work. It should fulfill its purpose.

On August 13 Latimer was completing preparations for returning to Hartlebury when Cranmer came in, waving a letter. "From Cromwell," he cried. "His Majesty has consented to the printing and selling of the Bible to all men. In contrast to his attitude toward our book, he is quite cordial to this request."

Latimer stood stock-still. Then his joy bubbled up into laughter. The two men spontaneously embraced and almost danced around the room, laughing with the abandon of schoolboys.

In a more sober frame of mind Latimer recalled the burning of Bibles at Paul's Cross in years past. He thought of the grim searches, the laws passed to prohibit possession of the book. He thought of Bilney, burned, at least in part, for distributing copies of Tyndale's New Testament.

"When Tyndale was burned at Vilvorde," said Latimer, "his last words were 'Lord, open the eyes of the King of England.' His prayer is answered."

This last victory sent Latimer toward Hartlebury in a better frame of mind. Cromwell had approved his plan for the Ecclesiastical Visitation of his diocese. Cranmer had helped him work out the Injunctions to be used. A fresh outlook and a vigorous spirit replaced his discouragement. At last he was about to go to his work, his real work. Now he could begin to *be* a bishop.

18

[1537]

Early September was a delightful time. Latimer's physical vigor was at a high level. He recognized the impossibility of visiting each parish. A more realistic plan called for a stop in each deanery where the priests would meet him. An unusual circumstance might necessitate a visit to a particular parish.

"What joy to be able at last to fulfill my duties as a true Father-in-Christ to my diocese," he exclaimed. "Now I may absolutely forbid the abuses. The fact that the Bible will soon be available in English makes an extraordinary difference. The ignorance of the clergy must give way to knowledge of the Truth. The Word of God set free will bring in a new day."

His chaplains were amused at his enthusiasm. Yet they felt a bit apprehensive at his extreme optimism.

"Sir," said Garrett, "I hope you will not be disappointed if all you envision does not come about at once. The old ways are deeply ingrained. I do not belittle your authority, but you may note only slight change, except with the passing of time."

"Ah, Garrett," replied Latimer, reining in his horse and stopping under the shade of an oak, "you would pull me back to earth when my heels take wing and lift me above the clouds. It *will* require time. The Lord told Joshua he would drive out the wicked inhabitants of the land 'little by little.' I must be reasonable, even while I praise God for the power of his Word."

He savored the aroma of hay drying in the fields. He looked across at cherry trees laden with fruit. "Harvest time," he said. "Is it not time for the Lord's harvest as well?"

Things moved more or less smoothly. At each stop he offered counsel and encouragement to those genuinely devoted to their ministry. He sought to stir up the lax and careless. Some objected to the burdens imposed by the Injunctions.

Latimer and Cranmer had based the Injunctions upon the needs Latimer had previously observed. The results were not stabs in the dark, but remedies to be applied to existing ills.

First, he gently reminded them that they had not heeded the King's Injunctions of the year before. He followed with a stern warning: "Take care that you do so at once. To these you will add the further Injunctions, which your bishop now issues."

Each priest must provide himself with a whole Bible both in English and in Latin. This he must do before Christmas.

Murmurings became voiced objections. "The whole Bible, my lord? In both languages? You forget our impoverished condition. It is impossible that it be done before Christmas."

Latimer had foreseen the objection and made provision for it. "If you cannot afford a whole Bible, obtain a New Testament. Christmas is three months away. You have ample time to comply."

He did not intend the new Bibles to gather dust. "Read at least one chapter a day in both languages, comparing the two. Begin with a chosen book and read day by day to the end."

"Could we read in Latin alone? To read both takes so long. I am unaccustomed to English and don't understand it well."

"Are you certain," asked the bishop, "that you understand the Latin? The Injunction is clear. You must read both. By comparing the two you will come to a better understanding.

"You will obtain as soon as possible a copy of the book called *The Pious and Godly Institution of a Christian Man.* It will provide you with clear explanation of the Ten Articles issued last year."

A glare from the bishop silenced the groans that invariably followed. "The matter of the Injunctions is not debatable. Restrict your questions to the meaning, not the content. Compliance is not optional.

"When you follow the practices outlined, you will better understand what it means to live as a Christian. At the same time you will put aside practices that work against true Christian living."

They must encourage works of charity. When a parishioner came to confession, the priest must instruct him to make restitution for the wrong done when possible, rather than require some meaningless exercise of penance. When a man came to make his will, the priest should urge him to leave his property to his family or to the poor, rather than for masses said for his own soul.

"Do you really expect a priest to do this?" inquired Bradford in private. "He will be depriving himself of income."

"They must all learn to do it if they are to live as Christians. They must grow in their faith. Once they have learned to read the Bible, they will do so."

He insisted upon the importance of preaching. The sermon must not be cut short or omitted to make room for bead-telling or processions or interminable prayers for the dead.

A young person must learn the Lord's Prayer in English and recite it in public before he could receive the sacrament of the altar. The priest must seek to strengthen the marriages of his people. Chantry priests should teach the young to read in English. All were to be encouraged to read the Bible and other religious books.

With his own devotional life in mind Latimer included what seemed a minimum requirement. Each priest was to use the Lord's Prayer, the Creed, and the Ten Commandments for meditation in his private devotions. Latimer coveted a richer devotional life for them, but a beginning must be made.

Seeing how long the explanation of the Injunctions required, Garrett had asked, "Sir, will you also preach?"

"Need you ask?" replied Latimer. "Whatever else I do, I always preach. It is the most necessary thing of all."

Invariably, there were those who desired to speak privately with the bishop. He listened patiently and was often able to help. These conversations gave him information too that would be of value to Cromwell.

"I begin to understand," he said to his chaplains, "what it means that a bishop is 'the King's man.' I deal with the spiritual problems of the people, yet I must always keep an eye and an ear out for matters that concern His Majesty."

The bishop's party reached Warwick in the middle of October. He had spent six weeks in the Ecclesiastical Visitation. He turned back toward Hartlebury feeling a measure of satisfaction at the progress made. Much territory remained and great were the distances. Greater was the distance between the actual state of affairs and the attainment of his vision for the church.

19

[1537]

Just as they came in sight of Hartlebury, clouds began to roll together. A sudden downpour caught them as they hurried their horses up the avenue. They managed to reach the shelter of the castle before they were quite drenched.

Latimer's back had him once more in agony. After supper he sat before the fire. "When this torment begins," he said, "I find more comfort here by the fire than in bed."

"I wish, my lord," said Garrett, "that I could relieve your pain. Were we in London, Dr. Butts could doubtless help."

"Constant traveling takes its toll," replied Latimer. "I set out with high hopes. I felt confident that the work of Christ would go forward with great strides. Is it the weariness that brings me pain and dims my optimism?"

"As we told you at the start, my lord," said Bradford, "it will take time, even quite a lot of time, before we see definite results. Can't you trust God to bring it about?"

Latimer sighed deeply. "I want to be a true bishop, a pastor to the diocese. But the distances are great, the time short. I counsel with the priests, read them the Injunctions, preach to them, and move on. I need time in each place, time to train the clergy. Administrative duties consume my energies. I must try to prod others into preaching and am left with little time to do the work for which I am best equipped."

At last Latimer rose stiffly, wincing with pain. "The Word of God in English must be the one thing to turn the tide. I may be bound and frustrated, unable to reach all I would with my preaching, but St. Paul wrote that the Word of God is not bound. Tomorrow brings a new day, which must surely be a better one."

Toward noon next day Latimer heard the sound of hoofbeats. A King's messenger rode across the moat and up to the gateway. He presented an official letter.

Latimer broke the seal and scanned the contents of the Lord Privy Seal's letter. Weariness and painful back were forgotten.

"Glory be to God!" he cried. "England has a royal prince. Ring the chapel bell. We must assemble for thanksgiving and prayer. Send word for the bell in the parish church to be rung. Spread the glad tidings."

Queen Jane had given birth to the little prince on October 12 at Hampton Court. The coming of this child brought relief as well as joy to the hearts of the many loyal subjects of the King.

Henry's subjects loved him well. But he had reigned for twenty-eight years and was weakening in body. Parliament had declared illegitimate Mary, child of Catherine, and Elizabeth, child of Anne Boleyn. Should one of them succeed her father, civil war would almost certainly result. One of the old lords would lay claim to the throne rather than let it go to a woman.

Now there was a male heir of indisputable legitimacy. It meant the difference between a secure throne, in a thriving and peaceful land, and civil war, in event of the King's death.

To the Reformers it meant more. They could hope for the prince to be taught in the Reformed way. A strong Reformed Church should make forever impossible the return to Rome.

A letter from the archbishop described the wild excitement of London. Te Deum was sung at St. Paul's. Bonfires burned all over the city. Banqueting took on the most extravagant forms. Day and night the sound of guns was heard. Cranmer himself had baptized the infant when he was three days old. His hopes were high as to what this could mean to the Reformation.

20

[1537]

Another hard-riding messenger from the Lord Privy Seal brought news that dimmed the joy. The Queen was dead. She had lived only twelve days after little Edward was born.

Latimer was grieved, although he had not known Queen Jane personally, as he had Queen Anne. The King had loved her dearly and would be overcome with grief.

As was inevitable, Cromwell summoned Latimer to London. Masses and services of mourning would be held all over the nation. Sermons must be preached from every notable pulpit in the vicinity. Latimer would be responsible for one of these.

The chaplains were puzzled at the overwhelming proportions of Latimer's grief.

"I confess to selfishness of which you are unaware," he said. "I grieve in part for the loss of the Queen, but my chief dolor is for myself. With no time to recover from the Ecclesiastical Visitation, I must start off in this month of November on a three-day journey. My problem is self-pity. I am ashamed."

The weather turned cold. Bradford and Garrett made the journey with Latimer. Rain slowed their progress, so that the journey required four days. Each evening found Latimer in so much pain that his companions hardly saw how he could go on.

Through some slip-up, he was not expected at Stroud Place. They found the hearths cold, the rooms damp, the beds musty and unaired. The thick stone walls retained the chill, even after fires roared in the chimneys. Latimer was put to bed in pain, suffering from nausea and unable to eat. It was a sad arrival in a city already in deep mourning.

All efforts to ease the bishop's pain failed. In spite of firewood piled on the flames, hot stones and warming pans in his bed, quilts heaped upon him, the terrible chill remained.

Garrett sent for Dr. Butts, only to find he was out of the city. At this point a visitor entered, giving his name as Statham. His slightly bent back made him appear less tall than he was. Keen eyes peered out from beneath heavy eyebrows.

"My wife and I have known the bishop a long time," he said. "We live in Milk Street in the parish of St. Mary Magdalen."

"It is good of you to come," said Bradford. "You may speak to him, but I must warn you that he is in great pain."

"That," said Statham, "is why I am here. My wife has some skill in nursing. I've come to fetch him home with me."

Latimer was in no position to object. Mistress Statham met them at her door and took charge. A fire blazed on the hearth of a cozy room to which she directed them to carry the bishop. They settled him gently into a thoroughly warmed bed.

By the next afternoon he felt an improvement. His nurse pampered him in every way. She propped him up in bed, so that he might write to Cromwell. He explained to the Lord Privy Seal about his illness, praising the Stathams for their care. He expected to preach on the thirteenth as scheduled.

On Monday, November 12, at five o'clock in the morning, the funeral procession moved out from Hampton Court toward Windsor. Latimer did not attend. The burial took place in St. George's Chapel.

The next day, against Mistress Statham's protests, Latimer preached according to plan. Londoners may have been weary of the long mourning, but a crowd assembled to hear the message. Latimer urged them to support their grief-stricken Sovereign and to consider the promise embodied in the prince God had given. He did not neglect to urge diligent study of the Bible in the common language.

21

[1537]

When Barnes' broad-shouldered form appeared in Latimer's door and his boisterous laugh rang out, it was as if the sun had burst from behind a dark cloud.

"You must come home with me to Hartlebury," said Latimer.

With a clap on the shoulder, which made Latimer wince, Barnes said, "Of course I will. I wondered when you would invite me."

It was a merry party that rode out of London two days later. Latimer felt little pain. Barnes was no stranger to the chaplains. The three had earlier engaged in smuggling and distributing forbidden literature. They could laugh now at Barnes' escape made possible by feigning suicide.

"The miles pass quickly," remarked Latimer. "I do believe they have shortened the road while we were in London."

"The answer," said Garrett, "is that you are ten years younger than when we last passed along here."

"I feared then that another funeral might be necessary."

"Leave funeral thoughts behind," said Barnes. "You have to show me your diocese. I am a stranger to these parts."

"You'll see it," replied Latimer. "I'll take you out into the blind ends where they rarely hear preaching, and never such preaching as yours. You'll have to work for your keep."

The sun was just sinking behind the castle as the horses plodded up the hill. At the moat they paused. The glow of sunset enhanced the pink limestone of the old castle and dyed the moat the same color. Barnes seemed entranced.

"I'll give you the grand tour tomorrow," said Latimer. "Let me welcome you to Hartlebury. We live simply, but comfortably. An appetizing repast and a roaring fire should await us."

Latimer smiled as he extinguished his candle and lay in the darkness. What joy to have Barnes here for Christmas. His merry tales would shake up the old castle and do it good. He slipped quickly into a dreamless sleep.

22

[1537]

Barnes held Latimer to his promise of a tour of the castle. The land surrounded by the moat had belonged to the bishops of Worcester since the ninth century. The present buildings dated back over three hundred years.

"Some parts have had little attention since the start," said Latimer. "That ruined fortress was put up at the northeast corner by one of the bishops. The King required him to keep a hundred men-at-arms, to protect the area against Welsh invasion."

"A bishop was the King's man even then," said Barnes. "A hundred soldiers. Where did he quarter them?"

Latimer took his arm and led him into the Great Hall. "Here. Ample space, wouldn't you say?"

Barnes measured the vast expanse with his eye. Not only was there tremendous length and breadth, but the handsome hammerbeam roof stretched up and up.

"Yes," said Barnes, "for keeping a hundred soldiers, I can see it. But Latimer! This is a bishop's palace. The floors and walls are bare and cold. No hangings? No rich furnishings?"

Latimer laughed. "Why would I need those? This is a marvelous site for a Christmas celebration for the neighborhood. A thick layer of rushes softens the floor. No need for tapestries when we deck the walls with evergreens and holly."

Barnes cocked a quizzical eye. "Maybe. I suppose enormous logs give a big enough fire. It's still awfully bare though."

"Trestles loaded with food and drink occupy much of the space. When the people crowd in, the place fairly blooms with color. The singing, the laughter, the fun and feasting should warm your heart for a long time to come."

Knowing the two old friends had much to discuss and having their own duties, the chaplains had taken themselves off. Others were not so kind. News of the bishop's return had spread.

Barnes watched with growing concern as Latimer sat at his desk and saw his visitors, one by one. A priest could not get his flock to deliver their tithes. A small leaseholder reported that his landlord refused to renew the lease. A widow told a sad story. A sturdy yeoman from a nearby parish claimed his priest continued to make prayers for the Pope. Latimer listened, giving comfort, advice, or reprimand. He noted cases he would refer to the Lord Privy Seal. The sun hung low when the last one departed. With a sigh and a rueful smile at Barnes he rose with great care and straightened his back.

"How often does this sort of thing go on?" asked Barnes.

"They come every day. Usually there are not so many. I have been away, you see."

"But must you see them all yourself? Couldn't Garrett and Bradford take care of some of them?"

"They do at times," said Latimer. "But the people want to see *me*. They come with spiritual problems, personal difficulties, civil and political matters. They have some favor to ask of the Lord Privy Seal. They expect me to intercede in their behalf."

The conversation continued after supper. "When I was appointed bishop, I looked forward to an opportunity to demonstrate what a true bishop should be and do."

"You talked about it long enough. Remember your *ex tempore* sermon before the Bishop of Ely? Twelve years ago this month."

"I have even more ideas now. My failure is the ability to put the ideas into practice." He leaned forward and refilled their cups with the well-watered wine he drank with his meals.

Barnes shifted in his chair and stretched his legs out before him. "What particular failure do you refer to?"

"For one thing, I'm physically unable to oversee the diocese. Were I as strong as you, it would still be impossible. The diocese is too large. I found that out with certainty when I began an Ecclesiastical Visitation."

"You've got to have help. Didn't Parliament pass a statute permitting bishops to apply for suffragans in such situations?"

"They did," said Latimer. "Cranmer agreed that I should ask for someone to take care of the Bristol end of the diocese."

"You need to remember Moses. He sat day after day, hearing every case himself until he couldn't take it any more. His wise father-in-law showed him the remedy. Use the help God provides."

"I am determined not to be an *unpreaching prelate*. Preaching is my life. It is the way salvation comes to a person. 'Faith cometh by hearing, and hearing by the word of God,' as St. Paul says. And, 'How shall they hear without a preacher?' "

"You're right to put that first. You have a way about you that makes you the best preacher I know. And I've heard many."

"Between your preaching and mine, there is little difference, so far as doctrine goes. Only I feel *you* do a better job."

"The difference, my friend, in your preaching and mine," said Barnes, "is the man who does it. We may preach similarly, so far as words go, but the way those words come through makes the difference. Even when you speak hard words, they are more palatable because they come from a warm and caring heart. I could preach the same words and raise a great controversy because they don't come from the same kind of heart."

"You're too hard on yourself," replied Latimer, "and too kind to me. We both preach to the glory of our Lord. Few of my clergy are capable of preaching. Their lack of spirituality appalls me. They need training. But I have the feeling that many need first to be led to faith in Christ."

"At least you can require them to read the Scriptures. Only now have they been allowed to read the Bible in English."

"*That* is the greatest thing God has done for us toward advancing the Reformation. I can never be grateful enough."

"Bilney gave his life for distributing the forbidden New Testament," said Barnes. "I almost lost mine. You kept urging the King until we feared you would end up in the Tower."

Latimer changed to a more comfortable chair. He was determined not to give in to his painful back.

"Another time-consuming feature of being a bishop, as you mentioned, is that he is the King's man as well as God's man. I am determined to be God's man first. But even so, it is frustrating to be called continually to London."

"But you have a chance to exert your influence all over England by appearing in London, preaching at court and at Paul's Cross. At Convocation and Parliament you can speak and be heard. They may not always like what you say, may feel you show them up, but at least they hear you. As for the common people, how often as I walk along the street, I hear someone quoting you."

"You encourage me, Robert. I talk with Cromwell and Cranmer about some things. Others I discuss with my chaplains. But I can open my heart to you in a different way. You are a true friend and brother who is not officially related to my job."

Barnes rose and laid a hand on Latimer's shoulder. "Don't worry about the job you are doing. This diocese rocked along for fifty years with no resident bishop. Anything you give is more than it had then. Since God put you here, he means to use you."

23

[1537]

Barnes was to preach at Worcester Cathedral. The horses moved briskly, their breath puffing out white clouds before them. As they neared their destination, Latimer reined in and called to Barnes to do the same. The rest of the party moved on ahead.

"Why does a bishop have to travel with such a retinue?" asked Latimer. "When I was a poor parson at West Kington, I usually traveled alone. I'm the same person. Why all this?"

"At least you don't travel like our old friend the cardinal. He traveled with a small-sized army of servants and officials."

Latimer drew his horse to an even slower pace. "No need to hurry. The bells are only now ringing. Yes, those are days we shall not forget. You were a firebrand."

"Wolsey just naturally made the best target for my remarks. I paid dearly for the privilege. I think I've learned better."

Latimer knew Barnes was remembering the humiliation of his recantation and the fagot he had carried to Paul's Cross.

The cathedral came into sight, towering majestically above the surrounding buildings. Prior Holbeach welcomed them. The monks were in their places in the choir, hidden by the stone screen that separated choir from nave. The nave was crowded.

Barnes held the attention of the crowd from the first word. His voice made the arches and high vaulting ring. The message from the Word of God poured forth with earnestness and seemed to touch every heart. An awe-filled silence hung over the place as the service ended.

They remained overnight. The temperature had moderated by morning. As they set out, the sun broke through the clouds.

"There must have been a number of good bishops here over the centuries," said Barnes. "Why should two be singled out for canonization and enshrinement in the cathedral?"

"It brought in sufficient funds in the twelfth and thirteenth centuries from pilgrims to rebuild what fire damaged and destroyed. That's the purpose of shrines, isn't it—to attract pilgrims? Pilgrims mean money, whether miracles are performed by the enshrined saints or not. This is an example of what I have preached about since the time of my conversion."

"These things follow a pattern. Claims are made of miracles at the tombs of two bishops. The Pope canonizes them. The word spreads that St. Oswald and St. Wulstan perform miracles. Pilgrims flock to the shrines. The monks spread the rumor about the miracles because they need money for a building program."

"They may or may not have believed in the miracles," said Latimer. "But they would feel that some benefit must come to pilgrims who pray to the saints and give of their money."

"The stories grew," continued Barnes. "Such powers were ascribed to these saints that truth and falsehood became intermingled. The important thing was that money kept coming."

"What was happening to the souls of those who told the lies? What of the souls of the pilgrims who turned worship into superstition and idolatry?"

"How do you feel," asked Barnes, "about the image of the Virgin in the Lady Chapel?"

"It illustrates what I preached at Convocation last year. There it stands decked in silks, jewels, and gems. How many of the worshipers make the distinction between worshiping Our Lady and worshiping the image? At the start I spoke not against pilgrimages and invocation of saints but against the abuses."

"I remember well. Even with such a mild approach, you stirred up a hornet's nest at Cambridge."

"First, I thought it a question of priorities. Works of charity should come first, then pilgrimages and the rest."

"As I recall, you didn't hold that idea long."

"I soon saw that all the practices had built-in abuses. People must be taught to distinguish between worship of the image and worship of the saint and that true worship is only for God. They may only call upon the saints for intercessory prayer. They must recognize the difference between idolatry and true worship."

"I believe that theory fell by the wayside too. You stuck with it for quite a while."

"I move slowly. I want to know the Truth, but I have to be convinced. I was thirty-eight years old when I first saw the light of Christ."

"Youth or age has nothing to do with it," objected Barnes. "It's that obstinate head of yours. Think how long you resisted the Truth in defending the old ways."

"You're right about the obstinacy. But the fact remains that I move slowly."

"I can't be exactly sure how fast my own opinions changed," said Barnes. "I suppose it was Bilney and Stafford who opened up for me the Scriptures I was already expounding without understanding. I don't know what finally led me to join you."

"As I recall, it was when you saw a chance for a good fight," said Latimer. "The Bishop of Ely had tied my hands."

"I was ready enough by then. I offered you my pulpit over which he had no control. My trouble with the cardinal followed."

"We have an amusing reversal in the present situation. There I was suspected of heresy and silenced by the bishop. You, Prior of the Augustinians, offered me your pulpit."

With a laugh Barnes continued. "Now *you* are a bishop and offer *me* the freedom of pulpits under your control."

"The real irony is that the rule that gave me freedom to preach in your pulpit now shuts me out of certain pulpits in my own diocese. A bishop still has no jurisdiction over the affairs of abbeys and monasteries."

"Do you find this a great problem?"

"Not so much as formerly. The dissolution of the smaller monasteries broke down some of the obstinacy. The larger houses read the handwriting on the wall that tells them their days are numbered. Some are making plans to surrender voluntarily before they are required to do so."

"It need not work any particular hardship on the true Christians among them," said Barnes. "When the blow falls on the establishment at Worcester, the prior will probably be named dean of the cathedral. The monks will find places as parish priests. The unworthy will still have their pensions."

Latimer looked at the gray skies now hiding the sun. "The temperature has dropped. We'll have snow before morning."

24

[1537]

He was not mistaken. Soon after dawn Latimer put on his heaviest wraps and stepped out into the white-blanketed world. He walked briskly around to his favorite spot—the wall behind the fortifications overlooking the moat. The waters lay hidden. Each branch of oak and beech was outlined in white. A snowbird flew by, uttering its cheerful cry. Latimer leaned his elbows upon the wall and felt the crunch of the snow.

Barnes slipped up behind him and threw an arm about his shoulders. "Like a schoolboy, you couldn't wait to get out into the first snowfall. I'm surprised you're not throwing snowballs as we used to do in our undignified days at Cambridge."

"Now would that be fitting behavior for a bishop?" asked Latimer with a laugh. "You tempt me."

Later in the day Latimer assembled his household staff. "Christmas is barely two weeks off. I assume preparations are under way. This shall be the most festive celebration yet. Dr. Barnes must report that he was surrounded with every possible treat for eye and ear, touch and smell, and most particularly, taste. As for the Hall, no bareness of floor must be visible; no area of wall is to be left unadorned. Bring in the largest Yule log to be found."

The celebration of the Lord's birth should be the most joyful of the year. No one hungry or sad or lonely. He wanted his family about him, and he would be the merriest of them all. Immanuel—God with us—Incarnate in the Babe of Bethlehem.

As the household threw itself into frenzied activity, Barnes and Latimer set out for Evesham Abbey for Barnes to fulfill a preaching engagement. Between Worcester and Evesham, Latimer pointed out the towers of Pershore Abbey off to the right.

"The grand structures of the old abbeys and monasteries certainly dominate the landscape," said Barnes.

"My feelings about the dissolution are mixed," said Latimer. "Perhaps it is the only way to deal with widespread laxness and corruption. Attempts at reform proved ineffective."

"The direct hand of the Pope upon them through the years has been unfortunate. Now with the King as the Supreme Head of the Church, the problems are insurmountable. Loyalty is still to the Pope."

"No one seems to remember," said Latimer, "that the property was originally given for sacred purposes. Now it is turned over to the King, who often passes it on to greedy courtiers. I would see some of it reserved for schools for the young. We shall never have an educated clergy if schools continue to diminish."

"Make your plea to the King," said Barnes. "Employ your eloquence on the floor of the House of Lords. Use your God-given opportunity. The rest of us can't be heard. You can."

"Did you ever find me silent in the presence of a live issue? I use you as a sounding board upon which to try out my thoughts and ideas."

"We are too much alike for this to be entirely safe. You say I am rash. You too display a rashness of a certain stripe. Or is it fearlessness? No matter whether I'm right or wrong, I speak out. You first determine that you are right, then you speak. At times you have the sense to keep your mouth shut."

"Cranmer is the one who, though timid and quiet, speaks with utter fearlessness when the time comes," said Latimer. "He is the gentlest soul alive, but there is iron in him."

"He told me once," said Barnes, "that as early as 1525, he prayed daily for Papal power to be abolished in England."

25

[1537]

Christmas at Hartlebury! Latimer loved it. His heart was so full of joy, he knew this must be the happiest Christmas of his life. The whole countryside turned out. The chapel was packed to the walls for the service. Afterward, the Hall with its festive dress and tables laden with food and drink welcomed the throng for a day of merrymaking.

When the last guest had departed and the last candle had been extinguished, Latimer turned to Barnes. "You can never know what it means to have you here. This is my third Christmas at Hartlebury. Perhaps I shall have many more, but none will ever compare with this one."

Arm-in-arm they went to Latimer's small sitting room, followed by the chaplains. A time to relax and be quiet was welcome after the noise of a crowded day. The room was lit only by the flames on the hearth. Shadows leaped high on the wall behind them, then sank low as the flames rose and fell.

"Almost takes you back to the White Horse Inn," said Barnes. "We are fewer but we enjoy the same fellowship."

"There is one big difference," said Latimer. "No need to keep the door bolted nor to feel uneasy at a step on the stair. We need not hide the books. Praise God for that."

"Garrett, you still mean to ride with me to London tomorrow, I suppose?" asked Barnes.

Latimer answered for him. "Yes, he has some things to attend to for me. And he will be good company for you."

"Leaving tomorrow," said Garrett, "I should be back by Twelfth Night."

"You will convey my New Year's gift to His Majesty," said Latimer, "and deliver an important letter to Cromwell."

"Speaking of His Majesty," said Bradford, "I know he is still in mourning, but has anything been said about a possible choice of a new Queen?"

Barnes, always restless, rose and paced about the room. He poked the fire, sending a shower of sparks up the chimney. As he returned to his chair, he said, "You have touched on a matter of utmost importance. Have you considered its seriousness?"

"Is it not possible he may look across the Channel for a bride?" asked Garrett.

"It is likely," replied Barnes, "and that is why it is such a serious matter. The Romists will urge a match with a French or Spanish lady, almost certain to be Catholic."

"He can't move all the way back to Rome," said Bradford. "He has come too far. To renounce his supremacy would be unthinkable. He still claims to be Catholic but not Papist. He closes his eyes to the extent to which he has permitted the church to move toward Reformation."

"A Catholic Queen could move him to reverse the progress of the Reformation. It would be a disaster," said Barnes.

"Cromwell has an idea about a bride from the German area," said Latimer. "Perhaps he can guide things in that direction."

Barnes leaned forward in his chair, so that the others were all in his view. "Something tells me the year we are about to enter will be a crucial one, perhaps a turning point. The direction of the turn lies in the hands of the King."

Latimer shook his head in disagreement. "You surely remember, 'The King's heart is a stream of water in the hand of the Lord; he turns it wherever he will.' The King is mighty, but God is mightier. We need not be anxious. But the door is open *now* as never before. Let us not be slack about entering."

"You are right," said Barnes. "Perhaps we need to keep before us Cranmer's dream that all Reformed Churches be united 'in one sound, pure, evangelical doctrine, conformable to the discipline of the primitive church,' to use his own words. It is a dream not impossible of fulfillment."

Sadness attended the farewells in the morning. Latimer wondered when he and Barnes would meet again. The roar of his laughter would long echo through the halls of Hartlebury, but it was not heard this morning. Instead, a glow lit his face, kindled by the light in his eyes, as he raised his hand in silent salute. A smile, and he and Garrett were off down the path and across the moat with a clatter of hoofs.

26

[1537–1538]

Too much work faced him at year's end for Latimer to have time to feel lonely. He kept meticulous books on his income and expenditures. Whatever lack his record keeping might show in other areas, he was never lax in the financial department.

The general belief that bishops were immensely wealthy proved false in his case. Properties brought in considerable amounts in rent, it was true. More cash flowed through his hands than at any other period of his life, but his expenses were enormous. Tithes and rents were not always paid on time.

He lived comfortably, something he had never quite been able to do before. What he preached about charity to one's neighbor, he practiced. Innumerable poor ate from his kitchen each day. The Christmas feast had consumed food that would have lasted his household alone for months. All was part of following Christ as the pages of the New Testament portrayed him.

Tangible evidence of the people's esteem for their bishop appeared in their New Year's gifts. It was customary to remember him at this time, but it was obviously their pleasure as well. He received food and money from some. Those of some means presented him with plate and ornamental art objects of value. These handsome gifts added to the beauty of the castle. He had no objection to beautiful furnishings, but he preferred to spend his own money for others rather than himself.

Cromwell planned an all-out attack on images and relics. The Injunction against extolling images and encouraging pilgrimages had proved ineffective. This meant another trip to London for Latimer.

He leaned back in his chair, listening to an icy wind howling about the castle turrets and whistling down the chimney. It drove smoke and sparks into the room.

He thought now of the larger monasteries, soon to go. He considered those in his diocese. The Abbey of Worcester was in better condition than most, under the leadership of Prior Holbeach. Hailes was in real trouble. What about Great Malvern? Pershore was unfriendly and not run too well. At the thought of Evesham he stopped. Yes, Evesham was worth a try.

"Nevell," he said to his man, "our departure for London must be set for the day after tomorrow. I shall spend two nights at Evesham, instead of one. Let's hope the wind dies down."

27

[1538]

The wind did die down, and the temperature rose slightly. But snow clouds hung low.

"Perhaps it will hold off, sir," said Nevell.

"And perhaps it will not," replied Latimer grimly.

The roads were in their usual miserable condition. They traveled slowly, pitying the poor horses. Just past Worcester, snow began to fall in large, lazy flakes. Latimer chose to continue. A few miles farther along it became quite heavy.

When the shadowy towers of Pershore loomed up on the horizon, Latimer called to Nevell, "We'll put in here. Friendly or unfriendly, they won't refuse us on such an evening."

The monks received the bishop graciously, made him warm, prepared for him a simple meal, and saw him to a bed, which was dry, though not the most comfortable.

The snow had ceased, and a silent white world lay before them as they made an early start for Evesham. In a reasonably short time, considering the conditions, they turned their horses into the path toward the abbey buildings.

When Latimer was ushered into the abbot's presence a little later, he did not waste time on trivialities. He guided the conversation at once toward his real business.

"As always when I pass this way, it is a pleasure to stop. But this visit involves more than an overnight stop on the way to London. If you are agreeable, I would like to ask you some specific questions. I hope we may be frank with each other."

Hawford, a short, stocky man with an erect carriage, had served as abbot for a number of years. His countenance was stern, but his manner was friendly enough. Seating the bishop near the fire, he sent out for something hot to drink before replying.

"I think we may well be honest with each other," he said. "What do you have in mind?"

"Doubtless you know that the vicar-general's Visitors are already in process of examining the remaining religious houses."

The abbot nodded in the affirmative.

"What do you expect the outcome to be?" asked Latimer.

Hawford fixed his eyes on Latimer's face for a long moment, as if trying to discern the reason behind the question. At last he answered, "We agreed to be honest. I assume that, in time, the larger houses will go the way of the smaller."

"Do you think it inevitable that all of them go?"

"Eventually. The reasons are complex. Sometimes the charge of corruption is justified, but not always. Unfortunately, such a charge cannot be easily disproved."

"And the other reasons?"

"I hesitate to answer, knowing your close association with the vicar-general. One has to be careful of one's words."

"I can only assure you that I have no intention of using your words against you. On the contrary, I seek information. The association I enjoy with Cromwell may put me in a position to salvage some things worth salvaging. I intend to make suggestions in the proper place at the proper time. Trust me. I shall speak my mind freely once you have answered my questions."

Hawford came close to a smile and relaxed perceptibly. "One hears that the King again has need of money. The religious houses are wealthy in lands, property, and rich furnishings."

"You might look at the situation from the King's point of view. How can he let such vast amounts of property remain in disloyal hands? The rule of centuries that the religious houses answer only to Rome is hard to break. His Majesty is Supreme Head of the Church in England. You have taken an oath to uphold him as all have been required to do. But you know even from troubles in your own house that many subscribed to the Act while in their hearts they cling to the old loyalties."

A monk entered with refreshment the abbot had ordered. They remained silent until he had served them and left the room.

"Yes," said Hawford, "the uprising in the North in 1536 brought punishment upon some who were in religious orders."

"You must be aware that monks in your house persist in doing what damage they can. They disregard the Injunctions authorized by the King and speak against the ecclesiastical authorities set up by His Majesty. That is not within my jurisdiction, but I mention it because it is relevant to our discussion. On that point I *have* spoken to Cromwell. If you handle it before he steps in, it could be to your advantage."

At this, Hawford's expression hardened. He had no wish for the bishop to interfere in the affairs of his house.

"You mustn't take offense," said Latimer. "We agreed to speak honestly. But let me get to the heart of my inquiry. We seem to see eye-to-eye as to the fate of the monasteries. I can justify doing away with corruption that resists reform, but I desire that what is good be salvaged. When I consider the houses within the bounds of my diocese, yours, on the surface, gives me some reason for optimism. Can you name the good features? Will you agree to let me visit all parts of your establishment?"

"I begin to see what you are driving at," said Hawford. "The houses must fall, even mine. But perhaps what is good may be preserved for continued usefulness to religious purposes."

The abbot appeared to be in thought. "Our buildings," he said, "are large and in good repair. We enjoy a healthful location. One of the great roads to Wales runs beside us. The King and his court would find ample space and comfortable quarters, should they come this way."

"What about debts?"

"Except for a debt of eight hundred pounds to the King for first fruits, we are solvent. Few houses can say as much. This monastery supports the town of Evesham, which is well inhabited. This insures a sufficient army of laborers always at hand."

"Are there inns in the neighborhood? Others, besides the diocesan, must have need for a night's lodging in journeying."

Hawford shook his head. "The local inns are few and poor, not of the quality to accommodate noblemen and church officials. Our house has a wide reputation for hospitality. We make our guests comfortable, as you are in a position to know."

"What of your relationship to the sick, the poor, and needy of the neighborhood?"

"We are fortunate to have monks skilled in care of the sick. And we daily meet the needs of a throng of hungry and destitute."

"Should you surrender your house voluntarily, you could then request that it be made a collegiate church, retaining its present functions, with the addition of a school. An abbot of the monastery might well become dean of the collegiate church."

"I am willing to give the idea consideration. We have perhaps some months to improve the picture and prepare a good presentation. You may then channel the proposal properly."

Latimer went to his room feeling pleased with the way the interview had gone. By agreement they would make a tour of the establishment after dinner.

28

[1538]

Latimer pondered upon the situation at Evesham as he rode next day. He had been impressed with what he had seen. He smiled as he recalled the abbot's expression when he asked to see the kitchen, the scullery, and the vegetable gardens. The building housing the sick was reasonably clean. He thought of the horrors of the hospital at Cambridge. At Evesham some compassion and care were shown, whatever the quality of the medical skill.

The time for action was not yet. To say the right word at the right time to the right person would be all-important. Surely, God would guide the King's thinking in the right paths. He smiled again as he thought of a somewhat lesser person than God who was engaged in guiding the King's thinking even now. God could work through Cromwell to influence the King.

In London he found things in great commotion. Cromwell had begun his campaign against roods and relics with the highly reputed "Rood of Bexley" in Kent. One of Cromwell's Visitors had discovered its secret mechanism and had brought it to London. Plans were under way for a dramatic display at Paul's Cross.

Word had spread, and on Sunday, a jostling crowd was on hand. Hilsey, Bishop of Rochester, preached a masterful sermon, which showed evidence of Latimer's influence.

At the conclusion of the sermon the image was brought forward. "See your wonder-working image," Hilsey cried. "You supposed it to have the miraculous powers of Christ. See, it is only a wooden image manipulated by man-made devices. It rolls its eyes? Yes, when the proper string is pulled."

A helper pulled the string, and the eyes rolled about. He demonstrated nodding of the head, frowning of the face, shaking of the head, dropping of the lower jaw as if in speech.

"Of all the sick carried to Bexley," said Hilsey, "not one was restored to health by any power of this bit of trickery. You may recall that the image never moved until you had paid money to the priest. False priests have long deceived you."

The image was thrown to the floor where it splintered into bits. Those nearby rushed up to seize pieces of the wreck.

At this point Latimer rose from his seat. He stooped to pick up a small object he had kept at his feet and strode purposefully forward. The noise died down as he stood motionless.

"You have heard of the 'Rood of Ramsbury,' which would require eight oxen to move it from its place. I hold it in my hand." He lifted it high. "If that claim is false, surely no other is valid. I will cast it away as I would a stone or a rotten fruit."

He walked toward the street, the crowd making way before him. He hurled the image high into the air. It sailed in an arc over the heads of the crowd and landed with a thud in the street.

Latimer and the other dignitaries accepted the archbishop's hospitality for dinner. They spoke with excitement of the morning's events as they sat about the table.

"Today is but a beginning," cried Latimer. "How much more remains! I can think of a dozen images and relics in my diocese, which are ripe for exposure. Who can estimate how many have been deluding the minds of the people these many years? Praise God that this part of the Reformation can now advance boldly."

Cranmer remained silent. When all had spoken, he looked about the table. "Images and relics must go," he said. "But let us be careful that our zeal does not exceed its limits and spill over into destruction of what should be left intact."

29

[1538]

To Latimer's great satisfaction, the King responded favorably to his request that Henry Holbeach, Prior at Worcester, be appointed Suffragan Bishop of Bristol. This relieved him of the responsibility of a sizeable section of his diocese.

He became ill again but refused to let this keep him from his duties. Mrs. Statham took charge, insofar as he would permit, and nursed him back to a reasonable degree of health. His chief remaining complaint was inability to sleep.

"I feel such a light-headedness," he wrote to Cromwell. "It comes from lack of sleep. How terrible it is to wish to sleep, to try by every means to sleep and find sleep ever eluding me."

Cranmer called Latimer in on the case of John Forest, a friar accused of using the confessional to teach treason to his penitents. He openly denied the lawfulness of the King's title Supreme Head of the Church in England.

As Forest stood before them, Cranmer asked, "Did you not take the oath acknowledging the supremacy of the King?"

"Yes, my lord, I took it as required. But I gave assent only with my outward man. My inward man never consented."

Other questions brought out that he had taught on subjects condemned as heretical by Convocation and contrary to the royal Injunctions. The law was plain. He could only save his life by a full abjuration of his heretical teachings.

They tried every persuasion to convince him that he should retract his words, submit to the censure of the church, and thus, perhaps, save his life. Their efforts seemed fruitless. Then suddenly, his body went limp and he agreed in a trembling voice to abjure and submit. Great was the relief of his interrogators as they returned him to prison to await the King's pleasure.

Unfortunately, their relief was short-lived. A bit later Cranmer summoned Latimer. "Forest's friends had too ready access to him," he said. "They berated him for cowardice and apostasy. When the formal abjuration was presented, he refused to sign. He stands again by his old treason and heresy. The case is clear-cut. Our feelings do not alter the facts."

"How often one's friends turn out to be enemies," said Latimer, thinking of Bilney.

Cranmer was exceedingly burdened. "I have never been the instrument for delivering a man to death," he said.

During this time, the King was engaged in meetings with a commission from the German confederated princes, at which he required Cranmer's presence. The official mission of the Germans was to persuade the King to work with them in establishing a firm and lasting league between the Church in England and their own churches in Germany. The King prided himself on his knowledge of theology and took part in the arguments. Cranmer labored earnestly to promote unity, but Henry would not compromise.

Cranmer handed Latimer copies of two of Bullinger's books, a gift brought by the commissioners. They were *The Authority of Holy Scripture* and *The Duties of Bishops*.

"How could they know anything about me?" asked Latimer.

"That you are known on the Continent," said Cranmer, "should not surprise you. You have made a reputation for yourself."

"I am grateful for the compliment. Please say to the commissioners that nothing in the course of my life has pleased me so much as this gift."

Latimer was glad for that one bright spot because he now discovered that Cromwell had chosen him to deliver the sermon at Forest's execution. Someone must perform the ungrateful task, but Latimer wished with all his heart that it not be he. He considered pleading illness, but this would be the coward's way out.

To Cranmer he expressed his feelings. "Since I must do this unwelcome job, I take it as from the Lord. Perhaps he will use my sermon to bring about an abjuration that may save the man's life."

"God works in his own ways," said Cranmer, "but I confess that I am not hopeful of any change of heart in Forest."

The execution was set for May 22. Latimer slept little the night before. He rose and lit his candle. Opening his Bible, he sought comfort for his troubled heart. At last he flung himself to his knees beside his bed and poured out his heart in prayer for the man who was to suffer. Daybreak found him still there.

By the strange and awful provision of the law, Forest must suffer twice. For treason he must be hanged; for heresy he must be burned. He hung now, suspended by his armpits.

Latimer found a pulpit set up just opposite. Horror gripped him as he stood facing the man who, in his last extremity, refused to look in Latimer's direction, unwilling to listen.

Breathing a prayer for guidance, he sought to convince the man of his errors. He pled with him to repent, to turn to Christ and seek forgiveness. It was not just a matter of saving his life for a few years, but of saving his soul from eternal hell. In closing he asked, "In what state, then, will you die?"

Jerking at the chains that held him, Forest shouted, "Should an angel from heaven try to teach me a doctrine other than what I received from my youth, I would not believe him. Should my body be cut joint after joint or member after member burned, I would never turn from my old profession."

He turned to look Latimer full in the face and said, "Seven years past, you, who preach to me today, would not have dared preach such a sermon, lest it cost you your life."

At this point the authorities took over. A fire was kindled underneath the man. Once it was burning well, a wooden image was dragged forth and cast into the midst of the flames.

A voice cried, "We have thrown upon the fire the image from Wales, *Dderfel Gadern.* An old tradition held that one day it would burn 'a whole forest.' Today it is fulfilled."

Coarse laughter greeted this announcement. The fire, too far below to bring quick death, caused horrible suffering. A wave of nausea swept over Latimer. Almost fainting, he stumbled from the pulpit and pushed his way through the crowd.

When at last he slept that night from pure exhaustion, he again smelled smoke, burning clothing, scorching flesh. The crackle of flames and ugly laughter filled his ears. He saw the struggling agony of Forest.

Two days later he was on his way back to Hartlebury, despite Mrs. Statham's protests that he was in no condition to travel.

30

[1538]

Hartlebury had a wholesome effect upon him. He felt stronger. The summer breezes swept away the cares of the months in London, especially the concluding horror.

The arrival of the Lord Privy Seal's order to dismantle the image of the Virgin at Worcester sent Latimer hurrying to the cathedral. She stood resplendent in silks, velvets, and laces, ornamented with silver and gold. A crowd watched as Cromwell's clerks made ready to count and record descriptions of the finery. All must be transmitted to the King with no loss.

"The Devil has used her to bring many to eternal fire," Latimer muttered. "What a fire she and her sister images would make at Smithfield. That would be a burning I could approve."

One by one the ornaments were removed. When the final bit of drapery came away, a shocked hush fell over the onlookers. What stood before them was no female figure at all, but the representation of some long-departed bishop. For years people had asked favors of an impostor. Latimer could scarcely believe his good fortune. The task of discrediting the image was simplified and made almost a joke, though rather a cruel one.

Cromwell ordered it sent to London. He intended a public burning of this and others, not at Smithfield but at Chelsea.

One day Nevell placed an object in Latimer's hand. "A seal that I took from a priest," he explained. "He was operating as a 'pardoner,' still holding the license from the Pope."

Latimer examined the seal, then put it carefully away. "In spite of all the Injunctions such things continue. We remove the images to protect the people from deception and to guard them from thieving priests, yet a means is found. With a false paper from a false Pope he still pretends to sell pardon for sins."

"Should I have brought him in, sir?" asked Nevell.

"No, you did the right thing. If he comes for his seal, I shall have a chance at him. I must alert Cromwell to the situation. Where one is found, others may abound."

31

[1538]

In September Cromwell issued a second set of Injunctions to the clergy. Latimer summoned his chaplains to Hartlebury to acquaint them with the content of the new orders. To them would fall the task of distributing copies throughout the diocese.

"Cromwell's language is involved. Simplify it when you explain to the priests. Of utmost importance is the order that each parish church have an English Bible of the largest volume available in a place accessible to all. The priest is to encourage his people to read it."

"And a few years ago," exclaimed Garrett, "I had to hide in fear of my life just for selling copies of the New Testament."

"At least quarterly," said Latimer, "the priest is to preach the gospel of Christ and exhort to works of charity, mercy, and faith. He will continue to discourage pilgrimages, offering of candles, and kissing of relics. Such practices tend to idolatry."

"The words have a familiar ring," said Bradford. "One would suspect our bishop of having spoken with the Lord Privy Seal."

"All images that attract pilgrims," continued Latimer, "and to which offerings are customarily made are to be removed. They are an offense to God and a danger to the souls of men.

"If the clergy prove hard-of-hearing or thick-of-understanding, you must speak louder and more intelligibly."

Once he had sent them on their way, he had time to consider Cranmer's letter. The meetings with the German commissioners had failed. Under Cranmer's guidance, they had struggled to draw up articles that might serve as a common creed for both churches. But the King had insisted on denying the cup to the laity, on approval of private masses, and on celibacy of the clergy. The Germans, unable to compromise on these points, returned home without having accomplished their purpose.

In England they left an unhappy King, disgruntled that the commissioners had not sacrificed their opinions, rather than expecting him to give in. On top of this the Romish party indulged in a whispering campaign, saying that the King had forsaken his old faith. This stung him to the quick, for he prided himself on the orthodoxy of his beliefs. His irritation began to show itself in what Cranmer considered an ominous way.

As a further complication, Stephen Gardiner had returned from a three-year stay on the Continent, to the delight of the Romish party. Gardiner was no favorite of the King, but he was almost indispensable because of his knowledge of foreign affairs.

Cromwell understood the danger posed by Gardiner's return. In a sense, he and Gardiner became rivals for the King's mind. Both understood him well; both were skilled in using the King's power and convictions for promoting their own views. Yet their ends lay at opposite extremes. What would the outcome be?

When Latimer heard of the burning of a group of Anabaptists in London on October 1, he could not doubt the influence of Gardiner. Such an act offered an easy means for quelling the rumor that Henry had forsaken his faith.

Latimer found comfort in a letter from Martin Bucer, which Cranmer shared with him. Bucer had written encouragingly to the English Reformers, speaking for the leaders on the Continent. He recognized the progress the English Reformers had made in spite of many impediments.

"How remarkable, how extremely *Christian*," Cranmer had written, "for this man to write such words of encouragement. He knows how far behind we lag, how much remains to be set right. Yet he mentions that not at all, rather dwelling upon what he is able to commend. He counts us as brothers. I mean to have that man here in England one day."

The abbeys continued to fall, the wealth to be disposed of at the King's pleasure. Latimer watched for opportunities. Cromwell had answered his plea and given some help for Gloucester. Now the time was ripe for requesting assistance for Worcester. Two friaries in the city had recently surrendered. Their possessions could go far toward meeting outstanding needs.

He outlined to Cromwell the conditions in need of attention. Worcester was charged with the maintenance of the school, the keeping of the bridge over the Severn, and the care of the city wall. The school, formerly supported by a guild upheld by the Pope, had deteriorated since the Reformation. Latimer was at present paying the teacher out of his own pocket. The wall and bridge were in deplorable condition. No money could be found for repairing them, unless—perhaps the two friaries?

"In bestowing this assistance," he wrote, "His Majesty would do a thing worthy of a King, and your lordship would do a thing not unworthy of an excellent counselor."

He added a postscript asking Cromwell to thank the King for the stag he had sent. "I have made merry in these parts, for I eat not all myself. God save the King!"

Before October had ended, a commission was on its way to investigate the "Blood of Hailes." Latimer was one of four men appointed; the others Prior Holbeach, Richard Tracy, and Stephen Sagar, Abbot of Hailes.

The men entered the chapel where the relic reposed. The abbot removed it from its place and handed it to Latimer.

"So this is the very blood of Christ, shed on the cross," said Latimer with obvious sarcasm. "Anyone who looks upon it is assured of eternal salvation. Then blessed are we."

As he turned it about, the silver framework gleamed from recent polishing. Through the crystal vial, the contents did give a reddish appearance. Latimer handed it back to Sagar. "Remove the stopper," he said.

The man appeared frightened. "It has never been removed in my years here, no matter what the rumors may be to the contrary."

"Well, open it now," said Latimer.

With difficulty Sagar managed to remove the stopper. When Latimer turned the vial upside down, the contents remained in place. With the tip of a knife he removed a portion of the substance and placed it on a small dish.

"It looks yellow outside the vial," remarked Holbeach. He applied his finger. "It's sticky, like syrup or honey."

Tracy examined it. "It could be some sort of gum or even birdlime, highly colored," was his verdict.

At last they agreed that it was probably honey colored with saffron. It was certainly not blood of any kind. Latimer had Sagar coat the container with red sealing wax to insure against further prying.

"We shall report to the Lord Privy Seal," said Latimer, "that the object is left in your hands, Sagar, for safekeeping. He will instruct you as to its disposal."

32

[1538]

The time had arrived for Latimer to make his plea for Evesham Abbey. He wrote to Cromwell describing what he had seen on his last visit. He urged that the abbey be left standing and its properties used for godly purposes. At the same time he wrote to Hawford, advising him to send his plea to the Lord Privy Seal, so that the two letters would arrive in quick succession.

The so-called Sacramentaries, who challenged the doctrines connected with the sacrament of the altar, were becoming more outspoken. Gardiner advised the King to punish such offenders with the full penalty of the law. Heretics speaking against doctrines of the church would be dealt with and at the same time, the rumors persisting about changes in the King's faith would be put to rest. Gardiner was reported to be puffed with pride that His Majesty agreed to this advice.

When first sprung, the trap caught John Lambert, one of Bilney's old converts at Cambridge. Latimer was stunned. In 1536 Lambert had spent some time in prison for refusing to modify his belief that it was sinful to pray to the saints. Latimer had misgivings on the subject of praying to the saints but was not ready to declare it a sin.

Now Lambert was in more serious trouble. His statements were undeniably heretical according to the teaching of the church. Reluctant as

Cranmer might feel to act, he found no alternative. Lambert must either retract his statements or be condemned as a heretic. Lambert appealed to the King.

Gardiner immediately suggested to the King that this was his opportunity to make it clear to all his subjects that the reports against him were groundless. He had disowned the Pope but surely he was not going to make England a home for heretics.

Cromwell wrote to inform Latimer of this and to summon him to London. His Majesty desired his bishops and nobles to participate in a great theological tournament. The King would make open display of his firm orthodoxy. He expected to strike terror in the hearts of heretics and inspire joy in the hearts of true subjects.

Latimer was heartsick at the theatrical production the King made of the trial. His Majesty was clothed in white, pure and unrelieved, to symbolize his purity of doctrine. Cranmer, looking pale and unhappy, sat on the King's right. Cromwell, his face expressionless, sat on his left. The bishops occupied places beside Cranmer, and the nobles were ranged on the other side. A noisy crowd assembled to witness the performance.

The King's manner toward Lambert could only be described as brutal. Only one outcome was possible. But the trial provided the King with opportunity to show his prowess in theological argument and to demonstrate his firmness in punishing those who dared to disagree with stated doctrines.

"Is the sacrament of the altar," asked the King, lifting his cap as he spoke, "the body of Christ or not?"

"After a certain manner," Lambert replied, "it is the body of Christ, as St. Augustine said."

Impatiently the King shouted, "Answer me not out of St. Augustine. Tell me plainly, is it the body of Christ or not?"

Lambert replied that it was not the body of Christ. The King turned to the archbishop and bade him refute the heresy.

Cranmer did his best, but Lambert's arguments seemed to perplex him. Disputation had never been his strong point. The King, still impatient, passed on to Gardiner, who spoke readily and at length. Then Tunstal took a turn, followed by Stokesley and six others. Latimer sat in grieved silence throughout.

For five hours Lambert defended himself with ability, then he refused to answer further. The debate continued among the bishops. When darkness fell, torches were brought. The same weary arguments were repeated. At every pause the King bullied Lambert yet more. The crowd jeered and abused him verbally.

At last the King said to Lambert, "What sayest thou now? After all the reasons of these learned men, art thou yet satisfied? Wilt thou live or die?"

"I yield myself wholly to His Majesty's will," he replied.

"Commit thyself into the hands of God," said the King, "and not into mine."

"My soul do I indeed commend unto God, but my body I submit wholly to your clemency."

The King was in no mood for clemency. "If you commit yourself unto my judgment, you must die for I will be no patron of heretics." He then bade Cromwell to pronounce sentence.

Cromwell had not spoken during all the hours of the debate. He now rose heavily to his feet and did the King's bidding. The condemned man would die on the morning of November 20. His death as a heretic would be by burning at the stake. Such was the law.

Latimer would have preferred to turn his back immediately on London, but some episcopal matters kept him a few more days. He had little heart for seeing his friends. Was his utter dejection due solely to Lambert's trial and condemnation? He wasn't sure.

The day of the execution passed. Latimer finally sought out Cranmer. He had no desire to talk of Lambert, but inevitably they did.

"On the morning of the execution," said Cranmer, "Cromwell held a private interview with Lambert. Rumor has it that he asked Lambert's forgiveness."

"It is possible," said Latimer, "but I think it unlikely, knowing the Lord Privy Seal as I do. I hope I am wrong."

"At any rate," said Cranmer, "he permitted Lambert to have breakfast with the gentlemen of his Hall. That can only be construed as intended kindness."

The two men sat in silence, each with his own deep thoughts. Cranmer turned to Latimer in tears. "Why must it be like this? Right or wrong in his attitude toward the sacrament, Lambert was a brother in Christ. He loved the Lord; he served him to the best of his ability. Why did he have to die, and by such a death? He died by my hand, you might say. And I was his *friend.*"

Latimer reached out to take his hand. "I know, I know. I feel the same. But you must not blame yourself. The blame lies, at least in part, in Gardiner's vindictiveness and in the blindness of the King. You could not have saved Lambert. Bilney brought him to the Lord, but not even Bilney would have upheld him in the beliefs for which he died."

"Cromwell sent a report of the matter to Sir Thomas Wyatt in Paris," said Cranmer, "praising the King's inestimable wisdom, gravity, and benignity. He told him, 'I wish the princes and potentates of Christendom could have been here to see it.' He looked me in the eye as he told me this. No word betrayed him, but his expression did. He was speaking with an irony, which belied his words. It could never be proved against him."

"No," said Latimer, "the words were exactly what the King would wish him to say."

"The flames of persecution died down for a while," said Latimer. "I hoped it would be for good. I fear this may set off another such season. Gardiner will see to it."

"To change the subject," said Cranmer, "yet it really stems from the same subject, you will find it no surprise that His Majesty is issuing some other Injunctions."

"I already know of the proclamation issued on the day of Lambert's trial," said Latimer. "Anabaptist and Sacramentarian opinions are condemned. Only those who are counted as learned in divinity are permitted to dispute or argue upon the sacrament of the altar, on pain of losing life, goods, and chattels."

"There is more," said Cranmer. "Some of it pinches the Romists, but most of it we shall find unpalatable. Nevertheless, it is the King's word. We must follow it."

"What is it that will trouble us?"

"The clergy are to observe ceremonies, such as creeping to the cross on Good Friday, carrying candles on the Feast of Purification, holy water, consecrated bread, and the rest."

"But he's going *backward*," cried Latimer. *"Why* does he love creeping to the cross so? He continually reverts to that."

"It's a carry-over from his childhood," said Cranmer. "We have to make the best of it. It won't always be so."

"What next? This becomes more disheartening."

"Gardiner and the Romists will rage at this one. Thomas à Becket is denounced as a rebel and no saint. His image and pictures are to be destroyed, his name erased from service-books, and his festivals cut off. The clergy are to differentiate carefully between things commanded by God and the rites and ceremonies in the church to avoid further superstition."

"That brightens the picture. It also fills the King's coffers. Think of the wealth represented in that shrine at Canterbury."

"All married priests are to be deprived of their livings and to be hereafter reputed laypersons. Where does that leave me?"

"Just where you have been all along. His Majesty has a talent for ignoring what he does not wish to see. He has never seen your wife, so he will not admit her existence."

"I hope you are right. I am not sure how I would function as a layperson. Earning a living would present difficulties."

"Does Gardiner hope to persuade the King to bring back some of the ceremonies he has already left off?"

"I am sure he does," said Cranmer. "The Romish prelates are already at work on a book of ceremonies for the instruction of the people. Our prospects are becoming a bit clouded."

33

[1538]

December was not the ideal time to visit the Malvern Hills, but he had no choice. Latimer felt it imperative that he meet with the Prior at Great Malvern before the year ended.

"I did not find it convenient before," he said to Garrett and Nevell who were to accompany him, "nor do I find it so now."

He made the trip and accomplished his purpose. Back at Hartlebury, he sat down on December 13 to write to Cromwell on behalf of Great Malvern. He employed earnestness but was careful to exercise utmost diplomacy and courtesy as well. He was in no way hypocritical but felt that things were slipping a bit in his relationship with Cromwell. One had to tread carefully. It was the times.

Another task that he was determined to complete before Christmas was preparation of his annual financial report for Cromwell. It was not his favorite duty.

When his calculations were complete, he was not displeased with the result. In the time since he became bishop, the total receipts had been a bit over 4,000 pounds. The payment of first fruits, the repairs he had made, and the amounts applied to reducing his debts had amounted to 1,700 pounds. Cash on hand amounted to 180 pounds, of which 105 must go for his annual tithe. A New Year's gift to the King would be 20 pounds. That would leave 65 with which to get past Christmas and travel to London. He had food for his household for six months.

It was a relief to have his indebtedness reduced to 40 pounds. In January he would have his rents from the properties for the half-year. How good to be afloat rather than about to be dragged under. Who said a bishop had no money troubles?

The report was finished. It was Christmas Eve. He was about to celebrate his fourth Christmas at Hartlebury.

34

[1539]

Before the new year was fairly launched, Latimer's chaplain Bennett came with a report that upset him. Barker, Warden at Stratford-on-Avon, was talking against him.

Barker had said that anyone with whom Latimer had a falling-out should beware. The bishop stored up private malice and wrote to the Lord Privy Seal. He was overzealous in sending cases to the Court of Arches for trial before the archbishop. In short, Latimer liked to get people in trouble.

The accusation stung Latimer sharply. Nothing he had ever presented to Cromwell had been out of private ill will. He desired only to faithfully discharge his duty.

"As for the Arches," he said, "I could have sent fewer matters there and had more money in my purse. I could have settled many cases in my Consistory Court, had I been willing to follow the pattern of selling sin. That is what it amounts to when a man is permitted to buy his pardon."

The priest who had voiced the remarks of Barker had confessed his own error and written out a recantation. Latimer informed Cromwell of the matter, enclosing with his letter the priest's confession. He sent Bennett back to Stratford to hear the priest read a public recantation.

Near the end of January, the King, in reaction against the bad faith of the Emperor in the matter of a bride, had sent envoys to resume negotiations with the German Protestants. They were to say to the Elector of Saxony and the Landgrave of Hesse that the King assured them of his earnest desire for promoting the purity of the churches.

Taking this as a good omen, Cromwell began to urge the King toward a proposal of marriage to one of the Protestant princesses. Until now, the King had responded coldly to this suggestion. Cromwell had in mind Anne, second daughter of the Duke of Cleves, who was reported worthy both in beauty and in virtue. The King agreed to consider the matter.

In the euphoria brought about by these prospects, Latimer lost sight of the King's intentions about which he and Cranmer had spoken in November. At the end of February a reminder came as a sudden shock. A proclamation of His Majesty charged his loving subjects to observe and keep the ancient ceremonies.

"What a reversal!" cried Rudolph Bradford. "Look at the burden he puts on us: All bishops, deans, curates, and preachers are carefully to *explain* the true use of ceremonies."

"We are to teach the people," said Garrett, "that holy water is sprinkled to *remind* them of baptism and of the sprinkling of Christ's blood for redemption; that the giving of holy bread *reminds* them that Christians are one body, just as the bread is composed of many grains. We are to do the same for all the rest. What good will reminding them do?"

"I see good that *can* be in such ceremonies," said Latimer, "provided we are reminded by the reminders. Many through the ages have profited from the *proper* use of these things."

"The *proper* use," echoed Bennett. "The proclamation states that these ceremonies are only outward signs by which men remember Christ from whom alone comes salvation. We can preach that until we are blue in the face without convincing ignorant people who have been brought up to believe otherwise."

"I fear," said Latimer, "that many priests will read out these words with no heart's conviction as to their truthfulness. The statement is clear that men *are to observe them* until they be altered or abolished. When will that be?"

"How do you suppose this news will strike the German Protestants with whom the King's envoys are even now negotiating?" asked Garrett.

35

[1539]

Nearly three years had passed since Parliament last sat, as no necessary business had demanded it. This year it would meet at the end of April. Convocation was called as well.

Latimer reached London in the middle of April and went at once to Lambeth, eager for the latest news. He and Cranmer sat beside a fountain near a cherry tree, whose blossoms hung low. Climbing roses bloomed along the wall.

"Word of His Majesty's recent proclamation has reached the ears of those to whom his envoys went," said Cranmer. "It caused a burst of protest."

"I can well imagine," said Latimer.

"I confess to you, for I dare not to anyone else save God, that I do not understand the King's actions. He sends envoys begging to renew negotiations about a unified and pure church. Then he takes action that is sure to defeat that unity."

"His vacillations puzzle me equally."

"He has had a letter from Melanchthon and one from the Elector of Saxony."

"I'd like to know what Melanchthon said. Did he make his point with his usual reserve?"

"Melanchthon is ever the same. He is brave and firm, but not foolhardy. He maintains a discreet courtesy while saying as strongly as possible what he thinks. He warned His Majesty that a continued pushing of ceremonies will quite likely restore the reverence for the Pope that he has just succeeded in putting down. It was popes who introduced these things originally. He recommended that instead of compelling the use, the King permit some liberty in opinion and action in nonessential matters."

"Will the King hear him?" asked Latimer.

"I doubt it, especially in view of Melanchthon's closing words. He condemned the King's insistence on celibacy of the clergy, calling it a sure means for corrupting public morals."

"That would insure the closing of the King's mind to anything he might say," said Latimer.

"The Elector of Saxony was courteous, but firm in his remonstrances. He spoke for the other commissioners as well. He terms the ceremonies under discussion 'vicious and unprofitable.' He calls the act of confirming them 'impolitic and unscriptural.' They offend the light of the gospel, deter the weak from pure doctrine, and propose other worship than that delivered by God."

"Very well-said. I pray God His Majesty will hear."

"He won't," said Cranmer grimly. "Cromwell has to tread cautiously because of Gardiner, but he dared to suggest to His Majesty that the recommendations of the Germans were weighty and just. He was coldly ignored."

"Can His Majesty think he promotes the cause of unity when he takes these steps?" asked Latimer.

"He wants agreement on matters of religion. He dislikes the division of opinion that exists. Constant theological debates and controversies must cease. We must all become of one mind."

"A good theory, but his methods will not bring it about."

"Not in England, and not with our German brethren. The rift widens. Ceremonies, celibacy of the clergy, and the real presence in Holy Communion are points on which there is no agreement. And on those points, the King is adamant."

"Negotiations usually require give-and-take," said Latimer. "The King seems willing to take, quite unwilling to give."

"The negotiations will fail," said Cranmer. "Let us hope the other negotiations under way will be more successful."

"Is there any news on the search for a bride for the King?"

"The talks continue. Cromwell feels encouraged."

36

[1539]

As Parliament assembled on April 28, an abnormal tension was felt. Later in the week when Convocation came together at St. Paul's, a wariness manifested itself. By the end of the week those sensitive to such things saw the stage set for a pitched battle with regard to the religious issues in question.

The King spoke before an early session with deep feeling: "I consider it the most important part of my kingly office to reduce the people committed by God in my care to unity of opinion. I daily and painfully study means for accomplishing it." His unshakable intention was to secure, at whatever cost, absolute unity of opinion in religious matters.

"The man is unreasonable," cried Latimer.

"Shhhh!" said Cranmer. "Not so loud."

"But he *is*," insisted Latimer, "or is it that he is blind? Supreme Head of the Church he may be, but he is not in control of men's minds. How does he propose to obtain this unity?"

"I warn you to speak discreetly. These are not times for rash words. As to how he intends to achieve unity, he intends to throw it back upon a commission."

"Commissions!" snorted Latimer. "We've had enough of commissions. What can another commission do?"

"We shall be found trying."

"Does he really believe the situation is as he painted it in his address? He claims to see, at one extreme, a small group militantly intent on returning the church to the rule of the Pope. At the other extreme he lumps together Anabaptists and Sacramentaries as so zealous for their causes that they are easy to identify. These two groups he intends to deal with as traitors and heretics and be done with them."

"To a degree," said Cranmer, "he is right. But the two groups are not as clear-cut as he thinks. Variations in beliefs tend to moderate and blend with those of a larger number toward the middle."

"Just my point," said Latimer. "But, after describing the extremes, he sees in the majority between only a few insignificant differences that can be eliminated. Neither you and I nor Gardiner and Stokesley, for example, would ally ourselves with the extreme views. Yet we do not see eye-to-eye on some essential matters, nor will we ever come to agreement."

Cranmer's expression betrayed a sadness Latimer seldom saw. As he spoke now, Latimer realized that part of his sadness was due to concern for the King. A tender note, such as one uses in speaking of a beloved child, came through.

"His Majesty feels such a burden for his subjects. His earnest desire is for their good. He wants to lead them aright. When he discovers what he deems to be the right path and points it out, he expects them to follow without questioning."

"And he *will* find such a path and insist on its being followed?" asked Latimer.

The archbishop nodded. Latimer left with a troubled heart.

As Cranmer had foreseen, a commission was appointed, with caution exerted, to represent both parties. They were to meet at St. Paul's to devise a common bond of unity and religious harmony. "Mature discussion" to this end was urged.

From the Reformers were chosen Cromwell, Cranmer, Latimer, and Goodrich, Bishop of Ely. Representing the other side were Lee, Archbishop of York, Tunstal, Aldrich of Carlisle, Clark of Bath, and Salcot of Bangor.

Cromwell muttered gruffly to Latimer, "Obviously, the preponderance of ability is on the side of the Reformers, but the Romists have numerical majority, which counterbalances."

"And stalemates, as well," replied Latimer.

Even Latimer had to admit that both sides made an earnest effort. But as the men sat facing one another day after day, not one subject brought up for debate found accord. Tempers grew short as it became apparent they would present no articles of agreement to the King. Angry words were increasingly exchanged.

After two weeks of growing enmity Cromwell called a halt. "Let us admit failure," he said. "Were we to remain here for the rest of the year, we would arrive no nearer the goal His Majesty set for us. We are incapable of doing what he demands."

37

[1539]

The failure of the commission did nothing to enhance Cromwell's waning influence. The King now commissioned the Duke of Norfolk to obtain the opinion of the House of Lords on six controversial topics. These were stated as questions, but everyone knew that the King had already determined *his* answers.

A growing heart-sickness crept over Latimer as he heard the list read.

Was the King going to force these matters upon Parliament? Debate must surely follow.

Debate did follow, long and heated. The matters had able defenders in both camps. What was the manner of the presence of Christ in the sacrament? Should Communion be administered to the laity in one kind or in two? Was there benefit in private masses? Should celibacy of the clergy be continued? Was auricular confession necessary? Should those who had taken monastic vows continue to be bound by them?

The King attended some of the sessions and took part in the discussion. Cranmer, Latimer, Shaxton, and a number of others took a vigorous stand in defending the views of the Reformers. Due to their superior ability, it seemed for a time that at least some points would be swayed in their direction.

Hope diminished, however, as the King continued to make clear the conclusion he desired. His determination to have his way would yield to no opposition, however strong or reasonable.

Days dragged on to the middle of June. The Reformers lost heart. One voice after another grew silent. Only Cranmer showed no sign of weakening. He argued and protested; he cited Scripture and the Fathers against the royal measures. His friends begged him to give up. They feared for his life.

Cromwell had once said to Cranmer, "You were born in a happy hour, for do or say what you will, the King will always take it at your hand." But one wondered if possibly there was not a limit to what he would accept.

The six points had now ceased to be questions and had assumed the form of articles. The real presence of Christ in the sacrament was upheld. The laity was restricted to Communion in one kind only. The last four were simply affirmative statements of the questions asked.

What troubled Latimer more than the points themselves was the Bill of Pains and Punishments to be attached to the statute. This bill would provide for death by burning as a heretic for anyone who dared to deny or dispute against the first article. Abjuration would afford no escape.

The same penalty would apply to one opposing any of the other articles, but he might save his life by abjuration. The sentence could be translated into imprisonment at the King's pleasure. A second offense offered no escape. Any priest, monk, or nun who married would be pronouned a felon; he would lose his life and forfeit his goods to the King. All existing marriages of priests, monks, or nuns must be dissolved.

Latimer had no thought of denying the first article. He held to the old doctrine on that point, but the other five articles troubled him.

In the midst of the discussion Cranmer took time to quietly send his wife and children to the Continent.

"A curious thing," said Shaxton to Latimer, "is that only the bishops have taken part in the debates. The nobles are silent."

"They have their position to protect," said Latimer. "Not one would have dared speak on behalf of the Reformers. Neither did they raise a voice against us. I believe they are ready, to a man, to follow the King's lead. Such tameness is unnatural. This entire session of Parliament has been unnatural."

"Well," said Shaxton, "the Bill of Pains and Punishments was read for the third time in the House of Lords today. The Commons will offer objections, but in the end they must give in to the King's wishes."

Up to this time, Latimer had been faithful in his attendance at every session. Not only was he intensely interested in the debates, but he felt it his duty to be in his place and to do his utmost as a member of the Lords. But on the day after the passage of the Six Articles, his seat was vacant.

38

[1539]

Latimer had come to a crossroads. He must make a choice that would affect his own future and possibly that of the Reformation. Within a matter of days the bill would pass the Commons and go through the formality of being granted the royal assent. It would be the law of the land. The general consensus was that it would be in force by the middle of July.

He remained at Stroud Place in complete solitude, giving orders that he was not to be disturbed. Such a period of mental strain and spiritual agony he had never endured. He dared not err in the decision that faced him. To do God's will was the desire of his heart, but he was uncertain what it was. He spent hours on his knees in intercession for divine guidance.

"As a private individual, I have nothing to fear," he said, speaking into the silence of his study. "I do not deny the real presence. We have long lived with denial of the cup to the laity. I do not object strongly to private masses. Auricular confession is not obligatory, but it serves its purpose in some cases. As to my vow of chastity, I do not plan to violate it.

"But the fact is, I am *not* a private individual. How would my position be affected if I were a country priest?"

The wording of the law would not compel him to take an oath of agreement. He would not even be required to teach the matter contained in the articles. The only demand would be that he neither oppose nor deny them. He would face no problem.

"But I am *not* a parish priest," he thundered into the empty room. "Would God I were! I am a bishop of a diocese."

A groan escaped him, and he dropped to his knees, crying out to God in agony. After a time he rose to pace the floor.

"As a bishop, what will this statute require of me? I shall without doubt be compelled to preside on a commission in my diocese for the trial of offenders against the law. What then?"

His mind went back to the vanity of Lambert's trial. He could hear Lambert's voice courageously declaring his position again and again, though he knew it would cost him his life.

"Such men would be brought before me daily," he said. "I would be required to condemn them and hand them over for the punishment Lambert received. They might be men I know and love."

What of those who might be brought before him for protesting against the celibacy of the clergy? He would have to deliver up those who openly proclaimed what he himself believed.

He could see one important reason for remaining at his post. If he resigned, he would leave the archbishop to stand alone. *Could* he stand alone? For how long, with such a pack as Gardiner and Stokesley and Tunstal at his heels?

"How can I desert him? To do so might weaken what remains of the Reformation. It would appear that when trouble came, I hastened to quit the field. Who knows whether this setback is permanent? His Majesty has reversed himself before."

He was into his second day of deliberation. Suddenly, a new thought entered his mind. "Why cannot I resign and still support the Reformation? My health is too feeble for the load of a bishopric. My talent is not for administrative duties but for preaching. With the support of Cranmer and Cromwell I might be granted a post where I could preach as I long to do, under no obligation to enforce a law that in large measure I oppose."

At this point he heard a rapping on the door. A troubled servant faced him, saying, "My lord, I was in no case to disturb you. But the archbishop is here. Must I turn him away?"

Before Latimer could answer, Cranmer stepped past the man into the room. "For two days you fail to occupy your seat. When I send to inquire, I am told you are not to be disturbed."

A feeling of relief swept over Latimer, and he wilted into a chair. "How happy I am that you have come. A man can accomplish just so much by his own thoughts, even with the help of God."

For some hours the two went over the ground that Latimer had covered on his own. They viewed and discussed every angle.

"As for my own position," said Cranmer at last, "I dare not consider resigning. His Majesty would take it as a slap in the face, especially in view of the opposition I manifested to his wishes in the open debates."

"Yes, I see that."

"Even if it were possible, I cannot see that any good would come from my resignation. In spite of the setback this statute may cause, remember what we still have. Keep your eyes fixed on the gains. We have an English Bible and the freedom to use it. Even now a new and improved edition is rolling off the presses. Cromwell calls it 'The Great Bible.' It will be the one placed in every parish church. A Bible may soon hold an honored place in many a household.

"Relics and images are gone, pilgrimages suppressed. Parliament's recent action will sweep away the last of the monasteries. At least some of the ceremonies have been removed. The Pope's power is no more. Purgatory is on the decline. Let us concentrate on holding to these gains while we seek to reclaim the ground just lost and press on to new territory. God has not forsaken us."

"You give me new hope and renew my ebbing courage," said Latimer. "You show me where my duty lies. I shall not desert my post. You may count on me to stand beside you."

The hour was well past midnight when Latimer accompanied his friend down the path to the dock where his boat waited.

"Give me another day to get my heart and mind at one," Latimer said. "Then you will find me in my place."

And so it was. Latimer resumed his seat and made no explanation for his absence of three days. On June 28 the bill received the royal assent and became the law of the land. In the Statute Book it was entitled An Act for Abolishing Diversity of Opinions: But it immediately became known everywhere as "The Bloody Statute" and "The Whip with Six Cords."

On July 1 without warning to his friends, Latimer resigned his bishopric.

Part Four

TO THE TOWER

"I am Augustine Bernher, sir."
[1539–1547]

1

[1539]

Latimer thought the day's session would never end. As it closed, he slipped quietly away. He hoped to make his explanations at Stroud Place in his own rooms. *His own rooms?* Stroud Place was no longer his. He had not thought of that.

With a stab he recalled the words spoken so recently to Cranmer. Now it would appear that he had broken his promise.

He must leave Stroud Place at once. Cranmer would invite him to Lambeth Palace, but he could not accept. To do so might jeopardize his friend's position. Mrs. Statham had always made him sure of a welcome. She and her husband would care for him until he made plans. What would those plans be? His thoughts refused to come to focus. He felt immersed in a fog.

Friends began arriving at the gate only minutes after his own arrival. He gave orders that all be admitted. Amid the cries of consternation and remonstrance, he found it impossible to speak. When Cranmer arrived, Latimer drew him into the privacy of his study.

For a moment they merely stood facing each other. Cranmer opened his mouth as if to speak, then closed it. His eyes held the painful question he wanted answered.

"You are thinking that I broke my promise," said Latimer. "But you must believe me, it was not of my own choosing."

"My heart cries out for an explanation. Why, Hugh? Why?"

"It was His Majesty's wish," answered Latimer hoarsely. "Cromwell told me the King wished me to resign."

"Did you know that Shaxton too resigned?"

Shocked, Latimer replied, "No, I did not know. I wonder whether he received the same message as I."

"A different message came to me," said Cranmer. "His Majesty sent Norfolk and Suffolk and others to comfort me, lest I think my resistance had brought me under royal displeasure."

Back with the others, Latimer repeated what he had said to Cranmer. As he looked at the familiar faces, his eyes filled with tears. Barnes, his friend Jerome, Garrett, and the other chaplains, Holbeach and some priests from London churches, their shocked expressions changed to understanding and compassion as they listened. Did he detect something more? Was it—*fear?*

Some voiced regret; some, indignation. A silence fell, which became awkward. Latimer stepped into the breach to put his friends at ease. He thanked them for their love and friendship.

"Four years ago," he said, "I became bishop of a large and neglected diocese. Knowing little of administrative procedures, I did my best, God helping me. I sat in Convocation and the House of Lords and expressed my opinion. I felt a responsibility for the spiritual care of those in my great cure. I labored for reform and fought abuse, superstition, idolatry, immoral practices, greed, and gluttony among the clergy. I spoke without regard to person or position. I made enemies; I made friends. I amassed no fortune; I spent what came for furthering God's work. I am unashamed to render account of my stewardship."

No one spoke. His speech affected them so that some were in tears. He stepped to the center of the room. "Look at me," he cried. "It is your last chance to view me in that role. Before your eyes Hugh Latimer, Bishop of Worcester, will be transformed into Hugh Latimer, private person."

As he spoke, he began to remove his vestments. When he added the shimmering whiteness of the rochet to the pile, a chuckle broke from his lips. He gave a skip across the room.

"How light my shoulder feels," he cried. "To be relieved of so heavy a burden makes me feel like a schoolboy. With you as my witnesses I declare that I will never again wear the rochet."

Stripped of every item of episcopal regalia, he stood in an unadorned clerical gown. "Now what will Hugh Latimer do?" he asked with a forced smile. "Surely, my service for God is not at an end. But I confess that I have no idea where the path leads."

"You will come home with me," said Cranmer. "Never will you lack a welcome at Lambeth Palace while I am archbishop."

"No, it would do you no good to have me under your roof. But I thank you from the bottom of my heart. I shall go to the Stathams, away from the public eye until I know what to do."

His eyes moved about the room. "As I removed the marks of office from my person, so must I remove myself from this house, which is no longer mine. So friends, if you will excuse me . . ."

Barnes put an arm briefly about his shoulder and left. The others followed until only Cranmer and Garrett remained.

"We shall talk again," said Cranmer. "I am always your friend. Call on me for any need that I can meet. We shall work out plans for your future, never fear."

"You are kind to stay," said Latimer to Garrett as the door closed upon Cranmer. "You, better than anyone, can help me pack my books and papers. I can trust you not to generate confusion."

"Surely, you could spend the night here," said Garrett. "Would it not be better to wait until morning to leave?"

"I think it best to cut every tie quickly. Mrs. Statham will not be inconvenienced. My room is always ready."

"What of your staff here?"

"They must be dismissed with a month's wages. I plan to retain two who have been with me longest. My cash supply is not large, but I shall be able to pay them for a while."

"Since the King requested your resignation, he must be displeased with you. What will follow?"

"Not all questions can be answered at once. The Lord Jesus said truly, 'Sufficient unto the day is the evil thereof.'"

Darkness had fallen as the boatman pulled on the oars to carry the little party downriver. After a short distance by boat came the walk to Milk Street. Latimer leaned on Garrett's arm to keep from stumbling. It had been a long day.

His hostess showed no surprise. She threw the door open wide. The lamplight revealed traces of tears.

2

[1539]

Friends found the little house on Milk Street and brought gifts of money and food. The food Latimer turned over to his hostess; the money he put by for the wages of his men.

There was a general flight to the Continent of those holding Reformed beliefs, especially young scholars. When the storm passed, they could return, bringing with them great learning with which to benefit the church.

On July 7 the Chapter of Worcester petitioned for a royal writ to proceed to the election of a new bishop. When the paper was laid before the King, he roared, "What has happened to Latimer?" Informed that he resigned, His Majesty ordered that he be brought before him.

At a glance, Latimer took in the King's flashing eyes, angry mien, and clenched fists. He fell to his knees and bowed his head.

"Get up!" commanded His Majesty. "Why have you resigned? How is it that a week passes before this knowledge comes to me?"

"Your Majesty, it was represented to me as your wish that I resign."

"I expressed no such wish," thundered the King. "Who was so rash as to put words into my mouth?"

Latimer was silent.

"Answer me! I demand to know! Who was it?"

"Your Majesty, it was the Lord Privy Seal."

He received a curt dismissal. Misgivings filled his mind. He was not certain that the King believed him. An ominous thought struck him: It would be his word against Cromwell's. There were no witnesses.

Why had Cromwell told him the King wished his resignation? He had counted this man his friend. He felt betrayed. They had agreed that, while their aims might differ, the paths by which they would arrive at their respective goals would generally coincide. Cromwell's aims were in the nature of political moves to stabilize the throne and benefit the nation as a whole, but the Reformation of the church had a place in his plans.

Latimer had made enemies by sending Cromwell information on matters requiring his action. Diligence for the keeping of the law was a part of his duty to God. Because of his access to Cromwell, he had asked favors, but never for himself. He searched his mind for some act by which he might have offended Cromwell. He could find none.

Insistent in his thoughts was a nagging fear. The King had *not* wanted him to resign. Would he consider his resignation as censure of the royal policy? Latimer had opposed the measures, but when it became evident that the King would have his way, he had ceased opposition; Cranmer had kept on much longer. But that was another matter. The King could not do without Cranmer; Latimer was expendable.

Expendable? What was he thinking? The King would never beg anyone to recall a hasty action. It was well. Latimer knew he could never reconsider. He had been willing to remain at his post, even at personal discomfort and sacrifice. But having resigned, for whatever reason, he would not go back.

Barnes came with a suggestion that stunned him. "In view of the King's displeasure at your resignation, should you not join those who are crossing to the Continent? Little safety remains for you here. The Tower stands conveniently by."

Garrett gave the same counsel. The talk on the street, so he claimed, concerned the danger in which Latimer stood.

"Remember," said Barnes, "I found this a prudent step at one time. Had I not, I wouldn't be here to warn you now."

Cranmer agreed that his position was precarious. The fact that he had resigned would continue to gall the King. It made no difference that Latimer had been deceived. The King would see only that his wishes had been disregarded.

"None of us knows what a day may bring forth," said Cranmer. "I agree, Hugh, that you should go. You are too valuable for us to risk losing. God keep you and bring you back."

So the decision was made for him, yet he gave assent. His friends provided funds. Cranmer gave him introductory letters, though Latimer was known by reputation on the Continent.

A small vessel carried him down the Thames. At Gravesend he sought the ship on which he had arranged passage. His heart beat faster at the thought of the experience before him.

A sailor approached him, saying, "Sir, you may come aboard now." Latimer stooped to pick up his bundle, but the young man was ahead of him. Seizing it lightly with one hand, he placed it on his shoulder and motioned Latimer to follow.

Before he had taken two steps, Latimer felt a tap on his shoulder. Two men wearing the uniform of the King's guard stood there.

"You are Hugh Latimer?" inquired one of the men.

Taking care to keep his voice steady, he replied, "I am."

"By order of His Majesty the King we must take you into custody and return you to London."

3

[1539]

He was almost relieved to be on his way back. He did not doubt that he would go to the Tower. But the strong pulling on the oars took them past that forbidding structure. At the Bridge they transferred to one of the King's small barges and continued upriver. At the Temple Wharf the boatman pulled to the bank and skillfully spun the barge to the steps.

His guards led him past the Temple Church, across Fleet Street, and into Chancery Lane. Opposite Lincoln's Inn Fields, they stopped before the Bishop of Chichester's London palace.

Ah, yes, thought Latimer. *It would be safe for the King to leave me in the custody of Bishop Sampson.*

Latimer was restricted to the house. His rooms were on the front with windows that looked out across the greenness of Lincoln's Inn Fields. He had his books and papers. One servant was permitted him. Best of all, his friends were free to visit.

On July 14 the Pains and Punishment Law went into effect. News filtered in of prisons being filled and of one or two burnings. Undue publicity was discouraged, but the news spread.

"Tell me about the burnings," said Latimer to those who sat with him one evening in late July. "I have a particular interest there, for my heart tells me that such may soon be my fate."

"Don't joke, Latimer," remonstrated Barnes.

Some of his friends urged him to appeal for reinstatement in his bishopric. But having resigned, he had no freedom of conscience about submitting to the King. He would not be forced to acknowledge as just a measure he had so strongly opposed.

He was serious about expecting execution. The King would not leave him indefinitely in Sampson's custody. When he acted, would it be to free him—or would it be the Tower and Smithfield?

A more immediate worry concerned personal finances. He dispatched his commissary to the diocese to receive the Pentecostal offering, due to be collected at Whitsuntide while he was still in office. The commissary returned empty-handed. He was not allowed to collect the offering, lest he incite sedition.

Cromwell did not communicate with Latimer. For his part Latimer had nothing to say to the Lord Privy Seal. He suffered a great sadness because of this rupture with a man he had trusted.

Cranmer, not often free to come, arrived one day with welcome news. "His Majesty is softening. He has granted both you and Shaxton a pension of one hundred marks a year."

"I can hardly believe it!" cried Latimer.

"You would do well not to spend it until it is in your hand," cautioned Cranmer. "The King intends you to have it, but sometimes intentions miscarry."

"It may appear a small amount," said Latimer, "but it will be invaluable to me. Does he intend to keep me here long?"

"No one dares ask. Perhaps His Majesty does not yet know. Waiting is burdensome, but matters could be worse."

His servant made a journey toward Salisbury and returned full of talk. "They are saying, sir, that this has come upon the land because when the Bible was given, we did not apply ourselves to its study. It was as if we spurned God's good gift."

"They exaggerate," said Latimer. "Many people *have* availed themselves of the opportunity to read and study the Bible."

"They say, too, sir, that one of the best preachers in Christendom was the Bishop of Worcester. Now he is replaced by one never heard to preach, unless it were the Pope's law."

In September the King signed a marriage contract with Anne of Cleves. The Reformers felt a surge of optimism. Such an alliance *must* swing the King back toward the Reformation.

192

4

[1539–1540]

The consensus of popular opinion as to Latimer's promised pension was pretty well summed up in an alehouse prediction. "He'll never get a penny of it in his hands. Sooner or later he'll go to the Tower, then on to the block or the stake."

Such pessimism proved wrong so far as the pension was concerned. On September 29 he received payment for the six months previous, although his resignation had been in effect only three months. He paid his servant and had a bit for his needs.

He appreciated the freedom to see his friends and the comforts of his imprisonment, but the confinement grew frustrating. How long would it last? What came next? These questions plagued him in the night when he could not sleep.

The Continental Reformers began to shower the King with protests against the Six Articles. Melanchthon, usually so mild-mannered, made his wrath unmistakably evident in a letter against a measure he found both brutal and treacherous.

The letter was printed and circulated, which irritated the King greatly. He particularly resented Melanchthon's references to the disgrace of retaining in prison such men as Latimer and Shaxton, whom he deemed "very lanterns of light" to the church.

On the heels of this letter came one from the Elector of Saxony, expressing indignant astonishment. The passing of a decree so bitter and sharp could only have come about "by the conspiracy and craftiness of certain bishops, in whose mind the veneration and worshiping of Roman ungodliness is rooted."

Bucer wrote to Cranmer, "We are amazed more than I can express at those decrees. It is idle to suppose that we should not be offended by them." The archbishop had the wisdom not to share his letter with the King.

Preparations for his coming marriage mellowed the King's attitude slightly. Although unwilling to commit himself to the religious principles of the Schmalkaldic League, he knew his alliance with them could hardly fail to influence his domestic policy. As a result, the statute was not put into full force: He did not issue the threatened commissions for hunting heretics.

On Christmas Day Barnes and a host of others came to cheer Latimer. "Well, Robert," Latimer said, "two years ago we spent Christmas at the castle. This year you join me for Christmas in captivity. Hazard a guess as to where we spend the next one?"

Barnes shook his head and said ruefully, "I wouldn't hazard a guess as to where we may spend *tomorrow,* in these times."

On January 6 the archbishop solemnized the marriage of the King and Anne of Cleves. All England rejoiced to receive a Queen described as "an excellent woman and one who fears God." The Reformers cherished the hope that her presence would give a forward push to the spread of the Reformation.

Persecution had ended, at least temporarily. Barnes preached powerfully and widely; Garrett and Jerome spoke out in their respective parishes. Christian literature, other than the Bible, was offered for sale. The operation of the Bloody Statute seemed completely suspended.

Latimer chafed more than ever at his imprisonment, pacing like a caged beast. With such opportunities for preaching, how could he sit here looking out across Lincoln's Inn Fields?

Suppose I had not resigned, he mused. Then he jerked himself up short. *None of that,* he said sternly. *That is behind you. You would not wish to be again clad in rochet and miter. That was a burden you found almost unbearable. God relieved you of it. Patience, man!*

The happy state of affairs for the Reformation proved of brief duration. Latimer's heart sank when he heard that Barnes was once more in trouble with the King.

Cranmer related the beginning of the trouble back to February when Gardiner, Bishop of Winchester, had preached at Paul's Cross, attacking the doctrines of the Reformers. Three Sundays later, Barnes preached from the same pulpit.

In his sermon Barnes made an allegory in which he likened Gardiner to a fighting-cock and himself to another. "But the *garden*-cock lacks spurs," he said, and continued in that vein.

"Even so," said Latimer, "I fear I might have been tempted to take the same tactic. Barnes and I often follow the same patterns of thought."

"I have heard Barnes describe the difference in your preaching and his. You have a happy faculty of being able to say the daring thing without giving offense; Barnes can say the same words, and something in his manner makes it come out irritating."

"Gardiner's indignation knew no bounds, I am sure."

"He complained to the King, who ordered Barnes before him."

He continued, "There is something else you should know. I do not mean to carry gossip, but this is all common talk at court. His Majesty is not happy with his new Queen. This is reflected in his attitude toward those who were instrumental in bringing about the marriage, of whom Barnes was one."

Latimer groaned.

"Barnes hesitated for some time before agreeing to retract his teaching. He might not have balked as to what he had said about Gardiner; however, to retract the doctrine of justification by faith and the teaching against purgatory, simply because Gardiner wished it, was almost too much.

"He read his retraction at Paul's Cross as required. . . ." Cranmer broke off here. Latimer searched his face and detected a gleam of amusement in his eyes.

"Barnes will never pass up the opportunity to nettle an opponent," continued Cranmer. "His retraction required him to ask Gardiner's forgiveness. He read the request, then fixed his eyes upon Gardiner with a pleading look, waiting for an answer."

Latimer chuckled. "That's my friend Barnes, all right."

"He repeated the request for forgiveness. Gardiner sat as stiff as a poker and with a face as expressionless. A third time Barnes repeated his request, adding, 'I beg the Bishop of Winchester to give me a sign whereby I may be certain I am forgiven.' With no change of expression Gardiner at length raised the forefinger of his right hand in a brief gesture."

"He must have been furious at being forced to reply."

"Barnes thanked him profusely. But then he restated his former opinion, nullifying the effect of his recantation."

"So, of course, he's back in the Tower," said Latimer.

"It was inevitable. Garrett and Jerome took the same stand. So all three are there to await the King's pleasure and the determination of Parliament."

5

[1540]

Latimer stood at the window enjoying the freshness of the spring day, but wishing most of all to be out in it. Two men wearing the uniform of the King's guard entered the gates. His heart gave a leap. Had they come to conduct him to the Tower? Such a possibility was never far from his mind. He listened for footsteps approaching his door.

But no one came. A few minutes later the guards left, but not alone. The Bishop of Chichester was their prisoner. Sampson had voiced too loudly his leanings toward Rome. Before the Privy Council he was accused, questioned, and sent to the Tower.

Within a few days Latimer's circumstances changed. He must still return to the Bishop's house at evening, but during the daylight hours, he could go where he wanted in London.

His feet took him without hesitation straight to the Tower. He had little difficulty arranging to see Barnes. His old friend was overcome with joy. Between laughter and tears, he almost crushed Latimer in a bearlike embrace.

"I was beginning to feel I stood all alone," he said. "Garrett and Jerome are here, but we are not allowed to see one another. Others must agree with me, but no one else has come."

The guard allowed only a brief stay. Latimer's request to see Garrett and Jerome was denied.

By some quirk the King's ire was aroused against Latimer. With only a brief taste of freedom he was back in strict confinement, almost certainly marked for execution.

Cranmer went straight to the King. "Consider, Sire, what a singular man he is. Cast not away in one hour that which nature and art have been so many years in breeding and perfecting."

The King had not heeded Cranmer's plea for mercy with regard to Anne Boleyn. This time he did. The crisis passed. Latimer well knew that only Cranmer could have saved him.

Soon after the King's marriage, Gardiner had given a banquet. His keen eyes were already watching the King and his bride. One guest at the banquet was a young girl of unusual beauty, a niece of the Duke of Norfolk. Sprightly and charming, Catherine Howard stood out in contrast to the Queen. Gardiner did not miss the impression the lady made upon the King.

Talk in the streets turned to the King's visits by boat to see the new lady. They spoke of adultery, but in higher circles, speculation was about the King's intention to divorce Anne. No one could fail to note the frequency with which the Bishop of Winchester provided entertainment for them in his palace.

6

[1540]

On June 10 London was rocked to its foundations by the seizure of a new prisoner. Thomas Cromwell was accused of high treason by the Duke of Norfolk before the Privy Council. He was arrested and sent immediately to the Tower. Such action could not have been taken without the King's knowledge. Yet what word or deed of Cromwell constituted treason remained a mystery.

The man had few friends. The Lords despised him as an upstart of low origin; the Commons disliked him because of the great subsidies he laid upon them.

Latimer was greatly shocked. Indignant over the way people turned upon him, he cried, "They were glad to hover around him until he fell. Greedy petitioners had praise enough while they sought his favors."

A Bill of Attainder denounced him as a traitor in harshest terms. No proof seemed required. He was said to have freed persons suspected of being traitors. As a person of low degree, he had dared speak of "being sure of the King." He was accused of heresy and of being a patron of heretics, especially Barnes.

The man did not even receive a trial. By an infamous law for which he himself was responsible, persons accused of treason might be condemned without trial.

Only the Archbishop of Canterbury raised his voice in behalf of Cromwell. Cranmer knew him well and loved him as a friend. "He was such a servant in wisdom, diligence, faithfulness, and experience as no prince in this realm ever had," he declared.

All was to no avail. On June 29 the King gave the royal assent to the bill prepared by his legislators. But the execution was delayed.

The King's suit for divorce or annulment must be prosecuted before Convocation. They listened to the King's evidence, some of it shockingly indecent. By a unanimous vote they declared that His Majesty had never given "inward consent" to the marriage. Therefore, the sacrament of matrimony was incomplete, utterly null and void. Both parties were free to marry again.

In his delight at escape from the detested union, the King proclaimed that no further persecution should take place for religion. A general amnesty was declared for those in prison. Specifically excepted were Cromwell, Barnes, Garrett, and Jerome, but Latimer was free.

7

[1540]

Latimer's release did not bring unadulterated joy. The King attached conditions to his freedom: He must leave London immediately; he was prohibited from venturing within six miles of London, the two universities, or his old diocese. The crushing blow was that he was absolutely forbidden to preach.

"Perhaps I should feel grateful that I escaped the Tower and the stake," he fumed to Cranmer. "But why must he muzzle me, when preaching is the most important thing in my life?"

"It may not be for long. His Majesty's moods change. One day he will remember a happier time when he listened to your preaching. He will be moved to relent."

"You cannot be certain of that," replied Latimer. "If my tongue is to remain shut up in prison, what good is it for the rest of me to be free? How *can* I not preach? What am I to do?"

"What you *must* do," replied Cranmer in a grimmer tone, "is not preach. You *must* keep your distance from forbidden places. You *must* develop patience. You *must* trust the Lord for support."

"You give me a long list of *musts*," said Latimer. But Cranmer was right. He nearly always was.

"Accept His Majesty's terms as gracefully as possible. Your life will yet be brought into great usefulness in God's kingdom. Don't throw it away by refusing to obey the King's orders."

"Then I had better set about demonstrating my obedience by getting out of London as fast as possible."

"Where will you go?"

"To my niece in Warwickshire, the wife of Robert Glover. I can count on a welcome there." In a lower tone he added, "Their young son bears my name."

As he journeyed north, his thoughts were on Barnes, Garrett, Jerome— what would their fate be? Not released in the general amnesty. What would the King do? Cromwell's end was certain.

The thought of Cromwell troubled him. Cromwell had been his friend. Many found the secretary cold and hard to approach. Latimer had broken through this exterior. It was a mutually beneficial relationship. Why had this man betrayed him? Such a step had severed their friendship as with a knife.

With all his faults Cromwell was due a debt of gratitude from the English people. He could have blocked the progress of the Reformation. With wisdom and skill he had led the King even where he at times did not wish to be led. Without him the English Bible would not have been allowed at this time. He had kept up unrelenting pressure in that direction, drawing back when he saw the time was not propitious, but never giving up.

Word reached Latimer at the Robert Glover home at Mancetter that on July 28, Cromwell had gone to the block. He approached the scaffold, quietly committing his soul into the hands of God and saying, "I am altogether a miserable sinner. I have sinned against my good and gracious God and have offended the King." But his words about the King were pronounced coldly and with no ring of sincerity. This, Latimer knew, was quite in character.

Two days after Cromwell's execution, the three who were among the closest friends Latimer ever knew perished in flames at Smithfield. Barnes, Garrett, and Jerome were chained to one stake and died quietly without crying out.

Latimer experienced deep sorrow, a deeper horror and physical illness. He kept saying, " 'Little Bilney,' Bainham, Lambert—and now dear Barnes, Garrett, and my old friend Jerome."

Robert Glover grew concerned about him. Even Latimer's niece had no power to draw him from his dismal thoughts and terrifying dreams. Only when her little son who bore his name approached did the gloomy spell seem to dissipate.

Little Hugh would take his hand, and they would roam the green hills. The pleasant chatter reminded Latimer of another small boy who used to tramp the Leicestershire hills not far away, clinging to his father's hand. Such relaxation was like rainfall on dry ground. By degrees his spirits revived.

As the weeks passed, Latimer involved himself more and more in study of the Scriptures. He immersed himself in the Word in a way he never had time for in his bishopric.

8

[1540]

The King's marriage to Catherine Howard gave him such delight that he ordered public prayers of thanksgiving offered for so good a wife. This led the Romish party to consider themselves again in a favorable position. Gardiner must have been pleased to see the match he had promoted working out.

In the autumn Latimer moved to the home of John Glover, brother to Robert, four miles away at Baxterley Hall. John Glover was a man of deep piety, who walked close to the Lord. He gladly opened his beautiful mansion to his old friend Latimer.

Glover was quite wealthy in both lands and money. He built lovely Baxterley Hall, divided his lands with his brothers, and turned the rest of his property over to servants and officers to manage and care for. He wished to be free to devote his time to religious contemplation.

Anyone of the Reformed faith was welcome, and guests came and went at will. Besides houseguests, his neighbors made a habit of dropping in for an evening.

With Latimer's coming there developed a new custom. After the evening meal the family, along with guests and neighbors, gathered in the Hall for discussion of Christian topics. Latimer could not preach, but he could talk and answer questions.

This gave him an outlet for the new truths discovered in his daily perusal of the Scriptures. He found and swept away unsuspected remnants of Roman debris, which still clung to him. Difficult questions forced him back to the Bible to seek answers.

Tears often came to his eyes at the rapt expressions, the joy in having the

Truth made clear, difficulties lessened or removed. Each felt free to express his thoughts and ask any question.

At Glover's insistence he made Baxterley his base, though he would visit elsewhere. He made his first visit to his old home at Thurcaston, an easy day's journey on horseback.

He rode across the hills over which he had run as a boy. He visited the house in which he was born, a simple cruck dwelling with thatched roof and small windows. As he entered the front door, he could almost see his sisters going about their daily labors. The floor, the beams, the plastered walls were like those of many a country home, with the cruck frame exposed as it ran from ground to roof up through the walls.

In the kitchen much of the living took place. A huge fireplace provided warmth as well as means of cooking. Off the kitchen was the lead room with mutton and beef sides and great hams hanging from iron hooks, the winter's meat supply.

He stood at the foot of the stairway winding up to the bedrooms. He knew the rooms above would be just as he remembered. Small, cozy, with sloping roof coming down at such an angle that he would bump his head if he were not careful.

Out the back door he found the marigolds bright along the path. Salvia's flame glowed in the beds nearest the house. Across the Charnwood Hills he could imagine his father striding through the fields, coming home from a day's work.

His mother had died when he was quite small. But he recalled trudging along as she went with the servant girls to do the afternoon milking. He remembered there were thirty cows.

How often he had entered the great wooden doors of the stone church where he studied his lessons with the priest. He could see the stone font in which he, last child of old Hugh Latimer, had been baptized and given his father's name. Here he was confirmed and had participated in his first mass. Memories, so many memories.

Back with the Glovers, he joined in the celebration of Christmas. He thought of last Christmas and his question to Barnes about where they might spend this Christmas.

9

[1541]

Stokesley had died in the past year, and Bonner succeeded him as Bishop of London. He had been a follower of Cromwell, but upon Cromwell's fall he had made a quick about-face.

The new bishop seemed obsessed with the need to prove the whole-heartedness of his changed thinking. He began the year with a frantic search for heretics. In parish after parish he arrested offenders against the Six Articles. He imprisoned people for neglecting the ceremonies of the old church, for reading the Bible aloud, for speaking approvingly of Barnes, for eating flesh during Lent, and for even more ridiculous charges. His prisoners, more than five hundred, overflowed the prisons. Even Mrs. Statham was "noted" for having harbored Latimer and Barnes.

Happily for the prisoners, it was soon obvious that Bonner's zeal had overextended itself. No one could consider the possibility of burning five hundred offenders. A general emptying of the jails resulted.

Latimer took his walk on a May afternoon along a path through an apple orchard in full bloom. When he had fully drunk the beauties of this scene, he returned to the garden where his book awaited him. His senses seemed intoxicated with the miracle of spring. He felt well and strong as he had not in years. The hand of God was upon him and the peace of God was within him.

The sound of approaching footsteps brought him from his reverie. It was one of Cranmer's personal messengers.

"We do live these days moment by moment," wrote Cranmer, "as our Lord would no doubt have us do. Yet a bright spot has appeared. His Majesty has issued a proclamation that will cause you, dear friend, to rejoice. In strongest terms the King has ordered all parishes that have not yet provided themselves with Bibles to do so at once. They are to obtain a copy of the largest volume before November 1, under penalty of forfeiting forty shillings a month until they comply."

Latimer did rejoice. "Now every parish church will have its Bible, whether the priest wishes it or not. Gardiner has not been able to obstruct this blessing."

Gardiner returned from a mission abroad in October, just in time to witness the collapse of the King's fifth marriage.

10

[1541–1543]

On the basis of information brought to him, Cranmer was forced to inform the King that his young bride had not lived as a chaste virgin prior to her marriage. Indications were that her indiscretions had not ceased.

The news almost destroyed the King. He had spent sixteen months in one long honeymoon. It was reported that he wept openly when he received Cranmer's communication.

In January a new Parliament, summoned to deal with the matter, found the Queen guilty. On February 13 she went to the block. Parliament urged the King not to be overly troubled by his misfortune, lest grief shorten his valuable life.

Another year passed. Latimer was still at peace about his future. He knew God had something planned for him besides a pleasant country life among friends and with his books.

Then in the spring of 1543, a cloud appeared on the horizon. Foiled by Cranmer in his attempt to get a new version of the Bible—and delay its production indefinitely—Gardiner and his co-workers came up with another plan.

They persuaded the King to allow to be introduced into Parliament an Act for the Advancement of True Religion. "Seeing where it originated," snorted Latimer, "a more likely title would be Act for the Suppression of True Religion."

Certain translations of the Bible, especially Tyndale's, were to be abolished. No copy of Old or New Testament in that translation could be used in the realm.

After October 1, even reading the licensed versions would be limited. Noblemen and gentlemen were free to read the Bible to their families at home; merchants and gentlewomen might read by themselves. The common people must not read the Scriptures at all. Unless appointed by the King or ordinary, no one was to read openly any part of the Scriptures in English, under penalty of a month's imprisonment. Women (except of high birth), artificers, apprentices, and laborers should not read to themselves or others, openly or privately, under like penalty.

Latimer laid the paper before John Glover who read and reread the words of the act. Latimer was numb with shock.

"This is the most backward step the King has taken since the passing of the Six Articles," Latimer exploded. "Why should a nobleman be permitted to read the Holy Scriptures, but a weaver or a poor farmer's wife be prohibited?"

Glover seemed to be turning something over in his mind.

"Gardiner and Bonner must consider this a great victory for them and an equally great setback for us," said Latimer. "They are right. Where was Cranmer?"

Glover continued to hold his peace. "What do you think?" asked Latimer. "Is it not a terrible blow?"

"A blow . . . yes," said Glover. "Yet, do you not see certain implications? If the Romish party wishes to withdraw the Bible, it is because they know it *is* being read. And who is reading it? The common people. Therefore, they are not to be allowed to read it. The action is a sign of recognition by the Romish party that the Reformation is spreading. They seek to crush it."

Latimer considered. "What you say is true, but the act still cuts the common people off from the Book."

"It may not be as bad as it seems," said Glover. "As to the matter of Tyndale's translation, not many with his imprint are in circulation. Some of the later versions are substantially his, but without his imprint. Therefore, few Bibles will actually be called in. Even those approved by the King contain large portions of Tyndale's work. So that part of the act is useless."

"You are right. I *do* see signs of Cranmer's influence. A month's imprisonment is mild punishment. I envision many still daring to take the risk and continuing to read."

"I have a large number of laborers about my properties," said Glover. "Many are brothers in Christ. They say that, although Christians have used discretion in expressing their views under the Six Articles, most remain true to the faith. The number grows. They will read their Bibles, even in secret."

Latimer read the document through again. "I see in the list of exceptions and conditions that the wording leaves several loopholes. It is not as bad as I feared, praise God."

"Instead of a triumph of the Romish party over the Reformation," said Glover, "this act is merely an indication of their anxious desire to throw obstacles in the way of progress."

11

[1543]

Latimer removed the book from its wrappings and read the title: *The Necessary Doctrine and Erudition of a Christian Man.*

"After more than three years of intermittent work upon a revision of our old *Bishops' Book,*" Cranmer wrote, "this is the result. The final work was committed to me and to Thirlby of Westminster, Heath of Rochester, and Salcot of Salisbury."

"Those names," muttered Latimer, "bespeak the outcome even before I read. Cranmer was outnumbered."

"Gardiner could not be more pleased," continued Cranmer. "Do not judge me too harshly for my part in it. Sometimes I consider your lot by far the easier. Pray for me."

Latimer carried the book to a favorite corner of the garden where climbing roses perfumed the air. A bench beneath a huge oak provided reasonable freedom from interruption.

Transubstantiation was upheld. All seven sacraments remained, with no distinction between scriptural and unscriptural. The request for Communion in both kinds for the laity was described as "pestiferous and devilish." Prayers and masses for the dead were endorsed, but stress was put on the point that every mass was offered for the whole body of Christians and could not be limited to private persons.

Financial abuses of purgatory were deplored. The claim of the Bishop of Rome to sovereignty could not be supported by Scripture, general councils, nor consent of the Catholic Church.

"In spite of Gardiner's apparent change of views with regard to the Pope," murmured Latimer, "that last statement must have proved hard for him to swallow according to his conscience."

He read on. The only universal ruler of the church was Jesus Christ, whom Christians were bound to obey. Next to the Lord Christ, Christians must obey Christian kings and princes, who were constituted heads under him of the particular churches.

Matters that had not been touched upon in the *Bishops' Book* were few, yet of great importance. They struck a blow at fundamental Reformed doctrines. Poor Cranmer.

The doctrine of justification by faith was repudiated. Such a Lutheran doctrine was not to be tolerated. Man was not justified by faith alone, contended the book. He must *win* his justification by means of faith, hope, charity, fear of God, and repentance. Justification was a lifelong endeavor. A man could lose it by sin. No one could ever claim assurance of salvation.

Good works played a strong role in salvation. These were defined not as superstitious observances nor works done to earn human approval, but "all inward and spiritual works, as the love and fear of God, joy in God, godly meditations and thoughts, patience, humility, and such." Penitence and even the penance performed might count as good works for a converted sinner.

When he finished reading, his discouragement was greater than at any time since the passage of the Six Articles.

"Gardiner and his friends have done their work well," he said. "The Reformation will come almost to a standstill. The King has moved further backward than I thought possible."

Even John Glover could offer little encouragement.

12

[1543–1545]

One evening John Careless from Coventry arrived at Baxterley from a trip to London. He refused to speak of the news he brought until the hour when the household gathered.

A fire burned on the hearth, for even in July the evenings grew chilly within heavy stone walls. Glover made sure his guests were comfortable.

"Let's have it, Careless," he said, taking a seat beside his wife. "You are about to burst with whatever news you have."

"When things look darkest," said Careless, "God reminds us that he is still on the job. The first thing I should inform you of is the King's marriage to Katherine Parr."

"That *is* good news!" exclaimed Latimer. "Her piety is unquestionable, and she loves the true preaching of the gospel. Gardiner has acquired an adversary."

"After the *King's Book* appeared," said Careless, "Gardiner walked with new arrogance. People whispered that he had bent his bow to shoot at some of the head deer."

"Just which of the 'head deer'?" asked Robert Glover.

"He persuaded some Canterbury canons to make charges of heresy against the archbishop."

The group in the room gasped.

"The King called at Lambeth and took my lord Cranmer for an outing on the river. On the way he said, in a menacing tone, 'Ah, my chaplain, I know who is the greatest heretic in Kent.'"

Latimer chuckled. "I can picture Cranmer, a look of astonishment on his face, saying, *Who*, Your Majesty?'"

"The King's confidence in his primate could not be shaken. The conspirators had overshot the mark. To insure their own safety, they were required to make a humble apology."

"That *is* a story to cheer us," cried John Glover. "Your trip to London was worthwhile if only to bring us this news."

Robert Glover spoke. "Don't become too optimistic. Gardiner will seek another angle. Can the new Queen influence the King in spiritual matters? We must pray for that. Ill health does not give His Majesty a kindly disposition."

"The Queen is a wise woman," said Latimer, "possessed of a goodly supply of common sense. I think we may trust her."

Latimer's concern was for Cranmer. He knew the man's loyalty to and deep love for his Sovereign. He knew the King's attachment to Cranmer and his dependence upon him. Yet, Cranmer lacked the strength of a Cromwell. There were times when all the outspokenness of which he was capable did not register. Gardiner had a hold on at least one of the King's ears.

The strange part was that the King did not even like Gardiner. He recognized his ability and found him useful, so His Majesty let himself be influenced by him to a degree.

In the meantime Cranmer was swimming against the tide that sometimes threatened to drag him under. He was often swept helplessly along, hoping for a chance to turn the tide. He was the King's man, but he was first of all God's man. He was not weak; he was wise enough to know when to give in and wait for the chance to win out on greater issues. Cranmer's personal bond with the King was the strongest hope of the Reformers.

Cranmer must have been encouraged when Dr. Butts again made his voice heard by the King. Edward Seymour, Earl of Hertford, and John Dudley, Lord Lisle, were two able young men who began to take a stand for moderate reform. The Queen cautiously favored Protestant opinions, followed by several of the ladies at court.

The Queen's gentle persuasion perhaps did more than anything to urge the King further toward Reformation; however, she was not always successful. The King determined to be his own man, controlled or manipulated by no one. When the Queen saw that she was on dangerous ground, she was wise enough to desist.

The months slipped by. Latimer increasingly spent time with individuals seeking counsel. No one ever found him too busy. He found it reminiscent of the days in his diocese.

In the spring of 1544 Cranmer's efforts produced results. Parliament attached limitations to the operation of the Bloody Statute. Offenses older than a year could not be acted upon. Only by legal presentation on the oaths of twelve men could a person be brought to trial or imprisoned. Proceedings must be instituted within forty days to accuse a preacher for words spoken against the Six Articles.

"The King can overrule any one of these provisions in a particular case," said Latimer. "But we have cause to rejoice."

"Cranmer has succeeded," said John Glover, "in extracting the poison from Gardiner's fiery scorpions, to say the least."

A few evenings later, Latimer joined the group in the Hall with a small book in his hand. "The King has mandated the use of Cranmer's English litany for prayers in the churches."

Glover reached for the book and began to turn through it.

"It is to be used regularly in the services," said Latimer. "The priest is to explain it and encourage the people to worship God in their own tongue. The King reiterates an injunction that the priest read a chapter of the New Testament in English at Sunday and holy-day services."

Glover looked up from his perusal of the book. "Cranmer includes a number of Psalms, excellent models for prayer. His paraphrase of the Lord's Prayer should help people think what they are saying when they pray."

"The best feature," said Latimer, "is the litany. How conducive to worship it will be to have a real Prayer of Procession for use at the beginning of the service."

"Inclusion of invocations to the Virgin, to angels, prophets, apostles, and martyrs is a jarring note," said Glover.

"Cranmer would agree," said Latimer. "But he is wise. He had to make some concessions to gain the King's approval."

Glover handed the book to the next person, so that it might pass around the room. "It's a step forward," he said. "I don't know why we get discouraged. God is still working."

John Careless joined them one evening not long after. "I'm back again from London," he said. "Gardiner is in hot water."

"What's he been up to now?" asked Glover.

"He employed his nephew as secretary and now has reason to regret it. The young man worked against the royal supremacy, was seized, accused, and executed as a traitor. Suspicion attached to the bishop as having known about his kinsman's treason."

"That must have been a blow," said Latimer. "He would be enraged at his nephew's activity. And his pride would be injured that anyone would think that he was party to the crime."

"Gardiner was possibly behind another matter," said Careless. "Sir John Gostwick attempted in the House of Commons to bring a charge of heresy against Cranmer. The King reacted with no uncertainty. His message was, 'Tell the varlet Gostwick that if he does not acknowledge his fault to my lord of Canterbury, I will surely both make him a poor Gostwick and otherwise punish him, to the example of others.'"

"That should warn Gardiner off," said Glover. "Touch not the King's archbishop! Cranmer alone holds the door open for the Reformation, though he sometimes gets squeezed in the crack."

The last half of 1544 and the early months of the next year saw the Reformation again in the ascendancy. The King was engaged in war in France, then in Scotland. Gardiner and Norfolk were abroad with him. The Queen acted as regent with Cranmer as head of her council. At the King's return his sole concern was for replenishing his exhausted treasury.

Latimer grew restless. He wanted to go to London; he wanted to preach. Would the King never relent?

13

[1545]

Winter held on long. Heavy snow covered the paths and kept Latimer housebound. He pulled his chair close to the fire, and wrapping himself in a heavy cloak, applied himself to the Book.

He raised his head and spoke aloud from Philippians: " 'For I am in a strait betwixt two, having a desire to depart, and to be with Christ, which is far better. Nevertheless, to abide in the flesh is more needful for you. And having this confidence, I know that I shall abide and continue with you all, for your furtherance and joy of faith.' "

Then, softly, "Words of the apostle from his prison become my words from my 'prison' here. I shall live to preach again."

Someone knocked at the door. It opened to admit a well-built younger man who was surely no stranger. That unruly shock of brown hair, those piercing gray eyes, that hint of awkwardness in his manner—who was this man?

"Sir, you would not remember me, but I am—"

"You are Thomas Becon," cried Latimer. The voice had brought the name to him.

"Oh, sir, how could you remember? It is close to twenty years since we last met."

He pulled forward the chair Latimer indicated, and soon they were deep in reminiscences of Cambridge.

"I do remember," said Latimer. "You were quite young when you began to appear every time I preached. You were no more than fifteen years old. Your earnestness stuck in my memory."

"The three years I sat under your preaching were the most blessed and fruitful in my life. A common saying was, 'When Master Stafford reads and Master Latimer preaches, then is Cambridge blessed.' "

"But what brings you to Baxterley? I remember hearing some years back of your being caught for a time in Bonner's net."

"That was quite a time. After that, I became one of the archbishop's chaplains. In his most recent difficulty I was again brought under suspicion. When it seemed best that I disappear for a time, Glover graciously invited me here."

"Baxterley is a good place to come. I have been here the better part of five years. Is Cranmer in some new trouble?"

"Certain members of the council accused him of infecting England with unsavory doctrines through the men he patronized. They were convinced he could draw a large part of the realm into heresy; they wished him committed to the Tower. His Majesty permitted them to bring Cranmer before the council but would not send him to the Tower."

"He has not let them go so far before."

"The King secretly warned Cranmer of the proceedings and gave him his own ring with which he might appeal."

"Our Sovereign has a way of bringing a certain humor into a situation," said Latimer.

"The King and Sir William Butts concealed themselves in a spot from which they could see and hear. At the hour set for the archbishop's appearance, the council dallied and refused to call him. He stood waiting outside along with pages and footboys."

"How did they dare!" cried Latimer.

"At last they admitted him but kept him standing while they bullied him unbelievably and showed the greatest insolence."

"The Archbishop of Canterbury forced to *stand* in the presence of such as those?" cried Latimer indignantly.

"Their victim answered with his usual patience and without rebuke. When they ordered him conveyed to the Tower, Cranmer produced the King's ring and appealed his case.

"At that point the King, followed by Butts, came forth. Confusion became alarm. 'I thought you to be men of wisdom and understanding, but I see nothing of that. I gave you power to try this man, but not as you would a groom or some low varlet. How did you dare keep him waiting at the door among servants like some common criminal? I would remind you of the respect due an archbishop. I pray you, use not my friends so!' With a final glare he turned and left the room.

"The council quickly dispersed. Its members were fortunate to escape with only the King's ire. I think it will be long before anyone again troubles the archbishop."

14

[1545]

Becon was quite carried away by the evening discussions. He cried out with feeling, "You people are greatly privileged. In London one must look about to see who is near before such free expression as to the interpretation of Scripture and the purpose of the church. To be here is like being clean delivered from Egypt and quietly placed in the glorious new Jerusalem. To hear Master Latimer's lucid explanation of the Word is like hearing the golden voice of one of the prophets of old."

Pausing as he and Becon walked one afternoon, Latimer pointed to the southwest. "Across the miles lies my old diocese, which I may approach only in memory." Turning to the east he said, "Across those fields lie my Charnwood Hills and the valley of the Soar. Broad stretches of land that belong to my heart by God's gracious hand! But more than that, I have claimed great tracts of hearts for the Lord Christ. Much territory remains unclaimed. See to it, Thomas, that you gather your appointed harvest."

A large company was expected for supper that evening. The company gathered in the garden, made pleasant by a light breeze. As Latimer approached, his eye fell upon a young stranger. The face had a hard angle but was redeemed from harshness by a tenderness about the mouth. As the man's eyes met his, he saw that they were the deep blue of the summer sky.

The stranger detached himself from the group with which he stood and approached Latimer. "I am Augustine Bernher, sir," he said, his eyes shining. "I am a Swiss, recently arrived from the Continent. You are the reason for my coming here."

Suddenly, they were no longer two strangers, no longer an Englishman and a Swiss, no longer a young man and one growing old; they were friends. Their minds and hearts seemed to meet. Latimer could recall no experience like it.

They discovered that they had mutual friends. Bernher knew Coverdale and Hilles and others who had fled to the Continent after the Six Articles. He had met Cranmer on his way through London. He was now the guest of Robert Glover at Mancetter. What he had heard about Latimer had sent him to find him.

In the days that followed they were often together. Bernher joined Latimer and Becon on their walks. They laughed because Bernher, accustomed to the steeper slopes of his mountainous homeland, often outdistanced them. They would sit on some fallen log to rest.

"When I first knew Becon," said Latimer, "I was older than he is now. I had not long known the light of the true gospel, as it is in God's Word. That knowledge has come to you in your youth. You have the more years in which to learn of him and serve him. Long after I am gone, you will be helping to purify the church, to move it forward, and to spread the Truth."

"I daresay that will come about while you live, sir," said Bernher. "We may hope to work together in the Lord's vineyard. Surely the church's worst troubles in this land are behind her."

"The pendulum swings back and forth," said Becon. "Our King has not committed himself to the Reformation, although he has permitted it to advance within bounds. One never knows when he will change his mind and step backward, as he has often done."

Everyone was delighted with young Bernher and the pleasant contribution he made to the group. John Glover soon persuaded him to become his houseguest. So the unfolding of the friendship between Latimer and Bernher continued.

One September afternoon they walked alone, Becon being elsewhere. A companionable silence lay between them. It seemed to Latimer that Bernher, like his mountains, dwelt largely in silence. But when he spoke, what he said was worth hearing.

Now he broke the silence. "Sir, I would like to attach myself to you as a servant, if you would allow it."

Latimer wondered whether he had heard aright. *A servant? Bernher?* "I don't understand," he said.

"It is difficult to explain. We are friends, but to me it is more than that. You know so much that I too would know. I could say I wish to be your disciple. How better to accomplish this than for me to become your servant? I would be always at hand, to learn from watching as well as hearing you. I could act as your bodyservant and perhaps also as secretary."

"As you said," replied Latimer, "we are friends. What I know from the Scriptures I shall gladly impart to you. But for you to stoop to becoming my bodyservant? Unthinkable!"

"No stooping would be required, sir. I would count it a privilege. I am young and strong. You are not as young as you once were. Perhaps I could help preserve your strength for your labor in the Lord. I feel my extreme youth in comparison to your years but more so to your maturity in Christian matters. Might we not find such an arrangement mutually beneficial?"

Bernher would not be shaken in his determination. As of that moment, he spoke of Latimer as his master. He was unobtrusive, but always at hand when Latimer needed him. The strange arrangement proved eminently successful.

Latimer found himself indeed free to concentrate on the study of the Word without the distraction of certain mundane chores he had felt it necessary to perform for himself before. Bernher seem to know instinctively what needed to be done.

15

[1545]

A few weeks after Bernher entered Latimer's service, they started out with Becon for a walk. The weather threatened, but they decided this should not interfere with their outing.

As they reached the crest of a hill, Latimer said, "This is far enough. The wind is stronger than I thought."

They turned back down the hill to where the path wound through a wood. Bernher walked ahead, followed by Becon. Latimer trailed behind. The wind swept fiercely through the trees. Latimer heard a splintering crash and felt himself thrown to the ground.

The other two rushed back to find Latimer pinned face-down beneath an old elm. The trunk had missed him, but a large bough held him fast to the ground. The two younger men managed to maneuver the tree to one side sufficiently to free him.

The blow had stunned him. His first need was to recover his breath. Soon he was able to speak. He sought to reassure them that he was not badly hurt but felt far from certain himself.

"The extent of your injury remains to be seen," said Bernher. "Your back took a hard blow from that branch."

They tried to turn him, but he winced and almost fainted. "Perhaps the best way," he said, "is for me to try to rise to my knees. Then you could get me to my feet."

The first attempt failed. Latimer suffered more pain than he would admit. The next effort brought him to his feet. With their support he began a slow progress toward the house.

They soon had him in bed, but the pain grew worse. Bernher sat beside him through the night. Latimer slept little; Bernher did not sleep at all.

Within a week it was obvious that Latimer must have medical help. None existed in Warwickshire, or none worthy of the name.

"Butts could help, if I were in London," said Latimer.

"But going to London would break the terms the King put upon you," said Glover.

"If I don't get help," replied Latimer, "my back will break. Which matters most—a broken back or a broken agreement?"

Careless came when he heard of the accident. "With the present happy state of the Reformation," he said, "I doubt anything would be said if you quietly went to London."

"I *must* go," said Latimer. "I can't continue like this."

"Will you be able to ride that distance?" asked Glover.

"My old horse is gentle and slow," said Latimer. "Her age is telling on her. She will understand the need to go easy."

"Bernher is welcome to any horse he chooses from our stables," said Glover. "Shouldn't someone else go along too?"

Bernher spoke up in his quiet way. "I shall be able to care for my master with no help."

16

[1545]

Latimer remained three weeks with Butts, under whose skillful ministrations he felt steady improvement. At last nothing more could be done medically. Time would perhaps complete the cure.

He sent messages to Cranmer and Mrs. Statham. He did not wish his presence generally known. He decided to accept Mrs. Statham's insistent invitation to transfer to her house.

Cranmer had thought it unwise to visit him but had arranged for his pension to be delivered. They would meet at Lambeth as soon as Latimer could get about more comfortably.

According to her custom, Mrs. Statham put her patient to bed and pampered him in every way. Bernher made himself useful in the household, since his responsibilities to Latimer were light.

In November an unseasonable epidemic struck the area about Westminster. Whether plague or fever or a mixture of the two, no one seemed certain. It was less severe than usual, but the victims were numerous enough. Butts sent word that he was too much occupied with the stricken to visit Latimer.

Then Butts himself fell ill. On November 17 he died. Latimer grieved deeply. Butts had been his friend for many years and had done him innumerable favors. He had been a staunch supporter of the Reformation and had used considerable influence with the King. He would be missed in this latter capacity, but Latimer would miss him in a personal way.

An unutterable longing to see Cranmer seized him. He determined to risk a trip to Lambeth.

17

[1545]

It was a joyful reunion. Cranmer had little free time but insisted that Latimer remain. In that way they could use the available bits of time to catch up with all they needed to hear from each other. Latimer hesitated to remain overlong, lest news of his presence cause trouble. His objections were overruled.

Ralph Morice was still with Cranmer. Latimer found it good to renew his association with Nicholas Ridley, one of the archbishop's chaplains since 1537. Now Prebend of Westminster, he also served as one of the King's chaplains. Ridley, slow to reach his position as a Reformer, seemed intent on making up for lost time. He was an outstanding preacher.

"Weren't you instituted to the living of Herne some years ago?" asked Latimer as they conversed one evening.

"I am still there," Ridley said. "I come to London when duty requires, but I live at Herne. I believe that is one of your preaching points, that a man reside upon his living."

"Your years of study abroad must have been fruitful. You picked up where you left off at your return to Cambridge. Pembroke Hall is doubtless proud to have you as master."

"Clare Hall has cause to be proud of such a son as you."

"The years since my resignation as bishop have held little to be proud of. Not a sermon in more than seven years. Has the Lord retired me? You, of all people, must understand the frustration of not being allowed to preach."

"Don't say the years have held nothing. As I understand it, you may have touched as many lives away from the pulpit as you reached by your public preaching. You have had opportunity for study. What active preacher ever has time to fulfill a scholar's desire for deep study? Your voice will be heard again."

Latimer thought how the young face he first remembered had matured. The handsome features, the keen brown eyes were the same, but a depth of expression spoke of a close fellowship with Christ.

Parliament was to assemble before the end of the year. This accounted for Cranmer's busy schedule. Latimer returned to Mrs. Statham's. He must remain out of sight, though he fairly itched to be in the midst of it all.

In the early days of Parliament the King made a speech that sounded almost like a valedictory. Had he some premonition that his days were few? He expressed his devotion to his subjects, from lords and prelates to the least in the realm. He thanked them for their love and loyalty. His desire was for peace and harmony among his people. For this he still worked.

He put the blame for the discord still prevalent largely upon the "fathers and preachers of the spirituality."

"Alas," he said, "how can poor souls live in concord when you preachers sow discord by the sermons you preach? To you they look for light, but you bring them darkness. Amend these crimes and set forth God's Word, both by true preaching and example."

"He keeps me silent when I *would* preach," said Latimer.

18

[1546]

The King's determination to end dissension led to increased persecution of any who spoke out for a more sweeping Reformation. Latimer was acquainted with Anne Askew, a lady of good family who had often sat in his congregation. She loved the Scriptures and the doctrines of the Reformers. Because of this attachment to such teachings, her husband had driven her from home.

Her brother, a member of the royal bodyguard, arranged access for her to the court. The Queen and some of the ladies were already favorers of the same type of teaching.

In March 1546 Anne Askew was arrested on suspicion of denying the first of the Six Articles. When she was examined before Bonner, he ignored the protection enacted in 1544 for such cases. In defiance of the law he had her committed to prison.

Bonner continued his examination, trying without success to commit her to a denial of the Six Articles. At the end of March she was released, her friends being surety for her. Latimer was indignant over the affair but kept quiet; then he berated himself for not speaking out.

During Lent, Crome preached a sermon in which he said, "If masses avail souls in purgatory, as your bishops commonly preach, then it must be wrong in Parliament to abolish monasteries and chantries that were founded for saying masses for the dead. But if Parliament was right in dissolving the monasteries, then masses must be of no benefit to departed souls."

The inquisitors for detecting heresy seized him. When they could not reply to his insoluble dilemma, they referred him to the council.

Latimer, hearing of Crome's troubles, felt compelled to visit him. "I am grateful to you for coming," said Crome. "I hope you have not put yourself in danger. I must appear before the council, and who knows what the outcome will be?"

The outcome was that Crome recanted, as had happened before. Powerful he might be in logic and his proclamation of the Truth, but he weakened when faced by his judges. He was set free.

The matter was not at an end for Latimer, however. On May 13 he was summoned before the council. "You stand here accused," he was told, "as one who devised and counseled with Crome."

"I was in the company of Crome," replied Latimer, "after his first examination, and we did speak of his difficulties. He said something as to the matter of recanting or not recanting."

Such a reply made it impossible to prove anything against him. Having other cases to hear, they administered an oath to Latimer and handed him a list of questions he was to answer. They sent him to a quiet place to write his answers.

He turned through the papers. He let his mind go back to the faces about the table in the council chamber. Was it by coincidence or design that Cranmer was not among them this day?

He read the first question and wrote his answer. He pondered a bit over the second and scrawled an answer. At the third he put down his pen and read the rest of the questions. Frowning, he picked up his pen and considered once more the third question.

A troubling vision arose. He saw himself in another room, papers in hand. That time Stokesley had him in his power. Now Stokesley was gone, but were the others any improvement? He had feared to sign the articles presented by Stokesley, yet he had done so, had compromised his conscience and suffered in his soul.

The questions before him now were as sly as the articles had been. No matter how he answered, he might incriminate himself. His only crime was to return to London against the King's prohibition. Yet the questions required his opinion on subjects on which they had no right to question him.

He threw down the pen and called the guard. "Inform the lord chancellor and the other gentlemen that I earnestly desire to speak to them. I cannot proceed further until I do."

After some delay he was escorted to a room where Tunstal and Sir John Gage awaited him. "What is it, Latimer?" inquired Tunstal. "Why must you interrupt us at our business?"

"I confess, my lords, that I acted thoughtlessly when I swore to answer these questions before I had read them. I wish that some wise man had reminded me of the danger."

"Danger? What danger is there in putting down your clear answers to simply worded questions?" demanded Tunstal.

"Great danger, my lord," replied Latimer. "If I answer, I may be proceeded against more severely than I would under the rule of the Turk, though I live under the King's majesty."

"Explain yourself, Latimer. Enough of these riddles."

"I find it unfair to be called upon to answer for another man's fact," said Latimer. "I doubt whether it is his Highness's pleasure that I be so called and examined. Indeed, I should like to be permitted to speak with His Majesty."

His request seemed to stun the two men before whom he stood.

"Remember," said Latimer, "the Lord Cromwell represented to me as His Majesty's pleasure that I resign my bishopric. His Majesty denied it and pitied me for having been so deceived."

Tunstal left him with a promise to inform the rest of the council of his unprecedented request.

Having begun to exert himself, Latimer felt his old energies and a certain recklessness rising. When he stood again before the council, he added to his previous statements.

"I believe that some of your number," he began, resting his eyes upon Gardiner, "have procured this against me for malice. I would particularly name the Bishop of Winchester. As evidence of malice, I remind my lord of accusations against me of seditious preaching upon an occasion in the King's chamber at Westminster. More recently, I cite the letter he wrote to the Lord Cromwell against the sermon I preached at Convocation in 1536."

Latimer saw that the veins in the back of the bishop's hands were jumping, a telltale sign of anger. His tone was controlled.

"I harbor no malice toward you, Master Latimer. On the contrary, I possess a love toward you, in that I have done for you any kindness I could. You have no cause to be offended with me, though I admit that I am seldom content with your doctrine."

Latimer wondered whether Gardiner thought him taken in by such hypocrisy. They returned him to his quiet place, saying, "It is your duty to answer the questions."

He would have to comply. Once more he picked up the pen, with his jaw set. He would give them answers! He wrote slowly at first, but with increasing speed as he moved from one question to the next. Before nightfall, he turned the papers in. He was detained until the next day when he would again be called.

He spent a long time that night exulting to Bernher about having answered without really answering. "I would like to see their faces," he cried.

·Bernher feared the outcome. Finally, his master gave him the key to his attitude.

"Nothing I say or do will affect the outcome. They have already determined their course of action. Answering the questions as I did is only part of the game to confuse them. But they will win. My only hope lies in a plea before the King."

When he stood before them next day, Tunstal said, "You are a shrewd man, Latimer. You answered the questions, but in such a fashion that we know no more than we did at the beginning."

He was turned over to a committee, which spent the afternoon questioning him on the matter of the Six Articles. The lengthy interrogation produced nothing.

The King had Latimer brought before him. He covered the same material in a superficial manner. His lack of interest was a disappointment. At last they pronounced him "untractable." The fact remained that he had sympathized with offenders.

On a bright afternoon in mid-May the fields about Greenwich were clad in springtime majesty. But Latimer did not see it. He was led to a barge on the Thames and conducted to the Tower.

19

[1546]

He recalled as he was led across the green that his last visit here had been to see Barnes. Not for the first time the question came, Would his end be the same as that of Barnes?

The warder conducted him to what was called the Garden Tower, since it overlooked the lieutenant's garden. Bernher was permitted to remain to serve him. They even allowed Bernher to go to Mrs. Statham's and bring his belongings.

It was whispered that the council dispatched a man to Baxterley to search his possessions for incriminating evidence.

It was not the most disagreeable of imprisonments. The warders were friendly. When the weather permitted, he was allowed to walk in the garden. He had money from his pension, so Bernher could supplement his provisions. Even physically he was well enough, except for the persistent pain in his back.

But he soon had cause for keen anguish of mind on behalf of another. The chain of events and the details had to be pieced together, and it was long before he had the whole story.

Early in June, Anne Askew was summoned to Greenwich to appear before the same section of the Privy Council that had tried Latimer. For nearly a week the courageous lady was subjected to rigorous questioning. Gardiner and Wriothesley took the lead. They tried to get her to acknowledge that in the sacrament there was flesh, blood, and bone. This she refused to do.

Gardiner, always ready to employ his great learning, engaged her in metaphysical discussions until she was exhausted. Each council member took his turn at questioning, giving her no rest.

They threatened her with the terrible death of a heretic. She stood by her beliefs with inconceivable strength. At last she told them that she feared she was about to die and asked permission to speak with Master Latimer. Her request was denied.

When Latimer was told of this part of her trial, he was enraged. "To think of so treating a gentlewoman and not permitting her an interview with a preacher in her extremity."

She was transferred to Newgate Prison and arraigned at the Guildhall. Public indignation over her trial made it impossible to keep the proceedings secret. All London knew the details.

The accusation was the same as before. "That which you call your God," she replied, "it is a piece of bread; for more proof thereof, let it but lie in the box for three months and it will be moldy and so turn to nothing that is good."

When they utterly failed to make her change her views, they condemned her to the flames. She was returned to the Tower and at last permitted to see Latimer. He comforted her, reading from the Scriptures and praying with her. He also had the painful privilege of listening to the whole ugly story of her examination before the council, which she intended to commit to writing.

Her enemies on the council were not satisfied. She had not named others who might be implicated. They asked whether any ladies at court had helped her, and glancing at Cranmer, whether any of the council had maintained her. She did not answer.

Latimer was incensed when he heard what came next. The lord chancellor, along with that scoundrel Richard Rich, came to the Tower to question her. Obtaining no satisfaction, they put her on the rack and with their own hands turned the wheels. They kept her there a long time, angry because she refused to cry out.

When they finally had the lieutenant release her, she fainted. They took pains to revive her. Then Wriothesley kept her sitting upon the bare floor for two hours more, insisting that she reveal the names of others. At last she was carried to her cell and placed upon her bed, nearer dead than alive.

The lieutenant, who related the episode to Latimer, had gone to report it to the King. The King was outraged that his lord chancellor, whose duty it was to insure observance of the law, had taken it into his own hands and perpetrated this atrocity.

Called to the Guildhall at the same time as Anne Askew was Shaxton. What he had done to bring this to pass, Latimer never knew. Rather than face death at the stake, he completely reversed all his former opinions. In a stroke of pure malice they appointed him to preach the sermon at Anne's execution.

"I must refuse to judge him," said Latimer, "for I have not yet stood where he stood. But in the light of Anne Askew's good account of herself, it does make Shaxton look bad."

As if to bring the fist down more heavily upon the Reformers, a proclamation issued in July prohibited the circulation of the works of Frith, Tyndale, Becon, Barnes, and others of doubtful orthodoxy. It was all depressing.

On July 16 Anne Askew was carried to the place of execution in a chair. She could not walk as her bones had been dislocated on the rack. Pardon was offered if she would recant.

"I came not hither," she replied, "to deny my Lord."

"A very great lady," cried Latimer through tears. "No finer example of Christian constancy have we seen. But Gardiner will not yet be satisfied. His zeal has fed upon his victory."

That night the old dream of leaping flames and the faces of his friends returned. Bernher came to his side to wake him as he cried out in his sleep, "Bilney! Barnes! No!" He asked Bernher to light a candle and read to him from God's Word.

20

[1546–1547]

Latimer felt a compulsion to seek out the passages of Scripture dealing with the Sacrament of the Lord's Supper. He pondered upon the beliefs of the church concerning the mass and tried to put the two together. He had read what Bullinger and others on the Continent wrote in opposition to the traditional doctrine, but their arguments had not convinced him.

Could Anne Askew have been right in her courageous stand against transubstantiation? She had been certain enough of her belief to lay down her life for it. The question nagged at him.

An uneasiness began to stir in the back of his mind about viewing the mass as propitiatory sacrifice. As he pondered the New Testament passages, he felt increasingly disturbed.

Cranmer dared not visit the Tower, but he encouraged Bernher to come to Lambeth for books and special items of food for Latimer. The archbishop had utmost confidence in Bernher, knowing that his communication would reach Latimer's ears alone. When Cranmer was not available, Ralph Morice had his orders.

Bernher returned one day with an amazing story. Latimer had known that the Queen held Reformation doctrines and hoped to lead the King in that direction. Apparently she had taken a misstep. His Majesty, suffering constant pain from his ulcerated leg, took badly her vigorous defense of her opinions as opposed to his.

"Are you presuming to become a doctor," he asked, "and to instruct us rather than to be instructed of us? Must I face the prospect of being taught by my own wife in my old age?"

Gardiner, who happened to be present, moved at once. The King had not hesitated at other times to act against a Queen with whom he was displeased. They might now bring to death a great patron of heresy and strike terror into all Protestant hearts.

Gardiner and Wriothesley approached the angry King and persuaded him that the Queen was indeed a heretic. They urged that she be punished as an example to other heretics. He consented to her imprisonment in the Tower and signed the document they presented. Gardiner was confident that the step to the block would be a short one.

A friend of the Queen hurried to inform Cranmer that the Queen's life hung by a thread. Cranmer sought an audience and informed the Queen of her danger. She could hardly believe him. The matter with the King had seemed so trivial. Convinced of the seriousness of her position, she implored him to help her.

Cranmer outlined a plan and urged her to follow it. She must at once make peace with the King, using all her powers of persuasion and even flattery. She would say that to divert his thoughts from the pain he suffered, she had chosen to debate with him. She had no intention of offending him. She merely wanted him to confute her statements. Thus, she would learn from him.

When Gardiner and Wriothesley entered, with guards from the Tower, they found the King with his Queen happily by his side. He looked at them as if he had no idea why they were there.

Wriothesley hesitantly presented the paper that the King had signed. His Majesty snatched it from his hand and tore it to shreds. Turning to Wriothesley, he denounced him as a beast, a fool, a knave. He struck Gardiner's name from the list of his Privy Council and forbade him to appear in his presence again.

Latimer derived satisfaction from Gardiner's fall. Hope for his own safety rose a bit. But, knowing the King's changeable disposition, thought of the stake was never far from his mind.

Jealousy between the Duke of Norfolk and the relatives of Jane Seymour increased. Norfolk represented the chief family of the English aristocracy; the Seymour brothers claimed high position as uncles of the heir to the throne. A power struggle after the King's death could result in the loss of the throne to young Edward. True to form, His Majesty acted.

The Duke of Norfolk and his son, the Earl of Surrey, entered the Tower on December 12. They were accused of "conspiring to take upon them the government of the kingdom during His Majesty's life, and to get the lord prince into their hands after his death." The truth of the charge was debatable. But, seeming to realize his time was short, the King pressed on rapidly.

Surrey went to the block on January 21, found guilty of treason. He had assumed the armorial bearings of Edward the Confessor, thus threatening the established succession.

Hasty proceedings against Norfolk were completed with royal assent on January 27. The execution was set for daybreak.

It did not take place. Before daybreak, the King was dead.

Part Five

IN THE PULPIT ONCE MORE

"I have an appointment
with Her Majesty."
[1547–1553]

1

[1547]

Latimer received the news of the King's death with mixed emotions. The first response was a feeling of relief. For months, even years, he had lived in expectation of being called up for execution. Even when the threat was not imminent, the shadow remained. Next came the thought that now he would be free. Would he also be free to preach?

Yet within his heart was sorrow. He had never lost respect for the Sovereign, however they had disagreed and whatever treatment he had received. For the most part the King had shown him kindness and courtesy.

No one knew better than Latimer that Henry had not produced the Reformation. It had sprung up and made considerable progress long before Henry began thinking of divorce. If the Pope had permitted the divorce from Catherine of Aragon, the King might never have thought of breaking with him.

When it suited his purpose, the King had gone along with the Reformation. Cranmer had appeared on the scene at the right moment. And Cromwell. By their efforts the King moved in the necessary direction—to a point. But Gardiner was there too.

"When the archbishop reached the King, sir," said Bernher, "he was beyond speech, but he clasped Cranmer's hand. When asked for a sign that he did put his trust wholly in Jesus Christ for salvation, he tightened his grip on Cranmer's hand and was gone."

"Cranmer accepted this as assurance that all was well with the King's soul?" asked Latimer.

"He so reported to the council. He is deeply grieved; he loved the King."

Henry had appointed a council of sixteen to act during his son's minority. The chief four were Cranmer, Wriothesley, Tunstal, and Edward Seymour. Gardiner, to his chagrin, was excluded and termed "a willful man not meet to be about my son."

In December when Henry had drawn up the Council of Regency, Sir Anthony Browne had questioned the omission of Gardiner. "Hold your peace," the King had growled. "Of good purpose, I left him out. I could use him and rule him to all manner of purposes as you could never do."

A few days after the council first met, Wriothesley was removed and restricted to his own house. Edward Seymour was chosen to head the council and made governor of the King's person. He expected to continue moving with the Reformation.

On February 16 Seymour was made Duke of Somerset. Four days later the Archbishop of Canterbury crowned a little boy, not yet ten years of age, Edward VI, King of England. The Tower gates swung open at the usual general pardon. From this privilege, the Duke of Norfolk was specifically excluded, but Latimer was free.

A year in custody of the Bishop of Chichester; six years of banishment from places he longed to visit; ten dreary months in the Tower—now freedom. Suddenly he could not face it.

Bernher bustled about packing. Now he looked at Latimer who was making no move toward departure. "Sir, it is time."

With a lingering feeling of uncertainty, Latimer rose. He slowly crossed to the open door of his cell and stepped through. Everything was strangely silent.

Cranmer had arranged that he come directly to Lambeth. As the boat approached Westminster, they heard church bells ringing and other sounds of celebration. Latimer thought of the elation that had swept the land at the birth of this same small boy. No one had imagined he would be King so soon.

They said Edward was deeply devout. His teachers were from among the Reformers. Katherine Parr had exerted a godly influence upon him. He would be strong and godly, wise and worthy. Of this Latimer felt sure.

Latimer's friends rejoiced at his return. But for him, a sense of unreality persisted. He maintained a certain reserve, saying little. His friends found this totally unlike him.

At last he said, "I cannot step from the Tower to freedom and friendship so abruptly. I must adjust. Be patient with me."

2

[1547]

In March Somerset became Protector of the Realm and was largely in control, though the council still sat. The young King with red hair, fair skin, and rare beauty of face charmed his subjects. In public he received enthusiastic acclaim.

By degrees Latimer broke out of his shell, with Bernher to assist him. They visited the friends in Milk Street. As he conversed with those who clustered about him, he felt drawn back into the mainstream of life from which he had been cut off.

"The nobles who bought the abbey lands are arrogant in their treatment of us," they told him. "When a lease expires it is not renewed. Those who rent find rents raised, then raised again."

226

"My old farm," said another, "has been made pasture land for sheep. Even the common lands have been enclosed, and we are shut out. I came to London to seek work, but none is to be found."

"The wealthy are buying out the small landowners," said yet another. "My old landlord cared about his tenants; the new one does not even know us. All he cares about is the rent."

When Latimer asked about the situation in the courts, he was told that a poor man got no attention. His case was put off endlessly unless he had something to put in the judge's hand.

"Can't you do something for us?" asked one. "Time was when men brought their complaints to you, and you got them heard."

"I was Bishop of Worcester then with the Lord Cromwell as my friend. He would see justice done in cases I referred to him."

"Then can nothing be done for us? Are we without hope?"

"I will do my utmost," said Latimer. "God himself is our most powerful aid. Change is already under way with King Edward and the Lord Protector zealous for the Reformation. Improvement in our social and economic order must come. In the meantime I have access to a few ears in high places."

On Sundays Latimer visited the parish churches about London. In a few, old friends still preached the true gospel; in all too many, he found the same discouraging condition of years before.

He complained to Cranmer. "Priests *won't* preach, but truth is most of them *can't* preach, even if they would. They have no learning, no knowledge of God's Word, nothing to impart."

"What you say is true," replied Cranmer. "We plan to attack it in two ways. I'll need your help."

Latimer's heart beat faster at the prospect of a job to do.

"We are at work on a *Book of Homilies*, little sermons covering the major emphases of a Christian's daily life. People need help in knowing how to read the Bible profitably."

"Some priests have difficulty reading at all."

"They should be able to read these homilies. Each will be required to read one every Sunday, a ready-made sermon. If he has been preaching error, this will insure that he preaches the Truth."

"What help do you want from me?" asked Latimer.

"If you can put into a homily some of the substance of your preaching, think what it will mean. We'll have hundreds of 'Latimers' all over the realm preaching your sermon."

"It won't come out on paper as it does when spoken."

"But think what an improvement over what goes on now. I have written several. Ridley and Becon are helping. Would you write one called 'Against Strife and Contention'?"

"Sounds like a goodly topic for me," said Latimer, with a chuckle. "Could I see the ones already done?"

"You need not follow the pattern too closely."

"Have I ever done that?"

"I have more for you to do," said Cranmer. "We mean to send out all the solid preachers of the Word available to preach as often as possible. We need live preaching by living preachers."

"You'll have to get this muzzle off me first."

"It takes so long to work through all the channels. How would you feel about having your bishopric restored to you?"

Latimer looked up quickly. "Is that a possibility?"

"Almost certainly, it will be offered you."

Latimer meditated upon this. "I don't think so. My years are too many. I doubt I'll ever recover from the injury to my back. I suffer a great deal, though I try not to groan audibly."

"Your health will improve. You're no older than I."

"I am no administrator. I have no patience for spending long periods in Parliament. I am a preacher. God gave me that talent. I must employ it to the fullest in the years left me."

Cranmer shrugged. "I am not convinced. However, it is a matter that can come up again."

"It need not come up again," said Latimer. "You were present when I vowed never to wear the rochet again."

"People change their minds. The rochet is not so heavy. My burden is heavier. We bear the burdens God calls us to."

In July appeared a document entitled "The names of certain persons that have had license to preach under the ecclesiastical seal since July 1547." One of the names was Hugh Latimer. Now he was not only *free;* he was *free to preach.*

3

[1547]

"After the impatience of the past years," he said to Bernher, "you might think I would rush out, climb into the nearest pulpit, and preach. It isn't that simple. I spent eight years storing up knowledge of the Scriptures. Now I must shape it into sermons. The Truth God intends me to proclaim will emerge gradually. I want to preach no 'half-baked' sermons."

The council intended to advance slowly. It was important to get the bulk of the people behind the Reformation.

The *Book of Homilies* was a start. As Cranmer had planned, preachers were appointed by authority of the King. A living preacher could reach hearts more surely than a sermon read by an incapable priest. The list included Latimer, Rowland Taylor, Matthew Parker, Thomas Becon, Nicholas Ridley, and others.

"Rowland Taylor!" said Latimer upon hearing the names. "Where is he now? He was on your staff when I was bishop."

"I appointed him to the living of Hadleigh," replied Cranmer. "He wanted to marry when the pressure of the Six Articles slacked off. He is a powerful man in the pulpit."

"He's a powerful man physically," said Latimer. "He was one of Bilney's converts."

"He may have been Bilney's convert," said Cranmer, "but he spoke of your sermons as the source of his spiritual nourishment. Bilney had preached at Hadleigh, and Taylor found a well-established group of Christians, great lovers of Scripture."

In August the council sent out Injunctions similar to those issued by Cromwell and the ones Latimer used in his diocese. They needed to be restated in a new regime. An addition was that a copy of the English translation of Erasmus's *Paraphrase of the Gospels* be placed in every church for the use of the people.

Bishops were to preach at least four times a year and were to insist that their chaplains preach. Care was to be taken that no one teach against the doctrines set forth in the homilies.

"Telling a man what to do does not insure compliance," said Latimer. "Teaching a person what he should believe does not automatically change his convictions."

"We must start with a step in the right direction," pointed out Cranmer. "Some of the bishops won't like it much."

"I imagine Bonner and Gardiner will be the first ones you hear from," said Latimer.

A few days later as the two friends took an afternoon walk in the gardens, Cranmer said, "You were not wrong about protests. Bonner has already appeared, declaring that he will observe the injunctions and use the homilies *if* he does not find them 'repugnant to God's law and the statutes of the church.'"

"True to form. Always rough and never ready."

"Today he reconsidered, revoked his protest, and begged pardon. He was forgiven, but rather than risk having a precedent set for evil example, he will spend a time in the Fleet."

Latimer could not resist a chuckle.

"We can silence their protests," said Cranmer soberly, "but we cannot change their minds nor their hearts. We need men on the bench who will give wholehearted support to the Reformation."

Latimer sensed the archbishop's unspoken plea that he relent and return to his bishopric. He said nothing. For him this was a closed issue. He would not wear the rochet again.

When the visitors reached the Diocese of Winchester with the Injunctions, Gardiner instructed his subordinates to receive them and submit. He went to London to express his indignation.

He came before the council with a rather different air from Bonner. He would not promise to receive the Injunctions as given. The *Homilies* he found contrary to Scripture. The translation of Erasmus's *Paraphrase* was extremely inaccurate.

"Which," said Cranmer to Latimer, "is amusing, since the Princess Mary translated the Gospel of John into English. Surely, Gardiner would not question her orthodoxy."

Latimer laughed. "What was the outcome?"

"We found him quite untractable. . . ."

"The very word he used of me when he sent me to the Tower."

"He joined Bonner in the Fleet. As I said, we can silence him, but we cannot change his mind—or heart."

"There is a difference between those two," said Latimer.

"Quite right. Gardiner's innate superiority is plain to see. He usually defends the old learning in a dignified manner; he is wrong, but sincerely wrong. Bonner changes with the wind. His beliefs go no deeper than what is politic for his safety."

In that same month of September the archbishop was able to add a new name to supporters of the Reformation among the bishops. Nicholas Ridley was consecrated Bishop of Rochester.

4

[1547]

Parliament assembled in November. Most of their actions were to the advantage of the Reformation: the Bloody Statute was abolished; the excessively cruel additions to the treason acts were swept away; even the old enactment against Lollards went. Thus, the persecuting laws were removed from the books.

The most decisive step yet taken was the reforming of the mass. The sacrament was to be administered in both kinds to all Christians. Too long, the cup had been denied to the laity. The Scriptures taught that the Lord's Supper was meant to be a communion, not a solitary act of a priest. The sacrament should not be denied to anyone who devoutly and humbly desired it.

Latimer's mind was confused on the subject of the mass. He no longer saw it as a sacrifice made by the priest that truly averted God's wrath, but he could not abandon the doctrine of transubstantiation and of the corporeal presence.

A late evening hour presented an opportunity to bring up the subject to Cranmer, who was a bit evasive. "I must admit," he said, "that my belief on the subject has changed. I wish Ridley might talk to you. He has made a deeper investigation."

"It is *your* help I need, Thomas," said Latimer.

Looking straight into Latimer's eyes, Cranmer said, "In the closing months of last year I abandoned the Roman doctrine of the mass. Ridley produced convincing evidence that it was not a primitive doctrine of the church. I find no sign of it in Scripture; I now believe it to be blasphemous."

Latimer had expected something like this, yet he found himself profoundly shocked. His face must have shown it.

"You asked me to tell you, Hugh," said Cranmer. "The change did not come easily. Ridley described my first reaction as one of alarm. My inclination was to clutch the old teaching more closely, which I did. Then last year, I took a second look at Ridley's arguments. To my utter surprise, I found myself won over by his lucid thinking. I started to say, 'suddenly won over,' but it was not sudden. The teaching had been working in my mind for months; only my own realization was sudden."

"I would like to hear the arguments from you. You were convinced, not by Ridley, but by the Truth, if truth it is."

Cranmer stated the arguments in his own terms, telling how Ridley had come upon a book by a ninth-century monk in which were clear indications that the present doctrine had not existed in the time of the apostles and early church.

As Latimer lay in bed that night, he continued to mull over what he had heard. He was sure by now that the mass was not a truly propitiatory sacrifice, but what of transubstantiation and the corporeal presence?

Unable to sleep, he rose and lit a candle. The fire had gone out, and the room was chilly, so he wrapped himself in a cloak. Fixing his glasses on his nose, he read again the passages about the Lord's Supper from the Gospels and from 1 Corinthians.

After a time he said, "No *denial* of transubstantiation nor of the corporeal presence appears. But do I find an *affirmation?* Can it be that the doctrine is merely part of an old tradition? Can the teaching of the church be wrong? Have I assumed that Scripture teaches it simply because the church does?"

A chill swept over him, and it was not totally physical. The thought of deliberately breaking with a fundamental doctrine of the church shook him. Ceremonies and peripheral practices were one thing. This was a firm pillar of the church's teaching. He had not before actually considered making the break. Now he *was* considering it. Suddenly, he felt afraid.

He crept back to bed and eventually slept. Strange dreams disturbed him. Anne Askew appeared, looking at him intently. She vanished, only to reappear on the rack with Wriothesley turning the wheel. Her pleading eyes were again upon him. Next she stood at the stake, flames leaping about her. He could see the agony in her eyes, still fixed upon him. Then came the old dream of Bilney, Barnes, Garrett, and Jerome.

He must have cried out. He was suddenly awake but still engulfed in the horror this dream always brought. When he slept again, he was plunged into yet another dream.

He seemed to be on a journey. Walking determinedly along, he approached a boundary. Here he stopped, uncertain what to do. He must either return into familiar territory or he must step across into strange new ground. If he took that forward step, there would be no returning.

When he woke again, the sky was growing rosy. Bernher had a fire glowing on the hearth. He rose for his reading and prayer, but the spell of the final dream remained.

A bit later he said to Bernher, "See whether you can arrange a time for me to see the archbishop today."

"I am afraid, sir, that won't be easy. He is quite busy with the affairs of Parliament."

"He will know that I would not trouble him unless it was urgent. I rather think he will be expecting to hear from me. Ask that he arrange for Bishop Ridley to be present as well."

5

[1547]

Cranmer's stooped shoulders and tired eyes betrayed his weariness as they met that evening at nine.

How old he looks, thought Latimer. *His beard makes such a difference.*

Always clean-shaven before, he had let his beard grow since Henry's death, a token of his deep grief.

They settled themselves about the fire in Cranmer's study. No one seemed eager to speak. Then Latimer broke the silence. "I have reached a point at which I must make a decision. I am not yet certain what it must be. I need your assistance."

He told them of his thoughts as he searched the Scriptures for an answer to his questions. He mentioned the new questions that had arisen in his mind. He related the troubled dreams and the gripping reality of the final one.

"Will you state quite clearly for me your beliefs on transubstantiation, on the corporeal presence, and on the mass as propitiatory sacrifice. Tell me not only your beliefs, but the *basis* of your beliefs. I *must* know the Truth."

Cranmer indicated that Ridley should speak first. Ridley demurred in Cranmer's favor. In the end, each spoke, one breaking in to supplement or elucidate the statement of the other.

Only the low burning of the fire made them aware of the passage of time. Cranmer interrupted long enough to summon a servant to replenish the fire. Latimer sat completely absorbed. Finally, they ceased to speak and looked at him.

He sighed deeply. "I have been a long time arriving," he said. "The church has been wrong. I have long known the mass is no propitiatory sacrifice. When Christ died on the cross, it was the one and only time. When he said, 'It is finished,' he meant it. Now I am convinced that the bread and wine remain bread and wine. The priest performs no miracle. As the body is nourished by the bread and wine, so the soul is nourished by the body and blood of Christ. His presence in the sacrament is real, quite real, but it is spiritual, not corporeal."

"I told you," said Cranmer, "that I held out for a long time. I still need God's guidance into a fuller understanding."

"I too have much to learn," said Latimer. "But at this moment, I return to the point I reached in my dream. I take a deliberate step across the boundary into new territory, from whence is no returning. It is the final step in a long journey."

He sank back into his chair, surprised at the dimensions of his relief. "I have never gone into deep study of doctrine and theology as you two have," he said. "Yet from where I now stand, I have a clear view of something extraordinary. For the first time I recognize that two great doctrines of the Reformation stand like stalwart pillars. Both are in direct opposition to the old teaching of the church but both are firmly based in Scripture. One is justification by faith, which I discovered the night of Bilney's 'confession.' When I took that first step, I was far from realizing the full implications. I only knew that Christ's death on the cross was for my salvation and I had nothing to fear.

"From there I journeyed at a snail's pace. I had to release my hold on one thing after another as to the church's ceremonies and practices that were obscuring the Cross from the people. Not only the abuses but the practices that led to abuse had to go. As I read the Bible, I discovered the true meaning of the Christian life. Tonight I have laid firm hold upon the other great doctrine: the New Testament teaching on the Holy Communion. I admit the church has been wrong; I have stepped forward into the new Truth. It has been a long journey."

"More than twenty years, isn't it?" asked Cranmer.

"Nearly twenty-four," said Latimer. "God is patient. Now that I have in a sense completed my journey into faith, I hope to grow in that faith and be used as never before, God willing."

"I think perhaps God deliberately paced your journey," said Cranmer. "Had you reached this point much earlier, you might not be here to talk of it today."

"You may be right," said Latimer. "Yet within my heart, a voice even now whispers, 'This step will cost you your life.'"

"Not now," protested Ridley. "The persecutions are over. The church is well on the road to reform. It is only a matter of time before the doctrine of the mass is replaced by the Truth into which you have just entered."

"Perhaps," said Latimer, "but the premonition remains."

Cranmer looked thoughtful. "Strange how we stubbornly read into Scripture our own preconceived ideas."

"As to the issue of the mass," said Latimer, "you do mean to declare openly the Truth you have discovered? You admit that the mass is blasphemous. Can you remain silent?"

"Not silent," said Cranmer, "but careful. It took the Truth so long to get through to us. Can you suppose the people will be able to change quickly? And change by legislation is not the solution. I mean to assemble a group of the bishops early in the year to see what conclusions we can reach."

"What of the book you plan to write?" asked Ridley.

"The points I will attempt to refute are the corporeal presence, transubstantiation, the idolatrous adoration of the host, the teaching that even the wicked eat the natural body and blood of Christ, and the blasphemous sacrifice of the mass.

"Even now a few preachers will begin to teach the falsity of the doctrine of the mass and to instruct the people in the New Testament teaching. As time passes, it will take hold. If we make too big an issue of it, we will stir opposition. His Majesty cannot permit diversity of opinion on such an issue. At all reasonable costs we must avoid the revival of persecution."

Latimer went to bed exhilarated, but he slept immediately, dreamlessly, and deeply.

6

[1547]

On a morning early in December Bernher placed a letter before Latimer. He broke the seal and scanned the contents, then sat back in his chair and looked at Bernher without speaking.

"What is it, sir?" asked Bernher. "Pleasant news, I hope? The glow on your face would indicate as much."

Latimer rose from his chair, seized the astonished Bernher in a quick embrace, then handed him the letter. "Pleasant news, indeed! I am at last to preach. Four Sundays in January at Paul's Cross. What a place to resume my public ministry!"

Latimer spent hours in his room working on the sermons. The initial excitement simmered down into a warm glow. He spread out his sheets of paper and worked on four messages at once.

Bernher ventured to ask, "Upon what subjects will you preach, sir? You recall that I have never heard you preach."

"I find that hard to realize. You seem to have been with me always. I intend to preach all four sermons on 'The Plough.'"

"'The Plough,' sir? Four sermons on that subject?"

"I'm afraid I can tell you no more now. You might publicize my subject. A bit of curiosity could make for better listeners."

"Indeed, sir, I shall drop a hint here and there. But you will not lack for eager listeners. The talk is everywhere that Latimer will preach again after more than eight years' silence. You have quite a reputation, sir."

"That last statement could be taken in more than one way, depending upon who is discussing my reputation."

7

[1548]

At sunup on January 1 people were already moving through the streets toward St. Paul's. By the hour for the sermon the crowd in the churchyard overflowed into the street. The gallery reserved for upper clergy and noblemen was filled.

When the preacher began to speak, a hush fell over the throng. The lesson from the epistle for the day was from Romans 15. Latimer took his text from the fourth verse. According to his old custom, he read it several times. His voice rang out clearly, so that even those in the rear ranks must have heard.

"All things that are written, are written for our learning and knowledge," he said. "All things that are written in God's Book, in the Bible Book, in the Book of Holy Scriptures, are written to be our doctrine.

"I will speak to you today, and in future weeks, on what may appear a strange topic—'The Plough.' I propose to declare to you two things: one, what seed should be sown in God's field; the other, who should do the ploughing and plant the seed."

He proceeded, as of old, to pronounce condemnation upon sins of living, not merely of opinion. His native humor crept in, delighting his hearers. His words, so carefully thought-out beforehand, seemed to flow without effort from some deep place within his soul.

The sermon ended, and the enthusiastic crowd almost mobbed him. The common people were still hungry for the Word and heard it gladly, even as they had in Jesus' day. The thrill, the unutterable ecstasy of again proclaiming the Word of Life to eager hearers possessed him.

"Your preaching is the same," said Cranmer, "yet different. You have grown in these eight years. I perceive a depth, a richness, an increased insight into the Word, a clarity of expression that exceeds your old style."

Morice agreed and added, "John Cheke used to say, 'I have an ear for other preachers, but I have a *heart* for Latimer.' The heart is there—your heart, God's heart—and it overflows in the words you speak. Your sermons used to be like a spring of water; this one was like a deep, rushing stream."

"Such power," said Cranmer, "cannot but have its effect. Not only on the common people, but upon the council. With the mode of your expression now, we will see changes in matters upon which some of us have been hammering for years."

"What kind of changes?" asked Latimer.

"You spoke against the superstitious use of hallowed candles. You disapproved the giving of ashes on Ash Wednesday. You condemned images. You attributed to the Devil's influence the continued use of Latin in the service of the church."

"You think my sermons can bring about changes in those matters?" asked Latimer.

"Not just your sermons, the hand of God. When one attempts to break a large stone, he applies blow after blow with no evident effect. Then one more blow shatters the rock, and the work is done. I think you have struck some final blows. Rocks that have long seemed impervious may suddenly fall apart. Yet it is God's timing, God's work."

"Have you given him the other news?" asked Morice.

"Latimer, you will be asked to give a sermon each Wednesday in Lent before His Majesty and the court at Westminster."

Latimer caught his breath. "After all the silent years, it seems the Lord is overwhelming me with opportunities to preach. Nowhere am I so content as when I stand to proclaim the gospel of Jesus Christ."

8

[1548]

The day arrived for the final sermon on "The Plough." When Latimer rose before dawn, rain was falling and the temperature had dropped.

"This will mean preaching in the Shrouds today," he said to Bernher. "The crowd will be diminished. People will not venture forth in such weather; some must come from great distances."

"They will come, sir," said Bernher. "It will take more than a fall of rain to keep them away. I have heard their remarks. It is a blessing they would not miss. They will come."

"You could be prejudiced, you know. But we'll take with cheerful heart what God sends and trust him for the results."

The area known as the Shrouds was located at the side of the cathedral where a covering offered some protection from bad weather. A movable pulpit was placed against the wall.

Bernher was right. The people came. Some were doomed to disappointment, for space in the sheltered area was limited. But they stayed, in spite of the continued light rain.

Though cold without, a fire burned in Latimer's heart. "I liken preaching," he said, "to a ploughman's labor, and a prelate to a ploughman. Whom do I call a prelate? Any man who has a flock to be taught. And well may the preacher and the ploughman be likened to each other."

The term "prelate" generally applied to a bishop, but he would broaden the application. The lowest cleric had as great responsibility, according to his task, as the highest bishop.

He spoke from the memory of his boyhood in Leicestershire, describing the continual work required. He brought before their eyes the ploughman setting forth his plough, as many of his listeners had done, then the tilling of the land—breaking it in furrows, ridging it up again. At another time he must harrow and clot the field, put in fertilizer and plant a hedge about it. He had, in due time, to dig and weed, purge and make clean with never an idle day.

"Just as diverse," he said, "is the work of the preacher. He must first bring his parishioners to a faith that embraces Christ and trusts in his merits. I speak of a living faith, a justifying faith that makes a man righteous without respect to works. He must then confirm them in that faith, casting them down with the law and threatenings of God for sin. He must ridge them up with the gospel and the promise of God's favor, now weeding them by telling them their faults and making them forsake their sin. He must perhaps clot them by breaking their stony hearts, making them to have hearts of flesh apt for doctrine to enter in. He must teach them to know God rightly and to know and do with diligence their duty to God and neighbor. So, a prelate as God's ploughman has a continual work to do."

Latimer would forever after understand the fulfillment of John the Baptist's purpose in being "the voice of one crying in the wilderness." For he was conscious only of being a voice.

"Great are the labors of prelates," he said, "and they ought to have good livings, to feed more adequately their flocks. Preaching the Word of God to the people is called meat. Scripture calls it meat, not strawberries that come but once a year and last only a brief time. The people must have meat daily. Many make a strawberry of it, ministering it but once a year. But such is not the office of a good prelate. For Christ says, 'Who is a wise and faithful servant? He that giveth meat in due time.'

"It is God's work, God's plough, and that plough God would have still going. Those who loiter and live idly are not good prelates. Many such are now in England. 'But cursed be he that doth the work of God negligently.' A sore word for them that are negligent in discharging their office."

He shifted now to the condition of the poor in London and of its rich citizens, pointing out the extent to which pride, covetousness, cruelty, oppression, and superstition reigned.

"In times past men were full of compassion, but now there is none. For in London their brother dies in the streets for cold; he lies sick at the door and perishes for hunger. Charity is waxed cold. Oh, London, London! Repent, repent!"

He took a jab at bishops who esteemed their position in the House of Lords so greatly that they forgot their duties. "Ye that are prelates, look well to your office. For right prelating is laboring, not lording. Ye lords who live like loiterers, look well to your office. The plough is your office and charge. Preach and teach and let your plough be doing."

He hammered the theme home with words from his heart. "Since lording and loitering have come up, preaching has come down, contrary to the apostles' time: They preached and lorded not; now they lord and preach not. Ever since prelates were made lords and nobles, the plough stands idle. No work is done. The people starve. As the body wastes away for lack of bodily meat, so the soul pines away for default of spiritual meat."

Now he threw out a provocative question, "Do you know who is the most diligent bishop and prelate in all England?" He paused just long enough to be certain he had every ear.

"I will tell you: It is the Devil. He is the most diligent preacher of all. He is never out of his diocese or away from his cure. He is ever at his plough. No lording or loitering can hinder him. You shall never find him idle, I warrant."

A ripple of amusement was heard. But Latimer was serious.

"No words suffice to tell of his diligent labors, how he hinders religion and teaches all kinds of Popery. He devises a multitude of ways to deface and obscure God's glory. Away with books and up with candles. Away with Bibles and up with beads. Up with all superstition and idolatry: censing, painting of images, candles, palms, ashes, holy water, and new service of man's inventing. Down with Christ's cross and up with the purgatory pickpurse. Away with clothing the naked, up with decking images. Let all things be done in Latin. God's Word may in no wise be translated into English."

He followed with a call to unpreaching prelates. "Learn of the Devil to be diligent in doing your office. If you will not learn of God nor of good men, for shame learn of the Devil. Oh, that our prelates would be as diligent to sow the corn of good doctrine as Satan is to sow cockle and darnel."

Putting his hand to his ear, as if listening, he continued. "Do I hear someone say, 'What, sir, are you in on the Devil's counsel, so well acquainted that you know all this to be true?' I know him too well and have obeyed him a little too much in condescending to some follies. I know him as other men do, that he is always busy and always following his plough."

He now made his chief point about the Devil's work. "His great aim, of course, is to bring out of focus the institution of the Lord's Supper and Christ's cross. For that is the very place he lost his right. The Devil thought when he brought Christ to the cross, all was sure; he had won. But he was doomed to disappointment. For according to Christ's own word, that lifting up on the cross was the very point upon which the Devil's judgment was assured, his casting out was there made certain."

He had reached the very heart of his message. In 1539 when he last preached, he would not have spoken as he was about to.

"When Christ said, 'When I shall be lifted up from the earth, I will draw all things unto myself,' he meant the drawing of man's soul unto salvation. He said he would do it *per semetipsum,* by his own self. He meant his own sacrifice on the cross for the redemption of mankind, not the sacrifice of the mass to be offered by a church official. Who can offer him but himself? He was both the offerer and the offering. Yet this is the mark at which the Devil still shoots, seeking to make empty the cross of Christ and to mingle or mix confusingly the institution of the Lord's Supper. He cannot bring it about, but he has never stopped trying through fifteen hundred years. There are those today who would have us saved by a daily sacrifice."

A deep hush had fallen over the congregation. He moved on. "The Devil would have us put our faith in the so-called sacrifice of the priest, whereas Christ would have us to trust in his only sacrifice. He was 'the Lamb that hath been slain from the beginning of the world,' and therefore is called *juge sacrificium*, a continual sacrifice. This is not for the continuance of the mass as the blanchers, the hinderers, have wrested it, and as I myself once did understand it. Then let us trust only in his death and look for no other propitiatory sacrifice."

He expressed concern for the young King's guidance of the church. There would be those who would try to turn him aside from the Truth. He closed with a fourfold appeal for prayer for His Majesty. "Let us pray for him. Pray for him, good people, pray for him. You have great cause and need to pray for him."

9

[1548]

All London rang with the excitement caused by Latimer's preaching. His name was on every tongue. Bits of his sermons were quoted and argued about in every place. He was besieged with invitations to preach in numerous parish churches.

Wherever he went, it was the same story. Churches were crowded to capacity, and those unable to get in sought to elbow their way nearer to windows and doors in an effort to hear. In at least one place a window was broken by those determined to hear. At whatever cost the main thing was to hear Latimer.

On the first Wednesday of Lent Latimer began his series of sermons about "Restitution." The King was already an admirer of Latimer and had himself named him as one of the Lenten preachers. A pulpit had been set up in the King's garden at Westminster, where a larger crowd could be accommodated than in the chapel.

Latimer climbed the steps to the ornate pulpit and faced a gallery, which connected two wings of the palace. At a window, just opposite the preacher, sat Edward VI with an alert countenance and an eager expression. With him sat the Lord Protector and other members of the council. A throng of men and women of the noble classes stood about the garden with a few fortunate enough to gain entrance. Some moved up to sit upon the pulpit steps.

The preacher directed his sermon to the King, almost as if in private conversation. The lad's earnest gaze never left his face. This was Latimer's opportunity to speak God's Word to one who would continue to reign long after he himself was gone.

Yet as he addressed the King, he spoke to the needs of all his hearers. He called for repentance. This meant turning from unlawful practices, from illegal gain, from uncharitable ways, especially of those growing rich at the expense of the poor.

"You will say to me, 'What shall we do with the goods gotten by unlawful means?' I tell you, make restitution, the only way that pleases God. This may be done either by *affect* or by *effect*. In *affect*, that is by intention, when there is no means of restoring the goods. In *effect*, when it is possible and is so done. For unlawful goods ought to be restored. Without restitution, look not for salvation."

Aware of the displeasure he was causing a number of his hearers, he continued. " 'Restitution,' you will say. 'Why should he preach on restitution? Let him preach on contrition and let restitution alone. We can never make restitution.' Then if you will not make restitution, you shall go to the Devil for it. Now choose either restitution or else endless damnation."

His message was neither soft nor easy.

10

[1548]

It was Friday evening just two days later. Supper was served early on the short winter days, and Latimer had just excused himself from the table. Sermon preparation left him little leisure.

Fixing his thoughts upon the sermon of Wednesday past, he drew from his folio the outline for the next one. He pondered at the same time the remarks he had heard and those that others had passed on to him regarding the previous sermon. He would not follow his outline slavishly but would make alterations as needed to incorporate these reactions.

Just then Bernher knocked gently on the door. "I dislike to disturb you, sir, but you have a visitor. He gives his name as John Bradford and says his business is urgent."

"Then, Austy," said Latimer, removing his spectacles, "you must show him in. He is, I believe, a stranger, and strangers must be kindly received. We might entertain an angel unawares."

"A red-bearded angel then, sir," said Bernher.

The young man who presently stood before him was exceedingly thin. Was it this or something in his expression that made Latimer think of Bilney? It was not his height. He was tall and carried himself erect. The rich auburn beard was accompanied by the usual faintly ruddy complexion. Altogether Latimer's first impression of John Bradford was favorable even before he spoke.

"I made bold to come to you, sir," he said, "because I was in the King's garden on Wednesday, and my heart was stabbed as with a knife by what I heard. Since it was you, as God's surgeon, who made the wound, I am sure you will continue the treatment and offer the means of healing."

He identified himself as a student of Common Law at the Inner Temple. "But I am scarcely the man I was when I first came there. It pleased God to turn my heart to the true knowledge and obedience of the gospel of Christ our Savior. Through the kindness of your relative Thomas Sampson, I came to the understanding of the Scriptures and know my sins to be forgiven."

"Ah, yes, his wife is the daughter of one of my sisters. But what of this heartwound for which you hold me responsible?"

"For some years I was a servant to Sir John Harrington. As the King's treasurer at Boulogne, he made use of my abilities. Among other things, I served as paymaster. In 1544 Sir John committed a fraud to the deceiving of the King. I had no part in this, yet I am guilty for I knew of it and did not report it, but concealed it. Since I turned to Christ, this has caused me uneasiness. When you spoke of restitution, I was stabbed with the conviction that I must act. A wrong has been done; restitution must be made. But how? It is I who am convicted of the sin, yet another bears responsibility for it."

Latimer looked into the face of the earnest young man for some time before replying. The expression of the eyes as well as the tone of the words carried a sweetness Latimer found rare. Again he thought of Bilney.

"It is well that the sword of the Spirit has pierced," he said. "I suggest that you write to your former employer of your experience. Say that you believe he will want to right the wrong by returning the money. Another King is on the throne, but the fraud involved the treasury of the King, not the individual. You need not threaten but hint that unless he agrees to make restitution, you will go to the council with the story, taking your own part of the blame for having concealed the deed. God will doubtless honor such an effort to clear the slate."

Bradford appeared relieved. "If he agrees and returns the money, what then?"

"Secret restitution is acceptable. You may bring the money to me, and I will pass it along to the council without naming names. If I know the council members, they will be glad enough to receive the money without question."

"I thank you, sir," said Bradford. "I shall write the letter tonight. As soon as he sends any part of the money, I shall put it into your hands. A great burden has been lifted."

The matter settled, Latimer could have risen as a sign for the other's departure. Bradford could have made a move to leave. But neither stirred. Then the talk began again, and each seemed full of things to say. He felt, even in this first meeting, a comradeship akin to that he had with his older friends.

They parted with the expressed intention of meeting again, soon. When Bernher came in to see what his master's requirements were for the night, Latimer said, "Austy, you thought to bring me a visitor but you did more. You brought me a friend."

"But, sir, I thought you said he was a stranger to you."

"So he was when he entered; he departed a friend. Never have I been so quickly drawn to a man before unless it was to *you,* Austy. It was much the same. Do you remember?"

"How could I ever forget, sir? It was the finest day of my life except for the day I met my Savior."

Latimer bade him an affectionate good night. He knew the unshed tears he saw in the younger man's eyes were of gratitude.

11

[1548]

The word heard most about London during Lent was *restitution.* Bradford's heart was by no means the only one convicted as Latimer wielded the sword of the Spirit. But he made enemies as well.

With the court preaching behind him Latimer turned his attention to a matter that troubled him increasingly: the struggles of the poor against the oppression of the rich. The people in Milk Street had not exaggerated. Enclosures of common lands went on at a rapid pace. Landowners often resorted to "rack-renting," the practice of raising the rent until it was almost as much as the land was worth. Leaseholders were refused renewal when the leases expired.

The "new rich," especially, could not seem to get enough land. Monastery lands had come into the possession of many of them. The personal touch between landowner and tenant was lost.

Latimer could see an enormous change in the rural situation in his own lifetime. His father, a respected member of the yeoman class, had rented from the lord of the manor. He grazed his cattle on the common grazing land. He was careful not to let his sheep overgraze the land.

When Latimer and his sisters, as children, had trudged to the manor house to pay the rent, they were kindly received. The relationship between lord and tenant was cordial. They worshiped together at the gray stone church on Sundays and feast days.

Now absentee landlordism prevailed. The owner neither knew nor cared about the condition of his tenants. If high rents failed to bring in enough money, he turned cultivated land into pasture for sheep. One man could tend many sheep on land that had formerly been tilled by a dozen or more.

Latimer was appalled by the number of vagrants. No work was available. Many turned to petty thievery or worse to live. Vagrancy laws placed some in prison, but this in no way bettered their condition once they were released.

Sections of the city inhabited by the poorer classes were unbelievably crowded, and living conditions were indescribable. Many of these people had farmed until forced off the land.

As Latimer delved into facts and cases, he found others who were as disturbed as he. He began to meet with Thomas Lever, an outstanding preacher, Robert Crowley, another preacher, Bishop John Cory, Sir Thomas Smith, a Secretary of State, and John Hales, M.P. They discussed the problem, decided on a strategy, and mapped out plans.

The public soon designated them "Commonwealth Men." Their aim was to denounce the covetous landlords from the pulpit, in Parliament, and wherever else a word could be spoken and to demand a more equitable deal for the common man.

Their efforts bore fruit. June 1 saw a proclamation issued against enclosures, the neglect of houses that had fallen into decay, and the unlawful conversion of arable land into pasture. Commissioners were appointed to look into abuses and to spend time in the country explaining the law to the people and urging patience until it could be enforced as intended.

Increasingly, Latimer came to be looked upon as the friend of the poor and oppressed. Where possible he put in a word with the Lord Protector, who intervened in a number of cases.

In late summer Gardiner, who had been released from the Fleet in January, preached a sermon that got him in trouble again. He could not let disputed theological issues alone. This time he went to the Tower. Even there, he spent his time writing letters and papers denouncing Reformation beliefs.

"I have a strange feeling about Gardiner," said Latimer to Bernher. "Even as he was instrumental in bringing Barnes to the stake, I believe he will be preserved in the Tower for bringing me to the same place. He is being kept for a special purpose."

"God forbid, sir, that such a thing should happen. What could bring you under condemnation? The King is committed to the Reformation. I pray you to put the thought from your mind."

"Tuck it away in *your* mind, Austy."

The strain of constant preaching and of concern for others took its toll. Latimer began to suffer more with his back, and his headaches returned. He could not bear to think of slowing his pace. Preaching was his life. He *must* preach.

12

[1548]

Cranmer's plan for a unified Reformed Church took more definite shape as he continued his urgent letters to Reformers on the Continent. He shared his plan with them and asked their help in bringing it to reality.

Already the changed atmosphere of Edward's reign had drawn Ochino and Peter Martyr from the Continent. In recent months Francis Dryander and John à Lasco had arrived.

Since Cranmer envisioned a universal church, he wanted the assistance of all learned men available, so that they might do away with controversies and build up a system of true doctrine.

"A noble idea," said Latimer, "but learned men tend to have strong opinions with which they are often reluctant to part."

Cranmer reminded him gently that with God all things are possible. The love of God and the power of his Holy Spirit would make it possible. Latimer gave his friend an affectionate look.

Cranmer went to work in a practical way with bishops, notable divines, and as many of the Continental visitors as would sit with them. The *Book of Common Prayer* reached its completed form in time for Parliament to begin action upon it in November.

A new service book was needed, but not everyone agreed with Cranmer's solution. That it was in English ruffled some feathers. Cranmer had to make concessions to the conservative prelates if the work was ever to be passed by Parliament.

The chief bone of contention was the question of the Eucharist. For some days the House of Lords became a debating school. Bonner and Tunstal were the chief champions of the Romish position. Gardiner must have ground his teeth in frustration as he sat helplessly in the Tower.

Cranmer was the defender of the Reformed doctrine on the Communion. If they had not known before, men now learned that their archbishop no longer believed in transubstantiation. Cranmer surprised members of Parliament with his learning and skill in debate. Many had thought him ignorant of theology and knowledgeable only in matters of government.

The year ended with the issue still unsettled.

13

[1549]

The House of Commons on January 8 requested of Protector Somerset that Latimer be restored to his bishopric. For it to come from this unexpected source touched Latimer deeply.

"Many have spoken of me as a *quondam*—a has-been," he said. "Well, I am content to be a *quondam*. But I thank God that it is not so much as one who proved unworthy, but as one who of his own choice is become a *quondam*. It is too late to go back."

Ten days later, the Lord High Admiral, Thomas Seymour, brother to the Lord Protector, uncle to the King, was committed to the Tower on a number of charges. Latimer had long had his doubts about the character of this man.

In contrast to this dark matter, Parliament passed the Act of Uniformity. This established the authority of the new *Book of Common Prayer,* to be in use by Pentecost. This marked a victory for the Reformed party, but not a clear-cut one. Ambiguities remained that Cranmer wished he might have cleared up.

In February Parliament relaxed the laws against marriage of the clergy. The law declared with the apostle that "marriage is honorable in all."

Bankside in Southwark had long been notorious for its "stews" or brothels. The officials cleaned up the district and ousted the occupants of the houses. But Latimer discovered that they had merely relocated and were continuing their activities.

He was told of an immoral woman who had given birth to triplets whom she strangled. Taken to court for murder, she was let off when friends sent her money with which to pay the judge. In the same court a poor woman was dragged before the judge, accused of stealing a few rags from a hedge. Having no friends, she was condemned to death by hanging.

"The injustice of such things!" cried Latimer. "I shall certainly speak of bribery when I preach before the King."

Latimer now applied himself with zeal to preparation of his Lenten sermons. He would preach before the court on Fridays, beginning on March 8.

He had slipped into the habit of discussing his sermon plans with Bernher. The content of their daily conversations seemed to come forth sooner or later from the pulpit.

"What theme will you use this year, sir?" asked Bernher.

"I plan to use Romans 15:4 for all seven sermons. It says that the things written in Scripture are intended to teach us, so that through endurance and the encouragement we receive, we may have hope. I may be accused of weakening in my old age for choosing such a general text."

"Surely, sir, no one would dare to think that."

"The purpose of the Scriptures *is* to teach us. If the church is to be brought out of the evils that surround and even invade it, we need all the wisdom, encouragement, and endurance God's Word can supply. I mean to enumerate the ills and point out how certain passages in the Bible deal with them."

"Bishop Ridley speaks of you, sir, as the 'Apostle to the English.' He says that God's hand is so obviously on you that no one who hears can fail to be impressed. I can only agree."

"Such terminology should not be thus lightly applied. My friends see me for more than I am and praise me beyond my due."

"The people in the streets use like terms, sir. 'If England ever had a prophet, then good Father Latimer is the one,' and, 'Moses, Jeremiah, and Elijah did never declare the true message of God to their rulers and people with a more sincere spirit, faithful mind, and godly zeal than old Father Latimer.'"

Latimer closed his eyes. "This puts a burden upon me, Austy. I only want to declare God's message. When I see wrongs, I speak. Silence would be sin. I love my God and my country too much to permit God's will and Word to remain obscured. Any power I have is God-given. May I never fear to declare the message to all men, from the King to the beggar by the door."

"It is what the people want, sir. Thomas Becon says that no man can go away from your preaching unchanged. Either he will be convicted and let God change his life, or he will be enraged and become harder in his sinful ways."

"Enough of this! I have a sermon to prepare. Your business is to be my sounding board and help me organize my thoughts."

"Then let us proceed, sir. What will be your approach?"

"I will read the description laid out in Scripture as a model for Israel's King and apply the pattern to our King. He fits the specification that he be one of the brethren, no foreigner, and that he be a godly King. He is warned against excesses. He is not to multiply horses too much, nor add unto himself too much gold and silver, nor have too many wives."

Hearing a choking sound, he looked up. "What is it, Austy? You are trying, rather unsuccessfully, to restrain laughter."

"Pardon me, sir, but you may occasion amusement by warning the son of King Henry VIII against too many wives."

"I see the ludicrous aspect, but I do not intend it in a light way. Some may smile, but the advice is from God's Word."

"I see the point in the matter of wives, sir," said Austy. "But in horses, silver, and gold, how may one determine? What one considers too much could seem but little to another."

"You are right. No one will be able to tell the King. He will need a pair of spectacles, so that he may see for himself."

"A pair of spectacles, sir?"

"Yes, with two clear lenses. One lens must be a continuing faith in God; the other, fervent charity toward his Christian brother. With such spectacles he can avoid the greed that makes a man have too much to the detriment of those with too little."

"An admirable illustration, sir, that the King will not forget. May others of the court use the same spectacles."

"One has but to look about at the situation today," said Latimer. " 'Too much' wealth, 'too much' land, 'too much' power in the hands of too few. One 'too much' leads to another."

"It is as if men know not when to stop," said Austy.

"When the King comes of age, he will seek to put right the things so out of frame. He will set an example by letting down his own lands and urging his subjects to follow. I also find hope in my belief that the Day of Judgment is near, the time when God himself will set all things right. On that day the true King must say to some, 'Go, ye cursed, into everlasting judgment,' but to others, 'Come, ye blessed of my Father, possess the kingdom prepared for you from the beginning of the world.' "

"Well, sir, you seem to have your first sermon well in hand. I hear that one of your admirers has arranged for the messages to be written down and published."

"You manage to come upon information that escapes me. Now I shall need my writing materials, if you please."

14

[1549]

The pulpit was placed in the garden as last year. Latimer followed the theme he had outlined to Austy. A week later in preaching upon the need for justice in the courts, he directed a strong appeal to the Lord Protector.

"I desire my Lord Protector's grace to hear me in this matter, that your Grace himself would hear poor men's suits, and let them not be delayed. The saying is, money is heard everywhere. The rich man soon has an end of his matter; others go home weeping, for any help they cannot obtain at any judge's hand. Hear men's suits yourself, I require you in God's behalf."

The date for the execution of the Lord Admiral Thomas Seymour was set for Wednesday before Latimer's third sermon on Friday. The condemned man's friends among the courtiers insisted upon his innocence. They muttered that his brother had betrayed him, but the general opinion was that they were deceived.

Latimer tried to hold his feelings in check and his tongue under control. He had never liked nor trusted the man.

"One day when I was prisoner in the Bishop of Chichester's house," he said to Austy, "a cry came from a woman being brought along Chancery Lane toward Smithfield. As she saw me at the gate, she called out, 'They are leading me to my death. I am a wicked woman and have lived a sinful life. It was that fine gentleman Lord Thomas Seymour who first seduced me and sent me into a life of sin. But for him, I might not be facing my death today.'

"I began to watch the man. I have never seen anything to denote a change in his life's direction."

Latimer could not keep the facts from parading through his mind. Seymour's treachery in connection with the mint and sums he had taken for himself was undeniable. He had bargained with pirates who sailed the Channel, agreeing to look away while they robbed English vessels in return for a share of the spoils.

What angered Latimer most was Seymour's marriage to the Queen Dowager, Katherine Parr. He attempted to win, in order, the hand of the Princess Mary, the Princess Elizabeth, and even, so it was rumored, Anne of Cleves. His success in finally marrying a lady for whom Latimer had the highest regard rankled in his mind. She had demeaned herself no little by becoming Seymour's wife.

The previous summer the Lady Katherine Seymour had died soon after giving birth to a daughter. The circumstances of her death were questionable. A rumor, immediately hushed up, said that her husband had poisoned her.

His latest act had been in connection with the King's person. Seymour had corrupted the servants to gain their allegiance and conceived a plan for seizing the King. Obtaining a key to the royal bedroom, he arranged that no one be on duty on a certain night. What probably saved the King's life was the alarm given by the barking of his dog when his uncle entered the room.

These were the thoughts Latimer could not dispel as he sat at his desk on Tuesday morning, striving to concentrate on Friday's sermon. A note arrived informing him that the lord admiral requested Father Latimer to visit him in the Tower.

"Who am I," he said, "to begrudge a man on his way to hell a chance to repent and be saved? Yet, I could wish he had called upon someone else. May the Lord forgive me my reluctance."

Bernher never let his master go forth alone. For a man of his dignity, it was not proper, he said. Latimer knew it was because he worried over his increasingly feeble physical state.

Seymour was seated on a three-legged stool before a small fire. He rose and nodded as Latimer entered. The man strongly resembled his brother, with high, broad forehead and large straight nose. The features were regular and to a degree, handsome. But the hard eyes and arrogant expression abruptly differentiated his character from that of the Protector.

An hour passed before Latimer summoned the guard. His hands were clenched and his heart cold as he rejoined Bernher. He said nothing of what had passed between him and the prisoner. The talk had not been in the nature of a confession made to a priest. Still, Latimer determined to lock it within his breast and never speak of it. He had never felt so in dread for a man before.

He only said to Bernher, "I do not know why he sent for *me.*"

Some strange power compelled Latimer to attend the execution. He examined the face of the man intently. Just before he knelt to lay his head on the block, he turned to whisper something to the lieutenant's servant. Two strokes of the axe were required for the accomplishment of its purpose. Someone remarked, "He died bravely. He must have been innocent."

"Bravely or brazenly?" muttered Latimer as he turned away.

15

[1549]

The hue and cry over the admiral's death had not died down when Latimer stood to preach on Friday. Feeling was strong against the Protector for assenting to his brother's death. A cloud of animosity dimmed the brightness of a sun-filled day. An oppressiveness pushed against Latimer and made speaking difficult. He had to struggle to get his words out.

He preached the message against bribery that he had prepared, but he knew he must speak in some manner to the present situation. He breathed a prayer for guidance.

"A word or two more, and I commit you to God. I hear that you talk otherwise than becomes Christian subjects. You take upon you to judge the judgments of judges. The King may err, the council may err, the Parliament houses may err. I pray daily that they may not. But whatever they decree, we should stand by it and receive it obediently, if it is not manifestly wicked and directly against the law of God. Therefore, I exhort you, pronounce in good part all the facts and deeds of the judges."

A murmur of disapproval swept the crowd. "I would have you aware that God says, 'I will visit.' Indeed he comes with two visitations. The first is when he reveals his Word by preachers. When the first is accepted, the second need not come. The second is vengeance, when God comes in judgment. If his Word is despised, he comes with this second visitation. We have now a first visitation in England. Let us beware of the second."

After a slight pause he concluded, "I will leave off here, for I think you know what I mean well enough."

He was unprepared for the violent reaction. He was taken to task for his veiled remarks about the man who had died. Much of their anger was for his rebuking their judgment of judges.

He found himself bristling against their reaction. He had stated only the truth. They claimed Seymour was innocent, did they? He would be making some additions to next week's sermon.

16

[1549]

Before the day ended, a note arrived from Cranmer asking that Latimer meet him in his study before the evening meal. A formal appointment was almost a necessity for private conversation. The palace was full of guests, with the Reformers from the Continent and the usual ecclesiastical personnel who came and went.

"You preached under difficulties today," Cranmer said.

"You could sense that, could you?" asked Latimer.

"The currents of feeling were heavy. You managed well."

"You did not call me here just to say that."

"You are right. Some additional information has come to light. Seymour spoke to the lieutenant's servant as he knelt at the block, saying, 'Bid my servant speed the thing he knows of.' "

"I saw him speak, but I could not hear his words."

"Someone overheard, and a man was dispatched to seize the servant. Upon close questioning he admitted that his master had given him two little notes to deliver. They were found sewed neatly between the lining and the sole of his velvet shoe."

"Did you see them?" inquired Latimer, leaning forward.

"Not only that. I took the liberty of bringing them with me for further inspection. I knew you would be interested."

"Of course I am! Something so important that a man spends his last breath insuring delivery—don't keep me in suspense."

"Read them and tell me what you think."

The ink was pale, the pen poor. Latimer managed to decipher the words on the first paper; the second was almost identical. Utterly shocked by what he read, he looked at Cranmer.

"Unbelievable!" he said. "How fortunate they were found. Think of the damage they could have caused."

"If they had reached the hands of the Lady Mary and the Lady Elizabeth—but do you suppose they would have heeded the advice?"

"Who knows? To think of that wretch spending his last hours inciting the princesses to conspiracy against the Lord Protector. God knows there are those who would support such an effort."

"I fear you are right about that," said Cranmer. "The Lord Protector is a good man with fine qualities. Perhaps, he is *too* good. He is not a true politician. He lacks the instinct, the wariness, the sense of timing, even the patience of, say—a Thomas Cromwell. A gap yawns between his purposes and their carrying out. We live in a difficult world."

"Where did Seymour get pen and ink? His writing is barely legible. The paper I suppose he tore from his Prayer Book."

"The pen appears to have been a point plucked from an aiglet in his hose. A poor writing implement. As for ink—soot from the fireplace, blood from a prick of his finger, or wine from his meal? The important thing is that the notes were recovered."

"Some still insist, 'The man died boldly; he would not have done so had he not been in a just quarrel,'" said Latimer. "The boldness of his death proves nothing. The uncovering of this act proves that he persisted in his unrepentant way to the end."

"Yet it is not for us to pass judgment upon his final end. That is God's prerogative. Shall we not leave it in his hands?"

Latimer sighed deeply. "I suppose you are right. He suffered two strokes of the axe. Who can deny that he might have repented between the first blow and the second? So I leave him to God. But I have my own ideas about his final destination."

As Latimer rose, Cranmer laid a hand on his shoulder and looked earnestly into his eyes. "I feel for you, my friend. What they say is true. You *are* God's prophet. You see so deeply and must proclaim relentlessly the Truth he reveals. It is a heartbreaking task. The suffering is greater than most men ever imagine. Just remember to be as charitable as you know how."

Latimer glimpsed tears in Cranmer's eyes as they parted.

17
[1549]

A continuous rain fell on Tuesday afternoon. Gloom from the outside pervaded Latimer's heart as he huddled near the fire, trying to decide on the changes needed in Friday's sermon.

He found it difficult to concentrate. Though he rarely spoke of it, he was seldom free from pain. Damp weather aggravated his back problem, and today a throbbing pain in his shoulder added to his misery. Austy was away. With determination he picked up his pen and began to write.

A tapping sounded at the door, which opened to admit a tall dripping figure. It was John Bradford.

"John!" he cried. "Could I have chosen the person I most needed at this moment, it would have been you."

Latimer had learned more about Bradford since last they met. Apparently he came from a wealthy family. When he first came to the Inner Temple, he wore fine clothes and adorned himself with chains and rings of obvious value. After his conversion he sold his jewelry and used the proceeds in ministering to the poor.

He had adopted a frugal lifestyle, seldom eating more than one meal a day. He slept only four hours a night, engaging in study and prayer while others slept.

All this strengthened Latimer's first impression that Bradford was somehow like Bilney. The same habits, the same lifestyle, the same devotion to the Lord Christ and his Word.

"Are you finding Cambridge more to your liking than you did the Inner Temple? You are at Catharine Hall, I believe."

"Life at Cambridge is a great change, sir, especially since my studies lead in a different direction. I am preparing for the ministry, and that makes for a changed outlook on everything. I am at Catharine Hall, but I expect to transfer to Pembroke."

"Ah, so Bishop Ridley has been at you!"

"As Master of Pembroke, he insists I transfer. The Master of Catharine is eager that I remain there. But it seems settled that I go to Pembroke."

"Excellent! You follow in the train of godly men. I suppose the Reformers no longer gather at the White Horse Inn?"

"Hardly at all, sir. We can meet openly and freely. The White Horse would scarcely accommodate such a large group."

"Do you ever walk on Castle Hill? That was a favorite walk of Bilney's and mine."

"I walk there often. It is still known as Heretics' Hill. The prison stands nearby and the hospital. I visit them as often as time permits."

"As delighted as I am to see you, I can't help but wonder why you are here at this particular time," said Latimer.

He reached inside his shirt, untied a thin leather thong, and withdrew a bag that he dropped on the table before Latimer.

"It is the greater part of the restitution money we spoke of last year. Will you be so good as to deliver it to the council?"

Latimer untied the cord and emptied a pile of coins upon the table— crowns, sovereigns, nobles, angels, and a few shillings. Bradford stooped to retrieve two small silver pieces, which had rolled off onto the floor. When they finished counting, the coins stood in neat piles, shining in the firelight.

"Three hundred and twenty-three pounds for the royal treasury," said Latimer. "And a lighter heart, also a lighter purse, for your former employer."

"He was not eager to restore the money. I used a bit of a threat. This is all he could get together now. It may take another year to obtain the balance. *My* heart is lighter too."

"Neither his name nor yours will come into it," said Latimer. "God sees and recognizes the source. Man has no need to. The wrong is righted. I will deliver it to the council."

Austy returned as the coins were being restored to their bag. Latimer tied the mouth and handed the sack to Austy. "Put it in a safe place. I will have need of it on Thursday."

As Bradford reached for his cloak, Latimer said, "Your coming has been like the emerging of the sun from behind the clouds. You provide the medicine I need and make me feel strong and, if not young, at least less old."

18

[1549]

Latimer stood at his window and breathed the fragrance of daffodils. The effect of Bradford's visit lingered.

"Come, Austy," he said, turning from the window. "Get the little bag I gave you on Tuesday. Cranmer tells me the council meets this morning. We have a trip to make to the palace."

Admitted to the council chamber, he gave his usual cheery greeting. Without delay he dropped the bag on the table in front of the Lord Protector, saying, "A sum due His Majesty's treasury. My sermons last year on the subject 'Restitution' have borne fruit. I see no reason to reveal names or circumstances. Will you be so good as to make a count and give me a receipt?"

In his sermon next day he made mention of the crimes of the late lord admiral, with emphasis on the final deed of the notes. Any claim that the man had suffered unjustly he put to rest. As to his ultimate fate before God, he would make no pronouncement. Repentance *might* have come between one blow of the axe and another. Latimer's tone indicated his doubt. He held the man up as a warning to any who might be tempted to follow the same path.

These remarks made up only a small part of his sermon. He urged his hearers to let the Word of God as he preached it enter into their hearts and bear fruit. Someone had earlier pronounced his sermons "unfruitful." Fruitfulness, or lack of it, he reminded them was not in his hands.

"I am called by God to preach," he said. "God must work in your hearts to nurture the seed and bring it to fruitfulness. It lies not in me to make it fruitful. Yet preaching is necessary. Take away preaching and you take away salvation."

With deep feeling he spoke of faith as he understood it. "Faith is a lady, a duchess, a great woman. She is never alone. A gentleman-usher goes before her, and where he is not, there is not Lady Faith. This gentleman-usher is called Knowledge of Sins, or confession of the same. After Lady Faith a great train follows. These are Good Works wrought in Christ and for his glory."

He was disappointed that so many seemed to remember nothing of his sermon except his remarks about the late lord admiral.

"You should not speak ill of the dead," he was told. But how else could he speak of such a man as Seymour? And he had felt he must speak. Others needed to be warned. He recalled Cranmer's tears and better understood his words. Whether he qualified as prophet or apostle he was in doubt. God's instrument he was and must continue to be.

19

[1549]

On Monday a communication bearing the seal of the King's council reached Latimer. As he opened it, he gave an exclamation that brought Austy to his side. "Can you believe it, Austy? The council sends me a reward for returning the money last week. The King wishes me to have fifty pounds for my trouble. Fifty pounds, Austy, for doing my duty. It will meet my needs for some time."

Cranmer's *Book of Common Prayer* came from the printer and was ready for distribution. It was to be put into use in June on Whitsunday. Latimer held his copy lovingly in his hands. Whatever its lacks or imperfections, it was far superior to anything that had existed before, other than the Scriptures.

He preached his last sermon before the King on Good Friday. The fact that the messages would appear in print meant their witness would be multiplied.

Latimer took some time in these spring days to assess the direction of his preaching. He discerned a subtle change. For more than twenty years he had taken his stand against the errors, superstitions, and immoralities of the Church of Rome. While this was not yet finished, he now aimed his arrows at slightly different targets.

Even with the gospel light shining upon the church, the same old vices and sins prevailed, clothed perhaps in new dress. The sale of spiritual offices continued. Claims of loyalty to the Reformation moved hand-in-hand with breaking the laws of God in a scandalous manner. The nobility took first place in practice of open adultery. One wife was lightly discarded for another, even to the third or fourth. Graft and extortion were accepted means of enlarging one's wealth. Bribery was a way of life.

With sadness of heart Latimer spoke of it to Austy. "I supposed, rather naively, that turning to Reformed doctrine would produce a heart change in others as it did in me. I expected a resultant caring for one's fellowman and a loving effort to meet the needs of the unfortunate. But hearts seem harder than ever."

"It seems often the case, sir," said Austy, "with a popular cause. When the Church of Rome was in the ascendancy, many of the influential stood firmly behind it. When the Reformed Church came into prominence, a number of the same people aligned themselves with it. They could as easily change again, for there has been no heart change and their behavior is not affected."

"Yet I must continue to fight evil. I preach Christ's love for sinners and his willingness to save. But I cannot neglect the message of judgment against those who walk in wicked ways while professing a belief they do not hold in their hearts."

"Think of Isaiah and Jeremiah, sir," said Austy.

"How often I do think of them, and with more sympathy and understanding than I once did. They spent their lives preaching to men with sin-blinded eyes and sin-deafened ears and no willingness to repent. Yet, they preached on. So must I."

The *Book of Common Prayer* was well received, generally, in the London churches. Elsewhere it caused disturbances. Cranmer was kept busy refuting unreasonable objections. An army was sent to one or two places to restore order.

When Ridley made a visit in midsummer to Cambridge, he found the buildings of Clare Hall robbed of furnishings and stripped to the bare walls. Plans were on foot for incorporating it into a school for the study of Law. Ridley made an immediate appeal to the Lord Protector.

"I consider," he wrote, "not only what learned men may be brought up there in time to come but also how many have come there in the past, some such as I think it is hard for a whole university to match with the like. I will speak now of but one. I mean Master Latimer, who is, as I think, a man appointed of God and endued with excellent gifts of grace to set forth God's Word. In my judgment not only the King's Majesty and his honorable council but also the whole realm is indebted to him. He constantly maintained and defended God's Truth when Papists and persecutions assaulted the godly. Now in these days, he preaches the gospel so purely and earnestly and fears not to rebuke the worldly of his wickedness. Alexander, if I rightly remember history, in the course of his conquest, spared a city for the memory of the famous poet Homer's sake. Latimer far passes that poet, and the King's Highness, by your grace's advice, shall also excel that gentile prince in all kinds of mercy and clemency."

20

[1549]

In September the Bishop of London made disparaging remarks about the Prayer Book. More than that, he would not admit "unfettered authority of an infant King," a position taken by those who claimed that a King who is a child has not the ability to make decisions and approve changes. They did not want the Lord Protector and the council making changes, especially in matters of religion. Bonner was unwise enough to speak out on this issue.

When brought before a commission, he proved obstinate. As a result, he was deprived of his bishopric and sent to the Tower. His implied attitude toward the Lord Protector soon became expressed opinion by many in prominent places. Cranmer had earlier sensed Somerset's loss of popularity; Latimer had observed it in the reaction to his remarks about Seymour.

Somerset's consideration for the common people and the measures he took with regard to enclosures and the infringements of the laws on this matter displeased wealthy landowners. His open friendship with Latimer and others who spoke boldly for social reform worked against him. He was easygoing where many felt he should act with firmness.

The uprisings of the summer caused some to say that he purposely cultivated unrest among the common people. They claimed he sought to cause civil war and perhaps to seize power.

On October 13 Somerset was dismissed as Protector, charged with treasonable actions, and sent to the Tower. Cranmer presided at the council meeting. Latimer was shocked. Had Cranmer been outnumbered? Or had he felt compelled to do what he must?

"Who will succeed Somerset as Protector?" asked Latimer.

"Almost certainly," said Cranmer in a low tone, "it will be John Dudley, Duke of Warwick."

"Could this not bring about a dangerous situation? He is known to have Catholic leanings."

"Some expect Warwick to turn the church back to Rome."

"How can you speak so calmly? Can we sit by and let all we have accomplished collapse in ruin?"

"Can you suggest one thing we can do except pray? God is still on the throne. Unless Somerset had been removed, the country would have been embroiled in full-scale civil war. The noblemen are ready for violence. If we remain calm and cooperate to the best of our ability, we may at least preserve peace."

"Perhaps," said Latimer, "Warwick will not take a step that would bring him into conflict with the King. Our Sovereign has a mind of his own. That he will permit no drastic change in the church is our chief hope . . . that and, as you say, prayer."

Yet, he spoke of the King's staunchness with misgivings. The lad was often ill and unable to attend meetings of his council. It might be possible for the council to take a stand against him.

Presently, Cranmer spoke. "What will happen to the church if our beloved King dies? There is a possibility that he may not live long. No one wants to think about it, but it is there."

"I suppose that Princess Mary would succeed to the throne?"

"I see no other possibility."

Latimer did not sleep well that night.

21

[1550]

In early January Bernher entered the room one morning to find his master unable to rise from bed. A doctor sat near. Latimer said, "I am very ill, Austy. I am not able to move about or even to lift my arms."

The doctor's expression grew serious as he examined the patient. "We have a very sick man here. He will need constant care by someone who will follow my instructions to the letter."

"I am your man," said Bernher. "I will not leave him, day or night. You may trust me to do exactly as you say."

"I admire your zeal, my man," said the doctor. "But if you stay with him day and night, when will you sleep?"

Bernher stuck by his word. He scarcely left the room. A servant from Cranmer's staff came in to watch during the night while Austy got a bit of sleep on a cot placed in a corner. Yet he always rose several times to make sure all was well.

Cranmer, even amid the pressures of Parliament and Convocation, took time to come to the door at least once a day.

The patient drifted in and out of consciousness. His voice was weak and talking made him tired. For days there was no change. If anything, he grew weaker. One night when Bernher tiptoed to the bedside in the late hours, Latimer motioned him to sit, reached for his hand, and held it.

"Austy," he said, "I suppose I am dying." He silenced Austy's protest. "I have perhaps not much time. I want to thank you for all you have meant. You little knew what you were letting yourself in for the day you expressed your intention to serve me. Serve me you have, even going to prison with me."

He rested briefly, summoning the strength to continue. "I am not afraid to die. Once I lived in constant fear of death. That was before I knew that the Lord Christ had paid for my sins and that I need not struggle to try to pay for them myself."

He released his hold on Bernher's hand. "I am tired, so tired." He felt himself slipping into unconsciousness.

Of further events Latimer knew nothing until later. But Austy slept no more that night. He sat watching with a keen eye. Latimer did not move. The firelight played across his features, so drawn and worn.

At daybreak word went through Lambeth Palace and on to Westminster that Latimer was dying. Soon all London knew. Services were held, and prayer offered up on all sides for his life. It was said the King wept.

The doctor came, looked, and went away. Still, Austy sat; still, Latimer lay motionless. At last he moved his head and opened his eyes. Austy was on his feet at once leaning over him. "Austy," he whispered. "I am not going to die. Not yet."

22

[1550]

Recovery was slow. Latimer knew he would never be the same—too many years and too many ills. He maintained a keen interest in what went on, even though he could not be actively involved.

Warwick dismissed his Romish supporters and turned all out for the Reformation. Gardiner and Bonner remained in the Tower.

"He is showing himself zealous," said Cranmer. "Still . . ."

"Still what, my friend?" asked Latimer.

"I must not say it. Hooper calls him 'a faithful and intrepid soldier of Christ.' Perhaps he is right."

Hooper was a younger Reformer who had spent several years on the Continent, from the time of the Six Articles until his recent return. He was an outstanding preacher.

"The young," said Latimer, "who are coming up to carry on the work are in many ways strong and able. But sometimes they are gullible. Was it so with us?"

"Not with you," said Cranmer. "You have always had a shrewd insight into character. Sometimes I doubted your judgment and thought you cynical. Time proved you right in most cases."

"At times you see more deeply than any of us. You look so constantly through the spectacles of love. It was especially so in the case of the late King. You knew and understood him; you recognized his faults and weaknesses. But you loved him and hoped for the best, though you were often disappointed."

"I loved him, that is true," said Cranmer softly. "More than any man I ever knew, I loved him."

In the same week Latimer again received the offer of a bishopric. When Cranmer came for his reply, Latimer could only say, "I am deeply touched. It warms my heart and makes me feel loved and accepted, which is not always the case in these days. You know the answer. If I could not accept before, it is unthinkable in my present weakened condition."

"You will grow stronger. You will recover. I still need you. The King needs you. The church and state need you."

"I will grow stronger, God willing. But I will never be a well man again. What *you* need from me is my love and friendship, which you could never lose. Younger men are at hand to preach before the King. What the church needs from me, if anything, is preaching. I hope to continue that until my last breath. You know that it would be beyond me to serve as bishop. Explain it to His Majesty and the council. Express my gratitude."

On February 6 the Duke of Somerset was released from the Tower, but it was not a freedom without penalty. He was heavily fined and deprived of all his goods and offices.

"But he is free," cried Latimer. "The outcome might have been drastically different. Thank God he is free!"

Latimer was asked to preach at court on the Mondays of Lent. The old enthusiasm for preaching urged him on, but a strong pull to the contrary made him hesitate. "Possibly I should ask to be relieved of this duty," he said to Cranmer.

"You think you won't be up to it?"

"Preparation would be a joy. Delivery might tax me."

"His Majesty will be disappointed. He looks forward to your preaching above all others."

Latimer frowned. "The obvious solution is a compromise. You and I are old hands at settling for less than we would wish. Could I perhaps preach just once, say on March 10?"

"I shall communicate your request to the King."

"I should admit," said Latimer, "that my hesitancy about preaching is rooted in more than my physical condition."

"I knew that. I was waiting for you to tell me."

"I have served my time as court preacher. The King still listens, but the majority of the courtiers are increasingly impatient. They are willing to hear the Word of God, but only certain parts of it. Matters the Lord continually lays on my heart to preach are not pleasing to their ears."

"This is the first time I knew you to hold off because your listeners dislike what you preach."

"You do not represent quite accurately my attitude. Naturally some always reject my message."

"You have never liked to spend time at court, have you?"

"In 1530 when I first preached before the King, he was receptive and made me one of his chaplains. Responsibilities at Cambridge kept me going back and forth that year, but I found the atmosphere at court stifling."

"That was when you chose to go to West Kington."

"My friends could not understand my desire for a country parish. I could have remained at court and enjoyed the bestowal of some fat benefice, while preaching often before the King."

Cranmer sighed deeply. "I understand. How often I have wished I could slip off to some quiet rural parish and spend my days in ministry and study. It was never my choice to become archbishop. However, I recall that you did not find it so quiet in your country parish."

"I found trouble enough. I even asked you to arrange for me to preach again before the King, that he might hear my doctrine and know I was no heretic. But that was only temporary."

"Preaching during Lent is temporary," remarked Cranmer.

"The quality of the reaction against my preaching has changed. In the early days my attack was chiefly against institutional evils. I sought to reform the abuses in the church. That brought forth anger and indignation and cries of 'heretic.' Now my main thrust is against personal sins and social wickedness. That hits too close to home for some. The reaction is personal dislike and even hatred. To preach in such an atmosphere is unbelievably difficult. An impenetrable wall stands between us. I can do no more here. I would like to withdraw from public life."

"But your voice must still be heard," said Cranmer.

"I believe I have a ministry away from London. I shall find hearers. Hearts are hungry for the true gospel."

"People in the vicinity of London do have greater opportunity to hear the Word than those in remoter regions. Where do you plan to go? Shall I arrange something for you?"

"I have influential friends to the north. The Dowager Duchess of Suffolk has heard of my illness and insists that I come to Grimsthorpe in Lincolnshire. She has high standing and will open doors for me. John Glover urges me to return to Baxterley. Warwickshire offers a wide preaching area."

"You know how difficult I find it personally to let you go."

"I am not yet strong enough for travel. You still have me on your hands for a while. And I shall expect to return at intervals. We need anticipate no permanent separation."

"Bernher will go with you, of course."

"He insists that he will follow me wherever I go. He should be thinking more of his own usefulness to the church, rather than my personal needs. But he is a stubborn man."

"He serves the church in serving you. Companionship with you is a privilege. His day will come."

23

[1550]

On Ash Wednesday Latimer ventured forth for the first time since his illness. Austy stayed close by his side and made sure he was warmly wrapped. They crossed the river to Westminster to hear John Hooper preach the first Lenten sermon at court.

The sermon was one of a series on the Book of Jonah. On the way home Latimer exclaimed, *"That's* the kind of young preacher we need. He has courage and wisdom. God can use John Hooper."

He could hardly wait to get to the completion of his own sermon for the following Monday. "Get paper and pens in order, Austy. See that the ink is fresh. Plan to be available to listen to my ideas before I put them in final form."

"I'm happy to see you so eager, sir, but don't you think you should rest before beginning work? Was the trip not tiring?"

"You know I thrive on excitement, Austy. Today's excitement comes not only from hearing Hooper preach but from renewed contact with people. Getting out is just what I need."

"I can see that, sir, but you must not overdo," said Austy as he arranged writing materials. "As for listening, I am always ready. You have told me your subject will be covetousness."

"I have a little syllogism. I begin with St. Paul's utterance, 'Covetousness is the root of all evil.' When I want to speak of rebellion or any specific sin, I say, 'Rebellion is an evil; *therefore,* covetousness is the root of rebellion.'"

"Will your text come from a gospel or epistle reading?"

"Neither fits my subject well. I have chosen Luke 12:15, 'Take heed and beware of covetousness.'"

"You will see some sour looks, sir."

"Doubtless. But it needs hearing, so I shall preach it. This will be my *ultimum vale* before the court. It must be worth remembering. It ties in nicely with Hooper's sermon on Jonah."

Thus he spent the greater part of the next two days. He wrote, crossed out what he had written, and began again. He paced the floor at times, keeping up an animated discussion with Austy.

On Saturday morning he sat for some time in thoughtful silence. Turning to Austy, he said, "What I have to say is far too much for one morning's sermon. I should like to divide it and preach part of it in the afternoon."

"I should think the archbishop could arrange that, sir."

Later in the day Latimer proposed a walk in the gardens. It was warm for so early in March, the breeze soft and fragrant.

At a bend in the path Latimer caught a glimpse of someone approaching from the rear. It was John Bradford. His auburn beard glistened in the sunlight and his blue eyes shone.

Latimer threw his arms about him in a warm embrace and cried, "Bradford, you scoundrel! You never let me know when to expect you, yet you manage to arrive at just the right time."

"Bishop Ridley has something he wishes to discuss with me. I have also brought the balance of the restitution money."

Back in Latimer's room, they counted out one hundred and eighty pounds upon the table. They had no time to visit, for Bradford must find Ridley. He promised to return the next day. It was a disappointment to him that he could not stay for Latimer's sermon on Monday.

24

[1550]

Latimer was eager to be on his way early Monday morning, despite Austy's warning of dampness still on the river. He spent a moment in delivering the money to the council then followed the winding corridors through the palace to the chapel. The service would again be in the garden, but he wanted to compose himself in the silence of the sanctuary.

By the time he emerged from the chapel, people were already gathering. The moment arrived. He sought the face of the King and found it paler than before, yet marked by the same earnestness. Warwick sat beside him now.

He quoted his text in Latin: " *Videte et cavete ab avaritia.'* " Thrice he repeated it in English: " 'Take heed and beware of covetousness.' " He now had the crowd's full attention.

"What if I said nothing in all the time allotted me but these words, 'Take heed and beware of covetousness'? It would be a strange sermon before a King. Would it yet be stranger than that preached by Jonah, about which Master Hooper told us on Wednesday? 'Yet forty days and Nineveh shall be destroyed.' For three days he walked through the city with that sermon. The whole city was brought to repentance and judgment was averted. They believed God's preacher and were converted from their sins."

He expressed his wish that the preaching of the present day might produce like results. England must be brought to repentance for *all* its sins. Their root was covetousness. England must be willing to hear and heed the Word of God.

"Covetousness was the cause of the rebellion last summer. The gentlemen as well as the commons coveted. Both had an inordinate desire for what they had not, which is covetousness."

He preached to the end of the first section, conscious of a wall of resistance. He seemed to be battling, and Austy found him breathing hard when he came to take him away for a rest.

Cranmer touched his arm as he passed, saying, "The prophet speaks today in truth. The power stored up during your illness is now pouring forth."

The afternoon hour saw no lessening of the flow of powerful words.

" 'Beware of the leaven of the Pharisees,' our Lord said. Leaven is sometimes taken for corrupt living. Thus, one should be careful of his example, for one who lives corruptly will influence others to do likewise."

This was his opening for denunciation of the immorality and sexual looseness of the times. He deplored the fact that such lapses were looked upon lightly, even as laughing matters.

"Here," he cried, "I will make a suit to Your Highness to restore unto the church the discipline of Christ in excommunicating notable offenders. No man is able to devise a better way than God has done, to put them from the congregation till they be confounded. Bring into the Church of England open discipline that open sinners may be stricken thereby."

He made a thrust against bribery. "Think of this, you who are bribers, when you go secretly about such things: 'There is nothing hidden that will not be revealed.' That Word from God will prove true. He who took the silver basin and ewer for a bribe thinks that it will never come out, but he is now aware that I know it. Others also know it. Oh, briber and bribery! He was never a good man who will so take bribes." He cast a glance at the guilty party to observe his discomfiture.

Turning to the clergy, he said, "Sometimes leaven is taken for corrupt doctrine. So again we hear Christ say, 'Beware of the leaven of the Pharisees.' Christ intended to make his disciples teachers of all the world. Therefore, they were to beware of corrupt doctrine. Yet still, there are leaveners and mingle-manglers who sour Christ's doctrine with the leaven-of the Pharisees. Where there is any piece of leaven, they will keep that one piece more than all the doctrine of Christ."

He never stopped with denunciation of evil but called for repentance and for right living. He spoke of the responsibility of magistrates and judges to use their power and position as it was meant. He called for generosity on the part of the wealthy, especially landowners. They should do what they could to help their tenants and those in need. Great wealth did not assure peace and contentment. Sharing it with those less fortunate was more likely to insure those blessings.

"If God sends you abundance," he said in closing, "use it according to the rule of God's Word. Study to be rich in our Savior Jesus Christ, to whom with the Father and the Holy Spirit be all honor, glory, and praise for ever and ever. Amen."

Austy urgently steered him away from the crowd and settled him into the craft, which bore them across to Lambeth. He felt a sense of relief, then great physical weariness. It had been more of a strain than he had imagined. When Austy insisted on putting him to bed at an early hour, he did not protest.

25

[1550]

At Easter it became open knowledge that the Bishop of Rochester would be transferred to the Diocese of London. This pleased Latimer. Ridley would enhance this bishopric.

Delighted with Hooper, the King offered him the bishopric of Gloucester. To the dismay of all, he declined it.

"What's the matter with Hooper?" inquired Latimer.

"Plenty," replied Cranmer. "He objects to the Oath of Supremacy, calling it shameful and impious. He condemns the episcopal dress and ceremonies used in consecration, in spite of modifications recently made. He calls them Aaronic and Popish."

"Under those circumstances, he was quite right to decline the honor. I wish it were otherwise. He is a good man."

"The King is so eager to have Hooper a bishop that he is ready to strike out the obnoxious clause in the oath to accommodate him."

"But can he do that?" asked Latimer.

"I think he can. But he is now asking that I obtain the remission of the objectionable vestments and ceremonies."

"What will you do about that?"

"On personal grounds, I consider these matters as *adiaphora*, things indifferent. What does it matter what type of vestments are used or just how the statements are worded, so long as they do not conflict with the teaching of Scripture? But it is not a decision I can make on personal grounds."

"That's right. Parliament would have to approve any change."

"It goes deeper than it first appears. Serious dissension could result. If Hooper remains stubborn, this could get ugly."

The troublesome question of Hooper was put aside for the moment for Ridley's installation as Bishop of London. Latimer could not have been happier. Ridley confided in him plans that he meant to put into effect within a few weeks.

Latimer was not so nearly restored to health as he had supposed. Excitement had carried him through the Lenten sermon. Now he had to curtail some of his activities. The advance of spring lifted his spirits, but his body remained weak. He conserved his little strength for preaching on Sundays. He was preaching now in Ridley's diocese in the churches of London.

On the understanding that he would not be required to use the objectionable clause in the oath, Hooper accepted the offer of the bishopric.

He was duly elected and took the customary oaths, omitting the words that he felt to be sinful.

Cranmer came to Latimer in deep distress. "What is going to happen when time comes for his consecration? As I have said, I would not be averse to making the changes in vestments and ceremonies if it were a personal matter. But it is a legal matter. The King showed lack of wisdom in encouraging Hooper to think this would be an easy matter. Hooper should know better."

Latimer could only ask, "What does Ridley say?"

"He thinks Hooper is quibbling over nonessentials and that we should not even try to make changes to accommodate him."

"I deplore the thought of a division in our ranks upon such a minor question," said Latimer.

"I must write and ask our friends on the Continent for an opinion. Hooper spent the years of the Six Articles there. With his return so recent, he is out of contact with the thinking here."

"Suppose they align themselves on different sides? We could see the Reform leaders breaking into two opposition camps."

"What a rejoicing that would cause among the Romists," said Cranmer. "This comes about just when my hopes were high of obtaining a unified Reformed Church."

26

[1550]

June brought joy to Latimer, for it brought John Bradford. Again Latimer was in the garden when he looked up from his book to see the slender young man, whom he had learned to love so well.

"Come join me under the rose arbor," Latimer cried, "the most fragrant spot about. You come just as I am wondering what I will do about feeling so *old.* You make me feel ten years younger."

"Then you may grow younger all summer long."

"Splendid! But you must tell me what has been going on. You would not divulge even a hint of what Ridley wanted of you on that brief weekend in March."

Bradford laughed with the delight of a child. "First, let me inform you that you look upon a Fellow of Pembroke. This news came to me just at the end of the term."

Latimer reached out to take his hand. "Let me congratulate you. Not that I am in the least surprised."

"And the bishop plans to ordain me a Deacon of Fulham Palace and to appoint me a chaplain in his house. So you see why I shall be all summer in London. Once the Michaelmas term opens at Cambridge, I shall be in London as often as my studies permit."

Latimer would have detained Bradford for a much longer time. When he found he must go, he released him with a promise to return as frequently as possible.

"You will have your duties, but count this as a home whenever you can come. We must take advantage of these weeks. I expect to be moving on myself in the autumn, God willing."

He watched the young man stride away, turning before he passed from view to smile and lift his hand. Latimer resumed his reading, but it was some moments before he gave it his full attention. The sense of strength and well-being remained.

When Austy came to call him to dinner, he said, "I could, I think without sacrilege, quote, 'I have had meat that you know not of.' Bradford has been here." It was explanation enough.

Weeks had passed since Latimer had a real visit with Ridley. So he was pleased when the bishop sought him out one evening after supper and suggested a walk in the gardens.

"I want to share some more plans with you and get your reaction."

"Tell me," said Latimer. "I am eager to hear."

"I have prepared a list of Injunctions for immediate distribution. These, I hope, will be useful in cleansing the diocese of Papal customs still in use. Though the mass is abolished, I find priests who are unwilling to give it up. They continue to celebrate it in a veiled form."

"That must stop, assuredly," said Latimer.

"To mark the unmistakable change, I plan to set the Lord's board at St. Paul's as an honest table decently covered, not as an altar. Other altars and by-tables will be removed."

"I admire your courage in beginning at the heart of your diocese. What will the reaction be?"

"Doubtless, I will meet with opposition. But I am in a position to uphold my actions. I mean to launch immediately upon a visitation of every parish in the diocese."

"That's what it will take. Nothing like a personal visit from the bishop to get people on their toes. Make unannounced visits when possible. Then you find out what really goes on."

Latimer remained at Lambeth all summer, increasing his strength little by little. He spent hours with Bradford, quietly delving into the treasures of the Word of God and in speculation on the future of the church. They preached in many parish churches about London. Latimer insisted that Bradford preach as often as he did. Consequently, Bradford became beloved of the populace of London and its environs for his own sake.

One day Bradford arrived at Lambeth in particularly high spirits. "I have something here," he said, "that will increase your strength even more than you say I do by my presence."

"And what may be in that parcel you carry?"

"You often hear me speak of my friend Traves. He has sent me a cheese. It is certain to be a very special one."

"You are kind to offer to share it with me. Are there not those at Fulham Palace who would be pleased to enjoy it?"

"They are well provided for. As, of course, are you here. But since it is rather special, I would give it to you."

"How will your friend like your giving away his gift?"

"It will please him well to know I gave it to you. He knows how little food I require. For that matter, I am not giving it to you in its entirety. I plan to enjoy a small portion myself."

"Then let us lose no time. Austy, could you send for a knife and some small plates from the dining room?"

"Could you at the same time ask for some fruit?" inquired Bradford. "Then we could make a meal of it here and not go to the Hall for dinner. Or would that be sufficient for you?"

"Quite an excellent idea. I would want nothing more."

They spent a merry hour feasting upon the cheese and some peaches and cherries from the Hall. Austy beamed his approval at the effect Bradford had upon Latimer.

"You must tell Traves," said Latimer, "that this is quite the best cheese I have ever eaten. Express to him my thanks. Austy will see that the remainder is safely put away for later. I should like to give the archbishop a portion. I have so little to offer him in return for all he does for me."

Thus the summer slipped by.

27

[1550]

As Warwick's power increased and a new group appeared about him at court, Latimer was aware of the continued decline of his own popularity in those circles. He had seen it coming, but it still hurt. What grieved him most was the direction the church was taking under this new authority. Even Cranmer's popularity and influence had declined.

"The same flaws we found under Papal rule," said Latimer, "are reappearing under the guise of the Reformation. These new gospelers—I call them hot gospelers—are willing to accept any belief and push for Reform if there is something in it for them."

"A number are supporting the Reformation from ulterior motives," said Cranmer. "I know those who would like to simplify the order of worship, remove certain ornaments and vestments from use, just so they may lay hands on them."

"One would think the pillaging of the church was already complete with the distribution of the monastic lands and property, the removal of shrines and images. It was wrong for the riches to fall into greedy hands. So little was kept for religious and educational uses."

"Zeal for an extreme Reformation is often a cover-up for personal greed," said Cranmer.

"That and the desire to be on the winning side."

"Hooper seems convinced of Warwick's sincerity. He can't say enough good things about him."

"I have never trusted Warwick," said Latimer. "Nothing of late has moved me to change my opinion. I am afraid Hooper is deceived. I believe Warwick is a Papist at heart, but he is willing to jettison his beliefs for political advantage."

"I wish I could feel that he has the interest of the country at heart. I fear you are right, that he does use religious issues as a political weapon. He is not the man Somerset is."

"What about Somerset?" asked Latimer. "Will he remain in obscurity with what is happening to the church and the country?"

"If he speaks, it may mean civil war. I doubt he could return to power without it. Perhaps he should keep his silence."

Latimer walked to the window, restless and deeply unhappy. "Autumn is near," he said. "The Lady Katherine is renewing her invitation. She wants me to make her home at Grimsthorpe a center and preach extensively in that area. It is time I went."

"I was reluctant to think of your leaving. Now I feel it is wise. A sphere of usefulness is open to you."

"Commitments to preach hold me here for a few weeks. But by the end of October, Austy and I should be on our way."

"Just don't stay too long," said Cranmer with a tender smile. "We still need you here. *I* need you."

Bradford's return to Cambridge made it easier for Latimer to leave. His summer had been enriched by their frequent contact. He felt a sort of parental pride in Bradford's development as a Christian minister. In the back of his mind still hung the ghost of Bradford's resemblance to Bilney.

"You go your way and I go mine," Bradford had said, "but neither of us will ever be the same. Our meetings may be less frequent and of shorter duration from this point. I can never express what your friendship means. Nor can I thank God enough."

"Austy," Latimer said, "will it suit you to travel to Lincolnshire at the end of next month? We may be there for some time. Perhaps the change will do us both good."

28

[1550]

Latimer had made the acquaintance of Lady Katherine, Dowager Duchess of Suffolk, at court during his bishopric. She was then the very young wife of Charles Brandon, Duke of Suffolk. Her mother had come over from Spain with Catherine of Aragon. Her father, Lord Willoughby de Eresby, died, and she was given in ward to Charles Brandon. She succeeded to the fortune and position of her father, which made her quite wealthy in her own right. Soon after the death of his wife Mary Tudor, younger sister of Henry VIII, Brandon married his sixteen-year-old ward.

Lady Katherine was an ardent admirer of the Reformation preachers, especially of Latimer, and she was a special friend of Archbishop Cranmer. Latimer was impressed by her vivacity and charm and by her deep devotion to God and his Word.

He had lost touch with her in recent years. He knew she had two sons to whom she was devoted. The duke died in 1545, and the older son had succeeded to his father's title.

At the time of Anne Askew's trial Lady Katherine was again at court as one of the ladies of Queen Katherine Parr. She was among those suspected of heresy, whose names Wriothesley and Rich tried in vain to wring from Anne Askew on the rack.

Since Henry's death, she resided at Grimsthorpe Castle, part of the inheritance from her father. Brandon had restored the splendid Hall and furnished it in luxurious style.

On a gloomy afternoon Latimer and Austy guided their horses up the broad avenue toward the North Front of Grimsthorpe. Lady Katherine was watching and before they reached the gate, she had flung wide the doors and hurried unceremoniously down the path.

She soon had them inside before a roaring fire. The fireplace occupied the center of the longer wall of the Hall. The walls were adorned with fine

Gobelin tapestries that had come as part of the dowry of Mary Tudor, Dowager Queen of France. Other furnishings were in keeping. Yet, for all the luxury, Latimer felt at home. His hostess took it for granted and showed no tendency toward ostentation in awareness of her possessions.

With little delay she had them shown to their comfortable quarters. Time to rest and change from their travel-stained garments would be welcome.

"We sup early these winter nights, and with little formality. Come down when you are ready," she said.

Austy sought to take the position of an ordinary domestic. Lady Katherine would not hear of this. She insisted that he sit with them and join them at table on all occasions.

"You call Father Latimer your master," she said, "and you do serve him, but you are his Christian brother, as you are mine. And I understand that few of his sermons have been preserved. You and I must gather them all and prepare them for publication."

Latimer gave a rueful laugh. *"Gather* them! Where will you gather them from—the four winds? I seldom prepare a complete manuscript. When I do, you know my propensity for departing from it. I *plan* carefully, but a great part of it is in my head."

"From now on, Austy must prod you into writing your sermons out more fully. We both must take notes as you preach or write down afterward the additional material you bring in."

Austy attacked the collection of sermon notes and sought to organize the material. The dialogues in which they had engaged while preparing the sermons proved a great help. He could remember and fill in admirably what the sketchy notes lacked.

Latimer surprised himself. He was content to lean back and bask in the attention given him. For Lady Katherine had her eye not only on his preaching but on his physical welfare.

"Austy," she said, "we are going to feed him up until we get some flesh on that spare frame. It will be your responsibility to see that he sleeps and rests so much that he becomes quite lazy. He will be a changed man when we finish with him."

Latimer did find the peace a welcome inducement to complete relaxation. At Baxterley there had been peace, but Glover did not go in for the luxurious touches. Comfort he had enjoyed, but with a tendency toward austerity. For the present he had to admit that he reveled in luxury.

"You will spoil me beyond all remedy," he told his hostess.

"Nonsense," she replied. "You can do with a bit of spoiling. Besides, don't think it will be *all* rest and relaxation. Preaching is to be done."

She well knew that preaching was his chief joy in life. On November 9 he was to preach at Stamford, twelve miles away. His sermon would be in two parts, morning and afternoon. It was a crisp, cloudless morning when the party from Grimsthorpe set out for Stamford. As they neared the town they found the road full of people traveling in their direction.

Latimer found it easy to adjust his style to the rural congregation. It merely meant reverting to his native language, that of his childhood. As to subject matter, he knew what needed to be preached in this vicinity.

This shire had been the scene of uprisings after the dissolution of the monasteries and more recently in the rebellions concerning enclosures and the Prayer Book. "Render therefore unto Caesar the things which are Caesar's and unto God the things that are God's" (Matt. 22:21). The text would be no more popular here than in London, but he did not seek popularity.

As usual, he was God's man first, then the King's man. The King might do wrong. Yet the true subject must willingly abide by the King's word and pay his taxes, just or unjust. His listeners, landowners and farmers, would doubtless prefer to keep their money in their own pockets. But Jesus had said, "Render unto Caesar." He suggested that whenever an unjust exaction was laid upon them, it might be in punishment for their own sin, even as natural calamities and pestilences often were.

He insisted as firmly that they must "render unto God" and pay their tithes. "Of little use to say, 'Our curate is naught, an ass-head, a dodipole, a lack-latin, and can do nothing.'"

Withholding the tithe was not the solution. They should complain to the bishop. Then they might appeal to the council. Yet the major route for relief was that of diligent prayer.

"God may either turn your priest's heart and make him wiser, or he may remove him from you and send a better. In any case, you are not relieved of the responsibility of delivering the tithe. You give it unto God, not man."

Before the sermon he had led them in praying the Lord's Prayer in English. At the close he did the same, explaining that repetition would soon make the English words familiar.

As they journeyed back to Grimsthorpe in the late afternoon, the duchess said, "Your remarks upon the tithe were quite à propos. Many here have used unhappiness with the priest as an excuse to neglect payment of the tithe."

"Unfortunately," said Latimer, "good priests are scarce. We do need to pray for changed hearts in those already in place. We should also pray for the bringing of earnest young men into the ministry. We need a hundred or so like John Bradford."

"Would you prepare sermons on the Lord's Prayer for my household? To properly pray the Lord's Prayer, they need to know not only the words but the meaning."

"That is a project to my liking. Preaching to your household is preaching to a considerable congregation. How many men and women have you in your employ?"

She laughed gaily. "I cannot possibly tell you. The master of my household has rather a free hand. Probably there are far too many, but they need the pay and might suffer without it."

29

[1550–1551]

After a particularly joyful Christmas season at Grimsthorpe, Latimer informed his hostess that he should depart as soon as Twelfth Night celebrations were over.

"I have some unfinished business in London," he said. "I hope to return later, if you permit."

It was a bleak morning when he rode off down the avenue, Austy by his side. A wintry wind whipped the bare branches of the trees on either side.

"Come back in the spring," called Lady Katherine. "Grimsthorpe is at its finest then."

By urging their beasts on over the wretched roads, they were able to reach Ely and the bishop's palace by nightfall. Before the sun was well up next morning, Latimer insisted that they be on their way to Cambridge.

"Shall we tarry long at Cambridge, sir?"

"If Bradford is free today, we should move on tomorrow."

"Is the business that calls you to London urgent?"

"I do not know. I only sense that things are not going right. My presence may be required only for Cranmer's sake."

The reunion was one of mutual joy. As it happened, Bradford was free to spend the afternoon and evening with them.

In the remaining hours of the morning, Latimer introduced Austy to some of his old haunts. He grew silent as he entered the Church of St. Edward the Martyr. He approached the little wooden pulpit and with deliberation climbed the five shallow steps. Stepping inside, he closed the door. He stood looking first about the building, then down at the Bible lying open before him. His eyes misted as his thoughts carried him back.

"It is the same pulpit," he said softly. "Praise God, an English Bible now rests there. The altar is now a Communion table. I often preached to eager young men from this pulpit."

They made brief stops at the White Horse Inn and at Great St. Mary's before going to Pembroke to meet Bradford. Together they walked up Castle Hill.

As of old, Latimer found a sunny spot where they could sit and rest. The two younger men listened with rapt attention as Latimer recalled incidents and conversations, which had lain buried for years. The cold began to creep across from the fens.

"I had forgotten it was January," said Latimer. "I have been reliving the spring and summer of my life. Now the stiffness is upon me, and you will have to assist me in the descent."

"Must you go tomorrow, sir?" asked Bradford.

"It is better so. I have visited the old places and met the old ghosts. Another day would be anticlimactic."

Latimer gave a sigh of contentment as he relaxed in his bed. Austy had just checked to see that his covering was sufficient.

"It has been a strenuous day, sir. Are you sure we should travel tomorrow?"

"It has been one of the memorable days of my life, Austy. I would not have missed a moment of it. I am tired, but a night's sleep will remedy that. It is a healthy tiredness, no pain."

"I am glad for that, sir."

"The walk up Heretics' Hill was good for me. You know, Austy, I could almost feel that Bilney was by my side." A tear was on his cheek, not so much for sadness as for gratitude.

30

[1551]

Latimer's premonition of trouble had not been wrong. He was shocked to find Cranmer haggard and troubled.

"I should have come sooner," he said.

"No," said Cranmer, his expression softening. "It is well you were not here. You could have done nothing. You needed the time away. I see that you benefitted from the change of scene."

"That cannot be disputed. But I feel guilty that while I was being coddled, you were undergoing such severe trials."

"Put aside such feelings. Here you would have been worse rather than better. Now you can support me, even if only in a personal way. The problem is Hooper ... and Warwick."

"So Hooper has not yet been consecrated. Doesn't that man know the meaning of compromise? Why must he be so stiff-necked?"

"You will remember that Warwick and the council last summer ordered me to effect a dispensation whereby Hooper could be consecrated without the objectionable vestments and ceremonies. Upon consultation with Ridley I refused to do it."

"I remember that the council took your refusal ill," said Latimer. "I agree with Ridley's position. My first sermon in Lincolnshire was to the point that even if a man does not agree with the law, he has a responsibility to obey it."

"Most of the Continental Reformers who are in England believe as I do that these matters belong to the *adiaphora*. Only John à Lasco took Hooper's part."

"Does he think the form of ordination directed by Parliament can be dispensed with at will? Does he know so little about how difficult it is to get *any* changes passed?"

"The council requested him to withdraw his opposition to the ceremonies. Instead of retracting, he preached against the ceremonies."

"Surely the council didn't continue to stick by him?"

"No, the council placed him under house arrest and forbade him to preach. Unable to preach, he published a booklet in which he repeated all his offensive statements.

"At this the council committed him to my custody. In late February Hooper, still recalcitrant, was removed from my custody to the Fleet Prison. Gardiner, still in the Tower, was deprived of his bishopric in the same month.

"A few weeks in the Fleet brought Hooper to his senses. In March he submitted and was duly consecrated, wearing the very vestments and undergoing the exact ceremonies to which he had objected as sinful. It seemed utterly without sense that he should be the cause of terrible division and angry recriminations for nine long months and then finally give in so completely. The scars produced in Reformed circles will not be quickly removed."

"So Hooper is off at last to Gloucester," said Latimer. "That was part of my old diocese. Hooper will do a good job. Too bad he wasted nine months when he could have been at work."

Tunstal had remained for months under house arrest in London, away from his See of Durham. Warwick had accused him—falsely, so far as anyone could tell—of encouraging a conspiracy in the North. Tunstal had always been a consistent Henrician Catholic, but he was neither a conspirator nor a traitor. Cranmer further diminished his own popularity by defending him.

Latimer grew restless. He preached often and he gave what help he could on the revision of the Prayer Book and the articles upon which Cranmer asked his help. But he felt no great challenge in these works.

He was too shrewd a judge of character to be deceived by what appeared as zeal for the church among the courtiers. He could not understand the blindness of the younger Reformers who seemed utterly taken in by this group and eager to move along with them. Under the instigation of the grasping nobility, these Reformers made zealous attacks on all the ritual of the church that they considered even remotely tinged with Romist influence.

Latimer saw the affections of the people becoming alienated from the Reformation. The church had its opportunity while Edward reigned, yet it was being frittered away and the people untouched for Christ. The men in power wished only to enrich themselves, depriving the clergy of sources of revenue long consecrated to the support of the church. The council continued to make grants of church lands and livings to courtiers and those attached to them.

"In a short time," said Latimer, "the clergy, once overrich, may have to go back to the era of the apostles and earn their daily bread by the sweat of their brow. When will they find time for learning and preaching when that comes about?"

His friends regretted the depth of his misery but could not deny that his observation was valid. Courtiers raked in vast fortunes, but the royal revenue was steadily defrauded. The rise in price of provisions brought groans from every side.

To further darken the picture, the sweating sickness struck, raging with deadly violence. Latimer stayed in his place. He was not one to try to run to safety.

"Seven men dined together yesterday," said Austy. "This morning six were dead. It strikes with frightening rapidity."

A few days later word came of the death of Henry, Duke of Suffolk, and his brother Charles, sons of Lady Katherine at Grimsthorpe. Bright, attractive boys still in their teens, they had just been accepted at King's College, Cambridge.

"What a pity!" exclaimed Latimer, stricken with grief for his dear friend. "Such promise, wiped out within an hour."

"Will you write a letter to her, sir?" asked Austy.

"A letter, of course. I would go myself, but this is not the time." He pictured her radiance as he had left her. Her distress would be intense. "Yet she knows where to look for consolation. The God of all comfort is at her side."

Bradley came for the summer but spent most of the time on preaching missions. Occasional glimpses of him provided almost the only bright spots Latimer knew.

31

[1551]

Warwick made himself Duke of Northumberland. At this news Latimer gave vent to such violent anger that Austy was frightened. "That grasping, grabbing hypocrite! It is true that Somerset advanced himself when he was Protector. But whatever his failings, he could never be charged with the degree of selfish aggrandizement of which his successor is guilty. I not only distrust him; I dislike him intensely, God forgive me!"

In the same week, Somerset was again arrested and imprisoned in the Tower. The charge? He was seeking to recover his lost supremacy and plotting to replace Northumberland by violence. True or alleged? It made no difference.

To Latimer, this was the last straw. "The Tower! He'll not escape with his head again. Mark my words, Northumberland will see him tried for treason, found guilty, and sent to the block."

He turned abruptly to Austy. "Make our preparations to go to Lincolnshire. I have had all I can stomach of London."

32

[1551]

Once he had shaken the dust of London from his feet, Latimer's spirits rose. They bypassed Cambridge, taking a shorter route. By the second day he had relaxed perceptibly.

Like incense came the smell of newly turned earth from fields being readied for winter corn. Holly berries shone crimson in the hedgerows. Maple, elm, and birch were brilliant.

"This is where I belong, Austy," cried Latimer. "I am a countryman. It's my life and blood. I can breathe and expand."

Their arrival at Grimsthorpe was almost a repetition of the year before. Lady Katherine was paler and thinner. Deep grief had left its mark. She threw her arms about Latimer and clung to him as a child to a long absent father.

After supper she led Latimer into a small sitting room where a bright fire burned. "We must take this time to talk. Once I pour out my heart, we shall put it behind us. I do not mean this to be a sad visit." She tried to smile, but it wavered a bit.

"I should have come sooner. I *would* have come sooner—"

She stopped him. "Not a word! This is the right time. Had you come sooner, you would have found me so consumed with grief that I could not have heard what you had to say."

As she began to talk, the floodgates opened. Latimer was not disconcerted by her tears. He knew it was the best way.

Finally she was able to dry her tears. "You see," she said, drawing a deep sobbing breath, "it did seem such a waste. I loved them so dearly. They held such promise, perhaps for the ministry. Now they are gone. Why both? But how would I have known which to be ready to release? It is as well that they went together. They had always been together, almost like twins.

"I think I can dry my tears for good now that you have come. God knows best. I do not understand, but I trust him."

Latimer was deeply moved at her grief but confident of the staying power of her faith. He spoke the words she needed to hear and read to her the promises of God's Word. He placed his hand upon her head and committed her to God's tender care, asking that she be given strength and courage to face the future.

She was true to her word. She put it behind her, so far as outward appearance went. No more tears. She did not refer again to her loss, except in a matter-of-fact way.

As he sat with his book in the library one morning, Lady Katherine put her head in the door. "I must ask whether you have everything you need. Is there any special dish I might order for dinner? London almost undid my work of last winter."

He smiled. "I have everything I need. Never would I make a suggestion about food in this household where the variety and quantity rival what I saw at the Lord Cromwell's table."

She laughed a merry laugh. "You jest! The dishes served at that table will remain legendary in the chronicles of culinary accomplishment to the end of time."

"The series on the Lord's Prayer is almost ready," he said. "There are seven sermons. A few days' work will complete them."

"Wonderful! Once you have preached them here, you will be besieged with requests to give them in every parish church in the shire."

"Tush! Such exaggeration! Shall I preach one a week, giving time for it to be digested before the next is served up?"

"Exactly my thoughts! But I intrude on your time of quiet. I shall see you at dinner. Be sure to listen for the gong."

33

[1551]

Latimer spent hours at letter writing. Austy pored over notes and manuscripts, putting together the sermons. He now had a nice little stack completed. The duchess fluttered in and out, keeping an eye on what they were accomplishing.

A number of guests were usually in the house. Among them were deeply committed Christians, lovers of the Word of God and the Reformation. Their number increased with Latimer's arrival. Others came for the social aspects but they knew what to expect.

Instead of dances and plays and more boisterous forms of entertainment, the duchess planned musical programs or discussion of passages of Scripture with time for questions. Latimer was reminded of the old evenings at Baxterley.

He took pleasure in getting to know the friends who came. He found that more than one was drawn closer to Christ through the discussions. He gained a bevy of new admirers. The neighboring clergy regularly attended the evenings.

It amused Latimer somewhat that Lady Katherine always introduced him as *Dr.* Latimer, though she called him Father Latimer in private. She made such a point of it that he finally asked for an explanation.

"Of course you are *Dr. Latimer.* Why should I not give you the title which bespeaks your position as a scholar? I call you *Father* Latimer because I look upon you as a father. I lost my father when I was a child. You fill that void in my life, as well as that of my Father-in-Christ, my beloved pastor."

"I received the degree that entitles me to use *doctor* before my name," he said. "Somehow the records were lost or ill-kept, and no one can verify it from the Cambridge lists. The study I did profits me still. What does a title before my name add to it? Yet some speak disparagingly of me, as if I did not measure up because they find no record of that degree."

"How can they know whether or not it is on record?"

"There are those who took pains to search. Other discrepancies and omissions exist in the records, but that is not taken into account. No, old Latimer is a numskull, a know-nothing. I make no claim to scholarship of the caliber of Cranmer or Ridley, but as to the degree, I received it."

"I know that. It is only proper to make use of the title."

"It was strange," said Latimer, "that Sir Thomas More, who certainly loved me not, addressed me as Master Doctor Latimer."

"He was himself a man of quality and a scholar. He recognized in others what he was in himself and gave due credit."

She decided, since the Advent season was upon them, to postpone the sermons on the Lord's Prayer until the New Year. "I would like us to concentrate upon them with nothing to distract or detract from them. Some of my neighbors are begging to be allowed to come and bring their households. Will you mind?"

"The bigger the congregation, the greater my inspiration. I believe, however, we should not spread the sermons out quite as much as I first suggested. Might I give an introduction in a morning and the sermon on the first petition in the afternoon? The rest could follow two a week, but not in the same day."

"I like that. What about the last three weeks of January?"

"Quite agreeable. I have sermons to preach on Sundays of Advent, at Christmas, and through Twelfth Night."

"My, but they are keeping you busy. I shall grow jealous of your many engagements."

34

[1551]

December brought the first snow of the season. On the whole, the weather was good. Even the snow was a comfortable sort. Latimer continued his long walks accompanied by Austy.

"Sir," said Austy one day, as they crunched along snowy paths, "have you never thought of marrying?"

"Such a question, Austy! Actually I never have. I lived too long with the awareness that I had taken a vow of celibacy. When I found that nothing in Scripture prevented a clergyman from taking a wife, I still felt bound by my vow. At length I saw the sinfulness of a law forbidding the clergy to marry. For I saw what terrible conditions arose when priests could not or would not keep their vows and entered into all manner of unholy alliances. I knew the law must be abolished. I fought for such a change for years. The married state is a holy one, or should be. No law should keep a man from entering it, if he is so led."

"But you were never so led?"

"I suppose I was too old to entertain the thought by the time I felt free to marry. I have had the good fortune to have as friends a number of admirable ladies, most of them already happily married. I cherish such Christian friendships. But I never felt any inclination to seek the hand of a fair lady."

"Speaking of the hand of a fair lady, I am told that our hostess has a suitor."

"The lady had a marriage to an old man when she was little more than a child. She deserves a husband of her own choosing and one with whom she may have a congenial life. Not but what she made a good life for the duke."

Not many days after, as Latimer sat at his desk, pen in hand, he heard the musical laugh of the duchess. The door opened and she entered, followed by a man he had not seen before.

"Dr. Latimer," she said, "here is someone I wish you to meet. He is my gentleman-usher and very good friend."

Her eyes sparkled as she presented Master Richard Bertie. He was rather short, scarcely taller than the lady by his side. He was well dressed and meticulously groomed, as befitted his position in the household. Latimer considered his appearance not particularly striking, his features rather ordinary. He was probably in his midthirties, about the age of the duchess.

After this first brief meeting, Latimer took pains to cultivate the man's friendship and to win his confidence. Then when Mr. Bertie perceived that Latimer stood *in loco parentis* for the duchess, he was ready to declare his intentions.

It was his hope, he stated, to persuade the lady to become his wife. She had given him no promise, but she allowed him to believe that things might work out, if he were patient.

"And do you have the patience to wait?" inquired Latimer.

"I assure you, sir, that for such a lady I would spend the years Jacob spent waiting for Rachel, if necessary."

"Let's hope," said Latimer dryly, "that such a wait may be avoided. If you are a man of deep Christian convictions and of the character to merit her devotion, then nothing could please me more than to see you win her. Her life has held tragedies, or such events as men count tragedy. The Lord seems to have used them to deepen her faith and beautify her character."

As for the lady, she seemed to avoid any opportunity to discuss the matter with Latimer. Perhaps she wanted him to become better acquainted with Mr. Bertie before she spoke.

Then on an evening free of guests, she again led Latimer to her cozy sitting room. He liked this chamber with its altogether feminine atmosphere, from the pale blue draperies at the windows, to the tapestries upon the walls portraying Old Testament stories, to the soft sheen of the furniture. The books upon the escritoire were of a devotional nature.

But on this evening, the lady claimed his attention. She seemed somewhat at a loss as to how to open the conversation.

Then she said, "I have a proposal of marriage." He nodded understandingly. "But I feel no inclination to accept it."

"Oh?" he said in surprise. "But, then . . ."

She gave him her most dazzling smile. "The proposal of which I speak comes from His Majesty, the King of Poland."

This turn of conversation left Latimer completely confused.

She seemed amused at his reaction. "For a number of reasons I hesitate to accept this proposal. I do not know the man; I might not even like him. I have no desire to leave Grimsthorpe for an unknown habitation on the Continent. A strange land, different customs, another language . . . perhaps even a different religion. Has the Reformation touched Poland?"

By now Latimer had regained his composure. "Ah, but the chief reason for refusing the offer is that you have had another proposal that you find more attractive. Is that not true?"

She did not speak but raised her eyes to his and nodded.

"Do you intend to marry *this* man, my dear?" he asked.

"I am not sure. And I *must* be sure before I give him a definite answer."

"From what does this uncertainty stem?"

"I must make sure I am not marrying Richard merely because I am lonely and need someone to comfort me in my loss."

"No, that would not be fair to either of you."

"I hoped you could help me make up my mind. You have come to know him rather well. You have seen us in the same company. Do you think I will be able to make him happy?"

"You are aware, my dear, that he does not sparkle, so to speak, as you do. Could he be content to marry you and live rather in the background, while you stand out like a rainbow against a dark sky . . . or a sunset after a storm? Could *you* be content to have it so?"

"Perhaps he could learn to sparkle a bit," she said with a touch of wistfulness. "Or I could learn to be more subdued."

Latimer laughed. "No, my dear. If you marry expecting to change him into something else, you will be disappointed, and he will be miserable. Nor can you subdue the colors of the rainbow. You can never be other than the Lord has made you. You attract people to the gospel by your personality and devotion to Christ, just as a candle attracts a moth or an apple blossom, bees."

"Then you think it wrong for me to consider marrying him?" she asked, disappointment evident in her tone.

"I did not say that," he replied gently. "Indeed, I cannot tell you. You must find out for yourself. God will reveal it to you, if you seek diligently to know his will."

"Although I am of more mature years than many a young bride, I have never made such a decision. When I married Charles, I had little choice in the matter, though I was not unwilling."

"For him it was a marriage of convenience, to continue to administer your estate and to combine two fortunes. He received a lovely wife in the bargain, and I am sure you made him happy."

"I was genuinely fond of him and I tried to please him. I was happy, though it made me grow up rather quickly."

"A marriage of winter to spring. No mark remains to indicate that it is yet more than early summer for you. No longer a child, yet you are still young."

"Then, you have no advice to give me? No help to offer?"

"None," he said. "All I can say is that I like the man. He is not as mature a Christian as you. But it would be difficult to find a man who is your spiritual equal. It would be well for you to marry again. You need someone to love you, to cherish and care for you. But you need to be able to love him in return."

"I suppose you are right, but I can't help wishing that you could give me an answer. I need to set my mind at rest."

"You know my position on 'arranged' marriages. A Christian woman should have the privilege of deciding whom she will marry without being forced or urged into a loveless union. You are a mature Christian, well able to make such a decision."

"Then I say to you that I *do* love Richard sufficiently to marry him. I think we can work out our life together, so that the differences in our personalities will not matter to either of us. If they do not matter to us, why should they to others?"

"A good point. But others will have their say. Be prepared for remarks that will distress you unless you are able to brush them off."

"If I marry him, I shall love him and do all in my power to make him happy. Nothing anyone can say will change a thing for me nor, I believe, for Richard. We will have each other."

"When do you expect to give him an answer?"

"Perhaps soon, but that does not mean we will be wed soon. When all the matters of the inheritance are taken care of, I can turn to thoughts of my own happiness. Not before. Richard can be helpful in winding up the loose ends. He is experienced in such business. It will be a relief to have him handle it for me. I had never considered the possibility of both the boys being gone and my having such responsibility."

Latimer smiled. "Then you *do* intend to marry him."

She blushed and dropped her eyes to her hands, twisting a piece of ribbon in her lap. She had never looked lovelier.

"Yes," she said softly. "I did not know my own mind until this hour. My heart assures me it is the right decision. May we keep it a secret for a bit? At least until I tell Richard?"

Again he smiled. "Willingly, so far as speech is concerned. I am afraid you may have difficulty keeping people from reading your secret in your shining eyes and radiant face. Unless, like Moses, you choose to veil your face to hide the glow."

She made a mouth at him. "You tease me most dreadfully. Am I so transparent? In that case, I must talk to Richard at once."

"You should. It would be too bad for people to offer congratulations before Richard has reason to know he deserves them."

So it was generally understood that the Lady Katherine would wed her gentleman-usher in due time. As Latimer had predicted, disparaging remarks were not lacking. He hoped they did not come to her ears. People felt she was marrying beneath her: They made reference to "Lady Katherine and her little husband-to-be," as if he were a new pet she had acquired.

35

[1551–1552]

In the week after Epiphany he began the series on the Lord's Prayer. He preached so simply that a little child—or an ignorant servant girl—could understand. Yet his older and more learned hearers received an equal blessing and found the teaching to be that for which their hearts hungered.

"I heard you preach at court," said Lady Katherine. "The thundering prophet spoke with courage against the evils in our land. You denounced the evildoers in places of leadership, those responsible for curbing or enlarging the wrongs. Many rejoiced to hear the Word so proclaimed, but others reacted with anger and closed their ears. Yet you thundered on.

"Here you speak with even more power and with equal tones of certainty. But now you are the gentle apostle of love, encouraging and building up the simple and the weak. You teach the unlearned, rebuking still, but with a gentleness that must have been in the voice of our Lord himself when he preached."

"They love him," said Austy. "No angry looks, no jeering, no finding fault. As the Scripture says of our Lord, 'The common people heard him gladly.' I too note a difference here."

"You make too much of my preaching," said Latimer, feeling rather self-conscious. "I only try to fit my message to my hearers. I seek God's guidance in choosing the food his children need. Where condemnation is needed, it must be so. Our Lord thundered at the Pharisees. But he spoke in softer tones to the simple ones who came seeking healing for their ills or opening of their blind eyes. He is our example. We all do well to seek to follow him in this, though none of us does it to perfection."

For all the joy in his preaching, he still had that ominous sense of the approach of a dark cloud across the land. He spoke of it to the duchess and Austy.

"While it seems that the Reformation is progressing nicely and giving us much over which to rejoice, all is not well. As Cranmer often says, it is one thing to pass a law or hand down an injunction; it is quite another to change a heart. Many give lip service, but all too few have a real love for Christ in their hearts. Too few appear to live according to their doctrine."

"But surely you see changes in the lives of those about us," cried Lady Katherine. "You *must* see the fruit of your labors."

"I do see, and I thank God for it. But the church cannot grow strong until clergy of all levels, whether leaders in government, nobles in Parliament, or mayors and sheriffs in the country, have a true knowledge of salvation and are willing to put their faith into practice. The church is actually weakening at those levels. I fear that hard times are ahead, a season of great darkness. My prayer is that it may be brief and that God will quickly raise up those who will bring his church to strength and power."

"Perhaps you are too pessimistic, sir," put in Austy. "Surely what the archbishop is doing in the way of a revised *Book of Common Prayer* and his great work on the Articles of Faith will be a teaching instrument to strengthen the church."

"Dear Cranmer!" said Latimer. "Indeed, what he is doing will be of supreme value to the church. I only wish those in high places could recognize the greatness of the man and of his contributions. Still, I see that time of darkness approaching."

"Yet you are free to preach the gospel unhampered," said Lady Katherine. "God's preached Word cannot fall fruitless."

"Nor will it. After a time of lying in darkness it will spring up to a fuller blessing of lives. Probably Austy will see it bring forth fruit under his ministry after I am gone."

"Now," cried the duchess, "we surely must do something to cheer you up. You are not looking at the facts. You know you are counted the foremost minister in the kingdom. You are the Prophet . . . the Apostle to the English . . . the Preacher without peer."

"Yet, my preaching will be the cause of my death. I must work while it is day, for of a certainty the night comes. But you are right. We must speak of brighter things."

36

[1552]

Brighter things were not easily come by. On January 22, as Latimer was in the midst of the series on the Lord's Prayer, Somerset went to the block on Tower Hill, having been convicted of treason. The news saddened Latimer but came as no surprise.

"Northumberland could not afford to let him live," he said. "He was too popular. Northumberland is losing popularity with the people. Even the council is growing weary of him. Somerset was not a traitor, but many perish for crimes they do not commit."

With the approach of spring Latimer said to the duchess, "John Glover insists that I come again to Baxterley. I have too long imposed upon your hospitality. A little more and I will count this my permanent home, and you will never be rid of me."

"Would that such a thing could happen," she trilled. "My home is blessed when you are resident. If you must go to Baxterley, make your stay brief. We count on your presence here, especially toward the end of the year for the wedding."

"You are kindness itself, but I still feel it an imposition to stay such lengths of time. I shall send word to Glover to expect me around the middle of April."

So it was that he and Austy rode off through a cloud of pink fragrance wafting from apple orchards in bloom. Baxterley Hall presented itself with a beauty all its own amid green fields, apple and cherry orchards, flocks of sheep with new lambs frisking about, and then the stateliness of the Hall itself.

"This time," said John Glover, "we shall not have to limit ourselves to quiet talks about the Scriptures. You are free to preach now. The old church is wide open, beckoning to you."

"Nothing would please me more," said Latimer.

"When you left here, you ended up in the Tower. Let that be a lesson to you. Do not leave again."

"Ah, that was a time! My poor back gave me so much pain that I had to seek relief. Yet not much relief did I obtain."

"Largely because you showed sympathy for Crome."

"Which I had to do. There was no one else."

"Still, he recanted and went free. You went to the Tower."

"All that is behind us now," said Latimer. "What news from London? We've been out of touch while traveling."

"Parliament passed laws requiring church attendance. With each failure to attend, the penalty grows more severe."

"People should attend church," said Latimer, "but forcing them to do so bears too much resemblance to Papalistic rule."

"Sad news is that our King is quite ill with measles and smallpox. For a while no hope was held for his survival. The latest news is a bit more optimistic."

Latimer turned to Austy. "It is the beginning of the end of which I spoke. He will die, and the darkness will fall."

"God grant that you are wrong," said Glover. "He may yet overcome the effects of these diseases. We must pray that it be so. His death would be tragic in more ways than one."

"He has never been strong," said Latimer. "It will take a miracle. But let us pray to that end."

"The good news," said Glover, "is that Parliament has approved the revision of the *Book of Common Prayer*. It was included in the Second Act of Uniformity, which was passed at the same time. The book is to be put into use in November."

"That should make Calvin and Bullinger and others on the Continent happy. At Cranmer's request I read the book. I could suggest no changes. He is conversant with all shades of Reformed opinion. His mind is the best available for such work."

Latimer settled into something of a routine. He gave priority to preaching, and the weathered stone church on the hill could scarcely hold the crowds.

Near the end of May he one day startled Austy by announcing his intention of making a trip to London. The King had been restored to a measure of health but he continued in a weakened condition. Latimer felt the need to talk with Cranmer.

Preparations were made, but on the day of intended departure, it was clear the trip must be canceled. Latimer had become ill during the night. He was unable to leave his bed for several days. The strange illness left him quite weak. He continued to preach but he was able to do little else.

"The ills that plague my body may bring me down for a bit," he said to Austy, "but death will not take me that way. Gardiner will yet have his opportunity to deal with me."

37

[1552–1553]

Latimer gave up all thought of the trip to London. Until near the end of the year, he remained quietly at Baxterley. After preaching the Christmas sermons he informed Austy that they must leave at once for Grimsthorpe.

"Surely not such a journey at this time of year, sir."

"I promised the Lady Katherine that I could come. I must be there for the wedding."

"If you are determined to go, no one will be able to dissuade you. But it seems unwise."

"It may be my last opportunity to see Lady Katherine."

They were just in time for the wedding. At the insistence of the bride and groom Latimer agreed to remain for a while. It was well, for winter set in with a vengeance.

He preached often. When the weather shut him in, he still preached to the household at Grimsthorpe. Rarely, however, did the weather discourage those in the vicinity from coming.

"This is a happy time, Austy," he said one evening as he prepared for bed. "Winter brings its cold, but the outpoured love of those who belong to the Lord warms one's heart."

"They love the Lord, it is true," replied Austy, "but they love *you*, sir, for bringing them to the knowledge of him. They warm themselves at the fire of your preaching."

By the time April had brought a glorious spring to Grimsthorpe, Latimer was content to leave. He could see that Lady Katherine's marriage was a good one. It was time to go.

He knew with a strange certainty that this was his final departure from Grimsthorpe, but he made no mention of it. He would bring no sadness to these hearts. He wished to remember Lady Katherine in the fullness of joy her new life had brought.

38

[1553]

At Baxterley the news met him that the King was growing weaker. In London and at Parliament all thoughts were upon the succession. Should it be the Lady Mary?

The Papists favored her succession. She had refused to weaken her stand on the church and the Pope; she continued to have mass celebrated in her own quarters.

Rumors circulated of Northumberland's plans. Surely, he would not attempt to make himself King. The talk went on about the fireside at John Glover's. Latimer listened but said little.

"The Lady Mary will become Queen," he said quietly to Glover. "She will put down the Reformation for a time and seek to return the church to Rome."

After a prolonged time of intense suffering, which he bore bravely, the King died, not yet sixteen years of age. He commended the people of England to God with his last breath. He prayed that God would defend the nation from Papistry and would maintain his true religion.

Latimer said, "It is but a matter of time now. I listen each moment for the word that will send me on my last journey."

Five days after the King's death, Lady Jane Grey was proclaimed Queen. It was soon obvious that her cause was hopeless. Ridley's sermon at Paul's Cross in her defense had no effect. After nine days she was a prisoner in the Tower.

On July 19, in London, Mary was proclaimed Queen in great triumph, amid bonfires and shouting and the ringing of bells.

"How could it have happened?" asked Austy.

"It *had* to happen," replied Latimer. "The Lady Mary has a right to the throne. For the council and Northumberland to think they could have it otherwise was folly. They even pressed the dying King into agreement to such a scheme. The people are disillusioned about the Reformation; they hate Northumberland, so they are ripe to receive the lawful successor to the throne."

"But the archbishop signed the document for the Lady Jane," protested Austy. "Bishop Ridley preached on her behalf."

"Cranmer signed his own death warrant when he signed that paper. Ridley preached his own funeral sermon. They talk of the Queen permitting freedom in matters of religion. She will not."

Within a matter of days Bishop Ridley was in the Tower. Cranmer once more sent his wife and children to Germany. When Reformers from the Continent received orders to return to their homelands, many Englishmen in disguise fled with them.

Latimer waited quietly. He continued to preach, for no one had told him to stop. Hearing that many leaders of the church were joining in the general exodus from the country, friends urged him to do the same. He only shook his head.

"I have an appointment with Her Majesty," he said. "I do not know when her call may come, but I must be ready."

As the summer ended, he sorted out his few possessions. He was glad that the collection of sermons had been left with Lady Katherine, for she planned to have them printed.

September came. Haytime was well over, and the harvest was nearly ready to be brought in. As Latimer sat quietly in the library with his Bible one day, John Careless burst in.

"Oh, sir!" he cried, "you must flee! The Queen's messenger comes with a summons. He is yet several hours away. You must hurry. We will make plans for getting you away while you pack."

Latimer sat still in his chair and looked at his friend with a steady gaze.

"Sir," cried Careless, "do you not hear? They come to call you to London. You must flee."

"I hear you well enough, Careless. This was all settled long ago. Once before I sought to flee; the Lord returned me. I dare not try it again, even were I of a mind to do so. But an old man, feeble and ill, how should I flee? Austy, see to the rest of the packing. We must not keep the Queen's man waiting."

Six hours elapsed before the poursuivant reached Glover's gate. He was taken aback by his reception.

"My friend, you are a welcome messenger to me," said Latimer. "Be it known to you and to all the world that I go as willingly to London, being called by my prince to render a reckoning of doctrine, as ever I went to any place in the world. I doubt not but that, as God has made me worthy to preach his Word before two excellent princes, so will he enable me to witness the same unto a third, either to her eternal comfort or discomfort."

The confused messenger hastily concluded his errand and departed, declining to wait. "You are to follow," he said.

"Strange!" said John Glover. "But I think I read the meaning. They *mean* you to attempt flight."

"Doubtless," said Latimer. "That would discredit my testimony and the cause of the Reformation. Gardiner is not stupid. Not without reason has Her Majesty released him and made him lord chancellor. But I will not oblige him."

He led the gathered group in a moving prayer, committing them and himself to the tender mercies of Christ. After embracing each one in turn, he said to Austy, "We must be off."

As they rode past fields ready for harvesting, Latimer said, "There will always be a harvest, Austy. Be diligent in planting and do not despair if the harvest be delayed."

They came to London and were passing Smithfield. Latimer stopped his horse and stood. "Smithfield has long groaned for me," he said with a chuckle.

That evening Austy said, "I hear, sir, that Bishop Hooper is in the Fleet Prison. He too was warned when danger approached. He answered much as you did, 'Once I did flee and took to my feet. Now because I am called to this place, I am thoroughly persuaded to tarry and to live and die with my sheep.'"

On September 13 Latimer stood before the council. It was a distressing occasion but mercifully brief. Gardiner had obviously worked out the line of questioning.

Latimer had not, like Cranmer and Ridley, committed any overt act of sedition. Yet, the stoutness of his replies and the determined spirit he showed when required to make certain promises angered his inquisitors. They taunted and mocked him in a disgraceful way. He remained calm. For the steadfastness of his statements he was declared to have a seditious demeanor and committed to the Tower. Austy was allowed to accompany him.

"'Diotrephes, who loveth to have the preeminence,'" said Latimer to Austy as he was led away, "harped continually upon 'unity, unity.' 'Yes, sir,' said I, 'but in truth, not in Popery. Better is diversity than a unity of that sort.'"

As he was conducted across the green within the Tower walls toward his cell, he spied Rutter, one of the warders he knew of old. "What, my old friend," he cried, "how are you? I have come to be your neighbor again."

The next day Cranmer was brought to the Tower. Ridley and John Bradford had been there for some time.

Part Six

THE PROMISE OF A CANDLE

"It is time, Master Latimer."
[1553–1555]

1

[1553]

The council ordered close confinement. Latimer was denied the relative comforts of his former stay, only bare necessities being allowed. He fretted most at the knowledge that Cranmer, Ridley, and Bradford were near and yet inaccessible to him.

"May we hope that the Queen's devotion to the mass may not end in thrusting the church back under the Pope?" asked Austy.

"She will stop at nothing less," snorted Latimer. "She is determined to have things as they were at the beginning of her father's reign. She is more Spanish at heart than English, more Papistic than either. She must subjugate England to the Pope, even to the detriment of her own kingdom."

"The archbishop conducted the King's funeral according to the Reformed liturgy," said Austy. "But the Queen demanded a requiem mass here in the Tower Chapel as well."

"Already Gardiner is in charge of licensing preachers. Reformed preaching will be at an end."

"Except in secret, sir. Matthew Parker has not fled the country but is in hiding. He will not remain silent."

"Her Majesty should not imagine that the people's enthusiasm was due to eagerness for the old religion. They acknowledge her valid claim to the throne. They recognize her strong mind as somewhat like her father's. A stout-hearted Tudor on the throne gives a sense of security. But as for the old religion, their heart is not in it, nor entirely with the Reformation. We lost our chance. They hang between the two, waiting for a firm leadership to show the way. She *could* win them. I wonder about her wisdom to do so. If she tries force, she will lose them."

On October 1 the magnificent ceremonies surrounding the coronation of the Queen had London in a frenzy of excitement. A previous coronation day had also found Latimer in the Tower.

"Indeed, sir," said Austy, "that was a happy day. The gates opened, and you went forth to freedom."

"As will be true today for numerous prisoners. But not for us who uphold the Reformed faith."

As autumn deepened into winter, penetrating cold seeped through the stone walls with the dampness. No fire was permitted. The pain in Latimer's back intensified, and the headaches returned. Yet, he managed to retain his good spirits.

"I make quite a figure," he said as he drew a third cap down on his head "The Bishop of Winchester would be envious of my appearance." Yet when Austy had swathed him in all his clothing and wrapped him in the inadequate bedcovering, he still remained stiff with cold and shivered uncontrollably.

"How do you keep your sense of humor, sir," asked Austy, "and maintain the twinkle in your eye?"

"Ah, Austy! We do well to follow the example of St. Paul and remain content in whatever circumstances the Lord sets us."

One morning when frost was on the walls, the lieutenant's servant happened by. Latimer said, "Tell your master that unless he looks after me with more care, I am likely to deceive him."

Scarcely a quarter-hour later, Sir John Brydges burst into the cell. "What, sir, is the meaning of this message? Do you imply your intention to attempt escape? I will not allow it."

"You may not be able to prevent me, master lieutenant. You expect that I shall burn. But unless you let me have some fire, I am likely to deceive your expectations by dying from the cold."

Brydges eyed Latimer with uncertainty. His man came back, however, with material for a fire, saying, "The fuel supply will be strictly limited. You are urged to use it sparingly."

"Convey my thanks to your master," said Latimer. "Does the archbishop have fire? And Bishop Ridley?" The man nodded. Latimer ventured another question. "What can you tell me of Master John Bradford?" The man shook his head and departed.

He took the seat Austy placed near the fire. At least he had this luxury. He stretched his hands toward the flame.

2

[1553–1554]

As the days dragged by, Latimer's spirits drooped. One day while he sat staring at nothing, Austy approached with a paper for Latimer.

"Why have we not thought of this?" he cried. "Our trials will doubtless be upon the question of the mass. Ridley proposes to write out observations on the subject and to send them to Cranmer and me for comment. This will enable us to think through approaches our inquisitors might use. We shall thus be prepared to present a total agreement on the scriptural teaching."

"An excellent idea, sir. Their servants and I are permitted to move about freely, so passing the papers presents no problem."

Thus began weeks of writing and study. Latimer's Testament was constantly in his hand as he pored over Ridley's closely-written pages and dictated his responses to Austy.

The primary reason for the project was to refresh their minds on this important doctrine. It also put to good use their time. But perhaps of even greater importance was the sense of closeness the constant communication gave them, supplying warmth for their spirits as the fire on the hearth did for their bodies.

"When the papers are complete, sir," said Austy, "we could send them out to be circulated for the strengthening of others. In a sense, you will then be preaching even from prison."

When they had recorded their reasons for rejecting the mass with scriptural backing, Ridley proposed a second project. He would write out objections that an antagonist might make to their viewpoint, including the customary arguments of the Papists. Each would write what he deemed an appropriate reply.

At this point Cranmer was cut off from communication with Ridley and Latimer. His servant was warned to receive and deliver no more papers.

December passed and the early weeks of 1554. Shortage of paper hindered the project of Ridley and Latimer. They wrote in the margins of full sheets and hoarded every scrap of paper. As they approached conclusion, Latimer sensed a certain fear in Ridley's personal expressions. It struck an answering note in his own heart.

"You see, good father," Ridley wrote, "how I make in words a flourish before the fight. I prepare my weapons for the battle against the adversaries of Christ. I muse with myself how the darts of the old enemy may be borne off and how I may best smite him again with the sword of the Spirit."

Austy paused in his reading. "What a valiant warrior he is, sir. Yet as you say, a note of fear is apparent."

"Good father," continued Ridley, "as I pour forth these thoughts, I seem to see you suddenly lifting up your head toward heaven, after your manner, then looking upon me with your prophetical countenance. 'Trust not, my son'—I beg the honor of this name, so that I may think myself both honored and loved of you—'Trust not, my son, to these word-weapons, for the kingdom of God is not in words, but in power.'"

Tears rose unbidden and spilled over as Latimer listened. "He knows me well. I do indeed look upon him as a son, a strong son upon whom I may lean. He need never doubt my love."

"You will remind him, sir, that one need not plan ahead what to say in time of trial, as the Spirit will give him utterance."

Austy read on, "Pray, I beseech you, pray that I may enter this fight only in the name of God, and that when all is past, I through his gracious aid being not overcome, may remain and stand fast in him till that final victorious day of the Lord."

"He asks my prayers," said Latimer, "but little does he know how I covet his."

The final words seemed almost a sob. "Now, father, I pray you to help me buckle this gear a little better. You know the deepness of Satan, being an old soldier. You have wrestled with him many times, blessed be God who always aided you. I suppose he may well hold you at bay, even now. But he will not be so willing, I think, to join battle with you as with us younglings."

"The fear," said Latimer, "is of being tricked by insidious questions into a denial of the faith."

Latimer's voice trembled as he dictated his reply from the deep places of his heart. "I have caused my man not only to read your armor to me but also to write it out. It is no bare armor, but a well-buckled one. I see not how it could be better. Our common enemy shall do no more than God will permit him. 'God is faithful, which will not suffer us to be tempted above our strength.' Be at a point what you will stand to, stick to that, and let them say and do what they will. They can but kill the body, even that not when they please but when God permits them, at the appointed hour. To use many words is useless. Give a reasonable account of your faith, if they will quietly hear you. Otherwise, a man may keep silence, after the example of Christ."

"In the midst of the arguments," he wrote, "fear of death persuades a great number, as it did Shaxton, who once made a good profession. The flesh is weak, but the willingness of the Spirit shall refresh that weakness. The number of 'criers under the altar' must be fulfilled. If we are to be of that throng, happy are we. Surely, God gives no greater promotion in this world."

His voice broke as he reached this point. Austy looked up with some concern. "Never mind, Austy, just write."

Austy wrote. "Pray for me. For I am sometimes so fearful that I would creep into a mouse hole. Then God visits me again with his comfort. So he comes and goes to teach me to know my own weakness. Thus, I am reminded to thank him that is worthy."

He rose to stand with his back to the fire. "Your hand must be cramped by now, Austy. A bit more and you may rest."

"I am content to write as long as you wish, sir."

He concluded with, "I thank you, dear friend, from the bottom of my heart. My prayer shall you not lack. I trust you do the same for me. For indeed, *there* is the help."

3

[1554]

The Queen, in opposition to the advice of Gardiner and the council, insisted upon a marriage with her cousin Philip of Spain. Even the frowning of Parliament could not change her mind. She mistakenly interpreted the enthusiasm of her subjects in receiving her as *carte blanche* to do as she pleased.

"A Spanish match," said Latimer, "will diminish her popularity. She does not have her finger on the nation's pulse, as her father did."

"From what I hear, sir," said Austy, "she errs in another matter. The people are willing in things religious to return to the later days of her father but oppose a return to the Pope's rule. They want no foreign interference."

"She will have her way in that too. She is more eager to lay her crown before the Pope than to wear it herself."

The unpopularity of the Spanish match brought about a series of uprisings, the most serious led by Sir Thomas Wyatt. Concern had spread that the Queen would make Philip King and give him power to inherit after her. And a child she might bear him would be more than half Spanish, considering her own heritage.

The theme of Wyatt's rebellion was, "We are Englishmen." He rallied four thousand behind him and marched toward London. When the white-coated London militia met him at Strood, they joined the rebels, shouting, "We too are Englishmen."

Mary showed great personal courage and gathered forces sufficient to put him down. Wyatt was taken prisoner, along with nearly five hundred others.

Latimer leaned across the window ledge to look out toward the Traitors' Gate on that morning in early February. Wyatt and a number of his followers were being brought into the Tower.

Turning back to Austy, who was encouraging the fire to burn more brightly, he said, "No doubt there are numerous cells in this place, but I still wonder how they will house so many."

"I was having the same thought, sir. I only hope you are not called upon to share—"

Voices and approaching footsteps sounded outside the door, then the rattling of a key in the lock. As the door was flung open, Austy was on his feet, uttering a protest against the indignity of having common prisoners put into the cell with his master. Again his words were cut short and his mouth dropped open. Latimer only stood still, apparently struck dumb.

Before his uncomprehending eyes stood Cranmer and Ridley, their servants and their possessions. "I trust we may share your hospitality," said Cranmer, "for you seem to have little choice."

Latimer suddenly came to life. He moved across the room, almost stumbling in his haste, and threw his arms first about Cranmer, then about Ridley. All talked at once; then all grew silent. Latimer burst into laughter, joined by the others. Even Austy put aside his usual decorous demeanor to join them.

"It is unbelievable," cried Latimer at last, wiping his eyes. "They no doubt thought to inconvenience us by crowding us together. They have done us the greatest favor imaginable."

"Shall we make use of the chamber above, sir?" asked Austy.

"Ah, yes, up the narrow stairs. I had forgotten it. We will not be so crowded after all."

The cell door opened and closed again. John Bradford had joined them. The hubbub rose to a higher pitch. It was some time before they settled down to calm appraisal of their situation.

"Our cup is filled to overflowing," said Ridley. "God has blessed us beyond measure."

"Who would suppose," asked Latimer, "that prisoners could be so absolutely joyous?"

"We have this God-given opportunity to talk over the matters that will surely face us when we are brought to trial," said Cranmer. "Such discussion will be more valuable than the papers we wrote. Time may be short. Let us not waste a moment."

"Why not begin," suggested Bradford, "by reading the papers you have written."

"That would please me well," said Cranmer, "since I was cut off from participating in the latter series."

They clustered about the meager fire. Ridley produced the papers. They took turns reading, stopping frequently for discussion of a point. Cranmer made insightful additions.

"We are of one mind on these matters, then," said Cranmer. "We have individually found nothing in Scripture to substantiate belief in the mass. To insure beyond the shadow of a doubt that we are right, should we not read the New Testament aloud, taking time to ponder? We may detect something missed before."

"Certainty is essential," agreed Latimer.

Ridley and Bradford nodded agreement. The latter added, "We can count on the Holy Spirit to guide us in the study of the Word of which he is the Author."

Thus began a meticulous reading of the New Testament. Between reading sessions they spent time in prayer. Each knelt beside his stool or chair, and they poured out their hearts to the God they sought faithfully to serve. At times they remained so long at this blessed business that Latimer required help to rise.

"For all the length of time," said Ridley, "it seems but a moment. We have much for which to pray—the church, the land, the Queen. God can yet change Her Majesty's heart and mind."

Not all their time was thus spent. They took some hours, especially in the evenings, to discuss news that had come to their ears. Bradford, who had been shut off from any contact, was particularly hungry for information.

"Hooper is in the Fleet," said Latimer. "Rowland Taylor is in the King's Bench Prison. John Rogers was thrown into Newgate Prison. Not even his wife is permitted to see him."

A silence fell upon them as they remembered that Cranmer had sent his own wife and children to the Continent and was not likely to see them again. His heart must ache.

Ridley now turned to Bradford. "You've told us nothing of your imprisonment. It's time to break your silence."

Bradford sat with bowed head as he began to speak in a low tone. "I was brought before the Queen and council in August for acting to save the life of Bishop Bourn when he was threatened because of his preaching. They charged me with sedition and also found fault with my preaching. I was cast into a dungeon somewhere beneath the Tower. I saw no one except my keeper. It was doubtless better than I deserve from God's hand."

He lifted his head and gave them his touching smile. "Later I was moved into a cell known as 'Nun's-bower' with my Cambridge friend Dr. Sandys. What fellowship we had! We sought to engage our keeper, a perverse Papist, in conversation. With patience we were able to persuade him. At last he knelt to pray and make his profession of faith in Christ. On Sunday when they had mass in the chapel, he brought back a service-book, a small loaf, and a glass of wine. Dr. Sandys administered the Communion to us. The keeper became our son begotten in bonds."

4

[1554]

The Lady Jane Grey was imprisoned in the Lieutenant's House next to the Garden Tower. Her husband had been placed in Beauchamp Tower toward the far end of the Green. Due to the seriousness of Wyatt's rebellion, the Queen was willing to take no chances. Both were to be executed as traitors.

"Poor, gentle lady!" cried Ridley. "An innocent pawn! Northumberland was responsible for the whole unhappy affair."

On the morning of February 12 Guildford Dudley was escorted across the Green, down the steps, and through the gate beneath the Garden Tower. His execution would take place on Tower Hill.

"Look!" cried Cranmer. "They are putting up the scaffold on Tower Green for his wife's execution later today. There is sure to be much feeling against her death, poor lady."

From their vantage point, the prisoners could see the Lady Jane led forth. They did not remain to watch the sad scene.

"At least it was quick and merciful," said Ridley. "No doubt all of us are thinking what a *heretic's* death is like."

5

[1554]

When they reached the end of the New Testament, they began again. They found no evidence to lend support to any aspect of the Roman teaching on the mass. Their certainty that such teaching was foreign to Scripture increased daily.

On sunny days they were allowed to walk in the garden before the Lieutenant's House. To breathe the fresh air and have a change of scene restored a certain lightness of heart.

"At first," Cranmer said to Bradford, "we were restricted to our cells. Even before the extreme cold set in, my cell proved unbelievably damp and unhealthy. I am sure yours was more so."

"How you must have suffered," said Bradford.

"At length some kind soul—I shall never know who—made a complaint to the council against such treatment of an archbishop. From that time, we were all permitted some exercise on good days."

"It made a difference," said Ridley. "I, being younger, suffered less, but a claustrophobic sense can get to a man, no matter what his age."

"I experienced something of that," said Bradford quietly.

Friends outside sent food supplies at frequent intervals. "Our friends are kind," said Latimer. "They run a risk in undertaking to provide for 'heretics.' Yet, it is a saving for the treasury. When we eat our own food, it diminishes the outlay from the common prison supply, such as it would be."

Early days of March brought a lessening of the cold in the outside world, but not within the walls of the Tower. Walks in the sunshine were more welcome than ever.

Word came that commissioners were being selected for disputations to be held with Cranmer, Ridley, and Latimer at Oxford. Eminent minds from that university would be joined by others from Cambridge. The council would appoint those from the bishops' bench, whom it considered best qualified.

"I should like to know who the commissioners are," said Latimer. "Surely, Gardiner will take part, being 'Diotrephes' and loving the preeminence."

"I wonder what becomes of me," said Bradford in a rather forlorn voice. "Will I be left here? Or . . . what?"

"It is not a thing to worry about," said Ridley, putting his arm about the young man's shoulders. "Nor is the matter in human hands. It is in the best hands of all—God's."

"Gardiner may assume that it is in *his* hands," said Bradford. "But you are right. God is still sovereign. I am content in that knowledge. Yet, humanly speaking, I dread separation from you three who have been such a blessing to me. I don't know why God should have been so good to me."

That evening the lieutenant himself appeared at their door. "Tomorrow Bradford will be transferred to the King's Bench. You others will begin your journey toward Oxford. A barge will be at the steps quite early."

6

[1554]

Austy kindled a roaring fire before anyone was awake. There was no longer any need to conserve fuel. The small fire permitted them had only removed the worst of the chill from the constantly damp cell.

"I think," said Bradford, "that we shall not meet again this side of heaven. But what a glorious reunion that will be!"

Rutter, one of the warders they knew well, came with two others to escort them to the barge.

Austy was at Latimer's side to assist him. The descent of the steps would be difficult. The warders were patient. Down they went past Tower Green, the spot providing a grim reminder of recent tragedy.

Beside the steps, above the waiting barge, Sir John Brydges waited with Sir John Williams into whose hands the prisoners were formally committed for the journey to Oxford.

Cranmer's man assisted him into the barge and moved in after him.

Ridley stepped in, followed by his man. Latimer took his time, moving carefully lest pain cause him to cry out. Austy supported him as far as possible. Bradford took his place as Sir John and his companions stepped in behind him.

They passed under the Bridge, and the barge moved to the south bank. Bradford stepped ashore, then turned to fix his eyes briefly on the other three, his red beard seeming to tremble a bit. A sudden smile lit his face. "Pray for me," he said. "I will see you *soon.*" He mounted the steps, flanked by his guards.

Overcast skies contributed to the gloom. Wind whistled down from the north and stung their faces. Cramped and unable to move about, their discomfort increased. Finally, the towers of Windsor rose against the afternoon sky. They would stop here overnight.

After supper they huddled about the fire and looked at one another. "We may not be permitted to communicate after we reach Oxford," said Ridley. "What else do we need to speak of?"

"Before the commission," replied Latimer, "we should say no more than necessary. We are agreed upon what that is. Gardiner has said, 'I would the axe were laid at the root of the tree. The bishops and most powerful preachers ought certainly to die.'"

"It will be no *free* disputation," said Cranmer.

"The same freedom, no doubt," said Latimer, "as was with their forefathers at the trial of Jesus: 'We have a law and by our law he ought to die.' We must not let them lead us into vain discussions, lest we find ourselves unwittingly tripped up."

From Windsor they would travel on horseback. Latimer's back was so stiff from the river trip that he could barely stand. How could he mount a horse? Austy would manage. Dear Austy!

At Oxford they were turned over to the mayor who conducted them to the Bocardo Prison at the North Gate. The heavy bronze door clanged shut with a ring of finality. They were placed in separate cells, but their servants were allowed to remain. It was a miserable, filthy place.

7

[1554]

Easter fell on March 25. Austy approached Latimer's bedside with a hearty "Christ is risen!" With difficulty Latimer pronounced the customary response, "He is risen indeed!"

Latimer was alarmed, and Austy scarcely less so, at his state of mind and increased physical weakness. Day followed depressing day, and he did not improve.

"Even my memory fails me, Austy. What if they require Latin in the disputations? My knowledge of it is clean gone."

"Do not worry about it, sir. They can require no more of you than you are able to give. The Lord himself will stand at your right hand and give you what to say."

On Friday, April 13, the thirty-three commissioners arrived, with Weston, Dean of Westminster, appointed to preside. The proceedings opened next morning with a Mass of the Holy Ghost. Then came an elaborate procession, which ended at St. Mary's Church where the commissioners had seats in front of the altar.

In the afternoon the prisoners, followed by taunts from an unruly throng, were marched through the streets to the church.

"Never," said Latimer, "has such a city harbored an Archbishop of Canterbury and two bishops accused of heresy. Nor will it happen again. A great day, but not a godly greatness."

At the church they were placed in a small anteroom. Cranmer was summoned first. He did not return. Ridley went next. Latimer felt more fit today. God would grant him strength.

His turn came. He limped into the great church with a staff in his hand. When Dr. Weston saw his condition, he called for a chair and permitted him to sit for questioning.

The blaze of crimson and purple gowns produced a dazzling effect. The interested and merely curious filled every space. The unbelievable din diminished as the prolocutor began to speak.

"It is the Queen's pleasure that this commission bring you back to your former state of belief. I will now present to you the articles agreed upon by Convocation."

The notary rose and in a slightly nasal voice intoned with great deliberateness:

"1. In the sacrament of the altar, by the virtue of God's Word pronounced by the priest, there is *really* present the natural body of Christ, conceived of the Virgin Mary, under the kinds of the appearance of bread and wine; in like manner his blood.

"2. After the consecration there remains no substance of bread and wine, nor any other substance, but the substance of God and man.

"3. In the mass there is the lively sacrifice of the church, which is propitiatory as well for the sins of the quick as of the dead."

"What say you, Master Latimer?" asked the prolocutor.

"I deny them as false and contrary to the Scripture."

"Then I must advise you to prepare your opinions in writing and be ready for disputation on Wednesday next."

"I beg you, Master Prolocutor, to excuse me. I am an old man, and ill. My mind is not clear. I have no books for refreshing my memory. It has been long since I took part in a disputation. I am as fit to dispute as to be captain of Calais."

"You will not be excused on *any* pretext, Master Latimer. You must appear on Wednesday and take part."

"If there is no help for it," said Latimer, "I will declare my mind either by writing or word. I will stand to all you would lay upon my back. Yet, I have not been permitted to have pen nor ink nor yet any book, save this one." He held it aloft. "This New Testament I read seven times while in the Tower. I could not find the mass in it, neither marrow bones or sinews."

Dr. Weston said, "I will make you grant the presence of both its marrow and sinews in the New Testament."

"That you will never do, Master Doctor," replied Latimer.

He was taken to the house of one of the bailiffs. Austy had already transferred his belongings. He learned that Ridley was now in the mayor's house, Cranmer still in Bocardo.

The small room at the bailiff's house provided a measure of cleanliness and comfort. Latimer fretted about Cranmer, still in the filth and evil surroundings of the wretched prison.

The commission provided Latimer with paper, pens, and ink, but no books. He knew what he would write.

"The three articles were just what we had anticipated. We made our study and preparation along exactly those lines. I can write a refutation of each article with no difficulty. But to stand and dispute, perhaps in Latin, that I cannot do."

"Write," advised Austy. "They may permit you to read it."

"I am certain that they will not. What I write will resemble a sermon. Faith is contagious. To let me read would be dangerous. They know my reputation as a preacher."

"Write it, sir. At least there will be the record."

8

[1554]

Latimer awoke early on Wednesday morning, overcome by a dreadful attack of nausea. Gradually, the spell eased off.

"You should eat something, sir," said Austy. "It might settle your stomach. Perhaps one of these pears? Or some wine?"

Latimer closed his eyes and shook his head as another wave of nausea swept over him at the thought of food.

"You are so pale, sir. Should we not call the bailiff and ask to have you excused?"

"I must go. Another day might prove worse. The tempers of the commissioners would undoubtedly deteriorate. I *must* go."

A little before 8 o'clock they came for him. The bailiff, seeing his condition, let Austy assist him. Latimer leaned upon Austy's arm with his staff in the other hand. His only consciousness of the beautiful spring day was the welcome warmth of the sunshine.

The disputations were held in the Divinity Schools. One would have thought that the crowd might have responded to the sight of an aged man in a weakened condition with some pity and respect. But the reaction, as he made his halting way across the expanse of the chamber, took the form of hissings and mutterings.

He sank into the chair provided with a sense of relief. He could see the faces of the commissioners clearly, thanks to the flood of sunshine pouring through the stately windows.

After the prolocutor made his opening remarks, Latimer rose shakily to his feet. His voice was weak, yet he felt that the members of the commission could hear well enough.

"Mr. Prolocutor," he said, "it surprises me much to find you in the position of conducting this proceeding. Until Saturday last, I do not recall ever seeing your face. Yet, I knew of you and must say I did not expect to find you such a great cleric. During King Edward's time, I heard you were a curate beside Bishopsgate and seemed well content to feed your parishioners with the doctrine you here call heresy. You come now from the Queen to judge us as to that same doctrine."

Smiles played across the faces of some of the commissioners, as Weston flushed crimson. Latimer did not care that his speech had got him off to a bad start.

He lifted the sheaf of papers upon which he had written his opinions. "I ask your leave to read my answers to the articles, Mr. Prolocutor. As I told you before, I am unfit for disputation, especially for the use of Latin. I beg that my written words be taken as my arguments."

Weston brusquely denied the request. A notary took the papers from Latimer and handed them to Weston, who proceeded to examine them for some moments. Beckoning the notary to him, he indicated with his finger certain portions he should read aloud.

"I say that there is no other presence of Christ required than a spiritual presence. And the same presence may be called a real presence, because to the faithful believer I clearly state this, lest some sycophant or scorner should suppose me, with the Anabaptists, to make nothing else of the sacrament but a bare and naked sign."

There seemed no way to control the crowd, nor did anyone seem interested in doing so. Indeed, some of the rude cries issued from the lips of the commissioners themselves.

When Weston questioned him in detail, Latimer's mind was clear. The faintness of his voice still made it difficult for him to be heard. His strained efforts brought forth laughter.

Weston appointed Dr. Smith to dispute with Latimer but kept entering into the questioning himself. A great deal of confusion ensued. Sometimes questions were in Latin, sometimes in English. Latimer answered in the language in which the question was put.

"Is Christ's body really in the sacrament?" asked Dr. Smith.

"I trust I have obtained of Mr. Prolocutor that no man shall exact of me what is not in me. I have said that I am unable to take part in oral discussion. I am sorry that this worshipful audience is deceived of their expectations of me. I have given my mind in writing to Mr. Prolocutor."

"What you have given up shall be duly registered in the official accounts of the proceedings," replied Smith.

"Disputation requires a good memory, and my memory is clean gone. Doubtless, it is marvelously weakened and none the better for the prison."

"How long," broke in Weston, "have you been in prison?"

"These three quarters of a year."

"And I," said Weston, "was in prison six years."

"The more pity, sir."

"How long have you been of this opinion?"

"It is not long, sir."

"The time has been when you said mass full devoutly."

"Yes, and I beg God's mercy heartily for it."

"Where did you learn this newfangledness?"

"I long sought the truth in this matter of the sacrament and have not been of this mind past seven years. My lord of Canterbury's book especially confirmed my judgment in this belief. If I could remember all it contains, I would not fear to answer any man on this question."

"You were once a Lutheran," accused Weston.

"No, I was a Papist. I never could perceive how Luther could defend his opinion without transubstantiation. The Tigurines—those divines in Zurich—

wrote a book against Luther. I prayed that he might live long enough to make answer to them."

"Luther, in his book on the Private Mass," said Weston, "said that the Devil reasoned with him and persuaded him that the mass was not good. So it appears that Luther said mass and that the Devil dissuaded him from it."

"I do not take it in hand to defend Luther's sayings or doings. If he were here, he would defend himself well enough. I told you before that I am not fit for disputation. I pray you read my answer in which I have declared my faith."

His plea continued to be ignored. They went on to involve him in incomprehensible discussions on the famous passage from John's gospel, "Except ye eat the flesh of the Son of man, and drink his blood, ye shall have no life in you." As was customary, they brought up words of the Fathers that purported to give a mystical interpretation to this passage.

In the words of Mclanchthon, Latimer answered, "If the Fathers had foreseen that they would have been so taken in this controversy, they would have written more plainly."

They quoted from Cyril, Ambrose, Chrysostom, and Augustine in arguing against him. He held his impregnable position: To believe nothing as to the nature of the presence of Christ in the Communion except what Scripture plainly laid down.

"Augustine," he said, "was a reasonable man. He requires to be believed no further than he brings Scripture for his proof and agrees with God's Word. The doctors might be deceived in some points. I believe them when they say well. I refer myself to my lord of Canterbury's book wholly herein."

Smith sought to regain control of the disputation. "Then you are not of Chrysostom's faith nor of St. Augustine's."

"I have said, when they say well and bring Scripture for them, I *am* of their faith. Further than that, Augustine does not require to be believed."

Latimer turned now to Weston. "Sir, I have spoken in my time before two kings more than once, two or three hours together without interruption. But here I could not be suffered to declare my mind before you by the space of a quarter of an hour without snatches, revilings, checks, rebukes, and taunts, such as I have not felt the like in such an audience all my life long. Surely, it cannot but be a heinous offense that I have given. But what is it?" He tried once more to speak of what he called the "marrow bones of the mass" but was hushed up by the same sort of treatment he had just described.

He sat down, feeling very faint. Seeing his condition, Weston instructed that he be offered water to revive him. He declined the offer, fearing that he might vomit. The spell passed, and Weston asked him if he had any other words to say.

"No, I have answered your articles clearly enough in writing. I will stand unto what I have said, with God's help, unto the fire. I am able to declare to the majesty of God, by his invaluable Word, that I die for the Truth. For I assure you, if I could conform to the Queen's demands and still stand by the Word of God, I would rather live than die. But seeing they are directly against God's Word, I will obey God more than man, and so embrace the stake."

Weston proceeded to vilify the Reformers in a most undignified way. He made a last attempt to excite Latimer's fears. "Your stubbornness comes of vainglory, to no purpose. It will do you no good when a fagot is in your beard. By your own confession you have little cause to be stubborn, for your learning is in feoffer's hold since it lies in Cranmer's book. The Queen's grace is merciful, if you will turn."

"You shall have no hope in me to turn," replied Latimer. "I pray for the Queen daily, even from the bottom of my heart, that *she* may turn from this religion."

Weston cried, "Here you all see the weakness of heresy against the Truth. He denies all Truth and all the old Fathers."

With this, the affair ended, amid the same shameless and vulgar display as had characterized the whole. Latimer was led back to his prison, scarcely knowing what he did.

He had been three hours in the disputation. Now he was once more in his little room at the bailiff's house, the door closed and Austy by his side. It was perhaps the darkest day of his life. Never had he felt so ashamed of his fellowmen.

9

[1554]

The nausea passed, and Latimer could eat. Using funds from a friend in London, Austy searched the market for special foods to tempt his master's appetite and strengthen his body.

When Latimer saw what Austy had obtained, his immediate response was, "We must share this with Cranmer and Ridley."

"Each of them has as much as you have, sir."

"I should have known," said Latimer, his eyes resting on Austy's face. "How good God is to let me have you with me."

"It is my privilege, sir."

When they had eaten, Austy settled him comfortably before the fire that still proved necessary on late April evenings.

"Now, Austy, tell me what it is you have to tell. Ever since your return you have been bursting with news of some sort."

"Yesterday at the Divinity School I made the acquaintance of a young man of this university. He spoke rather boldly, but we had little time. I made an appointment to meet him today."

"No wonder you were so long."

"He says the Cambridge commissioners brought with them the full subscription of their scholars to the teaching of the mass."

"I wonder what means they used to force the subscriptions. Surely *some* would refuse. Perhaps they went into hiding. They would be wise to betake themselves to the Continent."

"Even in Oxford pressure is being applied upon all to subscribe. In his house, only he and his chamberfellow have resisted. Dr. Weston threatens any who refuse with removal from college and imprisonment. These two look hourly to be arrested."

"It is refreshing to know there are *two* Oxford men with courage to stand."

"This man attended the disputations on Monday and Tuesday. He found a place from which he could hear rather well."

Latimer sat forward in his eagerness to hear.

"The archbishop made an excellent appearance. He spoke with calmness and a respectful modesty that must have been difficult to maintain. The wisdom and dignity of his replies confounded them. They were not able to put him down at any point."

Latimer let out a growl. "In other words, he was just himself. How can he be anything else? But how was he received?"

"That is the sad part, sir. His opponents clamored so against him that his mild voice was often drowned. Yet he made an impression. Some, though differing with his opinions, were moved to tears at his gentleness in the face of such indignity."

"I am encouraged that some would react thus and be ashamed of the rest."

"As for Master Ridley, they could bring nothing, but he knew it as well as they. Yet he too received only shouting and hissing and the heaping of abuses upon him."

Latimer could almost see them. Cranmer, with his long white beard, staff in hand, would refuse to be seated in the presence of his adversaries. He would stand calmly, without losing his dignity or his temper. That sweetness of character, which was his trademark, would never desert him. Then Ridley. That intelligent light would shine from his eyes as he parried their thrusts and answered their questions. Not a man there would best him.

"Austy," he cried, "I am hungry. Are there more of those grapes? Where did you find grapes at this season? The cheese too was excellent. I could eat another slice."

Austy could not hide his pleasure. "The grapes must have come from Spain. The cheese was a special find."

"No doubt they required a handsome sum," muttered Latimer as he put a grape into his mouth.

"That is what the money was intended for, sir. I have no qualms about so spending it for your good."

"I admit those pears that come each day get tiresome."

As Austy settled him into bed that night, he was conscious of being almost free from pain. He had no trouble falling asleep. "I hope it lasts," he murmured as he drifted off.

10

[1554]

Friday brought blue skies, sunshine, and the fragrance of spring, a welcome relief from the odors that rose from Oxford streets. Latimer was stronger. As he moved along Cornmarket with Austy and the bailiff, he saw Cranmer and Ridley ahead.

They turned into High Street, for the commissioners in their bright robes were again at St. Mary's. The three prisoners were brought in together. The crowd was still noisy, but the ugly interruptions were fewer. They knew the matter was at an end.

The prolocutor addressed the prisoners on the dangers to which they exposed themselves by holding to their "vain heretical opinions." All three, according to him, had been completely overcome in the arguments. He renewed an appeal for submission.

Cranmer protested vainly against the statement that he had been overcome in argument. They were forbidden to make any reply beyond stating whether they would subscribe to the articles.

Each expressed determination to abide by what he had said in the disputations. Weston pronounced sentence: They were declared no members of the church and were condemned as heretics, unless even now they would turn. He stopped reading to give them opportunity to do so. They bade him read on.

"From this, your judgment and sentence," said Cranmer, "I appeal to the just judgment of God, trusting to be present with him in heaven for whose presence in the altar I am condemned."

"I be not of your company," said Ridley, "yet doubt I not but my name is written in another place, where this sentence will send us sooner than we should, by the course of nature, have come."

"I thank my God most heartily," said Latimer in a voice weak but still audible, "that he has prolonged my life to this end, that I may glorify him by such a death."

"If you go to heaven in this faith," said Weston, "then I am persuaded that I will not come there."

The next morning the bailiff's man called Latimer forth in great excitement. His heart gave a leap. So the hour had come. And with such suddenness that no further preparation was possible. But he was as ready as he would ever be.

A great throng had gathered in the street. As he reached Carfax, a procession came into view. All the commissioners and celebrities appeared in their finest apparel. At the sight of Weston carrying the sacrament, Latimer realized his mistake. It was not the hour of his burning.

He pulled away from his attendant and crossed the street to enter one of the shops. "I will not defile my eyes with such a sight," he cried. "They intend that I see in that magnificent procession the symbol of my defeat. I refuse to look."

11

[1554]

Condemned as heretics, they should suffer death by burning. But the Queen wanted it done legally. During Edward's reign, the old laws against heretics had been repealed. Too, the Queen wished to wait until the church was restored to Rome, so the jurisdiction would come from there, especially in Cranmer's case.

Not only were the three at Oxford left languishing. Countless others lay in London prisons and elsewhere.

One May evening as Latimer sat consuming the pears he tended to find tiresome, he said to Austy, "Weston accused me of stubbornness and vainglory. Was he right?"

"I think, sir, that perhaps he was right as to the charge of stubbornness. There is a proper time for demonstrating such a quality. But as to vainglory, he was quite wrong."

Latimer nodded in satisfaction. "I enjoy living, as much as any man. Sometimes when the pain in my back and the throbbing in my head are acute, I have a fleeting thought that it might be good to die. But in the ordinary run of things, I have no craving for death, though I do not fear it as I once did."

"At times, sir, it takes more courage to live than to die."

"Sometimes. But the death I am almost certain to face is no glamorous end to be sought for itself, no way to personal glory."

"Assuredly not, sir. In prison you have had opportunity to consider the matter and weigh the consequences. You sought the Truth in God's Word and prayed earnestly for guidance."

"I have taken my stand and I mean to hold my ground. But I shrink back when I think of facing such a death. I have witnessed the sufferings of those burned at the stake."

"Then look beyond, sir. The one on whose behalf you suffer has promised to be with you when you pass through the fire."

"I know, Austy. Confessing the dread occasionally seems to clear it away . . . until it returns in some midnight hour."

"You will remember Gethsemane, sir," said Austy softly. "Our Lord did not find it easy to face death."

"He was able to say, 'Thy will be done.' By his grace, so shall I. I have always said a man should not lay down his life unless the cause is worthy. I have a worthy cause."

"Since your cause is Truth, sir, I hardly see how any other course would be possible, whatever the end."

"The matter on which they force me to take a stand—the question of the real presence in the sacrament—is the proper ground for resistance unto death. It is the heart of the Romish system. For years I have dreamed of the importance of the question in the system of belief. I am no theologian."

"That is hardly true, sir. One who knows the Scriptures as you do cannot remain ignorant of theology."

"As to the systems of theological thought, I am not learned. Through Bilney, I came to know that salvation is not by my works, that I am justified by faith in the work of Christ on the cross."

"That is surely the starting point for any of us, sir."

"It took me years to fumble and stumble my way toward the other great Truth. Yet, it seems equally important."

"The years were not wasted. As your friends have reminded you, had you reached the second great Truth earlier, your life might have ended before now. God's timing is right."

"At least I see now the importance of this doctrine to the whole Popish structure. Remove it and the rest of the building will fall down of itself. Such matters as the pretended power of priests, the infallibility of the Pope, and the supremacy of tradition and the church over Holy Scripture would disappear. They all root back to the question of the manner of Christ's presence. It is not in Scripture, so they must find other means to bolster it up. Tradition must come above Scripture to insure the mass. If it is not so, the priest has no supernatural powers, nor is the word of the Pope infallible."

"It does seem clear that such is the case, sir."

"There is still much that I cannot explain, Austy. Some words of Scripture are difficult to understand. They sometimes lend themselves to being twisted by those who would make them say what they do not, in fact, mean. Still, as I view Scripture as a whole, the parts taken together and each part helping to explain another, I am absolutely sure of the Truth on this point."

"If, as we suppose, the Bishop of Winchester chose the questions for disputation, then, sir, he was wiser than he knew."

"He *knew* how wise he was. He is as determined on the Romish stand as I on the Reformed. Absolute and irreconcilable is the difference between their belief and ours."

"It is then the fundamental point at issue. I see it more clearly now myself, sir. There can be no compromise here."

"Ridley has apparently known for some years that he would end his days in this way. Bradford tells of a time when he accompanied Ridley in a boat. A sudden storm threatened to capsize them. They feared for their lives, all except Bishop Ridley. He said, 'Be of good cheer and bend to your oars. This boat carries a bishop who is not to be drowned but burned.'"

"You, sir, were once taken with a premonition that you would die at the stake. We remonstrated, but to no avail."

"I remember well. Even when I was so ill at Lambeth, I could not die. It is strange. God must give us these glimpses for a purpose. Perhaps to reassure us that it is his plan. He would not permit a horrible death except for a good reason."

12

[1554]

Austy attended to his master's needs with more than usual dispatch. "I should like to take the amount remaining in our 'treasury' to the market in search of more grapes, sir."

Near the middle of the morning Latimer looked up to see a white-faced and trembling Austy enter. He seemed in a state of shock. At Latimer's insistence he at last got the words out, "I am not to be allowed to stay with you longer, sir."

"What do you mean, Austy?"

"The bailiff stopped me when I came in to say he has been notified to that effect. Another man is to be sent to serve you. But, sir, how can I leave you? It is not as if ... as if ..."

"As if you were an ordinary servant who can be easily replaced." Latimer had risen from his chair at the recognition of Austy's distress. Now he sank again into it with a feeling of helplessness. He wanted to cry out, "What shall I do? How can I manage without you?" But he did not. He must think of Austy.

He motioned Austy to a seat. Struggling to keep his voice steady, he said, "Austy, dear Austy! What a blow! Earlier I feared this might happen. But since they left you so long, I began to feel secure. They mean to leave me no comfort. But, no matter. We must think about *you*. What will you do?"

Austy was struggling to regain his usual stoic Swiss mien. "I do not know, sir. What *will* I do?"

"You realize, Austy, that God's hand is in this. I do not say that he *wills* to take you from me, but he permits it. Whatever comes, he is able so to work that good results."

"I know he is sovereign and nothing comes unless he permits it. I find it difficult to see how good can come of this."

"I feel the same. For my part I would keep you with me to the end. You are friend, servant, son, nurse, confidante, adviser. You are my strong right arm. A man can lose his right arm and go on, I suppose, after a fashion."

"All my years in England, sir, have been at your side. I have no other life. No man could have had greater privilege. I came first to Robert Glover's house at Mancetter. But already I had heard enough about you to know that I must seek you out."

"The Glovers!" cried Latimer. "You must inquire of them what you should do for this time. After . . . after I am gone, that is another story. Until you can write and receive a reply, you must find means of remaining nearby in Oxford. No doubt they will refuse permission for you to see me, but there are ways."

Austy's face took on a more hopeful expression. "Oh, sir! They will find it impossible to keep me from contacting you. I *will* stay nearby. But I shall write to the Glovers."

Austy rose to his feet and stood looking down at his master. "Now we must talk about *you* and see what arrangements are to be made. The archbishop and Master Ridley are in the same situation. You will all be left to the care of strangers."

Latimer growled, as he found himself more and more in the habit of doing. "With instructions to spy upon us and to refuse to deliver messages or give us any news, I warrant."

"That will be the intent, sir, but you will gain the man's cooperation. He will grow to love you and desire to help you. I must set your things in order."

"What do I have, Austy? My clothing is mostly upon my back. My New Testament rarely leaves my hand. My spectacles become more useless as my eyesight fails. There is little else."

"I may be able to more easily find things you need, sir, if I am free to move about a bit. I can certainly obtain news more readily. A way will be found to communicate, never fear."

"Ah, that's my Austy! You'll manage. Your usefulness will extend to Cranmer and Ridley as well. Be careful not to attract attention. It would never do to let them clap you in prison."

"I shall endeavor not to worry about you, sir. If you can keep your sense of humor active, I shall worry less. For that assures me that you are not overborne with illness and trouble."

"You are *not* to worry, Austy. Would you disregard the Lord's own command? 'Be not anxious!' The same Lord will keep my spirits up by giving me of *his* Spirit. So no worrying."

Austy presented the new man to Latimer. He paid no heed to Austy's instructions, indicating that he had his orders. In exasperation Austy sent him to the kitchen for Latimer's supper. The time had fled, and Austy must make his unwilling departure.

"Kneel beside me, Austy." Each poured out his heart to God. Austy helped Latimer to his feet. They stood looking at each other for a long moment. Latimer drew his friend to him in a strong embrace. Austy turned and walked quickly from the room.

Only then could Latimer drop into his chair, let his head fall into his hands, and give way to his true feeling of grief and desolation. He could grant himself the luxury now of crying out, *"What shall I do? How can I manage without you?"*

13

[1554]

The first days were difficult. The servant took little notice of Latimer, performing his duties with no unnecessary words. About the third day, he began to soften. Latimer thought it was partly from sympathy for a feeble old man who, forced to exist under dreary circumstances, yet managed to remain cheerful.

Perhaps it was pity at the predicament of an old man kneeling so long in prayer that he could not rise without assistance. At any rate, he and Latimer began to converse. Latimer read to him from the Word of God when the light was strong enough to see. He questioned him about his faith and began instructing him a bit each day.

Then one day, by accident or design, he encountered Austy in the market. He agreed to deliver some innocuous verbal message to his master. It was then but a step for him to bring written messages and convey Latimer's replies.

After a time he began to take messages to Cranmer's man and to Ridley's. So, communication was restored. Latimer did not doubt that Austy rewarded the man with money from the little store that came to his hand from friends. Austy managed.

An answer came from Robert Glover. He realized that Austy could be in danger but felt that, as a Swiss, he probably would be safe if he refrained from drawing attention to himself. If he stayed in Oxford, trusting to the mercy and goodness of God, he might, in time, be permitted to rejoin his master. Until then, he could keep him in contact with friends outside.

With the letter came two shirts for Austy and two for Latimer. He also sent six pounds, thirteen shillings, and fourpence, left by "an honest gentleman" to provide things the prisoners at Oxford might need. Many considered it an honor to provide for their wants.

From all over England, letters began to come expressing sympathy and admiration and giving assurance of prayers. The courageous stand of the prisoners at the disputations inspired a new determination to stand firm for the Truth. Believers wrote to ask advice. Austy managed to provide writing materials for replies, most of which Ridley wrote.

Imprisoned, humiliated, looked down upon by the Queen, council, Convocation, and all in high places—but in the eyes of the people, they were still the leaders of the Reformation. It was to them God's people looked for guidance and instruction.

Finest of all were letters from other prisoners whose faith grew stronger through the courage of the three bishops. Their oneness in the Lord and in the cause of Truth would bear a witness far beyond the prison walls.

Austy had taken Ridley's full report of the disputations to London and brought back letters. Passing the letters required patience. Cranmer's man was not always cooperative.

Rowland Taylor wrote, "God be praised again for this, your most excellent promotion, that ye are counted worthy to be allowed amongst the number of Christ's records and witnesses." Latimer chuckled over his "promotion." "England has had but a few learned bishops that would stick to Christ *ad ignem inclusive*. Once again I thank God heartily in Christ for your most valiant proceeding, most constant suffering of all such infamies, taunts, open rebukes, loss of living and liberty for the defense of God's cause, Truth, and glory. Pray for us, for we fail not daily to pray for you."

Taylor, Hooper, Bradford, and Rogers were at times either in the same prison or had some contact with one another. They were able to communicate rather freely.

Bradford wrote to encourage them, believing their time of execution to be near, since the outcome of the disputations was so final. "Your staff standeth next the door," he had written. "You have the more cause to rejoice, as they that shall come to their fellows under the altar. To that society may God bring me with you in his mercy, when it shall be his good pleasure."

14

[1554]

Latimer thought often of Lady Katherine at Grimsthorpe. No letter came, but late in the summer she managed to send money in the amount of six royals, six shillings, and eight pence for their use. It was turned over to Austy to be used as needed.

A young man who loved the Reformation and had remained steadfast to the point of imprisonment wrote. Faced with the probability of the stake, he shrank back. In Latimer's opinion might he, without sin, purchase his freedom by payment of money?

Latimer determined to answer this letter himself. "The wise men of this world," he wrote, "can find shifts to avoid the cross. . . . But the simple servant of Christ looks only for oppression in the world. . . . Christ bore the cross not only for our redemption but also for an example to us, that we should follow his steps in suffering, that we might be partakers on his glorious resurrection. . . . Think not that it is lawful for money to redeem yourself out of the cross, unless you would go about to exchange glory for shame and to sell your inheritance for a mess of pottage, as Esau did."

He read the words he had written with tears in his eyes. This was the advice he must give. The issue was clear-cut. There was no acceptable compromise. As Ridley had said so bluntly, the command given them was, *Turn or Burn.* A follower of the Truth could not turn. He folded the sheets and wrote a note to Austy as to the letter's destination.

Late in July, Prince Philip arrived in England and the royal wedding took place. Queen Mary was said to take great delight in her spouse. The nation as a whole was less delighted.

Increasingly, Latimer spent time on his knees. Three petitions he kept foremost in his prayers. First, "O my God, as you have appointed me to be a preacher of your Word, so also give me grace to stand to your doctrine until my death, that I may give my heartblood for the same." He prayed that God would restore the gospel once again to England. Then he prayed for the Princess Elizabeth, that God would make her a comfort to his comfortless realm of England.

He prayed often with tears and always audibly. At first his man would slip out of the room. Then he began to remain.

One day he said, "Sir, when you pray, it is as if you talk with God face-to-face. When you ask him to restore the gospel to England, you repeat, 'once again, once again,' as if to beat against the doors of heaven."

"I *am* talking to him face-to-face, Thomas. I am so in earnest about the requests that I *must* repeat them again and again, not so much to beat against heaven's doors—for he always hears—but to pour out what throbs so strongly in my soul."

One crisp October afternoon the bailiff appeared at Latimer's door. "How would you like to go out for supper?"

Was it some joke? "I did not hear you well."

"How would you like to go out for supper with your friends? Come and we will go across to the Bocardo for a little."

Wondering, Latimer followed the man up the street to Bocardo, cringing as the bronze door clanged shut. The bailiff led him to where Cranmer sat.

They greeted each other warmly, if still a bit uncertainly. "What do you suppose is the meaning of this?" asked Cranmer.

His jailor replied, "We thought a bit of change might be good. Just be careful as to your topics of conversation."

Footsteps sounded on the stairs, and Ridley appeared. It seemed they were to be allowed an evening together and to enjoy the fellowship of a meal. It was not easy for them to speak naturally. They limited their talk to matters to which no objection could be raised. Their keepers remained near, yet the prisoners were clearly intended to enjoy themselves.

The meal itself was not different from what they usually received. Yet, shared, it seemed like a feast. There was bread and butter and ale. Two kinds of fish appeared, lyng and fresh salmon. With their cheese and pears, a wine was served.

"Do you suppose the authorities have a special fondness for *pears?*" asked Latimer.

Cranmer and Ridley laughed heartily. All summer, pears had been the sole fruit provided. Only Austy's efforts had supplied them from time to time with cherries, plums, apples, and grapes.

"It is an evening we shall not soon forget," said Ridley.

"Just to see and hear you is food and drink," said Cranmer.

In November at a similar evening they had news that boded ill for the Reformation. The Queen was expecting an heir. As they parted, Cranmer, who had been unusually quiet, said, "I should tell you that Cardinal Pole has arrived as Papal legate."

15

[1554–1555]

On November 30 the Papal legate absolved the nation from its heresies and assured it of the Pope's forgiveness. Parliament restored the penal laws as to heresy. Pole granted a commission to the bishops to proceed in the trial of heretics in prison and to judge them according to the rigor of the laws just reinstated.

In the last week of January Ridley sent Latimer a letter he had written to Bradford. "Austy is about to be off to London with the enclosed," he said. "You may wish to add a note."

He had written, "We all here be, thanks to God, in good health and comfort, watching with our lamps alight for when it shall please our Master, the bridegroom, to call us to wait upon him unto the marriage. Now we suppose that the day approaches. Parliament is dissolved and the burgesses of Oxford have come home. The only other news is that the King is made Protector to the prince to be born and that the bishops have full authority, *ex officio,* to inquire of heresies. We cannot but look for them shortly in Oxford, I trust to God's glory. Let them come when they will."

Latimer added a few words. The small effort caused a great weariness. But he must attend to one further duty. He wrote a note to Austy, assuring him of his prayers for the journey, bidding him be careful, and reminding him that he was to use money from the common fund for his needs. Latimer did not always know when Austy came or went, for daily communication was not possible.

One morning his man brought him letters. As he read, tears began to flow. He made no effort to check them. The good light would not last long. He could not delay in passing Austy's and Bradford's letters on.

"Thomas," he said, "will you place my chair again near the fire? And I should like you to convey this packet to Bishop Ridley. He will reward you according to your promptness."

He sat in meditation. "The sadness and the joy; the horror and the glory. Rogers, then, was the first. A long procession will follow. Where it will end, only God knows."

Austy had written an eyewitness account. On February 4 John Rogers was led forth from Newgate Prison to Smithfield. When asked whether he would revoke his abominable doctrine concerning the sacrament of the altar, he replied, "That which I have preached I will seal with my blood."

"Well," said the sheriff, "I shall never pray for you."

"But I shall pray for *you,*" came Rogers' quick reply.

A little before his burning, his pardon was brought if he would recant. He refused. A great crowd followed him to the stake, rejoicing at his constancy, praising and thanking God for it. He died calmly, committing his soul unto God.

"What an example for the rest of us," murmured Latimer. "A marvelous ministry he had! The Matthew Bible was largely his work. Many copies must still be daily read in secret."

Bradford's trial had taken place on January 31. As expected, he was condemned of heresy and delivered to the power of the law. He did not know when his time to suffer would come.

Latimer found himself between tears and laughter at the story of Rowland Taylor. Bonner came to degrade him from the priesthood. Custom demanded a blow on the breast with a crozier. In view of Taylor's size and awesome demeanor—for Taylor was ever ready to fight in a just cause—the bishop's chaplain cried, "My lord, strike him not, for he will surely strike again."

"Yes, by St. Peter will I," replied Taylor. "The cause is Christ's, and no good Christian am I if I refuse to fight in my Master's quarrel."

Bonner omitted that feature of the grim ceremony. Taylor mirthfully recounted the story, rubbing his hands together. "And by my truth, I made him believe I would indeed strike him."

"Would he really have struck?" Latimer wondered, smiling at the thought. "I would give a great deal to have seen Bonner's face. I daresay he was no less frightened than his chaplain."

He refused his supper that evening, bidding Thomas tend the fire and leave him. In the flickering light of the flames, he continued his meditations.

He thought of Rowland Taylor's work at Hadleigh. "He built upon Bilney's foundation," murmured Latimer. "Many women as well as men are learned in the Scriptures. He gave pains to teach children and servants. No edict of the Queen or law of Parliament or decree of the Pope can stamp out the faith of such a people. They must bide their time but they will stand forth to the restoring of the true church in the land."

Bradford had written, "I thought that your staves stood next the door, but now it seems otherwise. Our dear brother Rogers has broken the ice valiantly. Either today or tomorrow I think it will be that hearty Hooper, sincere Saunders, and trusty Taylor end their course and receive their crown. The next am I, who hourly look for the porter to open for me the gate after them. God forgive me for my unthankfulness for this exceeding great mercy that he chooses me to be one in whom he will suffer. Is this thy way, Lord, to send for such a hypocrite as I have been, in a fiery chariot as thou didst Elijah?"

Latimer cried out, "Bradford unthankful? Never! Bradford a hypocrite? I never knew a more sincere soul! So young—I think of him as a son. Yet so much has been accomplished in his years that number scarcely half of mine. I need not think of his accomplishments as only past, for he labors still. Austy says his correspondence is phenomenal. Many a sermon and treatise has come from his pen in these months of imprisonment."

Even as Bradford wrote, Taylor was on his way to Hadleigh to die in his old parish and Hooper to Gloucester. Austy heard of their deaths just before he began his journey back to Oxford.

Latimer bowed his head and wept. "They are burning the most godly men in the realm. How can God countenance it? The doom of those responsible is surely already sealed. Is it Gardiner? He sat at the trials of Rogers and Hooper. The Queen? Her share is large. Pole? He does not discourage the trend. Bonner? Ah, Bonner is only a weak tool in the hands of others. The guilt is known to God. Condemnation and judgment are certain. The Devil is, after all, at the root. And *his* doom is sure!"

16

[1555]

Latimer's imprisonment became more rigorous. His man was warned to allow no communication between him and the others. He was strictly watched. It was a lonely and frustrating time.

Near the middle of April, he and Ridley were transferred to the Bocardo. Latimer's tiny cell was filthy, and his man seemed able to do little to remedy the situation.

Austy would not be outwitted. His notes of encouragement soon found their way into Latimer's hands. News from across England removed the barrier erected by weeks of silence. Food, clothing, and writing materials arrived.

Latimer knew that it cost Austy much to stand by so faithfully. He must be laying his life on the line every day. Yet his zeal, inspired by devotion, never flagged.

The knowledge that he would never preach again brought Latimer unutterable sadness. Then an idea came. He *would* preach one more sermon. He would *write* it. Perhaps he would reach a wider congregation than any before which he had ever stood.

Getting it on paper would require patience, in view of his poor eyesight and weakness of body. He must plan first.

"I shall address it," he said, "to all unfeigned lovers of God's Truth." He tried to picture this, his greatest congregation. He must speak to special needs in a crucial time.

Then came the slow business of writing. "Brethren, it will now appear who has received God's Word in their hearts to the taking of good root therein. Such will not shrink from a little heat or sunburning weather. Rather, they will stoutly stand and grow, even in spite of the malice of burning shower and tempest.

"He who has played the wise builder and laid his foundation upon rock will not be afraid that every drizzling rain or mist shall hurt his building. He will stand, even in the face of a great tempest and drops of rain as big as fir-fagots. But they that have builded upon sand will be afraid. . . ."

When he arrived at the end of that paragraph, he laid his pen aside. "I began by addressing them as 'brethren.' I must not forget that a great number of sisters will be among them."

At the next session he began, "My dearly beloved brethren and sisters in the Lord, I am persuaded that you be in the number of wise builders who have made their foundation sure by faith in the infallible word of God's Truth. You will bring forth the fruits of God's glory, though the weather be never so foul. I urge you to go forward after your Master, Christ, not sticking at the stormy weather that has come or is likely to come."

The faithful faced a strong temptation against which he must warn them. The law demanded that every person attend mass. Many conformed, saying that they did not kneel at the elevation of the wafer nor did they in their hearts participate in the worship.

"Let not men beguile themselves," he wrote, "as I fear they do. This is a dissimulation and a seeking to deceive others."

He minced no words but described the mass as "an abominable idol, full of blasphemy and sacrilege against God and the dear sacrifice of his Christ."

Their path would not be an easy one, he told them, but a blessed one. They would not travel alone. The Scriptures spoke of the host of saints and martyrs on that road. Even Christ himself traveled a painful way from his birth to the cross.

"Pray for me, your poor brother and fellow sufferer for God's sake. Let us pray to God that he of his mercy will make you and me fit to suffer with good conscience for his name's sake. Die once we must. How and where we know not. Happy are they whom God grants to pay nature's debt (I mean to die) for his sake. Here is not our home. Let us, therefore, consider things accordingly, having always before our eyes that heavenly Jerusalem and the way thereunto in persecution."

One morning he arrived at the final paragraph. "Let us remember our

Savior Jesus Christ, how he rose again the third day. Even so shall we at the appointed time, when the trumpet shall blow and the angel shall shout. The Son of Man shall appear in the clouds in his majesty and great glory. The dead shall rise, and we shall be caught up to meet the Lord and to be with him always. Comfort yourselves with these words and pray for me for the Lord's sake. God be merciful unto us all. Amen."

He wrote his signature "Hugh L" and laid down his pen. *My last sermon,* he thought. *May God use it to the blessing of many hearts.*

Now he must get it to Austy. He would know how to get copies made and see to its circulation.

"Thomas," he said, "you must take part in the delivery of my last sermon. I charge you to find Austy and place it in his hand. A small matter, but it will bring a large reward."

17

[1555]

Before the end of May Latimer was returned to the bailiff's house and Ridley to the mayor's, without explanation. Cranmer remained in his dismal cell. He nodded and smiled from the window as Latimer left. It was a welcome glimpse, for there had been no suppers together of late.

One day a letter from Austy brought amazing news. No heir had been born to the Queen. Apparently, she had mistaken some physical ailment for a pregnancy, or perhaps her overwhelming desire for a child had led her to fancy herself pregnant. The doctors affirmed that she would never bear a child.

"I dare not say it aloud," mused Latimer, "but that news is more than welcome. It gives hope for the future of the church. Darkness may continue for a time, but there is light ahead."

The next bit of news caused him to laugh. "I have had a signal honor conferred upon me, Thomas," Latimer said. "My published sermons have been put on the list of condemned writings along with those of Archbishop Cranmer, Bishop Ridley, Luther, Tyndale, John Bradford, and others. It seems appropriate, I suppose, that since I am to burn up in flames, my books should do the same."

"Why should they want to burn the books, sir?"

"In the examinations of persons under arrest, many have quoted from these books. It is vain to silence the living voices if the written words still speak."

More than a month passed before another letter from Austy came with long expected news. Bradford was burned at Smithfield on July 1. In Latimer's heart was a conflict of joy and sorrow. Joy finally triumphed. For Bradford's suffering was past, and he was safely with Jesus. Nor would there be a long separation, for he must soon join him. There could not be much more delay.

Bradford had written a letter to Austy urging him to come. Austy reached London on the last day of June. He was with Bradford when the keeper's wife rushed in, quite out-of-breath.

"Oh, Master Bradford," she cried, "I come to bring you heavy news. Tomorrow you must be burned, and your chain is now abuying, and soon you must go to Newgate."

At that Bradford put off his cap and lifted his eyes to heaven, saying, "I thank God. It comes not suddenly, but as a thing waited for every day and hour. The Lord make me worthy of it." He thanked the woman and called Austy into his small room.

He put into Austy's hands some papers, telling what he wished done with them. Other friends came at evening. They talked and prayed until a late hour. About midnight, they came to take Bradford from the Compter to Newgate, hoping to avoid a crowd by going at such an hour.

At nine o'clock they led him to Smithfield. As the flames leaped up, he embraced the reeds, saying, "Strait is the way and narrow is the gate that leadeth to eternal salvation, and few there be that find it."

The hot summer dragged on. Near the end of August, Prince Philip returned to Spain. The Queen was reported inconsolable. Many predicted that he would not come again to England.

18

[1555]

In September Cranmer again faced commissioners at St. Mary's. After a good many hours he was returned to Bocardo. What did this mean? Would Cranmer be next?

One morning Thomas handed Latimer a paper on which Austy had written, "I am off to Coventry, concerning Robert Glover."

Within a few days Austy returned with distressing news. The authorities had headed toward Mancetter and Baxterley. Word preceded them, so that John and William fled from Baxterley to temporary safety. Robert was ill at his home in Mancetter. They arrested him in bed and carried him off to prison. Austy arrived in time to be with him and comfort him. He died at the stake in Coventry on September 20. John Careless was awaiting trial.

Latimer's emotions seemed all wrung out. "Too much, too much! I suppose the time comes when a man can bear no more. God makes it possible for him to hear and reflect without pain upon what would earlier have sent a sword through his heart."

19

[1555]

From that night he felt his body growing weaker while his will and his spirit grew stronger. On September 29 he awoke to the sound of a torrential downpour. Without letup the rain continued. In all his life he could not remember such a day.

The next day he was required to appear at the Divinity School before another commission. He and Ridley struggled along together through the mud of the flooded streets. They were not allowed to converse, but to be near one another was comforting.

Ridley was called first. Latimer waited as hours passed. Weariness and pain threatened to overcome him.

As soon as he faced his questioners, he burst into speech. "My lords, if I appear again, I pray you not to send for me until you be ready. I am an old man. It is great hurt to my age to tarry so long gazing upon the cold walls."

The Bishop of Lincoln, head of the new commission, replied that it was the bailiff's fault and would not happen again.

Perhaps Latimer's appearance inspired some feeling of pity. In an attempt to protect his head from drafts, which could cause severe pain, Latimer wore a nightcap with a kerchief over it and his black cap on top. His black frieze gown showed signs of wear. From a cheap leather girdle about his waist hung his New Testament. His spectacles, on a thin strap about his neck, rested on his bosom. It was not his intention to impress anyone. Let them see what it was like to remain in prison two years.

On the commission with White, Bishop of Lincoln, were Brooks of Gloucester and Holyman of Bristol. Cardinal Pole as legate had appointed them, so they directly represented the Pope.

The president declared their power to summon before them Hugh Latimer and Nicholas Ridley, pretended Bishops of Worcester and London. The commission was charged to examine them on various heresies maintained in the disputations of the previous year, as well as what the cardinal pleased to call "the times of perdition," the period during which the Reformation held sway.

The articles were the same as those of the year before. He might receive or reject them, at the risk of his life.

Before Latimer could speak, the Bishop of Lincoln continued: "I urge you to return like a strayed sheep to the unity of Christ's church from which you fell in the time of schism. Consider, Master Latimer, that *without* the unity of the church is no salvation and *in* the church can be no errors."

When Latimer moved restlessly in his chair and attempted to break in, the bishop silenced him with a gesture. He reminded Latimer that he should not hold back in confessing what all the realm had already confessed. He should not fail to forsake what the King and Queen had renounced and all the realm recanted.

At this, Latimer moved his head in a gesture of disapproval. He made no further move to speak, knowing it would be futile.

"Master Latimer, for God's sake, consider your position. You are a learned man. You have taken degrees in the schools and borne the office of bishop. You are an old man. Spare your body and accelerate not your death. Remember your soul's health. Should you die in this state, you shall be a stinking sacrifice to God, for the cause maketh the martyr, not the death. If you die in this state, you die without grace. For without the church can be no salvation. Let not vainglory have the upper hand. . . ."

Vainglory again, thought Latimer, *just like Weston.*

The voice droned on. "Humiliate yourself, captivate your understanding, and subdue your reason. Submit to the church. Do not force us to do all that we may do."

A persuasive appeal, thought Latimer. *What a feather in their caps if they could bring either Ridley or me to respond.*

Then he was permitted to reply. "Your lordship exhorts me to come to the unity of the church. I confess a catholic church, spread throughout the world, *in* which no man may err, *without* which unity of the church no man can be saved. But I know perfectly by God's Word that this church *is* in all the world and has not its foundation in Rome only, as you say."

As to the Pope's authority, he stated that the Lord had told Peter to *regere,* that is, to rule his people. The ruling was to be according to the Word of God, from which the bishops of Rome turned, making of it a ruling according to their own pleasure.

"I may illustrate," said Latimer, "by referring to a book published at the end of 1553, in which the Bishop of Gloucester argued from the words of Deuteronomy, 'If there ariseth any controversy among the people, the priests of the order of Levi shall decide the matter.' Only the bishop omitted entirely the important words, 'according to the law of God.'"

He got an understandable reaction from his audience, for Brooks, the same Bishop of Gloucester, sat in the commission. As Latimer spoke, Brooks rose to acknowledge his book.

"Was it your book, my lord?" inquired Latimer innocently. "Indeed, never did I see your lordship before. Nor yet do I see you because of the brightness of the sun shining betwixt us."

A burst of laughter greeted this statement. Latimer turned upon them, saying, "Why, my masters, this is no laughing matter. I answer upon life and death."

Brooks could not resist a taunt. "Master Latimer, hereby every man may see what learning you have."

Latimer answered in a manner reminiscent of his old style. "Lo, you look for learning at my hands, which have gone so long to the school of oblivion, making the bare walls my library. You keep me so long in prison without book or pen and ink, and now you let me loose to come and answer to articles. You deal with me as though two were appointed to fight for life and death. Overnight the one, through friends and favor, is cherished and has good counsel given him how to encounter his enemy. The other, for envy or lack of friends, all the whole night is set in the stocks. In the morning when they shall meet, the one is in strength and lusty; the other stiff in his limbs and almost dead for feebleness. Think you that to run through this man with a spear is not a goodly victory?"

The Bishop of Lincoln brought the proceedings back to order by reminding the assembly that they were not there to dispute but to hear from Latimer a yes or no concerning the articles.

Latimer managed one further protest. "Let the notaries register that I do not acknowledge the Pope's authority. I am a subject of the Crown only."

Then came a formal reading of the articles, one by one.

"We object to thee, Hugh Latimer, first, that thou, in this high University of Oxford, *anno* 1554, in the month of April, affirmed and openly defended and maintained that the true and natural body of Christ, after the consecration of the priest, is not really present in the sacrament of the altar. What say you unto this? I pray you answer affirmatively or negatively."

"I do not deny, my lord," Latimer replied, "that in the sacrament *by spirit and grace*, is the very body and blood of Christ. Every man who receives bodily that bread and wine, *spiritually* receives of Christ's passion. But I deny that the body and blood of Christ is in such manner present in the sacrament as *you* would have it."

The bishop directed the notary to record an affirmative answer and moved to the second article.

"That thou hast publicly affirmed that in the sacrament of the altar
remaineth still the substance of bread and wine. What say you to this
article?"

"There is, my lord, a change in the bread and wine, and such a change as
no power but the omnipotence of God can make, for that which before was
bread now has the dignity to exhibit Christ's body. Yet, the bread is still bread;
the wine still wine. The change is not in the nature, but in the dignity. That
which was common bread is no more common bread, neither ought it to be so
taken, but as holy bread sanctified by God's Word."

In a tone of slight exasperation the bishop asked, "Well, Master Latimer,
is not this your answer, that the substance of bread and wine remaineth after
the words of consecration?"

"Yes, truly, it must be so. Christ himself calls it bread, St. Paul calls it
bread. The doctors confess the same. The nature of the sacrament confirms it.
I call it holy bread, not that I make no difference betwixt your holy bread and
this, but for the holy office it bears. It is a figure of Christ's body, and not only
a bare figure, but effectually represents the same."

"Enter an affirmative answer," said the Bishop.

The third article was read.

"That you openly affirmed that in the mass is no propitiatory
sacrifice for the quick and the dead."

"No, no, my lord! Christ made one perfect sacrifice for all the whole
world. No man can offer him again. Neither can the priest offer up Christ
again for the sins of men that he took away by offering himself once for all
upon the cross. There is no propitiation for our sins except his cross only."

This too was recorded as an affirmative answer. The fourth article
declared that the foregoing assertions of Latimer had been condemned as
heretical by Dr. Weston and other learned men. To this Latimer made no
reply.

"Have you not heard what was read, Master Latimer?"

"Yes, but I do not understand what you mean by it."

"Only this, that your assertions were condemned by Dr. Weston as
heresies. It is not so, Master Latimer?"

"Yes, I think they are condemned, but how unjustly. He that shall be
judge of all knows."

This was taken as affirmative, and the last article read.

"All the premises are true and openly known by public fame, as well
to them near at hand as to them in distant places far off."

To this, Latimer replied that in his seclusion, he could not tell what men thought or said, and indeed he neither knew nor cared what men reported of him.

At this point the commissioners might have pronounced sentence. Instead, they informed Latimer that they would give him respite until the next day, hoping that he might seriously ponder everything, decide to acknowledge his errors, and recant.

"Nay, my lords, I beseech you to do with me *now* as it shall please your lordships. Trouble me not again tomorrow, I pray."

"Yes, Master Latimer, you must appear again tomorrow."

It was one o'clock when he was at last escorted back to his prison. He was weary beyond words and he ached in every part of his body. But at least the end was in sight.

20

[1555]

As he had promised, the commissioner did not send for Latimer until time for him to appear. Leaning upon his staff, he walked slowly up Cornmarket to Carfax in the company of the bailiff. A terrible downpour had come again during the night. He placed his feet carefully, fearing to slip and fall. He wondered whether Austy was inside the church. He longed for a glimpse of him but did not want to endanger him.

Ridley was led away just as he reached the church. They had difficulty moving through the crowd. Latimer found himself jostled and at one point rudely shoved against a wall.

The commissioners, in their finest robes, were seated upon a high throne placed before the altar. Festoons of tissue and silk gave a grand appearance to the whole scene.

As Latimer approached the table at which he was to stand, the silken cloth which had covered it was snatched away. His heart turned sick at such petty vindictiveness. The covering had been placed on the table for Ridley in recognition of his status as a doctor. They did not consider Latimer worthy of such honor.

As he stood facing the commission, he pointedly laid his old felt hat on the table and placed his elbows upon it. A memory stirred of the Lady Katherine's sweet voice speaking of *Dr.* Latimer. Much more valuable a tribute than a mere silken cloth!

He could not but smile at the contrast between the splendor of the men who would pass judgment on him and his own shabby appearance. So be it. There was an even vaster difference between what he and they represented.

The Bishop of Lincoln began by again urging him in strongest terms to revoke his errors and return to the Catholic Church.

Latimer interrupted. "Your lordship repeats often 'the Catholic Church' as though I deny the same. There *is*, my lord, a catholic church, to the determination of which I will stand; not the church that *you* call Catholic, which sooner might be termed diabolic. And whereas you join together the Romish and Catholic Church, stop there, I pray. For it is one thing to say 'Romish Church' and another thing to say 'Catholic Church.'" He was determined to battle them as long as he had breath.

The bishop offered Latimer one last chance to escape his doom. Latimer answered briefly, but with force. The bishop pressed him for a full answer on the third article, regarding the mass as propitiatory sacrifice.

"Christ made one oblation and sacrifice for sins of the whole world," he said, "and that a perfect sacrifice. Neither need there be any other, neither *can* there be any other propitiatory sacrifice." His words rang out in a remarkable way.

Since Latimer had made it plain that he refused to acknowledge that his teaching on these points was either heretical or contrary to the Word of God, the Bishop of Lincoln proceeded to the reading of the sentence of condemnation:

> "Forasmuch as the said Hugh Latimer did affirm, maintain, and stubbornly defend certain opinions, assertions, and heresies contrary to the Word of God and the received faith of the church, as in denying the true and natural body of Christ and his natural blood to be in the sacrament of the altar; secondly, in affirming the substance of bread and wine to remain after the words of consecration; thirdly, in denying the mass to be a lively sacrifice of the church for the quick and for the dead; therefore, the judges do condemn him as a heretic, adjudge him presently to be degraded from all ecclesiastical orders, declare him to be no member of the church, excommunicate him with the great excommunication, and commit him to the secular powers to receive due punishment."

The commissioners then broke up the court and dismissed the audience. The Bishop of Lincoln consigned Latimer to the mayor as his prisoner, to be safely kept until the appointed time. When Latimer complained again about being hurt by the crowd, the bishop gave instructions that he be allowed to wait until the crowd had dispersed before being taken back to his room.

Once back in his room, he asked Thomas to build up the fire so that he might try to dry his hose and slippers. His hose were in sad condition.

Because of the rain and the generally overcast condition, little daylight entered his window, even though it was still midday. He could not see to read.

A familiar passage flashed into his mind. "For I am now ready to be offered, and the time of my departure is at hand. *Bonum certamen certavi, cursum consummavi, fidem servavi*—I have fought a good fight, I have finished my course, I have kept the faith. Henceforth there is laid up for me a crown of righteousness, which the Lord, the righteous Judge, shall give me at that day; and not to me only, but unto all them also that love his appearing."

He found his heart comforted. *The grand old apostle faced an end similar to mine. Surely I may echo his words, "The time of my departure is at hand." Today is October 1. The mayor said the date set was the 16th. I believe God would grant me to say in spite of some setbacks, "I have fought a good fight."*

He thought of the battles over the years—back at Cambridge, with Stokesley, at Bristol, as bishop, before the King, on until now. He had often grown weary but he had never stopped.

Surely I can say, "I have kept the faith." God grant me to hold it to the end, keeping my eye on the crown that is laid up for me, soon to be given, when I come into his presence.

This thought pleased him, and he smiled. *What a great crown-giving time in heaven! So many all in a short space.*

21

[1555]

The rains continued, often accompanied by violent winds and thunder-storms. Never could Latimer recall such a time. "A sign from heaven?" he asked. "Is God using this means to show his displeasure at what is taking place in England?"

The days passed in unbroken quiet. No messages from outside reached him. He saw only his servant. Even Thomas left him more and more alone, appearing only at the times when he was needed.

Latimer did not find it burdensome to remain thus alone. He kept his Testament before him, though he seldom found light sufficient for reading. He need not see the words. They were written in his heart. Looking up and listening became a constant attitude.

Difficult as it was for him to place himself upon his knees, he still spent hours in that position. He held to his three main petitions but he prayed as well for the varied concerns of the church. He thought of his fellow prisoners all over England. He held them up in earnest supplication. He prayed for the refugees on the Continent, that they might be kept faithful.

"You manage to arrive at the right moment," he said to his man. "I cannot rise without help."

Thomas seemed to hold him in great awe. "How can you be so cheerful, sir?" he asked.

"Ah, Thomas, I have cause to be cheerful. Soon now I go to be with my Master, my Savior, my Lord, my King. I will no longer need help in rising from my knees. The stiffness of these old bones will be finished. My eyes will see clearly the marvelous things that await me. Is not that a cheerful prospect?"

On Monday the 14th he wrote a note to Austy, with a particular request. "Thomas, you must take this to Austy with all urgency. It is the last errand I will ever send you on."

As the door closed, Latimer said, "I hope I am not too late." Thomas brought the reply, "I will take care of it."

He awoke at his usual early hour next morning with the realization that he was beginning his last full day upon earth. He spent the time much as he had the previous days.

A certain dread came upon him as evening fell. He had been sentenced to be degraded from all his ecclesiastical orders. It would be a wretched interruption to be endured.

The hour grew late before the unwelcome visitors arrived. The Bishop of Gloucester, the vice chancellor, and a couple of other university officials entered his small room. They ordered him to dress in the apparel they had brought. He refused. They said they would do it by force, unless he cooperated.

"So be it," he said.

He stood still while they went through the absurd ceremony, dressing him in the robes he had discarded long ago, placing the miter upon his head, forcing his fingers to clutch the chalice. The bishop forbore to strike him on the chest with the crozier as he pronounced the words of degradation. The other features proceeded according to the ritual. The chalice was seized from his hand and the garments were stripped from him with the accompanying words. It was soon over.

22

[1555]

He dismissed Thomas for the night. Taking his place before the fire, he settled in for a period of meditation. Then the door opened, and someone moved into the room. Austy stood before him.

At first he was speechless. He even wondered whether he was seeing a vision. Austy moved closer and with a gentle smile, said, "It is really I. It is no dream. See, I am here."

He fell to his knees before his master and put his arms about him. Only then did Latimer find his voice. As he spoke, tears flooded his eyes and ran down his cheeks. "Oh, thank God! He has granted me the final boon I craved."

"Before I undertake to explain my presence, sir, here is the article you requested." He placed a parcel on the table. "The morning will be time enough to look at it."

He had wanted to approach Latimer in person on the days of his appearance before the commission. "I was present in both places. I kept away from you, for I had this plan and was afraid I might spoil it, were I to be seen with you before."

"I felt sure you must be there."

"I went to the bailiff and begged permission to visit you. I reminded him that I had not seen you since he dismissed me. I mentioned the years in which I served you. It would be a kindness to us both, if I might see you. He agreed that I might slip in for an hour or two."

"Then we must not waste time," said Latimer. "I will not attempt to thank you for all you have done. You know my heart well enough. What are your plans? Will you go to London? Perhaps you wish to return to your own land."

"In time I may return to my own land, but not yet. When . . . when I am no longer needed in Oxford . . . ," he said, swallowing hard. "I had thought to go to London. I could be useful to the prisoners still there. The number diminishes day by day. . . ." He paused to regain control. "Yet others take their place. They will have needs, which I can perhaps meet."

"It is what I had hoped."

"In London a group of believers meets secretly for worship. When I join them, they ask me to preach. Ministers are few."

"Such groups must exist all over England. If they can hold fast, preachers will become available. Those on the Continent will return. What better pastor could they find than you?"

"They know, sir, of my long association with you. I have absorbed some of your knowledge of the Scriptures, but more, the spirit of your life as you have lived it before me in Christ."

"Those closest to a man usually become aware not only of his good points but of his weaknesses and faults."

"Your weaknesses and faults, sir, have been negligible. You have lived before me a pure example of the Christian life. If I can in some part follow that example—love God as you love him, walk with him as you do, love my brothers as you do, and love my neighbor as myself as you do—then my life will be worthwhile."

Latimer spoke softly and with head bowed. "Thank you, Austy. What you fail to realize is the profound influence you have had upon my life. This is as it should be, that we be mutually encouraged by each other's faith, as St. Paul said."

"You must know, sir, how I feel about what is to transpire tomorrow. If I could by some means take your place, I would. That is not possible. Afterward, I may find peace. Until then it causes me the greatest agony of heart and mind and spirit. . . ." Here he broke down completely.

"I am sorry, sir," he said, after a moment. "I can be of no comfort to you when I let myself fall apart in this way."

"No, no, Austy. It is well that we reveal our inmost feelings to each other. God has given me great peace in these last days. Yet at times I still shrink back at the prospect of the ordeal. I pray for strength to abide the fiery trial without flinching. You told me once to look beyond. This I try to do."

"He will hear you, sir. My prayers for you go up constantly, as do those of countless people all over the land. God will not fail you in the hour of darkness."

"I am sure of that. Now, Austy, I put my New Testament in your hands. It is worn and falling to pieces, but you may want to keep it by you. I shall no longer need the written Word when I stand face-to-face with the Living Word. I give you, too, my spectacles. You may know someone who can benefit from them. Tomorrow I will have new eyes and see clearly, praise God!"

"I may not be permitted to approach you tomorrow, sir, but you will see me. Many are expected from a distance, for it is known that you and Master Ridley will face the fire. Special guards will be about to avoid trouble from any who might attempt to prevent the execution. Familiar faces will be in the crowd."

"The hour grows late. You must not overstay your time. Come, let us kneel in prayer before you go."

One last time they knelt. One last time they voiced the petitions of their hearts together. One last time Austy helped his master rise from his knees.

Soon a tap came at the door. "I must send you away now," said the bailiff. He sounded regretful. "No one knows you have been here. Slip out as quietly as you entered."

Latimer placed his hand upon his friend's shoulder and looked into his eyes. "Good-by, Austy," he said, drawing him close in a farewell embrace.

The door closed. He was alone once more, how very much alone, save for One who would never leave nor forsake him.

23

[October 16, 1555]

After a few hours of sound sleep he awoke strangely refreshed. A peculiar joy and anticipation filled him. He slipped from bed to his knees. "O Lord! This is the day! Thank you for bringing me to it."

He found strength to rise by himself when his brief season of prayer was ended. He felt uplifted by calmness of spirit, quietness of soul, and an assurance of the presence of his Lord.

He unrolled the bundle Austy had left and held up the garment it contained. "Just what I wanted," he murmured. He slipped the simple white shroud over his head and smoothed it out. It fell in soft folds down to his feet.

Thomas entered upon this scene and stood in open-mouthed astonishment. "You don't look the same, sir! What is it?"

"It is my wedding garment," said Latimer. "I must begin my journey shortly. I would be clad in white for the happy event."

He wore his black gown over the shroud, not disturbed over its tattered condition. Then he was ready, except for his cap.

"It rained much during the night," said Thomas. "But it appears to have stopped now, and the sun shines."

"That is good news. It might prove difficult to make a good fire in the pouring rain."

"The streets are crowded, sir. Not just the usual people. A great many strangers are among them."

"Yes, Master Ridley and I have friends who have come to bid us farewell as we begin our last journey."

"Where is your Testament, sir? And your spectacles?"

"I won't need them again. I gave them away last night."

The bailiff appeared at the door. "It is time, Master Latimer." He too seemed awed by the folds of the shroud hanging down below the black gown.

"Let us be on our way," said Latimer, with a smile. He took his staff and preceded the bailiff and Thomas out the door.

"It isn't far," said the bailiff. "Just outside the North Gate, past the Bocardo."

They had not gone far when Latimer saw Ridley up ahead. He walked between the mayor and an alderman. He was handsomely dressed in a rich black gown trimmed with fur. Latimer recognized it as a garment he would have worn as bishop in an informal situation. Upon his head he wore a corner-cap.

Latimer thought, *He is demonstrating the fact that he did not accept the degradation ceremony. He is still a bishop! But certainly not a Popish bishop.*

Ridley, as he reached the Bocardo, looked up toward Cranmer's window. Latimer could see that no one was there. What prevented Cranmer from making a last farewell to his friends?

Ridley cast a glance back at this point and spied Latimer. "Oh, are you there?"

"Yes, coming along as fast as I can follow."

Ridley entered the prepared area where the stake stood. As Latimer came up, Ridley turned to him with a wonderfully cheerful face. He embraced and kissed him. "Be of good heart, brother, for God will either assuage the fury of the flame or else strengthen us to abide it."

Approaching the stake, Ridley knelt and kissed it. Latimer knelt close beside him. They earnestly prayed. Then they rose and spoke to each other for a time.

They were interrupted by the announcement that they must now listen to the sermon. Looking to see who the preacher was, Latimer said, "It is that wretched Smith."

Smith had been one of the commissioners with Weston. He gave as his text, "Though I give my body to be burned and have not charity, it profiteth me nothing." Mercifully, he preached only fifteen minutes. Latimer had endeavored not to listen, spending his time searching the crowd for familiar faces.

As Austy had predicted, a force of extra guards held back the throng. None were allowed to approach the prisoners. Austy stood as near as possible. Latimer could see his face well.

Ridley asked permission for each of them to say a few words to the people.

"You may speak," he was told, "only to recant your errors."

They were instructed to make themselves ready. Latimer permitted the keeper to remove his hose, gown, and cap.

As he stood arrayed in the white shroud, he no longer felt old and crippled in his joints. A sense of well-being replaced his weakness. He stood quite straight. He felt young and strong. He detected a look of astonishment on the faces of those near him. Was it possible the change he felt was visible to others? A smile appeared on Austy's tear-stained face.

Their preparations complete, the two men looked once more at each other, then took their places beside the stake, back-to-back.

Ridley voiced a prayer of thanksgiving to God and then begged his mercy upon the realm of England and deliverance from all enemies.

The smith brought the chain about Latimer's waist and on about Ridley's.

Ridley bade him fasten it firmly. Shipside, Ridley's brother-in-law, was allowed to tie a small bag of gunpowder about the neck of each.

The wood was laid and the reeds stacked. A man stepped forward with a fagot and kindled the fire. Latimer spoke once more in a ringing voice: "Be of good comfort, Master Ridley, and play the man. We shall this day light such a candle, by God's grace, in England as I trust shall never be put out."

A hush fell over the crowd. He saw tears on Austy's face again. "Ah, Austy! No tears!" he whispered. "No tears!"

As the flames shot upward, he heard Ridley's voice, *"In manus tuas, Domine, commendo spiritum meum. Domine, recipe spiritum meum."* The words of the Lord upon the cross. "Into your hands I commit my spirit." He repeated in English, "Lord, Lord, receive my spirit."

Latimer cried out once, "O Father in heaven, receive my soul!" He reached out his arms to embrace the flames. After that he stroked his face with his hands, then put them forth to bathe them once more in the fire.

Strange, he thought. *There is heat, but no pain!* Darkness seemed to come in from all sides, though he knew it was midmorning and the sun was shining. The glow of the flames grew dim, as if the darkness would extinguish them.

Now he became conscious of a brightness from above, such a light as had no relation to the sun. A sound as of singing came from a distance. Unseen hands on either side lifted him up, up.

Once they paused, and he felt compelled to look down. In the dimness below, he saw two figures standing in the midst of dull flames, surrounded by a growing darkness.

He felt a tug at his arm and a voice spoke, "That is behind you. Come!" Again they moved upward toward the brightness.

"You may look once more," said the voice.

At first he saw nothing. Darkness prevailed; the flames had vanished; the two figures had disappeared. Then in their place rose what appeared to be a tall candle. It was tipped with a steady and unwavering flame that grew in brilliance as he watched. Its beams reached out through the darkness to illuminate the whole of Oxford, all England—and far beyond.

Joy washed over him like a cooling summer shower. The voice whispered, "For you, Hugh Latimer, time is no more."

He threw back his head in the old gesture, listening intently, lifting eager eyes, as the unseen hands moved him steadily upward toward the Light.

SELECT BIBLIOGRAPHY

Baker, John Austin. *The Living Splendour of Westminster Abbey.* Norwich, 1977.

Becon, Thomas. *The Catechism with Other Pieces.* Parker Society Edition, 1844.

Burnet, Gilbert. *The History of the Refomation of the Church of England.* 4 vols. Edward Nares, ed.

Burton, Elizabeth. *The Pageant of Elizabethan England.* New York, 1958.

Butler, Arthur F. *Hugh Latimer: the religious thought of a Reformation preacher.*

Carlyle, R. M. and A. J. *Hugh Latimer.* 1899.

Chapman, Hester W. *The Challenge of Anne Boleyn.* New York, 1974.

Chester, Allan Griffith. *Hugh Latimer, Apostle to the English.*

Cranmer, Thomas. *Writings and Disputations Relative to the Sacrament of the Lord's Supper.* Parker Society Edition. Cambridge: The University Press, 1844.

Darby, Harold S. *Hugh Latimer.* London: The Epworth Press, 1953.

Demaus, Robert, *Hugh Latimer: A Biography.* London: The Religious Tract Society, 1881.

Dickens, A. G. *The English Reformation.* London: Fontana/Collins, 1967, 1978.

Erickson, Carolly. *Bloody Mary.* New York: Doubleday & Company, Inc., 1978.

Foxe, John, *The Acts and Monuments of John Foxe.* 8 Volumes.

Hackett, Francis. *Henry the Eighth.* London: Jonathan Cape, 1929.

Hartley, Dorothy and Elliott, Margaret M. *Life and Work of the People of England, A Pictorial Record from Contemporary Sources, The Sixteenth Century.* New York, London: G. P. Putnam's Sons, 1926.

Hayes, John. *London, A Pictorial History.* New York: Arco Publishing Company, Inc.

Hughes, Philip Edgcumbe. *Theology of the English Reformers.* Grand Rapids, Michigan: Baker Book House, 1965, 1980.

Latimer, Hugh. *Sermons.* Parker Society Edition, 1844.

Latimer, Hugh. *Sermons and Remains.* Parker Society Edition, 1845.

Latimer, Hugh, *Sermons by Hugh Latimer, Sometime Bishop of Worcester.* London: J. M. Dent & Company and New York: E. P. Dutton & Company, 1906.

Latimer, Hugh. *Selected Sermons of Hugh Latimer, Bishop and Martyr.*

Loane, Marcus L. *Master of the English Reformation.* London: The Church Book Room Press, 1954, 1956.

Morris, Christopher. *The Tudors.* New York: The Macmillan Company, 1957.

Muir, Richard. *The English Village.* New York: Thames and Hudson, Inc., 1980.

Pollard, Albert Frederick. *England Under Somerset.* New York: Russell & Russell, 1900, 1966.

————. *Thomas Cranmer and the English Reformation.* London and New York: G. P. Putnam's Sons, 1905.

Quennell, Marjorie and C. H. B. *A History of Everyday Things in England.* New York: Charles Scribner's Sons.

Ridley, Nicholas. *A Brief Declaration of the Lord's Supper Written by Nicholas Ridley, Bishop of London.* London: Seeley and Co., Limited, and New York: Thomas Whitaker, 1895.

Robinson, Hastings, ed. *Original Letters Relative to the English Reformation.* 2 vol. Cambridge: The University Press, 1846.

Ryle, John Charles. *Light from Old Times.* Welwyn, Hertfordshire, England: Evangelical Press, 1980—first published 1890.

Smith, Lacey Baldwin. *Henry VIII, The Mask of Royalty.* Boston: Houghton Mifflin Company, 1971.

Strype, John. *Ecclesiastical Memorials of the Church of England.* 3 vol. Oxford: Clarendon Press, 1822.

————. *Memorials of Thomas Cranmer.* 4 vol. Oxford: Clarendon Press, 1812.

Walker, Williston. *A History of the Christian Church.* 1959 revision. New York: Charles Scribner's Sons, 1918.

Williams, Penry. *Life in Tudor England.* London: B. T. Batsford Ltd., and New York: G. P. Putnam's Sons, 1966.

Guidebooks, Maps, etc.

Booklets

A celebration of 1300 years of the Diocese of Worcester. Halesowen, West Midlands: Baber Rollaprint, 1980.

Bond, Shelagh. *St. George's Chapel.* London: Pitkin Pictorials Ltd., 1975.

Booth-Clibborn, Stanley, ed. *Great St. Mary's, The University Church, Cambridge.* St. Ives, Huntingdon, Cambridgeshire: Photo Precision Ltd., 1975.

Brain, Ralph. *Oxford, The Golden Guide.* Oxford: The University Press.

Brooks, John. *Historic Cambridge.* Norwich, Norfolk: Jarrold & Sons Ltd., 1978.

Butler, Colonel Sir Thomas. *Her Majesty's Tower of London.* London: Pitkin Pictorials Ltd., 1975.

Cox, Angela. *Sir Thomas More.* London: Pitkin Pictorials Ltd., 1977.

Fox, Canon Adam. *Westminster Abbey.* London: Pitkin Pictorials Ltd., 1972.

Grimsthorpe Castle, History and Guide. Sleaford: F. M. Morton and Son Ltd., Printers.

Hartlebury Castle. Stockport: The Cloister Press Ltd.

Hedley, Olwen. *Cambridge, The City and the College.* London: Pitkin Pictorials Ltd., 1975.

Prisoners in the Tower. London: Pitkin Pictorials Ltd., 1972.

Hill, B. J. W. *Windsor Castle.* London: Pitkin Pictorials Ltd., 1972.

Kemp, Dr. E. W. *Worcester Cathedral.* London: Pitkin Pictorials Ltd., 1975.

Randall, Roland E. *Trees in Britain, Broadleaved, Book 1.* Norwich: Jarrold & Sons Ltd., 1974.

Trees in Britain, Broadleaved, Book 2. Norwich: Jarrold & Sons Ltd., 1975.

Slanville, Philippa. *Tudor London.* London: Museum of London, 1979.

The Tower of London. Department of the Environment Official Guide. 5th ed., 1974. London: Her Majesty's Stationery Office, 1953.

Watts, Michael. *Oxford, The City and University.* London: Pitkin Pictorials Ltd., 1975.

Woodward, G. W. O. *King Henry VIII.* London: Pitkin Pictorials Ltd., 1972.

Worcester Cathedral, A Guide to Appreciation. Worcester, 1980.

Maps

Hollar, Wenceslaus. *Long View of London from Bankside, 1647.* The British Museum.

London, 16th Century. Greater London Council Publications.

Lyne, Richard, Engraver. *Cambridge in 1574.* Cambridge City Council Tourist Office.

INDEX